SUPERPOWERS
AND REVOLUTION

SUPERPOWERS AND REVOLUTION

Edited by Jonathan R. Adelman

PRAEGER

New York
Westport, Connecticut
London

Library of Congress Cataloging-in-Publication Data

Superpowers and revolution.

   1. United States – Foreign relations – 1945–
2. Soviet Union-Foreign relations-1945–
3. Revolutions – History – 20th Century. I. Adelman,
Jonathan R.
E744.S985 1986   327′.09048   86-21273
ISBN 0-275-92166-2 (alk. paper)

Library of Congress Catalog Card Number: 86-21273
ISBN: 0-275-92166-2

First published in 1986

Praeger Publishers, 521 Fifth Avenue, New York, NY 10175
A division of Greenwood Press, Inc.

Printed in the United States of America

♾™
The paper used in this book complies with the Permanent
Paper Standard issued by the National Information Standards
Organization (Z39.48-1984).

10 9 8 7 6 5 4 3 2 1

In loving memory
of our *tante*,
Sophia Falkenstein,
who cared

LIST OF CONTRIBUTORS

JONATHAN R. ADELMAN, the editor, is associate professor in the Graduate School of International Studies at the University of Denver and Lady Davis Visiting Associate Professor in the Department of Political Science at Hebrew University for the spring semester, 1986. He has written *The Revolutionary Armies* (1980) and *Revolution, Armies and Wars* (1985), and edited *Communist Armies in Politics* (1982) and *Terror and Communist Politics* (1984). An authored volume, *The Dynamics of Soviet Foreign Policy,* will appear in 1987 and another volume, *Endgame: The Soviet and American Destruction of the Third Reich,* will appear in 1988.

JENNIFER BAILEY is a doctoral candidate in the Graduate School of International Studies at the University of Denver.

MARTHA L. COTTAM is assistant professor in the Graduate School of International Studies at the University of Denver.

ALEX N. DRAGNICH is professor emeritus in the Department of Political Science at Vanderbilt University. He has written *Tito's Promised Land: Yugoslavia* (1954), *Serbia, Nikola Pasic and Yugoslavia* (1974), *The Development of Parliamentary Government in Serbia* (1978), *The First Yugoslavia: Search for a Viable Political System* (1983), *The Saga of Kosovo: Focus on Serbian-Albanian Relations* (1984), and *Major European Governments* (1986).

LUBOV FAJFER is a doctoral candidate in the RAND/UCLA Center for the Study of Soviet International Behavior.

MICHAEL FRY is professor of International Relations and director of the School of International Relations at the University of Southern California. He has authored *Illusions of Security: North Atlantic Diplomacy 1918–1922* (1973) and *Lloyd George and Foreign Policy* (1977).

CRISTANN LEA GIBSON is a postdoctoral fellow with the Avoiding Nuclear War project at the John F. Kennedy School of Government at Harvard University.

JACK A. GOLDSTONE is assistant professor in the Department of Sociology at Northwestern University. He edited *Revolutions: Theoretical, Comparative and Historical Studies* (1985).

ROGER HILSMAN is professor in the Department of Political Science of Columbia University. He has written *Strategic Intelligence and National Decisions* (1956), *To Move a Nation* (1967), *The Politics of Policymaking in Defense and Foreign Affairs* (1971), and *The Crouching Future: International Politics and U.S. Foreign Policy* (1975). He has also coedited *Foreign Policy in the 1960s: The Issues and the Instruments* (1965).

ANDRZEJ KORBONSKI is professor in the Department of Political Science at the University of California at Los Angeles and codirector of the RAND/UCLA Center for the Study of Soviet International Behavior. He has written *Politics of Socialist Agriculture in Poland* (1965) and coedited *Soldiers, Peasants and Bureaucrats* (1982).

ERNEST MAY is Charles Warren Professor of History in the John F. Kennedy School of Government at Harvard University. Among his numerous works are *The World War and American Isolation 1914–1917* (1959), *Imperial Democracy: The Emergence of America As a Great Power* (1961), *From Imperialism to Isolationism 1898–1919* (1964), *American Imperialism: A Speculative Essay* (1968), *Lessons of the Past: The Use and Misuse of History in American Foreign Policy* (1973), *The Making of the Monroe Doctrine* (1975). He has recently edited *Knowing One's Enemies: Intelligence Assessment Before the Two World Wars* (1984).

DANIEL McINTOSH is a doctoral candidate in the Graduate School of International Studies at the University of Denver and a research analyst for Science Applications, Inc.

CONDOLEEZZA RICE is assistant professor in the Department of Political Science at Stanford University and a fellow at the Council of Foreign Relations. She has authored *The Politics of Client Command* (1984).

BARRY RUBIN is currently working on the staff of Senator Gary Hart. He has written *The Great Powers in the Middle East 1941–1947* (1980), *Paved With Good Intentions: The American Experience and Iran* (1980), and *The Arab States and the Palestine Conflict* (1981). He coedited *Human Rights and U.S. Foreign Policy* (1979) and *The Israel-Arab Reader: A Documentary History* (1984).

CAROL R. SAIVETZ is fellow in the Russian Research Center at Harvard University and currently visiting associate professor in the Department of Political Science at Tufts University. She coauthored *Soviet-Third World Relations* (1984).

JIRI VALENTA is professor and director of the Soviet Studies Program at the Graduate School of International Studies at the University of Miami. He has written *Soviet Intervention in Czechoslovakia 1968* (1979) and coedited *Euro-communism: Between East and West* (1980) and *Soviet Decisionmaking for National Security* (1984).

ACKNOWLEDGMENTS

It is always a pleasure to acknowledge those who helped to make this book possible. My colleagues in the global conflict concentration here in the Graduate School of International Studies at the University of Denver, and especially Karen Feste, have been most helpful and stimulating. The various and numerous contributors to this volume have displayed unflagging intellectual interest and enthusiasm in this venture. I would especially like to single out Andrzej Korbonski, Barry Rubin, Jennifer Bailey, and Dan McIntosh in this regard. The patience and encouragement of my editor at Praeger, Dottie Breitbart, has been exemplary.

And on the indispensable home front I wish to mention the support of my wife Nancy and the ever-entertaining diversions offered by my son Joshua.

CONTENTS

PART III: THE SOVIET UNION AND REVOLUTION

I: INTRODUCTION

1 INTRODUCTION
Jonathan R. Adelman

The subject of superpower intervention in the postwar era in countries both in and outside their spheres of influence is a critically important topic in world politics. For several hundreds of years major threats to world peace arose from large-scale intra-European conflicts. But the end of World War II and the wave of subsequent decolonization marked an end to European predominance in international politics. The development of nuclear weapons and the military division of the world into the camps of the two superpowers with differing ideologies and histories created a new world order. The growing destructiveness of nuclear weapons has made a direct, planned nuclear war between the two sides mutually suicidal. The more likely dangers to peace come not in Western Europe, where the Soviet Union and United States have been at peace for the last 40 years, but in other areas of the world. These crises especially arise from revolutionary movements threatening superpower control or hegemony in areas considered to be in or near the superpowers' perceived spheres of influence. It is to the conflict between these two powerful forces—superpowers and revolutionary movements—that this volume dedicates itself.

The power of neither side of this contest can be denied. That of the superpowers is considerably more tangible and evident. Both the United States and Soviet Union dispose of enormous military power, conventional and nuclear, far greater than that possessed by any other powers in the world. Both are vast economic powers with huge populations and reservoirs of natural and human resources. And neither has shown a shyness in the postwar era in the use of force to maintain its position in the world.

At first glance then any attempt by a revolutionary movement, which we can define as one aiming at a radical transformation of the political and

3

social structure of a country, would seem hopeless, especially if it occurs in a smaller country penetrated by the superpower.[1] This is even more true since revolution in a lesser state poses a serious threat to other states in the system. The hatred and even loathing of revolutionary movements by leaders of established states has been deep and profound. Historically this was true of the great revolutions and it remains true today. For as El-baki Hermassi has delineated the dangers that such revolutions pose to the international order as convention shattering movements,

> The world historical structure of revolutions means, among other things, that they introduce new political ideals and principles of legitimacy which threaten existing power arrangements by their explosive novelty or demands for societal restructuring. They exert a demonstration effect beyond the boundaries of their country of origin, with a potential for triggering a wave of revolution and counterrevolution both within and between societies.[2]

As a consequence, revolutions have tended to pose some of the most critical and intractable problems for the superpowers in the past four decades since the end of World War II. By the very depth of their popular support, by their seizure of existing or creation of new political institutions, by their emerging radicalism and often xenophobic antisuperpower nationalism, they pose a serious and dangerous challenge to the existing international order. The depth of their local support and frequent control of the instruments of violence ensures that the superpowers would not find the suppression of revolutionary movements an easy matter. Too, there is certain international condemnation and possible countermoves with which to contend. Yet, at the same time, to do nothing would represent a diminution of superpower political influence and set a dangerous precedent for the other countries to emulate. Given the highly contagious nature of revolution—as seen in the spread of revolution from France after 1789, 1830, and 1848 and from Russia after 1917—this would be a very serious matter for the superpower to consider.

Indeed, much of the history of the postwar era could be written in terms of the confrontation between superpowers and revolutionary movements. Nearly every U.S. president since 1945 has had to confront at least one such brutal decision over how to deal with a rising revolutionary movement in an area of importance to the United States. The roll call is impressive: China (Truman), Guatemala (Eisenhower), Cuba (Eisenhower/Kennedy), Vietnam (Kennedy/Johnson), Chile (Nixon), Iran (Carter), and El Salvador and Nicaragua (Reagan). As this list makes clear, there was a wide diversity not only in geographic locale and economic and geopolitical importance of the countries but also in the political nature of the revolutionary movements. Khomeini's Islamic fundamentalism had little in common with Maoist communism or Arbenz's nationalism.

At the same time the Soviet Union has also faced some of its most severe challenges from revolutionary movements within or near its predominant sphere of influence. Here too the roll call recaptures many of the most significant events in postwar Soviet foreign policy: Yugoslavia (1948), Hungary and Poland (1956), Czechoslovakia (1968), China (1969), Iran (1979), Afghanistan (1979), Poland (1980–85). And, as in the U.S. case, there is a fairly wide range in economic and political significance of these countries as well as the nature of the revolutionary movements. Dubcek's "socialism with a human face" had little in common with Khomeini's Islamic fundamentalism or Polish Solidarity.

A brief review of the superpower decisions in those cases does little to reinforce relatively simplistic notions on the Right and Left about the nature of Soviet and U.S. foreign policy. Those on both the Right and Left who have emphasized the innately brutal, imperialistic, and repressive nature of Soviet foreign policy have naturally pointed to the military invasion of Hungary, Czechoslovakia, and Afghanistan. But, in a broader perspective, it is equally important to assess why the Soviet Union did *not* undertake to militarily crush the challenges posed by Yugoslavia, China, and Iran and why it settled for a substitute for invasion in Poland. At the same time revisionist critics, who have assailed U.S. imperialism abroad, have naturally focused on the U.S. role in crushing the Guatemala revolution of Arbenz and attempting to crush the Vietnamese revolution. But, equally important, it is necessary to assess why the United States did *not* militarily intervene to smash revolutionary movements in China (1948), Iran (1979), and El Salvador and Nicaragua (1980–85). Thus, an important question to which this volume is devoted is not only why the superpowers intervened in given revolutions but even more importantly why they often did not intervene.

In the rest of this chapter we will examine a number of overall questions relating to the themes of the volume. We will look at how great powers traditionally treated revolutions, at the characteristics of superpowers, their rules and modes of intervention, and at the framework of this book.

Great Powers and Revolution

Historically, of course, great powers never hesitated to use military force to crush threatening revolutionary movements. Indeed, in the aftermath of the final defeat of the French Revolution, the Congress of Vienna enshrined the legal right of sovereign states to use force to repress revolution to protect the international order. And, until its defeat in the Crimean War, Tsarist Russia, as in the case of the 1849 Hungarian Revolution, acted as the reactionary gendarme of Europe to quell all revolutionary outbreaks.

However, a brief review of great powers' intervention in the major Western revolutions shows a markedly inconsistent pattern of reaction to revolution. The English Revolution of the 1640s, which culminated in the regicide of Charles I in 1649 after a public trial, involved a major radical challenge to the established order. Too, Charles I repeatedly and urgently pleaded with the crowned heads of Europe to come to his aid to save his throne. Yet no aid was forthcoming and Charles I was beheaded after losing three civil wars. The reasons for this lack of foreign military intervention, even when requested by a sitting monarch challenged by an openly revolutionary movement, are of contemporary interest: the military exhaustion of Europe after the devastation of the Thirty Years' War, Europe's preoccupation with the Thirty Years' War, England's isolation from the Continent, Parliament's control of the navy and major ports, national rivalries, and a reluctance to aid an unpopular king.[3]

The French Revolution is of even greater interest. Despite violent foreign hostility to the regicide and radicalism of the French Revolution, it was France who declared war on its enemies in 1792 rather than the other way around. Furthermore, the varying and shifting coalitions against revolutionary France were so ineffectual that after the Treaty of Tilsit in 1807, Napoleon held sway over Europe in a manner and grandeur not seen since Charlemagne. Only the catastrophic Russian campaign of 1812 and overextension of French resources would lead to the final disasters of 1814 and 1815. But, in the process revolutionary France had existed and even thrived in a very hostile, largely monarchical environment for over 25 years and mainly could blame only itself for its ultimate demise.[4]

Finally, there was the remarkably erratic record of foreign intervention against the Bolsheviks in the Russian civil war. The initial stated objective of the interventionary activity until November 1918 was not to overthrow the Bolsheviks but to restore the eastern front against the Germans. The number of Allied troops landed in Russia were relatively insignificant, numbering only in the tens of thousands, except for Japan's large-scale intervention in the Far East. And, the places of occupation—French sailors in Odessa, English and U.S. troops in Arkhangel and Murmansk, Japanese soldiers in Vladivostock—were relatively peripheral to the civil war. By 1919 Allied resolve waned and the main effort consisted of large-scale military aid to the Whites. At no time, as Lenin later noted, was there a large scale, coordinated direct Allied military effort to overthrow the Bolsheviks. Thus, many factors inhibited efforts to throttle the nascent revolution—Allied rivalries, exhaustion from World War I, Bolshevik resistance, the unwillingness of soldiers to fight in an alien land after the prolonged exhaustion of the war.[5]

Superpowers

Now we turn to an examination of the extent to which we can consider the superpowers as comparable in relating to revolutionary movements. The final outcome of World War II brought with it the destruction of the European balance of power system, the elimination of Germany and Japan as great powers and the emergence of two heretofore peripheral states, the United States and the Soviet Union, as dominant actors in the international political order. The term superpower, coined by W.T.R. Fox in a 1944 book (that incidentally included England as one of their number), denoted the new phenomenon that emerged from the war.[6] It indicated an especially high military and economic capacity and concomitant capability to undertake a predominant role in international politics. This role was conceptualized as one significantly greater than that played by any of the traditional six to eight mainly European powers before 1945.

Throughout the postwar era the two powers have shared a number of common attributes that have set them apart as superpowers. Most important of their similarities is their effective governmental structures. As Samuel Huntington wrote in *Political Order in Changing Societies* about the two superpowers and Great Britain,

> Communist totalitarian states and Western liberal states both belong generally in the category of effective rather than feeble political systems. The United States, Great Britain and the Soviet Union have different forms of government but in all three systems the government governs. Each country is a political community with an overwhelming consensus among the people on the legitimacy of the political system. In each country the citizens and their leaders share a vision of the public interest of the society and of the traditions and principles upon which the political community is based. All three countries have strong, adaptable, coherent political institutions: effective bureaucracies, well-organized political parties, a high degree of popular participation in public affairs, working systems of civilian control over the military, extensive activity by the government in the economy, and reasonably effective procedures for regulating succession and controlling political conflict. These governments command the loyalties of their citizens and thus have the capacity to tax resources, to conscript manpower, and to innovate and to execute policy. If the Politburo, the Cabinet or the President makes a decision, the probability is high that it will be implemented through the government machinery.[7]

Equally important, the other lesser powers have acknowledged them as superpowers and they themselves have openly accepted the label. By the late 1960s their military power was roughly equal and the gap in nuclear weapons between them and the rest of the world had grown. Both countries openly proclaimed their desire to avert nuclear war or any confrontation between the two sides that might lead down that fateful path. In a sense, this awareness of their own great military strength also served to inhibit their actions and to encourage them to act in tandem in dangerous situations. Similarly, they were economic giants with the two largest economies in the world.

The two superpowers also shared some historical features as well. Both were huge continental powers with large populations that had traditionally functioned on the periphery of the European balance of power system. Both had undergone great revolutions that had created new political orders and a commitment to manifest destinies as new worlds contemptuous of the old decadent European order. Neither had significantly participated in the colonization of the Third World and could thereby strongly denounce colonialism. Both emerged reluctantly from a relatively isolationist past through Axis attacks in 1941 and suddenly and surprisingly found themselves enshrined as great powers by 1945 with minimal preparations.

The two superpowers have maintained relatively clearly demarcated spheres of influence, replete with doctrines and formal organizations for at least a significant part of their spheres. They have strong ideological commitments to their allies. And, despite their great power, each has suffered major defections, not always permanent, to the other side. While the Soviet Union "lost" Yugoslavia (1948), China (1969), and Egypt (1977), the United States "lost" China (1949), Cuba (1962), and Vietnam (1975).

And yet, there are also a series of factors that make the concept of superpower an inadequate variable to explain Soviet and U.S. behavior solely in its own terms. Most importantly, the power of the United States is and has been overall much greater than that of the Soviet Union. While Soviet nuclear capabilities achieved parity with U.S. capabilities by the late 1960s, there remained and still remains a great asymmetry in political, economic, and cultural power. Politically, all of the world's medium powers—England, France, West Germany, Italy, Japan, Canada, and China—are aligned, usually by formal treaty, with the United States. None are aligned with Moscow. While the United States is a truly global power with strong political ties to many Third World countries, the Soviet Union remains largely a vast Eurasian regional power whose ideology has lost most of its appeal in the last several decades. Too, the scope and geographic dispersion of the United States' sphere of influence is far greater than the Soviet sphere of influence. While the Soviet sphere is almost solely limited to its geographical periphery, the American sphere of influence encompasses much of the world and several continents.

The gap between the two powers is, if possible, even greater in the economic realm. The United States continues to be the economic engine of the Western world with an economy more than twice as productive than the Soviet Union. The power of international capitalism, and its agents as the multinational corporations, World Bank and International Monetary Fund, is vastly greater in the world economy than that of the socialist bloc. The contrast between the economic power of such U.S. allies as West Germany, France, and Japan on one hand and that of such Soviet allies as East Germany, Poland, and Vietnam, is staggering. Indeed, the economic dependence of much of Eastern Europe on the West is quite considerable. The trade pattern of the Soviet Union, which exports raw materials (as oil, natural gas, and gold) and imports high technology-finished goods, resembles that of a typical underdeveloped country rather than a superpower.

The gap is equally great on a cultural level. The extent of U.S. penetration of much of the world—through movies, music, television, consumer goods, and ideas—is at times awesome while that of the Soviet Union is minimal. The problems of the "Ugly Russian" have well nigh replaced those of the "Ugly American" in much of the world. Overall, then, there is a great asymmetry in the power and levers of influence available to the two powers.

Second, there is a significant difference in the nature of the revolutionary threats faced by the United States and Soviet Union. For the United States the main threat comes from antiregime radical forces who over a long period of time have built up strong guerrilla forces to overthrow friendly regimes. Occasionally this process may occur through elections (Chile) or massed street demonstrations (Iran). By contrast, it is precisely the indigenous governments that have often posed the greatest danger to the Soviet Union. For the bulk of these anti-Soviet revolutionary movements have been led by such dedicated Communist party leaders as Josip Tito (1948), Imre Nagy (1956), Wladyslaw Gomulka (1956), Alexander Dubcek (1968), Mao Zedong (1969), and Hafizullah Amin (1979).

Third, there is a pronounced difference in the way the decision-making process has worked in Moscow and Washington. The asymmetry in power and influence of the two powers and the difference in ideology have lent a more pressing and urgent tone to Soviet decision making in such crises than U.S. decision making. Even though the process is rather isolated in crises, there is a far greater sense of accountability to external groups, such as the Congress, media, and public opinion, in Washington than Moscow. Furthermore, the Soviet Union sees itself more as custodian of the small, embattled, and territorially adjacent socialist order than the United States does of the far larger and more dispersed capitalist order. This has been reinforced by the greater nonmilitary levers available to the United States than the Soviet Union and Washington's demonstrated success in the 1970s at wooing major regional actors (Egypt and China) out of the Soviet camp and into the U.S. camp.

Thus, while superpower status is an important and necessary condition for global involvement, nevertheless, as John Girling has observed,

> The form involvement (or intervention) takes in any specific case cannot with certainty be deduced from the structure of super-power, because of the operation of contingent factors—i.e. elements that are not determined by (outside the control of) that structure. These contingent factors and their relative importance can only be established by empirical investigation; they are not deducible from the superpower model.[8]

Superpower Intervention

During the 1970s there were several notable attempts to develop an analysis of superpower intervention, and especially military intervention, in the postwar era. Andrew Scott and Carsten Holbraad have developed superpower "rules of the game." In the aftermath of the Czech invasion Andrew Scott elaborated a series of superpower rules that gave superpower behavior a degree of predictability. These rules, which evolved over time, dealt with three kinds of intervention: intra-bloc intervention; inter-bloc intervention; extra-bloc intervention. Scott emphasized that a rough cost/benefit analysis could be applied to superpower decisions, in terms of such factors as the existing situation, its seriousness, probable future seriousness, policy options available, the effectiveness of each option, present and/or future costs and benefits associated with each option.[9]

More recently Carsten Holbraad has elaborated in depth some rules of the game. He has found 10 major rules which are:

1. No military intervention in the other's clear sphere of influence.
2. Keenest rivalry in gray areas rather than on the fringes of better demarcated spheres of influence.
3. Conflict by proxy more desirable than direct confrontation.
4. Encourage clients and allies only up to the point of a real danger of major war and then check them.
5. Urge or compel rival to restrain his proteges in dangerous situations.
6. Do not intervene militarily in local conflict if the rival might be compelled to follow.
7. Urge or compel rival to stay out of local conflict if he would be compelled to follow the rival's intervention by one of his own.
8. Use great restraint in direct confrontation.
9. Compel rival to use self-restraint.
10. Invoke nuclear threat to deter superpower restraint.[10]

There has also been some work on intervention by each superpower. Herbert Tillema has developed a detailed analysis of U.S. military intervention. Tillema's work is especially interesting as it focused on the puzzle of "Is there a pattern in America's appeal to force that a theory can explain both military intervention and the more frequent absence of military intervention?" He developed an intricate list of conditions that must be met before intervention was possible. These included:

1. perception of a threat of a new Communist government;
2. intervention not entail fighting the Soviet Union or using nuclear weapons;
3. the president not permit others to veto his decisions;
4. intervention not become unnecessary by an early end of the threat, burden taken up by another government;
5. a formal request from a government for military aid.[11]

Similarly in a recent study of four Soviet crisis decisions I have found a low-risk bureaucratic incremental decision-making style for Soviet foreign policy in which military force was used only as a last resort.[12]

Framework for the Study

Our basic orientation in this volume is taken from the work developed over time by James Rosenau. We agree with his stress on the need to approach intervention "through assessments of behavior probabilities rather than through adherence to moral or legal imperative" and especially his early and still relevant critique of the literature,

> For all the vast literature on the subject, in other words, not much is known about intervention. There is an abundance of specific detail but no general knowledge; a profusion of elaborate impressions but no verified findings. . . . The factors that foster, precipitate, sustain, channel, constrain and/or curb intervention simply have not been scientifically explored with the result that the literature is barren of any established generalizations.[13]

If this is largely true of the field of intervention studies, then it is still more true of studies dealing with intervention and revolution. Indeed, we could find no significant studies of the subject of intervention and revolution that dealt with the topic in any systematic way.

In order to differentiate superpower interventions from the more normal modes of international politics, we find especially useful his definition of interventionary behavior. He defines this as convention-breaking behavior directed at changing or preserving the structure of political authority in the target country. This is particularly apt since revolutions aim to alter the structure of political authority in the target country. Rosenau's definition allows us to isolate a series of intervention decisions, largely but not necessarily involving the use of overt or covert force, over time by the superpower. At the same time the use of revolutions as the key variable in the target country allows us to isolate a series of cases in which the power must respond to these threatening cases. Thus we can generate a series of discrete cases of superpower reactions to revolutionary situations.

Next we proceed from some of the postulates in his more recent work. Rosenau stressed that interventions can only be understood as a convergence of internal and external factors with multiple causality. These internal and external factors combine under varying circumstances for varying cases in varying ways. Interventions are usually associated with the outbreak or continuation of civil strife in the target nation. And in light of cost-benefit analysis, interventions can best be perceived as allocative decision for intervening societies in which domestic resources are redistributed by the intervener for foreign purposes.[14]

Finally, Rosenau emphasizes the need to stress the role of individual and bureaucratic variables in intervention decisions. The premise of this study of decision-making processes in the two superpowers in a series of revolutionary situations flows quite ineluctably from his concept that in the absence of public pressure and with the advantages of surprise and secrecy,

> Interventions are very much the product of the perceptions, calculations and decisions that occur within decision-making organizations and their leaderships . . . interventions are more exclusively a consequence of decision-making activity than any other type of foreign policy, that assessments of the need for and probable outcome of interventionary behavior are more subject to the whims of individual leaders and the dynamics of bureaucratic structures than the diplomatic, economic, military and political policies through which nations conventionally relate themselves to the international systems.[15]

In this volume we will examine a series of superpower intervention decisions with regard to threatening and developing revolutionary situations. For each case the authors will look at the formulated goals, policy options, policy choices, and implementation of the decision. Our stress is on the content of the interventionary policy and the decision-making and bargaining process that led to the choice. Information is derived from available documentary evidence and historical accounts. While there is far more information extant on the U.S. side than the Soviet side, there seems to be adequate material for constructing relatively comparable case studies for both powers. From this material we hope to answer three basic questions:

1. What determines Soviet and U.S. interventionary policy with regard to revolutions that threaten their interests?

2. Are U.S. and Soviet policies sufficiently similar that an overall superpower policy toward revolutions can be discerned?
3. Is there anything unique about revolutions that affects superpower policy toward them?

We begin with a series of introductory chapters. While Jack Goldstone looks at the view from the revolutionary states, and Jennifer Bailey analyzes the nature of the international system, Martha Cottam gives a useful psychological review of the nature of decision making. This is followed by a series of cases covering U.S. decisions with regard to China (Ernest May), Guatemala and Chile (Martha Cottam), Vietnam (Roger Hilsman), and Iran (Barry Rubin). This is followed by a series of cases covering Soviet decisions with regard to Yugoslavia (Alex Dragnich), Hungary (Condoleezza Rice and Michael Fry), Czechoslovakia (Jiri Valenta), Iran (Carol Saivetz), Poland (Andrzej Korbonski), and Afghanistan (Cristann Gibson). From these cases we should be able to draw some conclusions about the nature of superpower activity.

Notes

1. For Theda Skocpol's definition of revolution as a rapid transformation of the social structure of the country, see her *States and Social Revolution* (London: Cambridge University Press, 1979).

2. Elbaki Hermassi, "Toward a Comparative Theory of Revolutions," *Comparative Studies in Society and History,* vol. 18, no. 2 (April 1976), p. 175.

3. For a good view of English foreign policy, see G.M.D. Howat, *Stuart and Cromwellian Foreign Policy* (New York: St. Martin's Press, 1974).

4. For an excellent overview of the French Revolution, see Georges Lefebvre, *Napoleon: From 18 Brumaire to Tilsit 1799–1807* and his *Napoleon: From Tilsit to Waterloo 1807–1815* (New York: Columbia University Press, 1969).

5. For the classic view see George Kennan, *The Decision to Intervene* (Princeton: Princeton University Press, 1958).

6. W.T.R. Fox, *The Superpowers: The United States, British and the Soviet Union* (New York: Harcourt Brace, 1944).

7. Samuel Huntington, *Political Order in Changing Societies* (New Haven: Yale University Press, 1968), p. 1.

8. John Girling, *America and the Third World: Revolution and Intervention* (London: Routledge and Kegan Paul, 1980), p. 109.

9. Andrew Scott, "Military Intervention by the Great Powers: The Rules of the Game," in *Czechoslovakia: Intervention and Impact,* ed. I. Zartman (New York: New York University Press, 1970), pp. 85–104.

10. Carsten Holbraad, *Superpower and International Conflict* (New York: St. Martin's Press, 1979), p. 110.

11. Herbert Tillema, *Appeal to Force: American Military Intervention in the Era of Containment* (New York: Thomas Crowell, 1973).

12. Jonathan Adelman, "The Soviet Use of Force: Four Cases of Soviet Crisis Decision-making," *Crossroads* 16 (July 1985).

13. James Rosenau, "Intervention As a Scientific Concept," *Journal of Conflict Resolution,* vol. 13, no. 2 (1969), p. 150.

14. See James Rosenau, "Foreign Intervention as Adaptive Behavior," in *Law and Civil War in the Modern War,* ed. John Moore (Baltimore: Johns Hopkins University Press, 1974), pp. 129–51.

15. James Rosenau, "Intervention As a Scientific Concept," *Journal of Conflict Resolution,* vol. 13, no. 2 (1969), p. 166.

2 REVOLUTION AND THE INTERNATIONAL SYSTEM

Jennifer Bailey

Revolution has an international as well as an internal context and foreign intervention is an integral part of the ideal-typical revolutionary process. The nature of foreign intervention in social revolution is related to the position of the revolutionary nation on the "maps" of both the International State System and the International Economic System.

Social revolution is fundamental change in the structure of society although controversies rage over the necessary degree, nature, and direction of that change. But one potential area of dispute has been neglected: the International System. It has been assumed that the most important point of departure of revolutionary change is the former domestic status quo.

The most common theoretical approaches to revolution focus exclusively on prerevolutionary society within the revolutionary country. They treat this society as a closed unit and ignore the international context and consequences of the revolution as well as the international connections which domestic actors in the revolutionary drama usually have. At the heart of traditional theorizing, whether the frustration-aggression approaches of Gurr and Davies, the "anomic" approaches of Schurmann and Dunn, or the disequilibriated social system of Johnson, lies the conviction that revolution stems from an essentially internal social disharmony between what people want and what their political or social systems provide.[1] The resolution of this disharmony, too, lies within the society. This is true even of Marx despite the internationalist orientation of his work. The disharmony in his analysis stems from the tensions between the relations and the forces of production.[2]

Students of peasant revolution were the first to consistently incorporate the importance of external influences by linking the outbreak of peasant-based revolutions to peasant reaction to new, externally generated

15

social forces. These writers concentrate on the process by which peasants *qua* peasants change or are incorporated into a revolutionary process but they are not sensitive to the effect that the degree or nature of dependency has upon that process or the extranational character of the resources of some of the groups directly involved in the revolution.[3]

Theda Skocpol has explored more systematically the importance of international context with regard to both the causes and the outcome of revolution.[4] In her analysis of France, Russia, and China, she points primarily to the importance of the International State System in the outbreak of revolution. States engage in international competition within the International State System which may on occasion weaken them. The weakened condition of the state, in conjunction with a particular agrarian structure, means that omnipresent underlying social conflict cannot be contained and that no structures exist to prevent that unrest from sweeping away the ancien régime. Continuing international pressure shapes the creation of the new society as much as or more than ideological principles.

Kay Ellen Trimberger accepts the idea of state competition as an impetus to "revolution from above" but she focuses primarily on the international economic conditions that hamper the implementation of the "revolutionary" programs of the modernizing elite and on the state's tendency to try to forge an alliance with the dominant economic class in the attempt to surmount these difficulties. The perceived need to forge this alliance at the same time that mass mobilization is avoided ultimately results in the defeat of the state goal of modernization to meet the international challenge.[5]

Let us here leave aside the question of the causes of revolution and focus instead on the factors that shape the revolutionary process once it has begun. Revolutions take place within international contexts that are not neutral. An understanding of the forces that shape the ideal-typical revolutionary process must include a theoretically grounded consideration of the implications of variously configured international systems and the positions of states within them. Let's look more closely at the two contemporary "maps"—the international context of postwar revolution.

The International State System

Kenneth Waltz observes that "a systems approach will be needed . . . if outcomes are affected not only by the properties and the interconnections of variables but also the way in which they are organized."[6] Every system has a structure, described by Waltz as "a set of constraining conditions, which acts as a selector." Structures select by "rewarding some behaviors and punishing others." The consequence of the selective process is the emergence of a long-term pattern of behavior despite changes over time in the motivations, intentions, and cast of actors.[7]

The International State System is the whole which emerges out of the relationships of both functionally differentiated and functionally undifferentiated states. The states of the most powerful nations, the political core states which lend the names "bipolar" or "multipolar" to an International State System, are functionally undifferentiated. They perform roughly the same domestic functions and exist in a competitive relationship with other primary powers with whom they have regular contact.

The state is "a set of administrative policing and military organizations headed and more or less coordinated by an executive authority."[8] Thus the state is a tangible organization with goals and interests not reducible to those of a particular class or social group. The primary goals of the state are: to maintain internal order and to compete with other actual or potential states.[9] The horizontal relationship of the most powerful nations is composed of states that are roughly equal in their abilities to pursue these two goals. These states are internationally sovereign and internally autonomous. In short, the states of the primary powers are fully autonomous.

But, as primary states seek to expand and demonstrate their power, their competition generates spheres of influence composed of less powerful nations. Nations integrated into a sphere of influence develop states that are not the functional equivalents of the core: They complement the core. These states do not compete internationally for power nor do they have the ultimate responsibility for occurrences within their political boundaries. They are externally dominated rather than sovereign at the international level.

The economic dependency literature suggests, however, that political domination is not something one actor imposes upon another but that the contact between the internal and the external is a dynamic relationship in which internal actors participate. Political dependency is a situation in which domestic actors are an integral part of the process of external domination—they accept a subordinate status for their country, create a state and armed forces which complement rather than compete with the dominant country and finally, adopt the ideological value system of the dominant country. These internal actors comprehend the world and their country's place in it through the value system and interpretation of the dominant country and they achieve success within the framework that interaction with the dominant country generates. This dynamic creates an internally generated block to the autonomy of the politically dependent state.

The International Economic System

The International Economic System here refers to the capitalist world economy, especially in the aftermath of the industrial revolution operating as a distinct system, according to its own logic. The concept of the International Economic System is derived from Braudel's "world economy": "An economically autonomous section of the planet able to provide for most of its own needs, a section to which its internal links and exchange give a certain organic [functionally differentiated] unity." The world economy is "the sum of individual economies" and is always marked by a hierarchy based on the international division of labor with a comparatively rich economy in the center.[10] Here I take "individual" economies to mean those economies existing within the political boundaries of the nation-state.

There are two levels of functional differentiation in the International Economic System: within the boundaries of a nation-state and at the international level. Ideologically based principles underlie the operation of the contemporary International Economic System. These principles are modified liberal economic principles.[11]

The division of labor suggests the nature of dependency. Theotonio Dos Santos defines dependency in a capitalist world system as

> The relation of interdependence between two or more economies, and between these and world trade, assumes the form of dependence when some countries (the dominant ones) can expand and be self-starting while other countries (the dependent ones) can do this only as a reflection of that expansion, which can have either a positive or negative effect on their immediate development.[12]

The dependent economy has a subordinate position in the international division of labor: it or a major part of its economy performs lower order functions in the world economy with decisions and dynamism coming into its economy from external sources.

The actors of the International Economic System are international economic agencies such as the World Bank and the IMF among others, multinational corporations, and also, again, states. That states are actors in both the international economic and state systems may obscure the operation of two distinct international systems. States have economic as well as political interests since state power is to some degree dependent upon the prosperity and productivity of its dominant economic class. Yet state interests are not reducible to the interests of the dominant economic class, especially in the core states. The pursuit of state goals may bring the state into direct confrontation with the most important economic interest of the country. When these two interests clash, the fully autonomous state pursues state interests.

The relationship between the Soviet Union and the Eastern European countries serves as a reminder that not all international economic communities constitute autonomous international economic systems. While the economic relations between the USSR and Eastern Europe do create a degree of autonomy and organic unity, the state domination of these economic relations prevents the operation of a distinct economic system. There are few entities that may serve as actors within this economic community outside of the state. International economic actors distinct from the state increase in importance as members of the COMECON community increase contact with the capitalist world economy which surrounds them. Economic relations between Eastern Europe and the Soviet Union may thus be considered more purely a function of the operation of the International State System, more exclusively political artifacts, than are economic relations in the capitalist world economy. The primacy of politics in the COMECON economic community may aid in the explanation as to why the USSR is a political core state but has what appears to be a dependent economic relationship with its East European Warsaw Pact trading partners.[13]

Revolution in the International Context

Social revolution as fundamental change is often directly related to economic and political development by theorists and practitioners alike. If greater productive power and consequently greater military power is the outcome of revolution, then revolution in a primary state may have the capacity to change the very nature of the international system itself by altering its structure, that is, by altering the relationships between its defining parts. Revolution in such a state may set off systemicwide war as the other primary actors work to increase their power at the expense of the nation in turmoil or as they act to defend themselves from the "revolutionary" intent of thusly transformed states.[14]

Revolution in nations dependent in either or both the economic or economic senses has a slightly different impact. By definition revolutionaries propose radical change in the domestic status quo. But the dependent nation-state exists within a particular international context. Its domestic political and economic systems have subordinate roles within international hierarchies. Revolutionaries, by rejecting the domestic status quo, are also rejecting their nation's role in the international systems, perhaps even the system themselves. The actions and rhetoric of revolutionaries pose a direct threat to the structure of the two international systems and to the nations that benefit from those structures. Driven by systemic imperative, primary nations intervene in revolutions as a matter of course. Intervention in the revolution becomes an expected occurrence which may vary according to the degree and nature of prior dependency.

Within the International State System, the hegemony of a primary power over a secondary or tertiary power represents an attempt to control the environment to the extent possible and in so doing, to augment its own capacities vis-à-vis other primary states. Rejection of the subordinate role is the rejection of the primary power's hegemony and constitutes a perceived loss of capacity on the part of the hegemony vis-à-vis the other primary powers.[15] Status as a primary power and ultimately unit survival and sovereignty are put into question. Successful revolution may be dangerous also in its demonstration to other subordinate states that rejection of hegemony is possible.

Revolution becomes very much an assertion of state sovereignty as revolutionaries seek internal autonomy over political actors closely related to or who identify with external actors of the international systems. The fully autonomous state apparatus consequently acts much as primary states do to insure unit survival and sovereignty, rejecting complementary existence for a competitive existence. The revolutionary state becomes a centripetal force pulling apart the vertical power relationship of the sphere of influence and thus ultimately a threat to the stability of the horizontal power relationship existing between the primary actors in the International State System.[16] Achievement of full state autonomy is thus both a precondition for revolutionary success and an implicit revolutionary goal.

Within the International Economic System, an economically dependent state occupies a subordinate position within the international division of labor. Rejection of this role implies the at least partial systemic loss of the performance of some tasks, endangering the stability of the division of tasks among the remaining members of the International Economic System. The very example of successful rejection of a subordinate role is again dangerous. The survival and success of an alternative economic system would create doubts regarding the need to participate in the International Economic System, especially on the part of states struggling to assert their sovereignty. Additionally, if the territory of an economic system is successively reduced, the system may be unable to continue or the tasks performed by its core economies may be altered so that their status as a core is endangered.

The assertion of state autonomy consists in part of the attempt to gain the control over the economy necessary to the implementation of revolutionary policies. Participation in an International Economic System means the relinquishing of some power to actors other than the state. The more economically peripheral the country is, the more power the state relinquishes when it participates in an International Economic System. As Alfred Stepan has described, the dominance of foreign capital in a dependent country inhibits state control over domestic economic policy because "the bulk of the assets and most important decision makers of foreign capital lie outside the boundaries of the nation" and only a small part of the enterprises' total assets can be affected by state policy. Consequently, most Third World governments must self-consciously avoid policies that might provoke state sanctions or circumscribe their access to the capital, technology, and markets which they do not control.[17]

Intervention in the International Context

The international systems create "pushes" to intervene on the part of actors located physically outside the boundaries of the state. While the concepts of political and economic dependency imply penetration and the limitation of state autonomy on a daily basis, an act of intervention is here defined as a *change* in the relationships between the revolutionary nation or groups and the other units of the international systems during a revolutionary situation. These changes are specifically targeted at the revolutionary nation rather than being general changes in a unit's standard operating procedures which affect that unit's relationship with all others. Intervention may or may not have an appreciable impact on the revolutionary process, and what impact it does have may conceivably improve or diminish the chances of revolutionary success.

While the international systems create incentives for intervention on the part of external actors, the legacy of the dependent relationship is the creation of "pulls" for intervention. To paraphrase British Foreign Secretary Canning, internal actors call external resources into existence to redress the balance of the internal. Skocpol writes of the weakening of the state which on occasion and under the right conditions allows revolution to occur. Yet in a dependent nation, two sets of state apparatus must prove inadequate to the task of repressing rebellion: the apparatus of the dependent state and the apparatus of its political core. A leadership—persons with intentionally revolutionary goals—may be required to continue internal unrest to the breaking point given this need to overwhelm two repressive apparatus. In opposition to Skocpol, one might say that in the dependent nations of today, revolutions must be made rather than "happen."[18] At the same time that the need for leadership increases, the consciousness that revolution is within the realm of possibility also increases. The Russian, Cuban, and Chinese revolutions provide images to emulate.

Dependency theory has illuminated the series of linkages between what is generally thought of as the external and the internal, so much so that the demarcation between the two spheres has become blurred. First, domestic actors such as the state may have a history of relationships with other states which both create a constituency supporting the continuation of those links and which permit the coalescing of preexisting support for such links around state structures. If a core state provides material support for the government of a dependent state, personal and organizational contacts, bureaucratic standard operating procedures and material flows create a network of ties which bind the two states together. When internal problems disrupt the dependent country, the core which dominates it becomes a logical ally in the struggle to repress the disorder.

Second, ideological affinities may link political groups in one nation to the state or political groups of another. Substantive support may subsequently flow into the dependent nations along the conduits that those bonds construct. Faced with a society or state policies that are at odds either ideologically or materially with its orientation, a domestic political group or the state itself may turn to previously established allies and lines of support in order to combat internal state policies or to redress the existing balance of power within the state, again with the object of effecting change in state policy. Preexisting ties favor the status quo because those links have had the best chance to flourish. The more dependent the country is, the less chance it will have to develop "balanced" connections with others.

With regard to the International Economic System, the plethora of ties between domestic businesses, international businesses, and government create constituencies within the country in support of certain kinds of domestic economic policies which harmonize well with the ideological orientation which underlie the operation of that system. When a revolutionary government comes to power and pursues policies that disrupt the prerevolutionary business patterns, internal opposition to such changes may find natural allies in their internationally based business partners. International economic opposition groups consequently may encourage foreign intervention in support of their own efforts to alter governmental policy consequently affecting the ability of the revolutionary government to follow its social program.

Revolution and Intervention

At the same time that dependency increases the chance of intervention, it also makes a country more vulnerable to intervention in its revolutionary process. Intervention in turn shapes the revolutionary process. It does not make revolutionary "success" impossible but it does make it more difficult and more likely to be a qualified success. Nor is the success of revolution solely a function of external intervention: It is intimately connected with the internal opposition to revolutionary policies.

Military intervention may directly affect the outcome of the political side of the struggle. Economic intervention, such as boycotts, may directly affect the efforts to implement revolutionary social policy by directly blocking the revolutionary state's ability to institute its social program.

Most intervention works indirectly, however, by altering the domestic balance of power. The supply of aid to one side or another is a use of internal actors to achieve goals of external actors. The military of a politically dependent country is usually linked to the military of the core. Lines of supply run directly to the core and fluctuations in the pattern and amount of support have an immediate effect on the ability of the dependent state to maintain internal order. The revolutionaries in a dependent state, then, must both defeat the indigenous state's military and police forces and outlast the willingness of the core state to reinforce its ally.

The economically dependent country has few internal resources upon which to draw in order to implement a revolutionary program and many of the resources that it does have are in the hands of people tied either materially or ideologically to the International Economic System. Driven by a need to interact with some external source of dynamism, the state may be forced to return to the International Economic System in the same hierarchical position it occupied before the revolution. Other alternatives are to return to the International Economic System in a modified role after a period of fairly autarchic social transformation, perhaps development; or to receive assistance from members of an alternative source, either from members of an alternative economic system or from another policial core. Development, especially industrialization, requires either "original accumulation" or credit and aid that can substitute for it.[19] Credit and banking institutions are unlikely to fund countries that propose development schemes which violate the principles of the system of which the institutions are an integral part.

Implications and Conclusions

The world is essentially politically bipolar, but with many marginally aligned or non-aligned second or third order powers. The United States and the Soviet Union each have developed its own sphere of influence both of which have experienced revolutionary movements. Both political cores intervened in these revolutionary movements.

But there are crucial differences between the U.S. and the Soviet spheres of influence which are reflected in the differing nature of intervention. The United States' sphere of influence has been generated by two international systems, the political and the economic. The United States has a military presence in the form of bases, advisers, and military supplies and sales. This is the realm of direct state domination. And the U.S. state has intervened directly especially in Central America and the Caribbean by landing U.S. troops, by "covert" support of rebel troops, or by supporting the indigenous established elite and its troops.

But the U.S. state dominates many countries of Latin America in a second, less direct fashion: By being a dominant member of the economic system within which Latin American states are dependent. The U.S. state in effect reinforces this less direct form of influence by working to promote the international capitalist system and to discourage economic models that alter or dispense with links to that system. This indirect form of influence permits the U.S. state to extend its influence beyond its ability to station troops.

The U.S. state uses economic tools as instruments of state policy but with an imperfect degree of control. The U.S. state can indirectly intervene against a revolutionary state by manipulating the International Economic System or a bit more directly by manipulating its own economy in an effort to utilize the power and leverage that the International Economic System accords its core economy. The U.S. state cannot command other actors in the International Economic System but it can bring pressure and influence to bear in the attempt to turn those actors actively against the revolutionary nation. The U.S. state may not need to apply much pressure if the revolutionary nation is challenging the principles of the International Economic System: Other actors may already be predisposed to action. U.S. ability to intervene economically thus varies with the degree of control that the U.S. state is able to exert over its own economy and with the degree to which the United States as a national economy dominates the International Economic System. The use of troops as a means of domination should increase as U.S. economic power declines relative to the other members of the International Economic System.

The Soviet state dominates its sphere of influence in a much more direct fashion. The Soviet sphere of influence consists primarily of countries in which it has troops such as Eastern Europe. When revolutionary movements threaten the status quo in Eastern Europe, the Soviet state acts directly to contravene such movements. There is no International Economic System that the Soviet state can manipulate: International relations in the Soviet sphere of influence are exclusively state to state. Yet, again drawing upon the concept of political dependency, the Soviet state, like the U.S. state, does work in cooperation with an indigenous elite whose personal achievements and well being, in addition to their ideological commitment, depend upon the continuation of their country's relationship with the Soviet Union. Thus the Soviet state intervenes directly by the use of Soviet troops and indirectly by influencing or pressuring indigenous elites to either suppress their own revolutionary situations or to assist in suppressing their neighbors'.

The U.S. state thus has more tools of pressure and influence but its control over those instruments varies. When the economic instruments of dominance can be used, intervention is more subtle and less spectacular than direct state to state action but perhaps also more insidious and powerful precisely because of its invisibility. The Soviet state has fewer tools at its disposal but its control over those instruments is more sure. Soviet intervention is limited to direct state actions and is consequently more direct, more blunt, and often more spectacular. Thus Soviet intervention tends to be more observable, lending an air of strength and decisiveness to the Soviet image while more forms of U.S. intervention may be overlooked, creating the image, when eventually direct U.S. state action does take place, of a sudden twist in an already erratic foreign policy.

Notes

1. Cf. Ted Robert Gurr, *Why Men Rebel* (Princeton, N.J.: Princeton University Press, 1970); James C. Davies, "Toward a Theory of Revolution," *American Sociological Review* 27 (February 1962): 5–19; Franz Schurmann, *Ideology and Organization in Communist China* (Berkeley: University of California Press, 1968); John Dunn, *Modern Revolutions: An Introduction to the Analysis of a Political Phenomenon* (London: Cambridge University Press, 1970); Chalmers Johnson, *Revolutionary Change* (Boston: Little, Brown, 1966). The "anomic" characterization is taken from Charles Tilly, *From Mobilization to Revolution* (Reading, Mass.: Addison-Wesley, 1978).

2. Marx often writes as if countries constituted closed societies. His analysis of revolutionary events in France treated them by isolating and analyzing the class struggle within that nation. Though men might have a common destiny, they may up to a point advance upon that fate in the company of only their countrymen. Peter Burke notes that "Marx explains social change in fundamentally endogenous terms by the international dynamic of the mode of production." See Peter Burke, *Sociology and History,* Controversies in Sociology, ed. T.B. Bottomore and Dr. M.J. Mulkay, vol. 10 (London: George Allen Unwin, 1980), pp. 90–91.

3. Joel Migdal notes that much literature which addresses the question of change in peasant society, including the seminal anthropological studies of peasants, employs the formulation he calls the "culture contact" theory. Its essence is that "contact between the old and new leads to the triumph of the new patterns" (compare to Peasants, Politics and Revolution (Princeton, N.J.: Princeton University Press, 1974), introduction, p. 7). The "new" in this case originates external to the peasant society and external to the country in which the peasant society happens to be located.

4. Theda Skocpol, *States and Social Revolutions: A Comparative Analysis of France, Russia and China* (Cambridge, Mass.: Cambridge University Press, 1979).

5. Kay Ellen Trimberger, *Revolution From Above* (New Brunswick: Transaction Books, 1978).

6. Kenneth Waltz, *Theory of International Politics* (Reading, Mass.: Addison-Wesley, 1973), p. 39.

7. Ibid., p. 74.

8. Skocpol, *States and Social Revolutions,* p. 26.

9. Ibid., p. 30. Stephen Krasner also develops this idea. See *Defending the National Interest: Raw Materials Investments and U.S. Foreign Policy* (Princeton, N.J.: Princeton University Press, 1978), chap. 1.

10. Fernand Braudel, *The Perspective of the World* (New York: Harper and Row, 1984), p. 22.

11. Fred L. Block has illustrated just how modified these principles are. In general, however, the international monetary order favors "open" nations (which allow the market to play a major role in the flow of goods and money across national boundaries) over "closed" nations (which allow the market little or no role). The international monetary order, or the governing set of rules and procedures of the international monetary system, reflects the influence of the most powerful capitalist nations that created it and the strongest capitalist nations have a "responsibility" to see that the system works according to the "rules." Cf. *The Origins of International Economic Disorder: A Study of United States Monetary Policy From World War II to the Present* (Berkeley: University of California Press, 1977).

12. Theotonio Dos Santos, "The Structure of Dependency" *American Economic Review* 60 (May 1970): 231.

13. Cf. Valerie Bunce, "The Empire Strikes Back: The Evolution of the Eastern Block From a Soviet Asset to a Soviet Liability," *International Organization* 49 (Winter 1985): 1–46, and Torbjørn L. Knutsen, *The Political Economy of Superpower Domination,* PRIO Working Paper 14/85, Peace Research Institute of Oslo, 1985.

14. The single study dedicated to the study of a revolution within an international system is the work by Kyung-Won Kim, *Revolution and International System* (New York: New York University Press, 1970). Kim notes that the revolution transformed the primary unit France from a status quo power to an aggressively revolutionary state. Not only were the motivations and goals of the French government altered, but the revolution transformed the capabilities of France itself, providing among other things, a reinvigorated French army which nearly matched capacity to goals.

15. Waltz suggests that a bipolar world engenders a zero-sum view of the world on the part of decision makers of the two primary states. A loss to one side is consequently automatically perceived to be an absolute gain for the opposition *Theory of International Politics,* p. 171).

16. Most systems theorists including Waltz and Morton Kaplan do not include second or third order powers in their schema and so miss one source of change with the system.

17. Alfred Stepan, *The State and Society: Peru in Comparative Perspective* (Princeton, N.J.: Princeton University Press, 1978), p. 231.

18. Skocpol, *States and Social Revolutions,* p. 17.

19. Alexander Gerschenkron, "Reflections on the Concept of Prerequisites of Modern Industrialism," in *Economic Backwardness in Historical Perspective: A Book of Essays,* ed. Alexander Gerschenkron (Cambridge, Mass.: Belknap Press of Harvard University Press, 1966).

3 RESPONDING TO REVOLUTION: WHY DO THEY DECIDE TO INTERVENE?

Martha L. Cottam

The proclamation that certain political events demand better policy consideration and decision making than others is a truism. Small mistakes in judgment in day-to-day policy adjustments can be corrected. But responding to dramatic political events such as revolutionary change and making delicate decisions concerning policy toward a revolution would seem to demand precise, careful, and well-considered decision-making practices. However, a growing literature in psychology and political science indicates that these are precisely the situations in which policy makers will be least able to follow ideal decision-making procedures. These are the circumstances in which policy makers are most likely to make mistakes and they may be situations in which policy makers are more likely to use coercive measures against a target government. This is the topic of this chapter: What is the likely response to revolution in another country and if the response is intervention, is it probable that such a decision was based upon a careful evaluation of ends and means, costs and consequences, long-term and short-term results, value trade-offs and the nature of the target state? The answer, to make a long story short, is no.

A number of political-psychological issues must be examined in order to address the major perceptual problems policy makers face in responding to revolutionary change. First, an idealized standard for decision making is presented. Second, a brief discussion follows concerning the extent to which all people are unlikely to achieve those ideal standards. Third, the problem of adaptation to change is considered with particular attention to the psychological difficulties involved in adapting to revolutionary change.

Optimal Decision Making Procedures
and Departures from Perfection

There has been considerable research by psychologists and political scientists alike as to the stages involved in optimal or ideal information processing and decision making. Janis and Mann have reviewed the literature and have compiled seven "ideal" procedural criteria [that] have a better chance than others of attaining the decision maker's objectives and of being adhered to in the long run."[1] The decision maker, to the best of his ability and within his information processing capabilities:

1. Thoroughly canvasses a wide range of alternative courses of action;
2. Surveys the full range of objectives to be fulfilled and the values implicated by the choice;
3. Carefully weighs whatever he knows about the costs and risks of negative consequences, as well as the positive consequences, that could flow from each alternative;
4. Intensively searches for new information relevant to further evaluation of the alternatives;
5. Correctly assimilates and takes account of any new information or expert judgment to which he is exposed, even when the information or judgment does not support the course of action he initially prefers;
6. Reexamines the positive and negative consequences of all known alternatives, including those originally regarded as unacceptable, before making a final choice;
7. Makes detailed provisions for implementing or executing the chosen course of action, with special attention to contingency plans that might be required if various known risks were to materialize.[2]

Unfortunately, for policy makers and analysts alike, there are numerous limitations on the ability of normal human beings to process information and make decisions in this manner. Several crucial psychological properties interfere with the decision making.

Moving from general to specific psychological processes, one should begin with the now commonly accepted assumption that individuals (and organizations) are not capable of understanding and evaluating the complexity of the environment that surrounds them in full detail. This notion is a classic in psychology and in political psychology as well.[3] Because of this limitation, people develop psychological screening devices that enable them to filter information and decide (often nonconsciously) which information is valid and should be accepted as true and which information should be ignored as false. Analysts differ in the analytical device chosen to describe this psychological screen but most accept the general argument that beliefs and "images" are the core screening device.[4] In this chapter and elsewhere it is argued that a useful analytical device that describes the psychological filter is the concept of images.[5]

Images are defined similarly by psychologists. Allport defines an image (category) as "an accessible cluster of associated ideas which as a whole has the property of guiding daily adjustment."[6] Zajonc defines them as "a class of events, objects, ideas" and Rosch defines them as "a number of objects that are considered equivalent."[7] In layman's terms, images or categories can be thought of as sets of ideas or beliefs about others that permit the perceiver to organize and simplify the world in which he lives. Allport explains the purposes of psychological images quite nicely:

> The human mind must think with the aid of categories. . . . Once formed, categories are the basis of normal prejudgment. We cannot possibly avoid this process. Orderly living depends upon it.
> Our experience in life tends to form itself into clusters (concepts, categories), and while we may call on the right cluster at the wrong time, or the wrong cluster at the right time, still the process in question dominates our entire mental life. A million events befall us every day. We cannot handle so many events. If we think of them at all, we type them.
> Open-mindedness is considered to be a virtue. But strictly speaking, it cannot occur. A new experience must be redacted into old categories. We cannot handle each event freshly in its own right . . . Bertrand Russell . . . has summed up the matter in a phrase, "a mind perpetually open will be a mind perpetually vacant."[8]

In short, we use categories to organize our knowledge of the environment in which we live. That knowledge, in turn, heavily guides the processing of information, vastly simplifying it nonconsciously. Categories permit the perceiver to assimilate information, to quickly identify an object (or person, or country), to ascribe to it certain qualities associated with the image, and to prejudge a course of action in response to the object's probable behavior. As Allport argues, "There is a curious inertia in our thinking. We like to solve problems easily. We can do so best if we can fit them rapidly into a satisfactory category and use this category as a means of prejudging the solution."[9] Although images are necessary, their use in processing information and judging others is similar to the use of a stereotype and can lead to similar judgment errors. Further, while an image holds certain characteristics always associated with the perceived object, person, or state, it also contains a record of the perceiver's emotional reaction to the perceived item. Thus, when one organizes the world of car salesmen into "new" and "used" car salesmen, one has different emotional associations with each image in accordance with common folk wisdoms and cultural stereotypes.

It is argued by some analysts that in international policy making as in all other arenas of life, images are used to organize an extraordinarily complex environment. The literature suggests that common images of other states include the image of the enemy, ally, dependent of the perceiver's state, the hegemonic or imperialist power, the dependent ally of the enemy, and the neutral.[10] Once political decision makers associate a state and its leaders with one of these images, the image permits them to screen information about that state. The tendency is to accept information that supports the expectations associated with the image. The need for psychological balance and consistency among beliefs accounts for this tendency. Although the psychological process does facilitate the management of a bewilderingly complex and ambiguous political universe, it leads to a number of deviations from optimal decision making as well. Several specific patterns emerge.

The first deviation from optimal decision making deriving from the use of images as information screens is the simplification of the political realities of other states. The more one associates another state with a stereotyped image, the more one tends to assume that the state has the characteristics associated with the image rather than, or regardless of, the actual political idiosyncracies of the individual state. Thus, those who impose the ideal-typical enemy image upon the USSR believe that it is irremediably aggressive, evil and harmful in its intentions, ruled by a small number of highly rational individuals who can carefully orchestrate and carry out their devious plots. They refuse to acknowledge evidence of political factions within the Politburo and evidence of incremental policy planning and errors. The enemy doesn't make mistakes. Similarly, those who perceive the states of Central America as the ideal-typical dependents, that is, the "banana republic" stereotype, see the leaders and people as nice but corrupt, culturally inferior, malleable, unwilling to resist U.S. pressure and incapable of doing so if they wanted to. To the extent that they depart from this behavior they are assumed to be controlled or duped by an external, superior, force.

The tendency to simplify the political realities of another state or the complexities of its leaders is compounded by the association of prototypical examples with the image. The ideal-typical enemy for Americans, for example, is currently the USSR and formerly Hitler's Germany. The ideal-typical example of an ally in American perceptions is Great Britain.[11] The prototypical example of an image is said by psychologists to "anchor" the image. People experience an "assimilation" effect in which objects associated with an image shift toward the anchor, appearing psychologically to be more similar to it than they are.[12] This makes differences among members of a category less distinct and increases the tendency to simplify. Traits associated with the category are imposed upon states associated with it. Missing information, unknowns, are supplied by the image despite the absence of confirming evidence.[13] Finally, once an object is categorized, the perceiver responds to it with more speed and confidence. This is further increased when the object (or state) is seen as being more similar to the ideal-typical example of the image. This, in turn, narrows the range of behaviors the perceiver expects from the state and the range of alternatives associated with responses to those behaviors.

Although all people use images and simplify others to some extent, some individuals are more extreme in their categorization of a particular state than others. Consequently, they tend to disagree about policy alternatives and information concerning a target state. Generally, the more extreme the image, the sharper the stereotype, the less amenable the decision makers to information conflicting with the image and the more they simplify the political realities of the target state. The tendency to push an image to a stereotyped extreme increases with amplified perceptions of threat or opportunity.[14]

The impact of the tendency to rely upon images to assess the validity of information and to make decisions concerning useful policies is cemented and confounded by a number of other psychological processes. Attribution theorists point to several including the use of the representativeness and availability heuristics and the problems of causal inference. The representativeness heuristic is simply the tendency to decide upon the nature of the characteristics of others by assessing the degree to which they are representative of, or similar to, the perceiver's stereotype of others. Certain key pieces of information are used to assess the extent to which a person (or a state's leaders) are similar to a stereotyped other. Information concerning the probability that the individual fits the stereotype is not weighted properly, sample size receives little consideration, as does an understanding of chance error in evaluation.[15] In political decision making one should therefore expect policy makers to look for and attend to characteristics of other states that are highly salient and that represent characteristics of stereotyped images of international actors. Thus, evaluations of other governments, particularly new, revolutionary governments, are quickly made with attention to potentially irrelevant or misleading clues as to their "true" nature. The danger to complex political analysis proffered by this tendency is clearly enhanced by the availability heuristic wherein people "assess the frequency of a class or probability of an event by the ease with which instance or occurrences can be brought to mind."[16] In short, we look for salient indicators as to the nature of other actors, and we assume a greater probability of those characteristics being present when they are easily brought to mind. For example, simple criteria have been used by U.S. policy makers to determine that the nature of the leaders of other states is Communist and an equally simple connection has been made between those characteristics and imagined control by the USSR with all the associated threat.

A curious and important corollary to the tendencies mentioned above is the predilection among policy makers of drawing upon the "lessons of history" in evaluating other states and in deciding upon policy. Jervis argues that policy makers learn most from firsthand experience and from events that were highly salient for them and their nation.[17] They learn important lessons from a small number of cases and they remember a small number of broad general factors as being important in the outcome of those events. These are the events that policy makers regard as representative of the internal characteristics and motivations of states associated with the image imposed upon states in earlier instances. In general, Jervis argues, people "pay more attention to *what* has happened than to *why* it has happened" and will misapply the lessons of history since they often are not learned correctly in the first place.[18] He goes on to note that "because of their predispositions, they see the present as like recent and dramatic events without carefully considering alternative models of the implications of this way of perceiving. They thereby fail to apply fully their intelligence to some of the most important questions they face."[19]

A final psychological process that deserves mention is the tendency to overestimate the role of "dispositions factors" in controlling behavior.[20] We assume that the behavior of others is determined by their dispositions (intentions, motivations) but that our own behavior is determined by constraints imposed by the situation. Thus, when in conflict with another state, we assume the behavior that we dislike is illustrative of the leadership's true nature whereas our own behavior is forced upon us by the situation and cannot and will not be interpreted as part of our own characteristics. For example, when Guatemala purchased weapons from Czechoslovakia in 1954 it was interpreted by U.S. policy makers as evidence of the leadership's pro-Communist leanings rather than as a result of repeated turmoil, rumors of a pending coup, and the arms boycott imposed by the United States since 1948.

Recognizing and Responding to Political Change

Given the importance of psychological "inertia," that is, the tendency to rely upon images derived from experience to help manage current events, it is not surprising that it is very difficult psychologically to recognize and adapt to important political changes in other states. The difficulties are multiple. Psychological studies show clearly that it is most difficult to adapt to incremental change. When dramatic events of an unambiguous nature occur, people are more able to acknowledge that the environment has transformed and some adaptation is called for. Jervis points out that when discrepant information "arrives in a large batch . . . the contradiction between it and the prevailing view will be relatively obvious" and change is more likely.[21] When information arrives slowly or in small amounts, it is easier to discount or ignore. Thus, policy makers are likely to recognize dramatic change as calling for a reassessment of their image of a state. Revolutions tend to be dramatic so policy makers should have little difficulty recognizing the need for change and adaptation. That does not mean, however, that adaptation is easy or will be appropriate.

Despite the fact that revolutions involve change that is relatively easy to recognize, the problems for policy makers do not end and they do not suddenly revert to optimal decision-making practices. The next task they are faced with after recognizing the need for change in image is the evaluation and reclassification of the new government they must deal with in the revolutionary state. Given the discussion above, it should be obvious that they will nonconsciously research through the images already composing their world view looking for a different category in which to place the new state. If the revolution they are observing is similar to some which have gone before and has resulted in a state fitting the types they are familiar with, they are lucky. If not, they will be caught in a nonconscious dilemma of misclassifying and therefore improperly responding to the new state, or of being completely perplexed by a state they cannot classify and of having no previous experience to rely upon for instruction in how to respond. The revolution in Iran provides an excellent example of the latter case. U.S. policy makers were faced with a phenomenon they had never recognized before and could not understand how a revolution could be so profound and opposed to the United States and the Soviet Union at the same time.

Revolutionary states are often classified into a preexisting category. If the revolution is seen as hostile to the perceiver's state's interests, it may result in an "enemy" or "dependent of the enemy" classification. The new classification is not undertaken after a careful evaluation of all the complex attributes of the new government, however. In fact, the classification of an object into a category ordinarily does not occur in after careful evaluation whether one is classifying a state or an individual. Instead, objects (states) are classified on the basis of the attributes that are most salient to the perceiver. This is an important characteristic of psychological images. Psychologists argue that some features are more representative of the image than are other attributes.[22] Judgments of states are made in an impressionistic manner and in terms of a vague assessment of similarities between the state being judged and the prototypical example of an image.

Further insight as to how a revolutionary state will be classified can be gained by referring back to the availability heuristic. Revolutionary states will be classified on the basis of salient characteristics into categories that are most readily available. Given the experiences of both U.S. and Soviet policy makers in the postwar era, the categories that should be most readily available to accommodate a new revolutionary state would be "dependent" and "dependent of the enemy" categories. Most revolutions in the post-World War II era have taken place in the

Third World and both the United States and the USSR have experienced difficulty recognizing the validity of and giving credibility to revolutions creating nonaligned states. U.S. policy makers have given particular attention to salient clues as to the intentions of revolutionary states believed to be perceptible in actions such as the proclamation of socialist or Marxist principles and the establishment of diplomatic relations with socialist countries, particularly the USSR. The discovery of these attributes can easily lead to the reclassification of a state and/or its leaders as dependents of the enemy. Information conflicting with that image is subsequently regarded as unreliable or simply is not acknowledged.

When a new classification results in an image imbued with emotional feelings of threat or opportunity the situation becomes more difficult for the policy makers. Not surprisingly, people assess risks posed by threats and opportunities in terms of past experiences. They cannot "conceptualize floods that have never occurred."[23] Hence one should not be surprised to find that they evaluate political threats in terms of past experience as well. Increased perceptions of environmental threat or opportunity can lead to increased simplification of other states as the policy maker moves away from optimal decision making and toward defensive avoidance. Judgments become self-fulfilling prophesies. It is assumed that the new state, particularly a state previously regarded as a dependent of the United States, will be subservient to a new master. Its people, having always been seen as inferior, will be expected to be unable to deal with the sly Soviets and will be expected to be destined to be agents of the Soviets. The stereotype grows stronger as disconfirming evidence is ignored or disparaged.

All of these patterns together only point to a tendency, a predisposition. They do not permit us to predict that a superpower will or will not intervene or with what instruments it will do so. At the moment, studies of decision making like other theoretical orientations in international politics have not reached the refined theory needed to make such precise calculations. Nevertheless, there is evidence that provides weak indications as to the tactical predispositions of the superpower's policy makers. Studies of bargaining have found repeatedly that power differentials are important in tactics chosen by adversaries in negotiations. Pruitt has found, for example, that negotiators who "see themselves as powerful and as having access to a potent set of competitive tactics will expect concessions from the other and will make few concessions of their own."[24] When a revolutionary state is seen as weak, therefore, superpower policy makers should not be predisposed toward cooperative tactics designed to forge a new understanding and *modus vivendi*. Further evidence of the tendency is available from a survey of foreign policy officials wherein they were asked which of seven tactics they would choose to use and in what order in conflicts with different types of states (enemies, allies, dependents, and so on). There was a clear tendency to move toward the selection of coercive measures in conflicts with weak states (dependents, puppets) much more rapidly than in conflicts with other types of states.[25]

Although one cannot predict with certainty that once a revolutionary state is classified as a state led by individuals under instruction of the stereotyped enemy a superpower will intervene, one can argue that such a classification is not improbable and should lead to a definite pattern of information processing that makes change in image quite difficult. Further, the predisposition should be toward coercive measures, particularly when the revolutionary state is weak. It will, of course, be seen as weakest when its presumed alliance with the enemy is in its formative stages, that is, in the early consolidation years of the revolution. When the environment and information about the "suspect" state is ambiguous, policy makers will tend to rely upon image for instructions. As studies of crisis behavior have shown, they will also be less inclined to undertake careful examinations of all available data. Lebow, for example, argues that several decision-making "pathologies" appear to be important in analyzing crisis performance including "(1) the overvaluation of past performance as against present reality; (2) overconfidence in policies to which decision-makers are committed, and (3) insensitivity to information critical of these policies."[26] Thus the nature of the situation itself reinforces the tendency to ignore conflicting information and to rely upon past experiences in dealing with current problems. Having painted this grim picture of human decision making let us return to the optimal decision-making processes discussed earlier. According to the description of optimal decision making, policy selection in response to a revolutionary situation in another state would require first an assessment of a wide range of alternatives. This would necessitate a full analysis of the relative power and positions of members of the target state's polity, a careful analysis of one's own goals and the implications of each policy alternative for those goals under a variety of possible contingencies. The acknowledgment of possible value trade-offs implied by policy alternatives are an important part of good policy making. Further, new information should be actively sought and attended to, particularly information that challenges one's assumptions and predictions about the behavior of the target government. Finally, the policy alternatives should be evaluated several times, including a review of options previously rejected.

Given the patterns discussed above, it is quite unlikely that decision makers will explore a wide range of alternative courses of action in deciding upon policies toward a revolutionary state. Instead, they will use a simplified image of that state particularly when they experience heightened threat or opportunity perceptions. They will use simplified images to evaluate the state's current behavior and to predict its future behavior. They will carefully select information that supports these ideas

and ignore or distort information that conflicts. The decision maker is unlikely to assess costs and risks associated with preferred policies since he
will rely upon past events for instruction and will fail to carefully search
for causal relationships between action and the outcomes of those earlier
events. He will not search for new and conflicting information but will become increasingly confident that his predispositions have led him to the
correct decision. Finally, when decisions are made with great secrecy, as
they tend to be when planning the covert overthrow of another government, policy makers are even less likely to receive and attend to information indicating that they have not correctly interpreted the situation, that
the policy option they have chosen will not succeed in achieving the goals
they have set or that those goals are not in the best interest of their own
state. Finally, one can see a hidden danger for revolutionary governments
for they may be completely unaware of the image of themselves held by
superpower leaders but that image, once set, is difficult to change and can
lead to disaster for the target government.

Notes

1. Irving Janis and Leon Mann, *Decision Making* (New York: Free Press,
1977), p. 11.

2. Ibid.

3. See Solomon Asch, "Forming Impressions of Personality," *Journal of Ab-
normal and Social Psychology* 41 (1946): 258–90; Gordon Allport, *The Nature of
Prejudice* (Garden City, N.Y.: Doubleday, 1954); Eleanor Rosch and Barbara
Lloyd, eds., *Cognition and Categorization* (Hillsdale, N.J.: Lawrence Erlbaum,
1978); Ole Holsti, "Cognitive Dynamics and Images of the Enemy," *Journal of In-
ternational Affairs* 21 (1967): 16–39; Alexander George, "The 'Operational Code':
A Neglected Approach to the Study of Political Leaders and Decision-Making,"
International Studies Quarterly 13 (1969): 190–222; Robert Jervis, *Perception and
Misperception in International Politics* (Princeton: Princeton University Press,
1976); Richard Cottam, *Foreign Policy Motivation* (Pittsburgh: University of
Pittsburgh Press, 1977); and Martha Cottam, "The Impact of Psychological Images
on International Bargaining: The Case of Mexican Natural Gas," *Political Psychol-
ogy* 6 (1985).

4. Alexander George, *Presidential Decisionmaking on Foreign Policy: The
Effective Use of Information* (Boulder: Westview Press, 1980), and Robert Jarvis,
Perception and Misperception.

5. Richard Cottam, *Foreign Policy Motivation*; Richard Herrmann,
"Analyzing Soviet Images of the US: A Psychological Theory and Empirical
Study" (Paper presented at the International Studies Association/West meeting,
Denver, Colorado, October 1984); and Martha Cottam, "The Impact of Psycholog-
ical Images."

6. Allport, *Nature of Prejudice,* p. 166.

7. Robert Zajonc, "Cognitive Theories of Social Psychology," in *The Hand-*

book of Social Psychology, ed. Gordon Lindzey and Eliott Aronson, 2nd ed. (Reading, Mass.: Addison-Wesley, 1968), p. 332; and Eleanor Rosch, "Principles of Categorization," in Cognition and Categorization, ed. Eleanor Rosch and Barbara Lloyd (Hillsdale, N.J.: Lawrence Erlbaum, 1978), p. 30.

8. Allport, Nature of Prejudice, pp. 19–20.

9. Ibid., p. 20.

10. Richard Cottam, Foreign Policy Motivation; Richard Herrmann, "Analyzing Soviet Images of the US"; and Martha Cottam, "The Impact of Images."

11. Martha Cottam, "Cognitive Limitations and Foreign Policy Decision Making" (Ph.D. diss., University of California, Los Angeles, 1983).

12. J. Richard Eiser and Wolfgang Stroebe, Categorization and Social Judgment (New York: Academica Press, 1972), p. 42.

13. Shelly Taylor and Jennifer Crocker, "Schematic Bases of Social Information Processing," in Social Cognition: The Ontario Symposium, ed. E. Tory Higgins, C. Peter Herman, and Mark Zanna, vol. 1 (Hillsdale, N.J.: Lawrence Erlbaum, 1978), p. 118.

14. The importance of threat and opportunity is discussed in Richard Cottam, Foreign Policy Motivation.

15. Amos Tversky and Daniel Kahneman, "Judgment Under Uncertainty: Hueristics and Biases," in Judgment Under Uncertainty: Heuristics and Biases, ed. Daniel Kahneman, Paul Slovic, and Amos Tversky (Cambridge: Cambridge University Press, 1982).

16. Ibid., p. 11.

17. Jervis, Perception and Misperception, p. 239.

18. Ibid., p. 228.

19. Ibid., p. 282.

20. Lee Ross and Craig Anderson, "Shortcomings in the Attribution Process: On the Origins and Maintenance of Erroneous Social Assessments," in Judgment Under Uncertainty: Heuristics and Biases (Cambridge: Cambridge University Press, 1982), p. 135.

21. Jervis, Perception and Misperception, p. 308.

22. Ross Martin and Andrew Carmazza, "Classification of Well-Defined and Ill-Defined Categories: Evidence for Common Processing Strategies," Journal of Experimental Psychology 109 (1980): 322–22.

23. Tversky and Kahneman, "Judgment Under Uncertainty," p. 465.

24. Dean Pruitt, Negotiation Behavior (New York: Academic Press, 1981), p. 22.

25. Martha Cottam, "Cognitive Limitations," pp. 179–80.

26. Richard Ned Lebow, Between Peace and War (Baltimore: Johns Hopkins University Press, 1967).

4 REVOLUTIONS AND SUPERPOWERS

Jack A. Goldstone

In 437 B.C. a revolution seized the Greek city-state of Corcyra. The outbreak of the conflict and its outcome were largely governed by the actions of the two superpowers of ancient Greece—Athens and Sparta.[1] The issues that arose in Corcyra—legitimacy, elite alignments, popular discontents, and relations with the superpowers—are largely the same as those that confront the governments of small nations today under the pressures of a politically divided world. The lesson of that ancient conflict, that superpowers' policies to secure foreign allies often founder on a misapprehension of the internal politics of those allies, remains critical. Yet it seems that lesson needs to be relearned in modern contexts.

Both the United States and the Soviet Union pursue foreign policies designed to secure the friendship of strategically important foreign states. Yet diverse economic and political pressures on allied states have often undermined those policies. Indeed such policies have often failed in spectacular fashion, with massive revolutions overthrowing the "friendly" governments and replacing them with hostile ones. To be sure, the Soviet Union, through its willingness to commit its own armed forces in massive proportions, has prevented hostile governments from fully supplementing allied governments. Thus, revolutions among the Soviet Union's strategic allies have been abortive—in Czechoslovakia in 1968, in Hungary in 1956, in Poland in 1980, in Afghanistan in 1979. The United States, on the other hand, less willing to commit its own forces to reverse revolutions, has seen the process completed. Most recently, Iran and Nicaragua, two linchpins of U.S. strategic regional support, have been transformed by revolutions from staunch allies to opponents of the United States.

Those arguing in favor of U.S. support of strategic allies, even if they have authoritarian regimes, have argued that authoritarian regimes make

38

stable allies, and may evolve into democracies, while totalitarian regimes never make such an evolution.[2] Yet the proponents of this argument have failed to fully confront the fact that precisely those authoritarian regimes that have received the greatest U.S. support have not evolved into democracies, but have succumbed to revolutions that moved those countries toward becoming hostile, totalitarian regimes.

This chapter examines the cross-cutting pressures on small nations caught in the superpowers' quest for strategic allies, and examines why revolutions have turned U.S. policy on its head, especially in Nicaragua and Iran. It then briefly considers the Soviet Union's responses, and considers alternatives for U.S. policy that may prove more successful.

The Causes of Revolutions in Neopatrimonial States

Revolutions occurred in traditional imperial and absolutist states— France in 1789, China in 1911, Russia in 1917—when those states faced either overwhelming foreign pressures, as Russia did in World War I, or moderate foreign pressures combined with paralyzing opposition to needed economic and administrative centralization and rationalization from autonomous traditional elites who held institutional positions of leverage within the Old Regime administration.[3] Failure to cope with war or paralysis due to the opposition of traditional elites opened the way for popular revolts that undermined the Old Regime. Modernizing elites drawn from urban professional and middle-class groups completed the dismantling of Old Regime institutions and sought to restructure state and society on a more modern basis.

Since World War II, a spate of revolutions and rebellions have sought to overthrow colonial rule or to dislodge traditional landed elites. A partial list includes those in Algeria, Angola, Bolivia, Columbia, China, Cuba, Ethiopia, Iran, Kenya, Nicaragua, the Philippines, and Vietnam. Comparative analysis of these revolutions and rebellions has taken several different directions. Wolf and Paige explored the rural peasant bases of revolutionary movements, and have shown how commercial development conduces to popular mobilization. More recently, Walton, following Skocpol, has stressed the complex international and domestic pressures on contemporary dependent states as crucial to revolution. Dix and Gugler have argued that the most significant recent revolutions, those in Iran and Nicaragua, were only partially "peasant" revolutions, and depended far more on interactions among urban groups, elites, and the state. Wallerstein has stressed the limited autonomy of dependent states whose economies play subordinate roles in the world-system, and the likelihood of revolutions aimed at gaining greater autonomy.[4]

Foreign pressures, conflicts with elites, and popular revolts have all combined in bringing about recent revolutions, and we shall return to many of the themes mentioned above. However, one of the key lessons of comparative studies is that the vulnerability of states to revolutions differs among states with different institutions. Thus we need to consider how contemporary states differ from traditional imperial and absolutist states.

Contemporary states generally have partially modernized governments in which the chief executive's and other officials' rule are based on some form of constitutional and parliamentary political arrangements rather than simply hereditary authority, and in which traditional landed elites have no institutionalized roles in administration. Instead the chief executive's rule is organized through political party mechanisms and sanctioned through a combination of electoral, bureaucratic, and military rule.

Among such states, the United States has often sought as regional allies states with strong personal leaders, such as the Somozas in Nicaragua or the Shah in Iran. These states, blending modern and traditional institutions, often have a political system that can be described as "neopatrimonial." To understand the processes that can lead such states to revolution, we need to examine their structure and their weaknesses.

The Neopatrimonial State and Its Vulnerabilities

Eisenstadt has described as neopatrimonial those partially modernized states in which the chief executive depends primarily on an extensive system of personal patronage, rather than acceptance of and obedience to impersonal law, to maintain state authority.[5] Such states may have democratic trappings, including parliaments and political parties, constitutions and elections. However, it is recognized by all that the decisions of the chief of state are quite secure, as the patronage system, plus coercion where necessary, secures the compliance of the legislature and the political parties, the favorable interpretation of the constitution, and electoral victories. Examples include Mexico under Diaz, Nicaragua under Somoza, and Iran under the Shah.

In such states, the masses are generally depoliticized. They may participate in periodic elections under the eye of local state servants; however, their interest in the economy and the polity is largely defensive. Their goal is merely to preserve their livelihood, with as little contact with the state authorities as possible. Whether in urban or rural settings, a secure if modest income and traditional habitations and culture are their requisites.

The elites in such states, by contract, are strongly politicized. The chief executive therefore is in a situation where he must broker among highly active elite segments. These generally include traditional oligarchs, new professionals, and military/bureaucratic elites. Traditional oligarchs are generally strong supporters of the state; they usually depend on ownership of land, and while they have traditionally enjoyed the support of the state they have also controlled their own networks of patronage and coercion. New professionals are the product of the introduction of modern systems of education, law, medicine, and communication. Engineers, journalists, lawyers, doctors, teachers, and businessmen, they are characteristically rooted in urban settings, and have strong contacts with international business and culture. If one adds skilled workers to these groups, they constitute the bulk of the urban middle classes. The military/bureaucratic elites comprise the arms of the state. However, they are a force unto themselves with their own interests.

They may support the old oligarchs, the new professionals, or the chief executive in the event of policy or financial conflicts. Or they may be rendered impotent by internal splits and corruption. In either event, their ability to secure the role of the chief executive by fiat is questionable, for their loyalty too depends on the workings of the patronage system. In short, neopatrimonial states rely on the support of a diverse assemblage of elites, themselves often divided, to maintain authority over a largely depoliticized population.

This kind of state thus has varied vulnerabilities. First, since it relies chiefly on elite support, rather than on mass support, alienation of too many segments of the elite can be fatal. Second, since the elites themselves are divided, the chief executive must perform a complex balance act to preserve the alliance of diverse elites while counterbalancing their conflicts. Third, since the populace is depoliticized, the state can be threatened by mass-mobilizing movements which place new forces in the political arena. Thus, the defection of elites, plus the willingness of elites to mobilize masses against the state, can leave the chief executive with few defenses other than sheer armed force, whose loyalty itself is never assured.

How does the chief executive maintain authority, indeed an authority that seems near-absolute, in such precarious conditions? The typical strategy is a mix of divide and conquer, carrot and stick, and indispensability approaches.

In neopatrimonial states, the chief executive generally faces elites with divided goals. Rather than attempt to unify them, the executive generally chooses to reinforce their divisions. The armed forces, political parties, urban professionals, landed oligarchs, and state bureaucrats, are each encouraged to form direct, competing links to the chief executives' patronage networks. The armed forces, political party leaders, and state officials may be encouraged to share in corruption or in secret deals and partnerships in order to isolate them from other groups. As a result, different elite segments find themselves in competition for the ear of, and the official power and financial advantages conferred by, the chief executive. The chief executive then becomes the crucial broker of power in the society, its sole political "center." The divisions among the elites make reliance on the chief executive essential for political coordination and conflict-management.

Of course, the ability of the executive to manage such conflict and provide central coordination depends on its ability to dispense resources valued by the elite, chiefly money and political power. Thus, chief executives seek to implement policies for rapid economic growth. Such growth enriches the executive, of course, but it also provides the essential fuel to power his political machinery.

Contemporary neopatrimonial states usually seek to turn economic growth to modernization of the armed forces, growth of enterprises requiring professional and skilled workers, and growth of the state bureaucracy. This gives the executive the ability to dispense the carrots of military and bureaucratic posts, and economic contracts that will profit the elite. In addition, securing the loyalty of the landed elite generally requires that land reforms be kept moderate. Depoliticization of the masses is also served by economic growth sufficient to allow growing populations to sustain themselves at rationally accustomed levels of food, clothing, and habitation.

Policies for promotion of economic growth are coupled with the "stick"—the threat of loss of wealth, position, liberty, or life, for opposing the chief executive. Potential opposition leaders are often jailed or exiled, political freedoms (including freedom of speech) are limited, and even loyal aides whose accomplishments or influence threaten to make them autonomous leaders find themselves promptly disposed of.

In addition to these strategies, the chief executive seeks to increase his "indispensability" by monopolizing key contact points in the society. The chief executive may be the only contact between the military and the civilian elites. He (and his close associates) may monopolize contact with foreign nations, seeking to become the indispensable conduit for foreign aid and investment. He generally seeks to avoid appointing, or even favoring, possible successors. Thus, the executive seeks to reinforce the fear that, if he or she is lost, political coordination and conflict management and the flow of foreign resources will fail, leading to chaos.

These are potent strategies. Provided that economic growth provides resources, a politically adept chief executive, by skillful manipulation of elite aspirations and rewards, forging of strong ties to foreign resources, and limited coercion, can achieve and maintain a substantial concentration of power. The Shah of Iran, the Somozas in Nicaragua, Marcos in the

Philippines, Batista in Cuba, Chiang Kai-shek in China, and Diaz in Mexico are examples of chief executives who typify this pattern.[6]

Pressures and Problems in Neopatrimonial States

Despite their success, the vulnerabilities of neopatrimonial executives do not disappear; indeed they may increase over time.

First, as economic growth continues, the ability of the executive to broker the conflicting demands of the elites becomes more difficult. After the initial stages of foreign investment, domestic urban and professional elites may seek greater domestic control of the economy. Nationalism thus becomes a potent ideology among a segment of the elites. The executive thus must balance increased reliance on foreign aid and foreign investment, which increases the resources that the executive controls but requires satisfaction of foreign investors and states, against satisfying the demands of its own professional and economic elite for national self-determination.

Second, the urban and professional elite, and skilled workers, may also seek a domestic economy more geared to satisfaction of domestic consumption than to export growth and luxury and heavy industrial import. Yet establishing light industry and a domestic consumer market generally requires improving the education and economic status of the populace, including the peasantry. This goal can come into conflict with the desires of the landed oligarchy to maintain its control of land and the rural labor force.

Third, as the state bureaucracy expands, it eventually comes into conflict with traditional organizations, including guilds, local village organizations, and religious organizations. Where the state is successful in absorbing the functions of these bodies, state power may increase. Yet this is difficult where the autonomy of these organizations is well established, and the traditional organizations control considerable resources and cultural authority. Conflicts between state and church may arise over secularization of economic life, over control of popular education and local justice, over disposal of church resources, and over cultural and ideological hegemony. Any of these conflicts can spur religious elites to seek alliances with other elite segments against the state, or to support popular mobilization against the state.[7]

Fourth, the temptation to monopolize resource may become a self-defeating one. If the chief executive concentrates power and the proceeds of corruption too closely in his hands, and those of a local circle, the flow of "carrots" to diverse elite segments diminishes. Where elites find themselves excluded from their traditional, albeit limited, share in government and wealth, dependency on the chief executive quickly turns to animosity. Overuse of the "stick" and restriction of "carrots" is one of the most common errors of neopatrimonial executives over the course of their rule.[8]

Fifth, the temptation to rely too heavily on foreign support may become fatal. Foreign support, both in terms of financial aid through grants and investment and in terms of military/political aid, is highly attractive to neopatrimonial executives. It is a source of economic and political resources and, most importantly, a source over which the chief executive can establish exclusive control. As it becomes more difficult to satisfy conflicting elite demands and aspirations, and since there is no mass popular base to counterbalance the elites, there is thus a temptation to rely increasingly on foreign support. Yet this can further alienate the elites by frustrating their nationalist ambitions, and leaves the executive in a highly extended and vulnerable position if foreign support should fall.[9]

Finally, the economic growth that fuels the patronage machine may falter. Growth may also fail to trickle down to the masses, resulting in growing inequality and failure to meet traditional popular aspirations for diet, habitation, and family life.

In combination, these problems can cause a neopatrimonial regime to unravel with astonishing rapidity. Economic setback and overuse of coercion may begin a trend of elite defection and attempts at mobilizing the masses against the state. Overdependence on foreign support may leave the chief executive isolated and vulnerable to nationalist movements. Finally, if elites overcome their division to unite against the executive, and if the loyalty of the army should falter or be pressed by widespread popular mobilization against the executive and urban or rural revolts, revolution becomes nearly inevitable. This course of events unfolded in the Mexican, Cuban, Nicaraguan, and Iranian revolutions.[10].

The very "indispensability" of the chief executive works against a smooth transfer of power to another, and against maintenance of existing institutions. These are too deeply identified with the chief executive and his or her system of personal rule for them to gain credit by simply adopting a new head. The solution of "Somozism without Somoza" in Nicaragua, or of a new minister (Bahktiar) at the head of the Shah's state in Iran, had little appeal to elites seeking to establish their autonomy, reverse their exclusions from control of the state, and satisfy the aspirations of their now-mobilized popular supporters. Once the chief executive has lost elite support, and the masses are mobilized against him or her, the result is almost certain to be transformation of state institutions, a revolution in the bases of power and the constellation to the dominant elites, and unpredictable turns in policy and economic organization as elite segments vie for state control, court popular support, and seek to reconstruct state institutions—in short, a full-scale revolution.[11]

Superpowers and Revolution

How do superpowers exacerbate or alleviate the vulnerability of neopatrimonial states? And what effect do superpower actions have once a revolution has begun?

Problems in U.S. Policy and Revolutionary Debacles

It should be obvious that U.S. policy has often exacerbated the vulnerability of the very regimes that it relies on for regional strategic support.

First, overdependence on the United States is encouraged. A massive flow of foreign and military aid precludes the need for a foreign executive to build a domestic base. Instead, the resource flow encourages the executive to continue to play the game of selectively dispensing or withholding patronage resources. The greater the resources available, the greater the temptation to control, rather than cooperate and rely on, domestic elites.

Second, overidentification of the executive with U.S. aid irritates feelings of nationalism among the elite. In their eyes, opposition to the dominance of the executive becomes synonymous with opposition to the United States and national self-determination.

Third, while the U.S. seeks to increase the dependence of foreign executives on U.S. aid, it seeks to impose domestic policies which weaken the executive—limits on coercion, greater political expression for professional elites and skilled workers, meaningful elections, restrictions on corruption. All of these undermine the system on which executive power is based. To the extent that the United States is satisfied with lip service on these issues, the executive may retain power. But the price is high; the United States comes to be viewed by domestic elites as an insincere and untrustworthy advocate of popular rights and national self-determination. Thus, in the event that the executive falters, successor elites are unlikely to view the United States favorably, either as a mediator for succession or as a continuing ally.

Indeed, U.S. policy has generally precipitated disasters by initially supporting neopatrimonial executives and giving only lip service to its insistence on liberal reforms, but then insisting more emphatically on such reforms, usually under threat of withholding economic or military assistance. Such policies place the neopatrimonial executive in an impossible position—if he enacts liberalizing reform, he undermines the basis of his rule; if he does not enact such reforms, he loses U.S. aid which is essential to his maintaining his rule. In short, such policy almost guarantees that the executive's power will falter, and that the United States will lack influence or credibility with likely successors.

Exactly this course was followed in Iran and Nicaragua in the late 1970s. After decades of almost unconditional support of the Shah and the Somoza family, during which time the privileges of domestic elites were gradually curtailed and the chief executive aggrandized through manipulation of growing foreign investment and aid, the United States began to insist on a "human rights policy" that undermined the neopatrimonial patterns of rule. The result was greater room to maneuver for the domestic opposition to the Shah and the Somoza. Yet the Shah and Somoza sought to enact only limited reforms, to change as little as possible while still satisfying the United States. Continued support for the Shah and Somoza thus brought a policy debacle: the domestic elites perceived the United States as hypocritically supporting reforms which changed little, and maintaining its support for a repressive regime; yet the atmosphere of reform and U.S. pressure hindered the chief executive and emboldened the opposition in its quest for major reforms. The increased vigor of the opposition, and the ambiguous, albeit vocal, support for the executive, initiated an escalation of opposition that culminated in 1979 in revolutions in both Nicaragua and Iran.[12] Both revolutions brought power elites that were hostile to the United States and that sought to realign the foreign policy of what had been a steadfast ally.

Superpower Competition and Revolutions

The USSR, through its willingness to intervene with overt and massive force in the event of revolutionary threats to allied governments, has largely avoided the loss of strategic allies. Its main competition with the United States therefore comes in courting new revolutionary regimes, and thus in taking advantage of U.S. policy debacles. In these instances—Cuba in 1958, Nicaragua in 1979—it was not Soviet support for the opposition to the Old Regime that resulted in the failure of U.S. policy. Instead, U.S. policy tended to promote both the failure of the neopatrimonial regime, and the hostility of successor elites. Such elites generally were initially broad-based and had few ties to the Soviet Union.[13] Yet their hostility to the United States was met by U.S. hostility in turn, including strict conditions on granting aid to the new regime, denunciation of Marxist tendencies among the revolutionaries, and trumpeting of the danger that the revolution poses to the region. The result was to exacerbate tensions between the United States and the successor elites, and to leave the latter forced to look elsewhere for support in the process of political economic reconstruction. The Soviet Union, taking advantages of such opportunities, then built ties to the new regimes. These resulted in further U.S. hostility (for example, embargoes) which forced further dependency on

Soviet support. The result was a self-fulfilling prophecy of eventually Communist orientation that could likely have been avoided had the United States built strong and credible ties to the domestic opposition prior to the revolution. In short, the very policies that precipitate the fall of neopatrimonial allied regimes generally produce opportunities for the successful spread of Soviet influence.

Conclusion

Superpower policy toward those regional allies who maintain neopatrimonial regimes, and are thus vulnerable to revolution, must therefore recognize a variety of factors in the domestic politics of such allies. First, the regime has a precarious dominance over diverse elites. Second, overreluctance on foreign support tends to alienate the nationalist aspirations of those elites. Third, lacking its own mass base, the regime is highly vulnerable to mass mobilization by domestic elites in opposition to the regime. Fourth, many trends in dependent economic development— growing inequality, failure of popular income to provide traditional levels of food, habitation, and family lifestyles, growth of urban professional and skilled workers, dependence on exports subject to cycles of boom and bust, international debt and inflation—are precisely those that encourage mass mobilization. Fifth, superpower influence is seen as beneficial in limited amounts, but as pernicious and threatening to national self-determination in large amounts. Sixth, foreign support for limited liberalizing reform, especially rhetorical support for reform combined with continued support for authoritarian regimes, undermines the credibility of foreign powers with domestic elites, including likely successor regimes should the neopatrimonial state falter.

These six points need to be kept in mind when considering the impact of superpower policies on foreign states vulnerable to revolution. Failure to keep these points in mind generally leads to the failure of superpower policy, in quite spectacular fashion.

Notes

1. Thucydides, *The Peloponnesian War,* the Crawley translation (New York: Modern Library, 1982).
2. Jean Kirkpatrick, *Dictatorships and Double Standards: Rationalism and Reason in Politics* (New York: Simon and Schuster, 1982).
3. Theda Skocpol, *States and Social Revolutions: A Comparative Analysis of France, Russia, and China* (Cambridge: Cambridge University Press, 1978).
4. Eric Wolf, *Peasant Wars of the Twentieth Century* (New York: Harper

and Row, 1969); Jeffery Paige, *Agrarian Revolution* (New York: Free Press, 1975); John Walton, *Reluctant Rebels* (New York: Columbia University Press, 1984); Robert Dix, "The Varieties of Revolution," *Comparative Politics* 15 (1983): 281–93; Josef Gugler, "The Urban Character of Contemporary Revolutions," *Studies in Comparative International Development* 17 (1982): 60–73; Immanuel Wallerstein, *The Capitalist World Economy* (Cambridge: Cambridge University Press, 1980).

5. S.N. Eisenstadt, *Revolution and the Transformation of Societies: A Comparative Study of Civilizations* (New York: Free Press, 1978).

6. This list includes nations highly varied in their social structure, culture, and history. In this chapter I focus on broad similarities in their recent political structure and development. For a more detailed treatment of many of these cases, including more attention to differences in the origins and outcomes of their revolutions, see Jack Goldstone, *Revolutions: Theoretical, Comparative, and Historical Studies* (New York: Harcourt Brace Jovanovich, 1985).

7. James Scott, "Peasant Revolution: A Dismal Science," *Comparative Politics* 9: (1977): 231–48.

8. Richard Kraus, William Maxwell, and Rowe Vanneman, "The Interests of Bureaucrats: Implications of the Asian Experience for Recent Theories of Development," *American Journal of Sociology* 85 (1979): 135–55.

9. Walter Goldfrank, "Theories of Revolution and Without Theory: The Case of Mexico," *Theory and Society* 7 (1979): 135–65; Jorge Dominguez, *Cuba: Order and Revolution* (Cambridge, MA: Harvard University Press, 1978).

10. On the precarious loyalty of the armed forces in revolutionary conflicts, see D.E.H. Russell, *Rebellion, Revolution, and Armed Forces* (New York: Academic Press, 1974).

11. This was quite evident in Cuba and Nicaragua. See Jorge Dominguez, *Cuba: Order and Revolution,* and R.E. Chavarria, "The Nicaraguan Insurrection: An Appraisal," in *Nicaragua in Revolution,* ed. Thomas Walker (New York: Praeger, 1982), pp. 29–37.

12. Thomas Walker, *Nicaragua: Land of Sandino* (Boulder, CO: Westview Press, 1981); Edward Abrahamian, *Iran Between Two Revolutions* (Princeton: Princeton University Press, 1978).

13. See Dominguez, *Cuba, Order and Revolution,* and Walker, *Nicaragua: Land of Sandino.*

II: THE UNITED STATES AND REVOLUTION

5 THE U.S. STYLE OF INTERVENTION

Daniel McIntosh

Intervention in the domestic affairs of Third World states—particularly states undergoing "revolutionary" political and social change—is a persistent feature of U.S. foreign policy. Yet for all its importance, it is remarkable how little progress has been made to place these actions within the context of a general theory of intervention, or to explain recurring patterns of U.S. behavior. The case studies of this section point in the direction of such a theory, and suggest that the decision whether or not to intervene as well as the form of the intervention, is the product of an evolving U.S. policy culture operating within the constraints of the international system. This policy culture has been routinized in contemporary institutions and beliefs, and provides a key for understanding and anticipating behavior. There is, in short, a U.S. style of intervention.

A Definition of Intervention

The concept of "intervention" has been used to label and describe a large set of dissimilar acts. James Rosenau has observed that, depending on the context, intervention often "appears to be synonymous with imperialism, aggression, colonialism, neocolonialism, war, and other such gross terms that are used to designate the noncooperative interactions of nations."[1] Acts described as interventions may be overt or covert, conser-

I wish to thank the Ford Foundation Fellowship Program in Combined Soviet/East European and International Security Studies, administered by Columbia University, for its support during the period in which I have written this chapter.

vative or revolutionary. They may be unilateral or collective. Analysts of
intervention have identified military interventions, economic interventions, political interventions, diplomatic interventions, and even structural interventions. Any concept associated with such diverse activities is
so vague as to lose much of its value. If it is to be useful, what must "intervention" mean?

The classic formulation of intervention, as derived from international
law, is "the dictatorial or coercive interference, by an outside party or parties, in the sphere of jurisdiction of a sovereign state."[2] But to try to understand intervention by focusing upon international law is like trying to understand urban crime by reading criminal statutes. Law is, at best, evidence of common norms—not an explanation.

A more useful approach is the definition of a small set of necessary
characteristics which are common to all acts of intervention and which
differentiate intervention from other interstate behavior. Rosenau's formulation is the point of departure for this essay:

> Two characteristics would appear to be necessary attributes of interven-
> tionary phenomena and, as such, to provide a basis for an operational
> definition. One might be called the *convention-breaking* character of in-
> terventions. The other is their *authority-oriented* nature.[3]

Thus, an intervention "constitutes a sharp break with the then-existing
forms" of behavior and is "directed at changing or preserving the structure of political authority in the target society."[4]

Intervention is not merely interference in the internal affairs of a
state. If for no other reason, intervention is not synonymous with interference because interference may not be intentional. Given the unequal
distribution of power in the interstate system, interference may not even
be avoidable. At least in principle, an intervention may always be avoided. As Hedley Bull has observed, "an intervention always implies a
decision to do something, when not doing something is also an option."[5]

Systemic Influences

Intervention involves a decision to change behavior. However, this
should not blind us to the relevance of systemic factors. While the structure of the international system does not make intervention necessary, it
does make intervention possible, and differing interstate systems are associated with unique opportunities and restraints.

The obvious systemic influence on the decision to intervene is the
distribution of power. "Power" is itself a broadly-defined concept, but to
have any meaning it must include not only the capabilities that may be

brought to bear by the intervening power and its target, but also the internal stability of each state. Technological or economic resources are important, but no less so are the requirements for domestic support and organization. The failure of U.S. "power" in Vietnam is but one reminder of its social basis.

In recent years both the military capabilities of smaller states and their willingness to defend themselves against intervention have increased. The growth of capabilities has prompted Richard Smoke to declare that the world is "entering an era of 'military plenty.' " Between 1960 and 1974, the military expenditures of states outside of NATO and the Warsaw Pact jumped from about $8 billion per year to over $20 billion per year.[6] In 1984 these expenditures totaled nearly $171 billion.[7] The Falklands war has demonstrated that advanced military technology is no longer solely the possession of the core states of the international system.

As the rise of Third World nationalism continues, there is no reason to believe that these new capabilities will not be used. In fact, they are already being used, both to make war and to intervene in the conflicts of others. Contrary to expectations, most of the interventions in the civil wars of the 1970s were not instigated by industrialized states, but by less-developed countries.[8] Given the growth of capabilities and will, a U.S. decision maker contemplating intervention must consider the possibility that his use of force will soon escalate beyond the price that he is willing to pay.

In addition to the distribution of capabilities, the pattern of norms that are applied across national boundaries affect the probability and the form of intervention. The normative structure is expressed in several ways. First, the acceptance of "spheres of influence" serves to limit direct competition between hegemonic powers and to legitimize intervention by each great power within its region. The boundaries of these spheres have by no means remained stable over time, nor do spheres of influence imply a balance of power. As Bull has observed, "the history of Europe's relations with the rest of the world in the age of expansion is less one of balance among the contending powers than it is one of a succession of hegemonies."[9] A more recent example of a marginal change in a sphere of influence is the attempt to restructure U.S. commitments following the fall of Saigon. Despite these changes, the use of spheres of influence as an organizing principle remains, and a theory of intervention must take this into account.

The reliance upon spheres of influence to regulate and legitimize intervention requires a minimum level of cooperation among hegemonic powers. If for no other reason than to discourage general warfare between them, the powers must tacitly agree to adhere to the "rules of the game." This minimal cooperation is not always possible. In some cases, an internal ideology is so defined that its application cannot be less than universal. As in the case of Europe following the French Revolution, the attempts of states to universalize their domestic ideologies can disrupt the normative system, thus promoting coercive acts within and between blocs. In these circumstances, the ideology does not merely legitimize intervention, but actively promotes it.

This is particularly true if the ideology explicitly links the domestic organization of a state with its foreign policy behavior. If a particular socioeconomic system is considered to be a necessary foundation for a "friendly foreign policy, intervention to create or preserve such a system is logically imperative. It is perceived not only as a historic duty, but as an act of self-defense.

As an ideal type, intervention transcends particular nations and ideologies. For example, Weede has suggested the "imperial order maintenance is a general phenomenon; the only thing special about the American empire is its informality and the American reluctance to define it as an empire."[10] Yet the variation that he dismisses desrves to be examined and explained. There is no reason to assume that capability requires action, only that capability permits it. Nor does ideological disagreement serve as an unmediated cause of intervention. In order to have an affect upon state's behavior, systemic factors must be perceived by the individuals within the organizations responsible for foreign policy. Political outcomes are the result of interactions within the international system, but foreign policy outputs are the result of decisions made by individuals within a state.

U.S. Policy Culture

There are several recurring patterns associated with U.S. intervention in the Third World which deny a purely rational or systemic explanation. These include the unwillingness to use overt military force without an invitation by the target government, the frequent use of covert operations against unwanted regimes, the tendency to associate Communist threats with nationalist movements, and the postwar definition of the boundaries of the U.S. sphere of interest. A more comprehensive explanation requires that we look at the internal motivations and constraints that affect the decision to intervene, as found in the "policy culture" of the U.S. decision-making elite.

The notion that there is an identifiable set of beliefs that have motivated and guided U.S. behavior since World War II is not new. Daniel Yergin, for example, has written of the role of the "Riga axioms" in U.S. foreign policy.[11] Herbert Tillema has linked the decision to take overt military action to "the containment way of thinking" found in the U.S.

elite since 1947.[12] The concept of policy culture is rooted in this perspective. "Culture" refers to the enduring products of social interaction, which exist independently of the individuals who created them, and which serve to influence subsequent behavior. "Policy culture" narrows the focus to the set of individuals whose roles enable them to act in the name of the state. Thus, negotiating a treaty is a social act, but once approved the treaty itself is a cultural artifact. Once it is decided upon, a policy affects future decisions. Indeed, one of the purposes of policy is to restrict choices, setting guidelines that allow decision makers to perceive order in chaos and take action according to rules. Over time, decisions cannot help but tend toward incrementalism, and governing takes the form of "muddling through."

The importance of the policy culture is reflected by the tenacity with which those enmeshed in it resist change, and the effort expended to shape it by those who wish to alter foreign policy. In a modern bureaucratized government like that of the United States, the debate over foreign policy ends and means is often transformed into a struggle to manipulate institutional roles and rules.

In this struggle, policy-making institutions are not a passive environment for decisions. They are an arena whose shape favors some alternatives over others, and which changes somewhat after each battle. Thus, a low-cost commitment becomes a guiding principle of foreign policy. A phrase inserted into a presidential address to end an internal debate returns to haunt the policymaker. An agency created to oversee feuding factions fails in that task, but becomes the advocate of a previously unrepresented position. Capabilities create motivations, just as motivations lead to new capabilities.

As a first approximation, intervention may be explained as a result of rational calculation, balancing the probable losses to the hegemony if a target state develops an unwanted domestic system and/or foreign policy against the probable costs of taking action to create or maintain a desired condition. But of course ideal types are not present in reality, and human decisions are at best the product of bounded rationality.[13] The U.S. policy culture of intervention, by providing a context for decisions, tends to shape those decisions in predictable ways.

The current U.S. policy culture influences the decision to intervene by two means: perceptual filters and institutional channels. These are in turn the products of history. The policy culture underwent an exceptional transformation in the first few years following the Second World War, which witnessed the creation of the cold war consensus and the national security state. However, neither the consensus nor the organizational structure emerged without regard to prior events. Two centuries of accumulated decisions and experiences underlie the present. If we are to understand the policies of today, we must first look at their foundation.

The U.S. Experience with Intervention

As the United States has grown from colony to superpower, it has experienced intervention as a target, as a revolutionary power, and as a hegemonic defender of the status quo. During the Revolutionary War, great power rivalry helped to set the stage for U.S. independence. "Covert" arms shipments from France made possible the victory at Saratoga; there were more French sailors than American soldiers at Yorktown.

The first military intervention by the new American state was, ironically, against the French in support of the Dutch at Curaçao in 1800. In 1803, Thomas Jefferson authorized the first U.S. "covert action," applying funds and marines to a troublesome government in North Africa. Perceived U.S. interests varied widely and quickly, but by 1823, U.S. and British interests had converged sufficiently that President Monroe could declare "that the American continents, by the free and independent condition which they have assumed and maintain, are henceforth not to be considered as subjects for future colonization by a European power,"[14] while relying on the indirect support of the British navy. The provision for noninterference in European conflicts was violated only four years later, when two landings were made in Greece to raid pirate villages. Nevertheless, the perception of the Western Hemisphere as the domain of the United States has become one of the guiding principles of U.S. policy.

Tillema has identified three conditions for overt military interventions prior to the Civil War: in response to pirates; to suppress the slave trade; and to protect U.S. citizens and their property in the Far East and Latin America. Of these rationales, the third was the least commonly invoked. In addition, a large number of actions seem to have occurred at the discretion of U.S. naval officers physically unable to consult with higher authorities.[15] There was not so much a consistent "U.S. style" as a set of low-level idiosyncratic decisions. In those cases when a decision to use force was made at the presidential level—as in the raids on the Barbary pirates or the naval skirmishes with France—it was generally, but not always, subject to congressional approval. The president was the dominant voice in the creation of foreign policy, but often lacked the authority to make and implement decisions that would be common a century later.

Between the Civil War and the Spanish-American War, the decision to intervene was still largely unpredictable, although improvements in technology and the centralization of authority increasingly made the relevant decision maker the president, not the military commander on the scene.

Despite the general tendency for imperial expansion, it is still not appropriate to speak of associating an identifiable policy culture with intervention in these years. Instead, the decision to intervene seems to be associated more with the swings of domestic politics and the personality of the president. The war powers associated with Lincoln were sharply curtailed during Reconstruction. One example of these swings in policy is U.S. relations with Cuba and Spain. After internal debate and the failure of a House resolution to recognize the Cuban revolutionaries, the administration of President Grant refused to intervene in the Ten Years' War of 1868–78. Twenty years later, and with less objective motivation, President McKinley bowed to popular pressure and recommended military action. Paradoxically, bowing to congressional pressure served in the long run to increase the authority of the commander in chief.

Between the beginning of the twentieth century and the end of the First World War, the growing power of the United States was matched by the increasing institutionalization of the policy process, and a consequent decline in the importance of idiosyncratic factors. The president remained the dominant voice, but general patterns and particular interventions began to survive changes of administration—particularly in Latin America.

Theodore Roosevelt was proud of his ability to affect events around the globe, as exemplified by his sending the marines to Beirut in 1903 and Tangiers in 1904, but the defining characteristic of U.S. interventions of the early twentieth century was the drive to establish its preeminence in the Western Hemisphere. Cuba, subordinated to the United States by the Platt amendment in 1901, was subjected to U.S. intervention from 1906 to 1909, and again in 1917, in order to protect U.S. investments and forestall interventions by European powers. Likewise, Nicaragua was occupied in an application of "dollar diplomacy" in 1909 and 1912, while the governments of Haiti and the Dominican Republic were replaced by U.S. military rule in 1915 and 1916, respectively. President Wilson repeatedly intervened during the course of the Mexican Revolution.

The general pattern survived the First World War. A 1924 survey found that only six of 20 Latin American states were free from financial or political domination by the United States, while another six were occupied by U.S. troops.[16] U.S. forces remained in Nicaragua until 1933, and in Haiti until 1934. But as the policy stabilized, it moved in a direction far different from today.

By the mid-1930s the institutionalization of foreign policy was sufficiently advanced for one to refer to a U.S. policy culture of intervention. Yet in contrast to post-1947 America, it was a culture that emphasized costs over threats. No new use of force was authorized between 1928 and 1941. The isolationist mood that denied an active global role for the United States was reflected and maintained by the government, and a tendency to avoid new military interventions became routinized within the foreign policy elite. The domestic economy was seen to be a far more immediate concern than the problems of either Europe or Latin America.

Although the circumstances were similar to events associated with intervention in the past, the United States avoided military involvement in revolts in Ecuador and Brazil, as well as in the Chinese civil war.

These 13 years without new interventions more than doubled the longest abstention from the use of force between 1800 and 1928. It is indicative of a modern, bureaucratized state. To change such a policy culture requires a substantial shock, and for the United States, that shock would be the Second World War. The war and its aftermath transformed not only the international system, but also the ideology and organizations of the United States. Short of a similar shock, it is difficult to imagine another such transformation.

The Postwar Consensus

In attempts to reconstruct the decisions of the past, the historian acts as an archeologist of ideas: assembling fragments of statements and actions to produce a picture of the mindset of those who took action. These fragments indicate that in the years immediately following the Second World War, the policy-making elite of the United States found themselves with the capabilities of a superpower, but lacking a clear idea of how those capabilities were to be used. The new consensus that eventually emerged provided direction for U.S. policy.

One source of new ideas was the lessons from the war. Reflecting upon the origins of the war produced a sensitivity to the costs of appeasing totalitarian leaders. In addition, strategy during the war reinforced three prior tendencies in U.S. behavior. First, in a choice between Europe and Asia, Europe remained the first priority. Second, economic resources were used whenever possible to save time and American lives. Third, the conduct of the war involved the cultivation of the public perception of a national mission against a totalitarian foe. All of these tendencies endured in postwar behavior.

The United States did not simply or immediately identify Hitler with Stalin, or the world war with the cold war. During the transitional phase the lack of a common worldview did not forestall the systemic opportunities for intervention. In particular, the decision not to send U.S. troops in support of the Kuomintang in the Chinese civil war was taken while the postwar consensus and its organizational instruments were still half-formed. The consequences of that decision—and the resolution to never "lose" another country to communism—helped to shape the emerging policy culture.

Ernest May's case study of the decision not to intervene in China supports the contention that the decision was the product of a government in transition. Institutionally, it was associated with a relatively uncomplicated executive branch, led by a president with a forceful personality. Moreover, executive-legislative relations were more simple than at any time since, and considerable expertise on China could be found outside of the normal institutions of foreign policy decision making.

Ideologically, the China decision highlighted deep disagreements over the ends and means of U.S. policy. The costs of war were part of the experience of everyone involved in the decision. Although the Truman Doctrine of 1947 committed the United States to opposing communist expansion, it was clear that the United States could not give equal weight to all threats. The trends seen in the war continued: economic aid to Europe was generally the first priority.

In 1947 there was still a sharp distinction in the policy culture between economic and military action, and the support for the latter was seen to require both a greater provocation and a greater probability for success than was perceived to exist in China. Following Marshall's testimony concerning the probable costs and the low probability of success, Senator Lodge voiced the common sentiment that "I will be willing to vote them some money, but I'll be damned if I want to send them manpower."[17]

Even as this line between military and nonmilitary action was being drawn in Congress, the institutional component of the policy culture was beginning to obscure it. An organizational keystone of the new policy culture was the National Security Act of 1947. As well as reorganizing the military, this act created the Central intelligence Agency and tasked it with the responsibility for not only intelligence collection and evaluation, but also "such additional services of common concern as the National Security Council (NSC) determines can be more efficiently accomplished centrally" and "such other functions and duties" as the NSC "may from time to time direct."[18] Like the Truman Doctrine itself, the National Security Act could not be implemented overnight. However, it did provide the organizational tool for a regular policy of covert action around the world. The extent to which that tool has been used is reflected in the CIA's budget. In 1974, Marchetti and Marks reported that roughly two-thirds of CIA funds and personnel were used for covert operations and their support, and that that level had remained stable for over 10 years.[19]

By 1950, a cold war worldview was clearly the unifying theme in both the statements and the organization of the U.S. government. NSC–68 summarized the essential features of U.S. policy:

> Our overall policy at the present time may be described as one designed to foster a world environment in which the American system can survive and flourish. It therefore rejects isolationism and affirms the necessity of positive participation in the world community.
>
> This broad intention embraces two subsidiary policies. One is a policy which we would pursue even if there were no Soviet threat. It is a pol-

icy of attempting to develop a healthy international community. The
other is the policy of "containing" the Soviet system. These two policies
are closely interrelated and interact with one another.[20]

The distinction between these two policies has been easier to maintain in doctrine than in practice. This is nowhere more apparent than in
the construction of alliances to contain Soviet power and regulate the international system. Some, such as the Rio Pact of 1947, were arguably
more concerned with the regulatory function.

Containment placed an emphasis on the military dimension of national security which, coupled with the expansion of the armed forces in
the Korean War, led to the rapid growth of the ability to use force to
achieve foreign policy objectives. At the height of the Vietnam War, the
United States was committed by defense pacts with 42 states, while 1.1
million military personnel were in foreign bases and 2.4 million more
were on U.S. soil.[21]

In the early 1950s, as relations between the United States and the
Soviet Union grew colder, the CIA came into its own as the means to respond in kind to "covert aggression." While there were certainly elements within the government who had a less Manichean view of the
world, the dominant opinion was voiced by Secretary of State Dulles:

> I recognize full well that there are plenty of social problems and unrest
> which would exist if there were no such thing as Soviet Communism in
> the world, but what makes it a very dangerous problem for us is the fact
> that wherever those things exist, whether it is in Indo-China or Siam or
> Morocco or Egypt or Arabia or Iran . . . the forces of unrest are captured
> by the Soviet Communists.[22]

Given this attitude, it is no surprise that the United States moved to
intervene in the internal politics of Iran. Barry Rubin's chapter in this section notes the differing approaches to Iran of the Truman and Eisenhower
administrations. These differences are certainly related to the personalities involved, but they also can be seen as part of the routinization
of the cold war. The CIA, for example, grew from 5,000 to about 15,000
employees between 1950 and 1955.[23] By June 1953, when Eisenhower authorized covert action to remove Mossadegh from power, the uncertainty
of the immediate postwar years had been replaced by self-assurance. U.S.
leaders believed they understood the situation, and that they had the
means to control it.

In the case of Iran, the means were remarkably limited: five Americans, six Iranian contacts, and a few hundred thousand dollars in cash.
That it succeeded was more a function of Iranian conditions than U.S.
power. However, the August 1953 overthrow of the Mossadegh government, as the first operation to accomplish such a change of regime, served
to make covert operations an even more attractive alternative.

The 1954 intervention in Guatemala attempted to duplicate the "success" in Iran. Like the Iranian operation, luck was at least as important as U.S. planning and resources. The two operations had a second common element: they helped to relegitimize within the U.S. government the notion of covert action to change a government in power. One flaw in the Truman and Eisenhower doctrines, if they were to contain communism, was the requirement that the target state request U.S. assistance. As a result, some type of written invitation has generally been required to legitimize the open use of U.S. force. With the advent of covert operations, this restriction did not apply. As Allen Dulles pointed out,

> In Iran a Mossadegh and in Guatemala an Arbenz came to power through the normal processes of government, and not by any Communist coup. . . . Neither man at the time disclosed the intention of creating a Communist state. When this purpose became clear, support from outside was given to loyal anti-Communist elements in the respective countries. . . . In each case the danger was successfully met. There again no invitation was extended by the *government* in power for outside help.[24]

Henry Kissinger summed up this attitude in 1970: "I don't see why we have to stand by and watch a country go communist due to the irresponsibility of its own people."[25]

Confidence grew in the ability to conduct cheap and deniable interventions. As confidence grew, so did the scope and complexity of the operations, until they ran afoul of the "friction" inherent in any quasi-military action. By 1958, opposition to Sukarno in Indonesia was increasingly difficult to conceal. But the first undeniable failure came at the Bay of Pigs.

The Bay of Pigs operation is particularly interesting because it illustrates both the influence of organizational structure and the power of policy statements to restrict future behavior. President Kennedy came into office with two competing imperatives. First was the unacceptability of the Castro government. This was not only Kennedy's opinion, but it had already motivated the planning in the last years of the Eisenhower administration of an invasion of Cuba by a refugee army, supported by the U.S. military. Second, Kennedy's campaign statements rejected the use of U.S. forces to overthrow the Castro regime. Taken together, the result was not a complete rejection of either principle, but a new plan: to land at the Bay of Pigs without direct U.S. support.[26]

Roger Hilsman, in his discussion of the Vietnam decision, describes a more significant case of institutionalized intervention. Instead of a single decision to intervene, there were a series of decisions. In fact, as the term has been defined, there were *several* interventions: each was intended to be the minimum necessary to avoid defeat, each was to create a new set of norms for the relationship between South Vietnam and the United States, and each was to prove insufficient. Eventually, the "controlled escalation" came to be seen as the U.S. policy in Indochina. When it did so, early in the Johnson administration, Vietnam crossed the line between intervention and war.

Even as the United States was crossing that line, the Johnson administration conducted a classically "U.S." intervention to shape the government of the Dominican Republic. At its height, the intervention involved 35,000 U.S. troops, of which nearly 23,000 held an area of only a few square miles. In his analysis of that action, Abraham Lowenthal emphasized the way in which this intervention appeared to be an irrational echo of past policies:

> It is time to ask whether the American impulse to act in the Caribbean stems from anything more than historic axiom and unquestioned habit. Unchallenged premises and preconceptions very largely determined the U.S. intervention in Santo Domingo, and constructive analysis should focus special attention on outlining those assumptions.[27]

The tendency of policy to endure can also be seen in Martha Cottam's analysis of the effort to prevent Allende from rising to power in Chile. Between 1958 and 1970 an estimated $1 billion were committed to preventing Allende and the Left from coming to power. Covert action was directed against Allende in the election of 1964, while open financial support was given to the ruling Christian Democrats. The United States manipulated covert payments and influenced multilateral lenders to put the Allende government under pressure from within and without, culminating in the coup of 1973.[28] The traditional role as the dominant power in the hemisphere had combined with the fear of left-leaning governments.

The "Lessons of Vietnam"

As we have seen, the policy culture changes, but only slowly. The shock of U.S. failure in Vietnam led to a reevaluation of the assumptions that supported the war. The "lessons of Vietnam" reflected a "never again" mentality, but the mistake to be avoided varied according to the premises of each critic, and a decade later the most striking lesson is how resistant the policy culture is to change. Intervention remains an accepted tool of U.S. foreign policy.

Within the policy culture, the reaction to Vietnam included adjustments of perceptions, attitudes, and institutions. The net effect has been a marginal increase in the perceived costs of intervention. The institutional component of the "Vietnam syndrome" is most clearly seen in the War Powers Act, which in conjunction with other legislation limits the ability of the executive to fight undeclared wars. Other institutional restrictions, as summarized by Michael Klare, include the end of the draft, legislative restrictions and oversight of covert operations, and greater reliance on regional "surrogate gendarmes."[29]

Klare has oversated the case by saying that "the nation adopted a 'never again' stance on the use of U.S. troops to control political changes in the Third World,"[30] but it is undeniable that calculations of political will are made today that were not addressed prior to Vietnam. It is also more commonly perceived that public support erodes as a commitment drags on. Samuel Huntington has stated, for example, that "if we have to become involved in fighting limited conflicts elsewhere in the world, the most crucial limitation from our point of view is not the limitation on weapons or geographical scope or goals, but rather the limitation on time."[31]

Grenada and Nicaragua

The invasion of Grenada in 25 October 1983 presents an opportunity to see if the "Vietnam syndrome" has had an impact on the U.S. style of intervention, or if some version of the pre-Vietnam policy culture remains.

The invasion was not unanticipated by its target. Three times between 1981 and 1983 the U.S. Navy conducted operations in the waters near Grenada. In March 1983, President Reagan announced that Grenada was "a threat to the security of the United States." Prime Minister Maurice Bishop visited Washington in the hope of preventing U.S. action.

Following factional infighting, which culminated in the death of Bishop on 19 October, the island found itself to be the target of a task force of 12 ships, including the aircraft carrier *Independence* and helicopter carrier *Guam*. This force supported a landing by 1,900 U.S. marines and rangers, which in the course of the battle grew to roughly 6,000 soldiers. Also taking part in the operation were several hundred soldiers from Jamaica, Barbados, and four members of the Organization of East Caribbean states. In three days "all significant military objectives had been secured," and by 15 December all U.S. combat units had been replaced by "training, police, medical and support elements."[32]

The Reagan administration described the Grenada operation as a "rescue mission," as if to draw a parallel between the intervention and the failed 1980 attempt to rescue Americans held in Iran. A better analogue from history is the 1965 invasion of the Dominican Republic.

The image projected by the Reagan administration was in keeping with the restrictions on the open use of U.S. force that have existed since 1947. By linking the action to the request of the East Caribbean states, the

United States has again made an effort to appear to be acting as part of a collective effort. In addition, the secret message by the Grenadan governor-general fulfills, at least in part, the requirement for a request by the "government." It is little different than the rationale presented in the Dominican operation, in which Benoit requested assistance to restore order.

One new element in the rationale for intervention was the admission that there were no major differences of ideology between the old and new regimes, but "rather, the struggle appears to have been almost exclusively personal." Instead, both regimes were condemned as Soviet allies:

> Bishop and his colleagues not only wished to establish communism in Grenada; they wanted to be active members of the Soviet Empire. To this end, they sought ways to curry favor from the Soviets and other bloc countries, and loyally followed the instructions that came to them through the Cubans. Thus on both the domestic and international levels, the Grenadans emulated the USSR and tied their destiny to the Kremlin.[33]

If there was no significant difference between the old and new Grenadan governments, it would seem at first glance to be a violation of Tillema's rule that "United States overt military intervention has occurred since World War II only when decision-makers perceived the possibility of a new Communist government."[34] If the United States is moving toward a policy of openly "rolling back" Soviet-aligned regimes, this would be more than a reversion to the postwar norm. Both Nicaragua and Cuba would be immediately threatened by such a move.

However, there is no reason to believe that the Grenada operation signals any such long-term changes in the U.S. style of intervention. Instead, it should be seen as a unique opportunity for low-cost victory, similar to the 1958 invasion of Lebanon and the 1965 intervention in the Dominican Republic. If the island had not already been in a condition of political disarray, it is reasonable to believe that the United States would not have crossed the threshold of overt action. Current statements of U.S. policy toward Nicaragua reaffirms the tendency to support "covert" action (even when such actions become an item of common knowledge), while linking overt military involvement with the possible use of Nicaraguan territory as a Soviet base. The U.S. style of intervention endures.

Conclusion

The fears and capabilities of the early years of the cold war transformed the organizations and policies of U.S. foreign relations in ways that continue to shape our present and future. Although the world has changed, the fear of nationalism, the identification of Marxism with a Soviet threat, and even the prerequisites of covert and overt intervention remain remarkably stable. Thus, the case studies of this section are not isolated incidents, but examples of an institutionalized set of perceptions and behaviors. Each serves to illustrate themes that remain relevant for an understanding of U.S. intervention in the Third World.

Notes

1. James Rosenau, "Intervention as a Scientific Concept," *Journal of Conflict Resolution,* vol. 13, no. 2 (June 1969), p. 153.

2. Hedley Bull, "Introduction," in *Intervention in World Politics,* ed. Hedley Bull (Oxford: Clarendon Press, 1984), p. 1.

3. Rosenau, "Intervention as a Scientific Concept," p. 161.

4. Ibid.

5. Hedley Bull, "Intervention in the Third World," in *Intervention in World Politics,* ed. Hedley Bull (Oxford: Clarendon Press, 1984), p. 154.

6. Richard Smoke, "Analytic Dimensions of Intervention Decisions," in *The Limits of Military Intervention,* ed. Ellen Stern (London: Sage, 1977), p. 27.

7. Stockholm International Peace Research Institute, *World Armaments and Disarmament, SIPRI Yearbook 1985* (London: Taylor and Francis, 1985), Appendix 78 served as the basis for this calculation.

8. Bertil Dunér, "The Many-Pronged Spear: External Military Intervention in Civil Wars in the 1970s," *Journal of Peace Research,* vol. 20, no. 1 (1983), p. 66.

9. Bull, "Intervention in the Third World," p. 146.

10. Erich Weede, "U.S. Support for Foreign Governments, or Domestic Disorder and Imperial Intervention, 1958–1965," *Comparative Political Studies,* vol. 10, no. 4 (January 1978), p. 520.

11. Daniel Yergin, *Shattered Peace* (Boston: Houghton Mifflin, 1978).

12. Herbert Tillema, *Appeal to Force* (New York: Crowell, 1973).

13. The idea that rationality is bounded is far from new, and provides a common thread in many of the essays of this section. See Martha L. Cottam, Chapter 3 of this book for an explicit treatment of these limits.

14. Documents pertaining to the Monroe Doctrine, Roosevelt "Corollary," and the Rio Treaty may be found in Robert Goldwin and Harry Clor, eds., *Readings in American Foreign Policy* (New York: Oxford University Press, 1971), pp. 193–214. President Monroe's statement can be found in Tillema, *Appeal to Force,* p. 9, 26.

15. Tillema, *Appeal to Force,* pp. 9–10.

16. Alexander DeConde, *A History of American Foreign Policy,* 3rd ed., vol. 2 (New York: Scribner's, 1978), p. 117.

17. Ernest May, *The Truman Administration and China, 1945–1949* (New York: Lippincott, 1975), p. 30.

18. Paul Blackstock, "The United States Intelligence Community and Mili-

tary Intervention," in *The Limits of Military Intervention,* ed. Ellen Stern (London: Sage, 1977), p. 263.

19. Victor Marchetti and John Marks, *The CIA and the Cult of Intelligence* (New York: Knopf, 1974), p. 78.

20. Thomas H. Etzold and John Lewis Gaddis, eds., *Containment: Documents on American Policy and Strategy, 1945–1950* (New York: Columbia University Press, 1978), p. 401.

21. Paul Schratz, "National Decision Making and Military Intervention," in *The Limits of Military Intervention,* ed. Ellen Stern (London: Sage, 1977), p. 353.

22. John Foster Dulles, quoted by Barry Rubin, *Paved With Good Intentions* (New York: Penguin, 1980), p. 62.

23. Marchetti and Marks, *The CIA and the Cult of Intelligence,* p. 23.

24. John Foster Dulles, *The Craft of Intelligence,* cited by Roger Hilsman, *To Move A Nation* (Garden City, NY: Doubleday, 1967), p. 85.

25. Henry Kissinger, quoted by Charles Kegley, Jr. and Eugene Witkopf, *American Foreign Policy: Pattern and Process* (New York: St. Martin's, 1979), p. 54.

26. Hilsman, *To Move a Nation,* p. 32.

27. Abraham Lowenthal, "The Dominican Intervention in Retrospect," *Public Policy* (Fall 1969), p. 147.

28. Richard Fagen, cited by Kegley and Witkopf, *American Foreign Policy,* pp. 81–82.

29. Michael Klare, *Beyond the "Vietnam Syndrome": U.S. Interventionism in the 1980s* (Washington: Institute for Policy Studies, 1981), p. 2.

30. Ibid.

31. Samuel P. Huntington, in Stanley Hoffman, Samuel P. Huntington, Ernest R. May, Richard N. Neustadt, and Thomas C. Schelling, "Vietnam Reappraised," *International Security,* vol. 6, no. 1 (Summer 1981), p. 7.

32. Department of State and Department of Defense, *Grenada Documents: An Overview and Selection* (Washington, D.C.: September 1984), Preliminary Report, p. 1.

33. *Grenada Documents,* Introduction, p. 14.

34. Tillema, *Appeal to Force,* p. 28.

6

A COMPARISON OF U.S. POLICIES IN CHINA, 1945–49, AND VIETNAM, 1961–65

Ernest May

The Factual Bases of the Decisions

Despite the resemblance between the China issue of 1945–49 and the Vietnam issue of 1961–65, the policy outcomes were wholly different. Why? For such a large prize as China, why did the Truman administration not make at least a limited military commitment such as Kennedy made in 1961 for the much smaller prize of Vietnam?

One hypothesis belabored by right-wing extremists in the 1950s was that a clique of Communists and Communist sympathizers in the executive branch conspired to bring about decisions desired by Moscow. Even when a testimony was unearthed by congressional inquisitors bent on proving its validity, this thesis seemed unlikely. Now that a large body of sources has become open for research, it seems preposterous.

In the 1950s and afterward, defenders of the Truman administration replied to such charges by arguing that the decision about China was simply products of rational calculation-decision which would have been made by any reasonable man similarly situated. This counterhypothesis appeared in two versions. One emphasized the magnitude and complexity of the problem in China. The State Department issued in 1949 a White Paper—a large collection of documents relating to U.S.-China policy since 1944. The introduction, signed by Dean Acheson, declared: "The unfortunate but inescapable fact is that the ominous result of the civil war in China was beyond the control of the government of the

Previously published as "If Vietnam, Why Not China?" by Ernest May, *The Truman Administration and China, 1945–1945* (New York: J.B. Lippincott, 1975), pp. 34–47. Reprinted by permission.

United States . . . it was the product of internal Chinese forces. . . ." (p. xvi).

The second version emphasized the relative military weakness of the United States at the time. Testifying in 1951, Marshall said:

> My recollection is that at that particular time there were one and a third divisions in the entire United States. I know I was concerned and the Chiefs of Staff were very much concerned over obtaining enough men to guard the air strips at Fairbanks against a possible drop there. . . . There was very little with which to do. When you judge decisions, you have to judge them in the light of what there was available to do it.[1]

The arguments in the White Paper and in Marshall's testimony once seemed to provide a convincing explanation. In post-Vietnam retrospect, this no longer seems the case.

One cannot explain the difference in outcome by observing that China was large while Vietnam was relatively small. In the Foreign Relations Committee, to be sure, Senator Lodge remarked that China was distinguishable from Greece because it was "so damned big." But this consideration cut two ways, for there was some correlation between size and importance. Most Americans took it for granted in 1947–48 that if the Communists won China, they would gain something of value. In 1961–65 few regarded South Vietnam itself as a major asset. The rationale for blocking its conquest depended on a domino theory which supposed jeopardy to other countries that could be counted as valuable. China's size should have been as much an argument for intervention as against it.

Nor can one any longer accept the White Paper thesis that rescue of the Nationalists was obviously a task "beyond the control of the government of the United States." We now know that the Truman administration's agents in China were advising that the contrary was true. Americans in the field were just about as optimistic as were those in Vietnam in the early 1960s. And if there were voices of caution in 1947–48, there were also such voices in 1961–65. The Pentagon Papers show not only that the CIA gave warnings about the probable difficulty of saving South Vietnam but that Secretary of State Dean Rusk cabled President Kennedy in 1961, "I would be reluctant to see U.S. make major additional commitment of American prestige to a losing horse."[2]

In 1947–48 and in 1961–65 policy makers in Washington were offered both encouraging and cautionary counsel. There was no inherent reason why those of the earlier period should not have decided, like those of the 1960s, to listen to advisers who said that the task was manageable.

Nor is the decision of 1947–48 explicable, as Marshall claimed, as a function of U.S. military weakness. The estimates put before the decision makers in 1947–48 did not describe success in China as beyond U.S. capabilities. In June 1947 the Joint Chiefs formally advised that a very limited U.S. military commitment could reverse the course of events. The best-qualified staff officers took the position that 10,000 officers and enlisted men could do the job. Had that number of troops been sent to China, it would have represented less than 2 percent of the soldiers and marines on active duty. In 1961 Taylor and Rostow recommended sending exactly the same number of men to Vietnam—10,000 "advisers." The Joint Chiefs, however, warned Secretary of Defense McNamara that acceptance of the Taylor-Rostow recommendation would entail committing more than 200,000 U.S. troops to combat.[3] This larger figure represented 20 percent of the ground forces then on active duty.

Although some civilians saw the military recommendations of 1947 as unrealistic, few questioned at the time that the United States could accomplish the desired end if it chose to engage its own manpower. Even Vincent once said that the Communists could be overcome if "we were prepared to take over direction of Chinese military operations and remain in China for an indefinite period."[4]

Members of the Truman administration discounted the optimism of their missions in China and the estimates of their military advisers that China could be rescued through a small commitment of U.S. military power. They chose instead to heed relatively cautious analysts and to assume that the military investment would have to be large. By contrast, members of the Washington-based analysts and military warned that Vietnam would require a lot of U.S. manpower. If one looks simply at what the two administrations were being told by presumed experts, it is not all clear why nonintervention should have seemed the rational choice in one instance while intervention seemed the rational choice in the other.

To be sure, there were many contradictory reports and estimates concerning China in the public media while there were few such reports or estimates in circulation concerning Vietnam. The latter policy makers were much more the prisoners of images conveyed to them through official channels. Even so, it remains difficult to explain the differences in outcome as products of different sets of objective facts.

The Perceptual Bases of the Decisions

As an alternative, it might be hypothesized that the general framework of perception was different in the two periods. This is, in fact, a thesis implicit in many histories that deal with events of 1945–49. These histories portray the United States as having emerged from World War II innocently or idealistically hoping for international cooperation and coming only reluctantly, slowly, and with considerable psychological stress to a perception that the Soviet Union and international communism were forces no less ruthless, aggressive, and menacing than had been the Axis powers. This change is described as not complete until after the Berlin crisis and Czechoslovakian coup of 1948, perhaps not until after the Korean conflict. The issue of whether or not to intervene in China, it would follow, arose too early in the cold war. The comparable issue concerning Vietnam arose, by contrast, after the cold war mind-set had fully hardened.

As indicated earlier, this hypothesis is made less compelling by documentary evidence that has come to light in the 1970s. Previously classified files show almost beyond question a consensus by 1946 among bureaucrats, high-level officials, and key legislators that the Soviet Union was a dangerous and predatory foe, that all Communist parties were its instruments, and that the preservation of U.S. values and perhaps of the United States itself depended upon containing the spread of Soviet power and influence. These files also show wide agreement that the Chinese Communists were at least allies of the Soviets, that their success in China would be a significant victory for America's cold war enemy.

To be sure, some U.S. officials questioned how much the Soviets would gain from a Chinese Communist triumph. Vincent argued that the costs to them might outweigh the benefits. Showing extraordinary foresight, Kennan forecast that the Soviets would face enormous and intractable problems in controlling a Chinese Communist state.[5] But the sparser documentation on the later Vietnam debate contains comparable memoranda, pointing out difficulties that the North Vietnamese would encounter in trying to govern South Vietnam and suggesting that North Vietnam's Ho Chi Minh might prove "an Asian Tito."

And it is simply not the case that cold war assumptions were more firmly fixed in the early 1960s than in the late 1940s. After all, members of the Truman administration were completely convinced by 1947–48 that inclusion of Communists in coalition governments led inevitably to Communist takeover. Not only to the public but to themselves, they denied that they had ever desired a Nationalist-Communist coalition in China.[6] They were also sure by 1947–48 that no Communist government could be trusted to keep its word and that purely diplomatic understandings were thus impossible. The Kennedy administration, by contrast, showed willingness to experiment with a coalition government in Laos, and Kennedy and Johnson both carried on the search for detente with the Soviet Union commenced by Eisenhower and later continued by Nixon.

In short, it is probably not the case that the Truman administration chose the alternative it did because members of that administration had not yet accepted the fundamental perceptions and assumptions associated with the cold war. In economists' language, the relevant preference curves of the Truman administration and the Kennedy and Johnson administrations were not so dissimilar as to account for difference in behavior.

The Economic Bases of the Decisions

Yet another mode of explanation would assume that the ruling class of the United States perceived its interests differently in the two situations. Insofar as one can judge such an explanation by tests of evidence, however, it does not seem persuasive. In gross quantitative terms, the U.S. stake in China was larger than in Vietnam. Not only in percentage of gross national product but in actual dollars, there was more trade with China in 1948 than with South Vietnam in 1961. Though figures are not easily accessible, it is almost certainly the case that U.S. capital investment in China was larger. Furthermore, as historians influenced by Marx have argued, China was visualized by U.S. financiers and businessmen as a huge potential market, the future exploitation of which would be immensely profitable for U.S. capitalism. Records relating to U.S. economic policy in 1945–49 indicate that this image survived.[7] Nothing of the sort held true for South Vietnam in the 1960s.

Even if one supposes that the policies of a capitalist state are likely to be determined by the special rather than the general interests of the ruling class, it is hard to frame a plausible explanation. For China had the eye not only of special interest groups such as owners of silver mines, growers of cotton, and producers of cotton textiles but also of specific corporations with well-founded reputations for being able to get what they wanted from the government. Sosthenes Behn's International Telephone and Telegraph Company owned public utilities in Shanghai and had aspirations for developing power, light, and communications networks throughout China. Pan American Airways and Trans-World Airlines were in competition for airline routes to and within China, and Pan Am was already in partnership with some high Kuomintang officials in owning the Chinese National Aviation Corporation. Standard Vacuum and the Texas Company were two U.S. oil companies with substantial holdings and ambitious plans in China.[8] If manipulative special interests could have had their wish, one would suppose that ITT, Pan Am, TWA, Stan Vac, Texaco, and their like would have brought about decisions to do whatever was necessary to keep the Nationalists in power.

To be sure, a resolute economic determinist could contend the U.S. capitalists did not uphold Chiang because they thought the Kuomintang party committed to a kind of nationalist socialism almost as antagonistic to "open door imperialism" as the Marxist socialism of the Communists. Complaints by U.S. businessmen about their treatment by the Nationalists could be cited as supporting evidence. By the time of the decision against military intervention, however, these complaints had died down. From the spring of 1947 onward, the Nationalists were making generous concessions to U.S. investors and entrepreneurs. They signed a commercial treaty with the United States which satisfied every desire of enthusiasts for the open door, and they passed legislation promising to keep at a minimum the government's role in the economy.[9] There was nothing in the stance of the Nationalists in 1947–48 to inhibit U.S. capitalists from supporting them to the fullest extent.

In regard to South Vietnam, one has difficulty identifying significant groups or corporations in the United States that stood to lose much if it went Communist or gain much if it did not. It is thus hard to sustain an argument that economic interests dictated military intervention there while they did not dictate it in China. Indeed, it may be that the line of argument is stronger if reversed: that is, if one supposes that actual economic interests are a disincentive for intervention because they make it harder to rationalize intervention as altruistic.[10]

The Critical Variables in the Decisions

If the differences in outcome in 1945–49 and 1961–65 are not satisfactorily explained by differences in objective facts, or general framework of perception, or economic determinants, how are they to be accounted for? Unfortunately for the social scientist interested in engineering future outcomes, the critical variables were probably interlocking psychological, structural, and environmental factors more or less specific to two time periods and not likely again to coincide, either by accident or by contrivance.

Psychological Factors

The following factors might be classified as psychological factors.

The Image of War

Although there had been limited wars and proxy wars in the past, including a whole series from the Crimean War to the Spanish Civil War, the two world wars dominated U.S. conceptions of international conflict. Consciously or perhaps more often unconsciously, Americans fancied that if their intervention on the side of the Nationalists led to Soviet intervention on the side of the Communists, the result would be all-out war like that with the Axis powers. Fear of such a war was plainly not an absolute deterrent. Truman accepted the risk of another world war when he intervened in Korea in 1950. Nevertheless one senses that apprehension of all-out war imposed an extra degree of caution on Truman, Marshall, Lovett, and even on Forrestal and the Joint Chiefs when intervention in China was under debate.

In view of the Soviet development of nuclear weapons, the rocket-brandishing of Khrushchev, the valor and competence shown by Chinese Communist armies in Korea, and the growth of Chinese Communist military power in the intervening decade, Americans in the 1960s should have had more reason to fear conflict. By then, however, they had experienced a major limited war and lived through or observed several episodes in which limited military intervention had not developed into anything larger. Consciously or unconsciously, they could say to themselves: If we go into South Vietnam and don't invade North Vietnam, as we invaded North Korea in 1950, we will run minimal risk of conflict with a major power. The possibility that military intervention might lead to a large-scale war scarcely entered into thinking about Vietnam.

The Absence of a Warning Precedent

The men who decided China policy in 1945–49 expected some criticism. They did not anticipate the ferocious and scurrilous attack that actually materialized, culminating in 1951 when Senator Joseph R. McCarthy, the most irresponsible of the anti-Communist demagogues, charged Marshall with witting participation in a pro-Communist conspiracy. Certainly, they did not foresee that the manufacturers of such nonsense would gain so much popular following that the Republican administration succeeding Truman's would feel obliged to conciliate them not only by rhetoric but by a purge of the State Department's China hands.

Democrats who came to office in the 1960s assumed that the venom of McCarthy and his like had contributed to their party's defeat in 1952 and 1956. The bureaucrats who advised them remembered no less well the consequences of Truman's China policy. Both groups were fearful of what might happen at home if another Democratic administration "lost" another part of Asia. In his memoirs Lyndon Johnson is quite explicit on the point. Listing reasons for not having deserted South Vietnam, he puts first in order: "A divisive debate about 'who lost Vietnam' would be . . . even more destructive to our national life than the argument over China had been."[11]

The Tough-Mindedness of the Decision Makers

Truman enjoyed making decisions. Had his principal advisers united in recommending military intervention in China, he would probably have accepted that recommendation with fewer qualms than Kennedy and Johnson displayed about acting in Vietnam. In 1950 he was to show little or no hesitancy about going to war in Korea to counter what he interpreted as an attempt by Stalin to repeat the tactics of Hitler. Truman was equally capable, however, of a decision not to act. With advice to such effect from Marshall and Lovett and evidence that Congress would not rebel, he made this choice.

Similarly, Marshall and Lovett were men given to confronting issues and deciding them one way or the other. As a professional soldier, Marshall was accustomed to envisioning the worst contingencies that could occur. During the war, Marshall had frequently said no to otherwise attractive proposals because he judged that, if the worst happened, the costs would be excessive. As a banker, Lovett, too, had had experience in saying no and in rejecting investment opportunities that entailed a high risk of having to send good money after bad. In the summer and autumn of 1947, Marshall and Lovett may have been uncertain about military involvement in China. By the winter of 1947–48 they had concluded that the commitment would be of uncertain magnitude and indefinite duration. They decided that the commitment should not be made, accepting the consequent certainty that the Nationalists would eventually lose.

Kennedy, Johnson, and the majority of their advisers were not equally decisive. Neither president was prepared to face up to the worst that might happen in Vietnam and determine whether he would or would not pay the price to prevent it. With only a few exceptions, the same was true of the men who gave them counsel. Rusk never translated his doubts into a resolute recommendation against committing U.S. prestige to the "losing horse." Until it was too late to be useful, McNamara did not press upon the president an argument that the rescue of South Vietnam would cost more than it was worth. Of course, a conception of possible consequences that included limited and sublimited war as well as all-out war made Kennedy, Johnson, and their advisers more adventurous, while memories of the domestic results of abandoning China made them more timid. Also, Marshall and Lovett had just fought a major war. They had no subconscious or conscious need to display machismo. Even so, one feels that there was an additional difference and that Truman, Marshall, Lovett, and perhaps also Vandenberg had a little more steel in their makeup.

Structural Factors

Also important were factors which might be classified as structural:

A Relatively Uncomplex Executive Branch

While the reader may feel that he has traveled a maze of missions, divisions, offices, etc., he would feel this much more keenly if the analysis had centered on Vietnam. For by the 1960s the National Security Council staff had become a bureaucracy unto itself, headed by assistants to the president who were sometimes more influential than cabinet officers. In the State Department, six to eight layers of undersecretaries, assistant secretaries, deputy assistant secretaries, and the like had grown up between the secretary and the desk officers who knew something about a place like Vietnam. The missions abroad were mini-governments with numerous specialized subunits. The office of the secretary of defense had expanded. Within it, an assistant secretary for International Security Affairs ran a little State Department, with a policy planning staff, regional division, and desk officers all his own. The Joint Chiefs of Staff had a much more elaborate structure. The services had not lagged in their own bureaucratic growth. And the Central Intelligence Agency not only housed thousands of specialized analysts but also maintained a vast network of overseas stations and facilities.

The fragmentation of the executive branch had created difficulties in 1945–49. Not only the embassy but also each of the advisory groups and military commands in China had made policy recommendations to Washington. Responses to their recommendations required reconciliation of views among various segments of the State Department and the armed services. Sometimes they produced interdivisional or interdepartment battles. The varieties of opinion elicited, the varieties of personal vanity that became engaged, and the varieties of interests that had to be reconciled all made it immensely difficult for busy, preoccupied men such as Truman, Marshall, Lovett, and Forrestal to determine which decisions had to be made and what their costs would be.

Even so, Truman and his chief advisers were dealing with a small circle of men. In most cases, they knew them well enough to calibrate their judgments and discount for their private or parochial interests. Though making decisions under conditions of high uncertainty, they could feel that they understood most of the factors perceived as critical by the men who had more intimate knowledge of the specific problem.

In the executive branch of the 1960s, this condition may occasionally have obtained during a brief period of crisis, as most notably, when the Soviets were discovered to have sited offensive missiles in Cuba. It probably did not exist for any long period of time with regard to any problem, and certainly not with regard to Vietnam. (At least until 1966, when, as it was said, Lyndon Johnson became the Vietnam desk officer.) As a result, the inevitable uncertainty surrounding any policy issue was magnified. The men with authority to make decisions were much less sure whom to trust or what to take into account. The gigantism of the executive branch thus joined with factors in the psychologies of men in power to promote avoidance of conclusive action.

Simpler Executive-Legislative Relations

In view of the Senate Foreign Relations Committee's role as a critic of involvement in Vietnam and the legislation subsequently enacted to curb "the imperial presidency," one might be tempted to conclude that an im-

portant difference was the relative power of Congress. In fact, this was
not the case.

Congress itself did not lose authority between the late 1940s and
1960s. It was only the Foreign Relations Committee that did. In 1947–48
the decision of Vandenberg and his colleagues about intervention in
China was conclusive. Not even the Appropriations committees could
successfully challenge them, and an appeal on behalf of Chiang from
members of the House Armed Services Committee had little more influence than if it had come from members of the Committee of Post Offices
and Post Roads.

In the decade and a half that elapsed before the intervention in Vietnam, this condition changed. It was due partly to differences in personnel. J. William Fulbright of Arkansas, the Foreign Relations Committee
chairman in the 1960s, was not like either Arthur Vandenberg or Tom
Connally. He had more brains than either but less diplomacy, managerial
skill, or capacity for influencing other legislators. Also, there were
changes in Congress complementing changes in the executive branch. As
aid programs became normal instruments of policy rather than new de-
partures, appropriations became more important than authorizing legislation, and the Appropriations committees gained strength. As the military establishment increased in size and multiplied its activities abroad,
the two Armed Services committees waxed in influence. The same was
true of the select committee that oversaw the CIA.

In 1947–48 members of the Truman administration could look to the
Foreign Affairs and Foreign Relations committees to voice the will of Congress. Once Marshall knew that the Foreign Relations Committee would
support him rather than Forrestal or Wedemeyer, he knew that his decision and the president's had been confirmed. It was United States policy,
and he could insist upon it. The same was to hold true in 1950, when Truman could consult informally with members of the Foreign Relations
Committee and come away confident that Congress would not only support his intervening in Korea but approve of his doing so in compliance
with a United Nations resolution and without a formal declaration of war.

In the 1960s, had Rusk been a resolute opponent of military intervention in Vietnam and had he secured the provisional backing of Kennedy
and then the full support of the Foreign Relations Committee, he would
not have been in the position of Marshall in the spring of 1948. Proponents of alternative Vietnam policies could still have obtained blessing
from the Appropriations or Armed Services committees. If so, the majority of Congress would have been at least as likely to side with these other
committees as with Senator Fulbright's. There was no longer a simple
way in which the executive branch could ascertain the will of Congress.

In fact, none of the organs of Congress took exception to the intervention in Vietnam. The Foreign Relations Committee only began to do

so after limited intervention escalated into large-scale warfare. The Appropriations and Armed Services committees registered little or no dissent until much later. Had members of one or another of these committees been asked whether preservation of a non-Communist Vietnam was so important an objective that it should be pursued even if hundreds of thousands of U.S. troops had to be sent into combat, they might well have said yes. That is not the crucial point. Rather, it is that by the 1960s no committee had the authority to speak for Congress in answer to such a question. Along with the psychology of the policy makers and the complex structure of the executive branch, this fact, too, contributed to making decisions more difficult than it had been earlier.

Environmental Factors

Finally, there were several factors which one might regard as environmental.

Some Americans Knew Something About China

This point needs little elaboration. Especially in the Office of Far Eastern Affairs, the State Department had functionaries who knew the Chinese language and had followed Chinese affairs continuously for two decades or more. They did not all agree: Vincent and Drumwright, for example, held quite different views. Debate between the two, however, was relatively sophisticated. In 1961–65, debate about Vietnam at a comparable level of government was much less well informed, more crude, and more abstract.

Moreover, some hundreds, perhaps even thousands, of private citizens knew as much or almost as much about China as did people inside the government. They were scholars, newspapermen, missionaries, businessmen, or the children of missionaries or businessmen who had resided in China. Like the China hands in government, these citizens held diverse opinions. With regard to the efficiency of U.S. military intervention, the scholars and journalists tended to be as skeptical as Vincent, or even more so, and they made their opinions known. John K. Fairbank, the leading U.S. historian of China, debated Judd and other interventionists on the popular radio forums, "Chicago Roundtable" and "Town Meeting of the Air." Theodore H. White and Annalee Jacob published *Thunder out of China* (New York: Harper, 1946) a best seller and Book-of-the-Month Club selection, which portrayed the Nationalists as corrupt reactionaries not worth rescuing.

Although the missionaries and children of missionaries were by no means united in support of Chiang, most of those who advocated intervention fell into this category. As with Judd and Luce, their experience of

China was some years in the past. Although there is no evidence to such effect, this fact may have been noticed by policy makers. To be sure, a Gallup poll reported 55 percent of the public favoring aid to Chiang and only 32 percent opposing it; and Vandenberg assessed public opinion as "deeply sympathetic with China . . . [and] her resistance against communism even more than Europe's against communism."

Even so, policy makers may have felt some concern lest articulate people like Fairbank and White criticize intervention and, because of their expertise, win a following. In any case, the very possibility of a public challenge from outside experts forced decision makers to think about the rationales for intervention or nonintervention that would meet such a challenge. Because almost no private citizens knew anything about Vietnam, the decision makers of the early 1960s had less cause either to reckon on a public debate or to reason out the pros and cons as they might be perceived by people outside the government.

Decisions Were Made by a Well-Settled Administration with an Election Close at Hand

Truman was in his third year of office when the question of whether or not to intervene in China came to a head. He had passed through his transition period in 1945–46. Like his predecessors and successors, he had discovered from experience that bureaucrats usually had parochial perspectives and that their judgment of the "national interest" was no better than his own. He had developed ways of identifying real issues and learned whom to trust and not trust. Although Marshall and Lovett were new to their jobs, they were old Washington hands. They, too, understood how not to be hustled.

In 1947–48, furthermore, Truman had a presidential election immediately ahead of him. Though there is not a particle of supporting evidence, it can be surmised that he would have seen even limited military intervention in China as potentially harmful to his candidacy. It would add to the armory of issues available for Henry Wallace, who was to challenge him as the candidate of the left-wing third party. Because of probable criticism from China experts in universities and among newspapermen, intervention might alienate anti-Communist and anti-Wallace liberals such as those who had recently formed Americans for Democratic Action. Worse still, it could produce some casualties or deaths, lead Republicans to revive charges that the Democrats were the war party, and disrupt bipartisan cooperation on aid to Europe and to other such politics. Though Truman could expect criticism for not aiding Chiang, he could have calculated realistically and accurately that most of the attacks would come later, after Chiang fell. Except at the margin, they were not likely to affect the presidential vote in 1948. In fact, Gallup polls as late as December 1949 were to show the public still uncertain about what was happening in China and divided as to what the response of the United States should be.

Whether or not the president himself took account of the approaching election, some of his advisers must have done so. Marshall and Lovett cannot have been unconscious that the course of action that they recommended did not run counter to Truman's interests as a candidate. Probably sharing the almost universal opinion that Truman would not be reelected and that a Republican would take over the presidency in January 1949, they may also have seen it as both prudent and patriotic not to precommit the next administration to carrying on a war. Even in face of a Soviet attempt to take over Berlin, they were circumspect about adopting a course of action that a new administration would be unable to reverse.

A further effect of the impending election was to diminish the sense of urgency among those who advocated intervention. Members of the missions in China, officers of the military establishment, and men such as Judd and Bridges may have felt that an effort to get a change of policy by Truman was not worthwhile. Instead, they should wait and work on the new president.

In the early 1960s, both sets of conditions were different. Kennedy in 1961 and Johnson in 1963–65 were presidents still settling in. Neither had reached the stage of knowing when and when not to trust advice from the bureaucracy, and neither had yet arrived at a final estimate of the strengths and weaknesses of his appointed advisers. Especially in view of the more complex structure of the executive branch, they were more likely to be influenced by cables from Saigon than was Truman by 1947–48 to be influenced by cables from his missionaries in China. In 1961, Rusk, McNamara, and men like them were in the same situation as the president. In 1963–65 these men had some experience, but none knew whether he possessed the new president's confidence. Hence, even if so disposed, they might have felt reluctant to force upon him a choice between their advice and that of the diplomats and soldiers nearer the scene.

Moreover, Kennedy in 1961 was three years away from another presidential election. Especially because of the "loss of China" syndrome, the apparent incentives for him were different from those for Truman. If bad consequences followed from intervention in Vietnam, they could be faced in 1962 and 1963. The question of whether the price was too high could then be reviewed. On the other hand, if the United States did not intervene and the Communists took over South Vietnam, that fact would remain in evidence in 1964. Even if such thoughts did not enter Kennedy's mind, they may have crept into those of men around him.

Johnson in 1963 was heir to the commitment Kennedy had made. His best opportunity to make a real choice between rescuing or abandoning South Vietnam came almost immediately after his accession, when Diem was assassinated and one military coup after another occurred in Saigon. But Johnson could hardly confront such a choice at the very beginning of a transition period and with an election less than a year away. What he did was to procrastinate. Until the election, he attempted neither to increase nor reduce the level of military involvement. Only after November did he face up to his options; and then, of course, he and his advisers were in a position like that of Kennedy in 1961.

The Chinese Were not the Vietnamese

If only relying on U.S. official reportage, one might regard Chiang and Diem as twins. Cables from China in 1945–49 and from South Vietnam in 1961–63 seem paraphrases of one another, characterizing either Chiang or Diem as leaders who had lost their dynamism and were losing their popular appeal; men who were unduly deferential to reactionary elements around them and unduly tolerant of corruption, especially by members of their own families; and men who would not institute reforms necessary to save their nations.

Probably, however, the chief likeness between Chiang and Diem was that Americans said the same things about them and the same things to them. Both leaders were beset by foreigners who nattered about reforms. Precisely what was wanted from them was seldom clear. For China, the most visionary summary was one put together in a working paper for the Wedemeyer mission. Compiled by Sprouse, it may have been deliberately overstated. In any case, it included abolition of the secret police; transfer of power from the national to local police forces; reduction and reorganization of the armed forces in order to make them efficient, professional, and nonpolitical; reduction in the number of government employees, discharge of those who were incompetent or corrupt or both, and formation of an honest and independent civil service; a fair and honestly administered system of taxation; freedom for the press; an end of government interference in universities; free elections in localities and provinces as well as in the nation as a whole; and some measures to bring about more even distribution of land and wealth.[12]

Although such programs were advocated as being in the interest of China and later of Vietnam, their proponents showed little or no comprehension of the specific needs of either Chiang or Diem. Like almost all heads of government, Chiang and Diem assumed that the paramount interest of the nation was their retention in office. To this end, it seemed crucial, for example, that there be some instrument of terror such as a secret police; that there not be efficient armies other than those whose loyalty was certain; that potential conspirators be bought off with jobs or bribes; that the press and university not be able to forment subversion; and the powerful landowners be placated rather than turned into malcontents.

Chiang and Diem had identical problems in that both wanted U.S. aid and both had to deal with Americans whose conditions for extending aid were such as to threaten their own holds on power.

In other respects, there were less resemblances between the two. Though the Chinese and Vietnamese had the same cultural heritage, their histories in modern times had been very different. Chiang came from a line of Chinese rulers who had managed barbarians by playing one off against another. As his situation worsened in 1947–48, he resorted to the expedient of letting the United States know that he contemplated turning to the Soviet Union for mediation and subsequent protection. He also tried to make them believe that, if they did not supply him with arms, the British would do so. He sought in various ways to get Americans into positions in which they would find themselves fighting the Communists. Despite some reports to the contrary by Stuart, it was only in late 1948, after his outlook became desperate and after Truman had been reelected, that Chiang began to suggest placing himself in the hands of the United States and giving U.S. officers powers beyond those of foreign advisers employed by previous Chinese rulers.

Chiang's rivals were equally circumspect. Except for Marshal Li Chien, who was in exile in Hong Kong and had no real base in China proper, none of them bid for U.S. backing by promising outright to be more obedient to U.S. bidding. At most, they attempted to persuade the United States that their programs were more consistent with U.S. ideals.

The Vietnamese, by contrast, were products of a colonial past. They were schooled in getting their way by manipulating foreigners whom they pretended to obey. For all his nationalistic rhetoric and independence of character, even Diem was prepared to make apparent concessions that Chiang would not make. And Vietnamese generals had little hesitation about trying to involve the United States in their plans for coups. It may well be that the principal reason why the United States did not intervene militarily in China, as it later did in Vietnam, was that the Chinese did not exert themselves as wholeheartedly and adroitly to bring about U.S. intervention.

Determining the Decisive Factors: The Limits of Historical Analysis

This list of variables is not exhaustive. One can imagine, for example, that the Kennedy administration might have viewed Vietnam differently had it not experienced humiliation only six months earlier in landing Cuban exiles at the Bay of Pigs and having them routed by Fidel Castro's forces. One can also imagine that Truman and even Marshall and Lovett might have felt differently about China if Chiang had been overthrown and assassinated as Diem was to be in 1963, and they felt that the missions in China bore some responsibility for having brought a successor regime into power.

But the crucial variables were probably neither random events of this sort nor wholly nonrandom factors such as realities of power, long-term historical trends, or economic forces. Instead, they were certain persisting ideas in the minds of decision makers, certain elements in their characters, certain qualities in the governmental structure, and certain features in the domestic and international environment.

To be explicit, I feel that the eight factors listed above were decisive. Had all been present in 1961–65, the Kennedy and Johnson administrations would not have intervened militarily in Vietnam. On the other hand, had the conditions of 1961–65 obtained in 1945–49, the United States would have found it harder to decide that nonintervention was clearly the preferable policy; but they might still have decided as they did.

Had Truman and his advisers not been able to obtain a conclusive verdict from Congress, they would have had a more difficult time. Marshall would have had to expend as much effort on the Pentagon initiatives of 1948 and the Tsingtao question as on the China Aid Act. If so, he and the others might have relented. On the other hand, they might equally well have stood fast.

Conversely, the Kennedy and Johnson administrations might have gone into Vietnam as they did even if the executive branch had been less complex and if there had been a way of having Congress face up to the issue and participate in the decision. The involvement of the congressional leadership had a good deal to do, to be sure, with the Eisenhower administration's decision not to intervene in support of the French in Vietnam in 1954. Even so, it is possible that Congress in the 1960s would have pressed the Kennedy and Johnson administrations to take military action rather than to refrain from doing so. Structural factors seem to me to have the least explanatory power.

Psychological factors probably made more difference. If Truman, Marshall, and Lovett had been accustomed to think in terms of limited wars or "brush-fire" wars, they might well have found it harder to resist the recommendations of Wedemeyer, Cooke, and the missions in China. Had they been men of less self-confidence, they would probably have looked more favorably on compromise formulae testing the possibility of putting military advisers into China. They might have been tempted, for example, by the idea of attaching such advisers to Nationalist units south of the Yangtse. Had Marshall and Lovett had reason to foresee a furor such as actually arose over the "loss" of China, they would surely have been more hesitant to advise the president as they did.

One can imagine without great difficulty that Vietnam decisions might have come out differently if members of the Kennedy and Johnson administrations had visualized war in terms of World War II rather than in terms of the Korean War or the counterinsurgency campaigns in Malaya and the Philippines; if Rusk had had the character and standing of Marshall (or perhaps even if Lovett had accepted Kennedy's offer and been secretary of state in place of Rusk); or if Kennedy, Johnson, and their advisers had been able to estimate public reaction to "losing" Vietnam without remembering what had followed the "loss" of China.

But most powerful of all in explaining the difference are the factors loosely classifiable as environmental. If Truman and his advisers had not had to expect a public debate about intervention in China, they would have been exposed only to the adversary process within the bureaucracy, and where the voices proposing action were stronger and more numerous than the voices on the opposing side.

If the Truman administration had been less experienced and less well settled, it would almost certainly have been more influenced by advice from Stuart, Wedemeyer, Cooke, and the Joint Chiefs. If Truman and Marshall had had to make their decision in 1949–50 instead of 1947–48, they might well have seen the arguments for military action as much more persuasive.

Almost certainly, Truman and his advisers would have seen the arguments differently even in 1947–48 if Chiang and other Nationalists had been steadily exerting themselves to persuade the U.S. government to assume responsibility for their military success against the Communists.

It seems equally likely that Kennedy and Johnson would have had second thoughts if they had reckoned in advance on the amount of character of public debate that intervention in Vietnam would actually provoke; that they would have been more skeptical or cautious if they had had to make the critical decisions on Vietnam later in their presidencies; that this might have been true if presidential elections lay just ahead; and that these administrations would have regarded the issues quite differently if the Vietnamese had been as proud and independent and seemingly uncooperative as the Chinese Nationalists.

These observations are no more than musings. One cannot run the facts of political history through a computer to test whether the outcome would have been different if one variable was changed and the others remained constant. To ask why the U.S. government chose the option of nonintervention when confronted with the prospect of Communist conquest of China is nevertheless a useful exercise not only for achieving better understanding of the past but also for gaining better insight into issues that may arise in future.

Notes

1. U.S. Congress, Senate Committees on Armed Services and Foreign Relations, *Hearings on the Military Situation in the Far East,* 82nd Cong., 2d sess., 1951, 382.

2. *The Pentagon Papers,* Senator Gravel ed., vol. 2 (Boston: Beacon Press, 1972), p. 105.

3. Ibid., pp. 108–9.

4. *Foreign Relations of the United States,* vol. 7 (1947), p. 849 (hereafter cited as *FRUS*).

5. Ibid., p. 849; FRUS, vol. 8, (1947), pp. 146–65.

6. FRUS, vol. 7 (1948), pp. 141–43.

7. See FRUS, vol. 7 (1945), pp. 1,235–36; FRUS, vol. 7 (1947), pp. 1,132–34.

8. FRUS, vol. 7 (1945), pp. 1,210–11, 1,246–47, 1,361–62, 1,388–90; FRUS, vol. 10 (1946), pp. 1,230–32, 1,238, 1,240–44, 1,374–77.

9. FRUS, vol. 7 (1945), pp. 1,229–30; FRUS, vol. 10 (1946), pp. 1,380–81; FRUS, vol. 7 (1947), pp. 1,373–76.

10. This point was suggested to me by Albert O. Hirschman.

11. Lyndon B. Johnson, *The Vantage Point: Perspectives in the Presidency, 1963–69* (New York: Holt, Rinehart, and Winston, 1971), p. 152.

12. FRUS, vol. 7 (1947), pp. 726–30.

7

DECISION MAKING IN "SUCCESSFUL" INTERVENTIONS: THE CASES OF GUATEMALA AND CHILE

Martha L. Cottam

One of the more perplexing issues in the study of intervention is the question of why some interventions are "successful" (that is, the achievement of goals with the means selected) while others fail. A logical answer to this question would be that the decision-making procedures in successful interventions were better than those in cases of failure. This is the issue addressed in this essay: Are successful interventions the result of appropriate "optimizing" decision-making strategies, or are they the result of luck, accidents, brute force, or other factors? In recent years the body of literature evaluating decision making by political elites has grown. In general the patterns of political behavior presented in that literature lead to the hypothesis that optimal decision-making strategies are followed rarely and are less likely to be followed in decisions to carry out covert, secret operations against another government than in ordinary bargaining situations. Further, the prospect of "good" decision making is even less likely when the target government is a revolutionary government portending real or imaginary damage to the interests of the perceiver's state.

This chapter will attempt to investigate the decision-making process in two "successful" interventions by the United States: Guatemala, 1954 and Chile, 1970–73.[1] The "images" of both states held by the relevant policy makers in the United States are examined first. Studies of political decision making indicate that in an effort to manage an exceptionally complex and ambiguous environment policy makers rely upon sets of beliefs about other states, that is, images of other states, to facilitate the processing of information and policy formation.[2] People tend to accept information that conforms with their preexisting images of others and reject information that conflicts with those ideas. In the process, they simplify the political realities of other states and may make errors in judgment.

In this chapter attention is directed to the extent to which images of Guatemala and Chile provided U.S. policy makers with simplified beliefs about those governments leading them to accept, reject, disregard, or distort information and ultimately to decide upon a policy of intervention. Following the discussion of images a detailed evaluation of the decision-making procedures in these seemingly successful interventions by the United States will be attempted in order to gain insight into the actual processing of information and examination of policy options by the policy makers who conducted these interventions. Ideal decision-making procedures would involve a careful assessment of all objectives and possible alternative courses of action for achieving those objectives. The decision maker should evaluate costs and benefits identified with each course of action, search diligently for additional information, listen to criticism with an open mind, and reevaluate the chosen course of action carefully before proceeding with a course of action.[3] Given the importance of images and preexisting beliefs, and given the tendency to see what one expects to see, to rely upon simple clues in identifying the characteristics of another government, and to rely upon lessons of history for instruction in responding to current problems, it is unlikely that these ideal decision-making procedures will be followed in decisions to intervene.

At this point, it is necessary to turn to the decision-making processes used in the cases of U.S. intervention in Guatemala and Chile. The cases are discussed with attention to four basic analytical questions:

1. How was the leadership of the target state perceived, that is, what image was held of that leadership and that state?
2. How was the decision to intervene made? Were optimal policy-making procedures used or did the decision making deviate from optimality along the lines discussed above?
3. How did the intervention proceed? Did it go as planned and was its progress the result of "good" decision making?
4. How should one evaluate the outcome?

GUATEMALA, 1954

Background

The story of U.S. intervention in Guatemala with the intention of overthrowing its government begins in 1944 and a little background information is necessary to provide the context for U.S. decision making in 1953–54. In October 1944 Guatemala experienced a revolution. This was a revolution that sought economic, social, and political reforms in response to a long history of repression, foreign economic and political domination, racial discrimination against the Indian majority of the population, and strong-man government. Guatemala's last dictator before the events leading up to the October Revolution of 1944 was Jòrge Ubico. His regime "made important contributions to Guatemalan life, contributions that also helped lead to his overthrow. These included a massive development of governmental activities (especially the building of infrastructure, such as roads) that created a new, nationalistic middle class and pulled some Indians out of their political isolation."[4] In 1944 he was overthrown by another officer who was then displaced by a coalition of dissident military officers and members of the urban middle class, in particular, university students. In late 1944, Juan Jose Arevalo was elected president. Arevalo was a reform-minded university professor who had been in exile in Argentina for a number of years. His administration followed four policy lines: agrarian reform, advancement of labor rights to strike and form unions, the development of a national education system, and the promotion of political democracy.[5]

Arevalo implemented a number of important reforms that antagonized foreign investors and the traditional Guatemalan oligarchs. His support derived largely from the middle class, labor, and the peasants who received some benefits. The major agrarian reform efforts of the revolution were left to Arevalo's successor. During the Arevalo era Communist activity and influence in the labor unions increased although the party itself was illegal.

Arevalo's reforms, pressures on foreign investors, and reliance upon left-leaning and reform-minded supporters combined with a massive public relations campaign launched by the United Fruit Company complaining of the "radical" nature of his administration caused increasing concern among U.S. officials as to the direction the revolution was taking. This resulted in increasing pressures from the United States, including the termination of arms sales to Guatemala in 1948. Tensions between the United States and Guatemala accelerated rapidly during the administration of Arevalo's successor, Jacobo Arbenz Guzman, elected in 1950.

Arbenz continued many of Arevalo's reforms and added more. Land reform was a major component of Arbenz's programs and in June 1952 an Agrarian Reform Law was passed. According to Blasier:

> The law provided for the expropriation of uncultivated land above a specified size with compensation in agrarian bonds. . . . The law was generally viewed as moderate, and specifically provided for compensation in contrast to earlier drafts supported by the Guatemalan Communists which had not.[6]

This law had a powerful impact on the United Fruit Company's holdings, resulting in the expropriation of 83,029 hectares. The expropriation of United Fruit Company properties was a source of increasing friction between the U.S. government and Arbenz, but the legalization of the Communist party was equally important. The extent to which Arbenz actually permitted and relied upon Communist activity and support has been reviewed repeatedly in analyses of his administration. Communist influence was located primarily in their relationship with labor. They were also influential in the peasant organization which ultimately held 400,000 members. Four out of 56 members of the Guatemalan Congress were Communists and Communists held posts in several government ministries including education and agriculture. At the end of the Arbenz era the Communists numbered about 4,000 in Guatemala.[7] Arbenz was essentially a reform-minded nationalist who accepted the support of the Communists. Further, as the strain between Guatemala and the United States grew and as segments of the military and middle class began to lose enthusiasm for Arbenz, he relied upon support from peasants, labor, and the Left more and more.[8] Communists were, therefore, present and legal in Guatemala and they supported Arbenz. But they held no cabinet positions and their political influence was limited. They did not, in the view of modern analysts, control the government or Arbenz. But their presence, as will be seen below, was disproportionately salient to the Truman and Eisenhower administrations and the Arbenz government was assumed to be subservient to the Communists despite all conflicting information.

The Truman administration began to look upon events in Guatemala with growing alarm by 1947. Throughout the remaining years of Truman's tenure in office a variety of pressures were imposed upon the Guatemalan government. The arms boycott instituted in 1948 has already been mentioned. In addition, the Truman administration discussed a policy of denying economic assistance, terminating agricultural research, and other measures but ultimately decided upon a more moderate policy of continuing assistance programs but refraining from funding new ones. U.S. diplomats, in particular U.S. Ambassador Patterson, applied irritating diplomatic pressure for more favorable treatment of U.S. investors and for the elimination of Communists. (Patterson was ultimately asked to leave Guatemala for demanding that Arbenz fire several cabinet ministers for being "Communists.") In addition, Truman briefly approved a covert campaign suggested by the Nicaraguan government designed to overthrow Arbenz in 1952. Approval was revoked before the plot was enacted. At the same time, the United Fruit Company was doing its utmost to convince the public and Congress that Guatemala was on the road to communism.[9]

With the advent of the Eisenhower administration relations between the United States and Guatemala deteriorated quickly. As will be seen, Eisenhower had no doubts as to the nature of the Arbenz government and employed strong diplomatic and coercive measures to isolate and ultimately overthrow that government. Jacobo Arbenz was overthrown in June 1954. It is often argued that his demise was the result of carefully executed policy by the Eisenhower administration. In fact, a careful examination of the policy-making process creates strong doubt about this conclusion. The decision making was far from optimal and the success of the operation was never really understood by the Eisenhower administration. This failure to understand the causes of the fall of Arbenz came back to haunt the United States at the Bay of Pigs. At this point it is necessary to turn to a close examination of the image held of Arbenz and the decision to intervene.

Images of Arbenz and Guatemala

The image of Guatemala and Arbenz ranged from simplified to extremely simplified and did not result in policy selection on the basis of careful evaluation of risks and probable success. It tended to be highly simplified at the highest levels of government in the United States and slightly more complex farther down the official hierarchy. It is fairly easy to characterize the image of Guatemala held by U.S. officials as typical of the patronizing view of a stereotyped "dependent" or "colonial" state. Immerman, for example, argues that United Fruit Company officials believed so strongly in their own racial superiority that they could not treat Guatemalan unrest seriously.[10] More importantly, State Department officials held an equally paternalistic view so that they were surprised when the 1944 revolution took place despite the fact that they knew opposition to the dictatorship was pervasive throughout Guatemala: "[T]hey seemed incapable of conceiving that his [the dictator's] 'children' might really oust him."[11] There was a chronic failure to consider adequately the causes of Guatemalan nationalism and to recognize the importance of anti-Americanism as a component of that nationalism. Nevertheless, there was some effort shortly after the 1944 revolution to explain the event. State Department officials argued that the Arevalo government would seek a "moderately liberal" form of government.[12] This assessment changed rapidly as reforms were instituted. Embassy officials began warning of Communist penetration of Guatemala particularly through the labor organizations. They expressed fears that Arevalo, who depended upon intellectuals, workers, and peasants for support, would fall victim to Communist influence with labor. This concern, that Guatemalan political leaders could not really understand and deal with Communists, is also reflective of the patronizing image of this stereotyped "banana republic."

With the Eisenhower administration one sees the most extreme simplifications of the image of Guatemala. In his memoirs Eisenhower refers to President Arbenz as a Communist who had attempted to establish a Communist state in Guatemala and, alternatively, as a puppet being manipulated by Communists.[13] Allen Dulles, director of the CIA, agreed, referring to Arbenz as a "stooge" of the Communists.[14] The U.S. ambassador to Guatemala appointed in December 1953 to help oversee Arbenz's overthrow, John Peurifoy, reported that after his first meeting with Arbenz he "came away definitely convinced that if President [Arbenz] is no Communist he will certainly do until one comes along and that normal approaches will not work in Guatemala."[15] Ambassador Peurifoy, incidentally, knew no Spanish and nothing about Guatemalan politics. His credential for his position as ambassador was his success in combating communism in Greece.

Generally, there was little understanding of Guatemalan politics at the highest levels of the U.S. decision-making circles. Guatemalan Ambassador Toriello reported that upon meeting Eisenhower he was surprised at how little Eisenhower knew about Guatemala.[16] Arguments by Arbenz and his ministers that the Communists in Guatemala were few in number, could be controlled, and were not supported by labor were simply discounted.[17] Arbenz is described by Eisenhower as ruling through a reign of terror rather than through popular support.[18] Other analyses, as will be seen, are a bit more sophisticated but hardly enough to be termed complex evaluations of Guatemalan politics.

It is interesting to note at this point the impact of the representativeness heuristic used to conclude that Arbenz was a Communist or a puppet of Communists who were controlled by Moscow. This assessment was clearly made by comparing Arbenz and his government to the stereotypical Communist with no attention to plentiful information indicating that Guatemala's revolution and its president were strong nationalists only. Most alarming is the explicit discussion by former Ambassador Patterson of his own reliance upon the famous "duck test." This is how he identified a Communist in 1950:

> Many times it is impossible to prove legally that a certain individual is a communist; but for cases of this sort I recommend a practical method of detection—the "duck test." The duck test works this way: suppose you see a bird walking in a farm yard. This bird wears no label that says "duck." But the bird certainly looks like a duck. Also, he goes to the pond and you notice that he swims like a duck. Then he opens his beak and quacks like a duck. Well, by this time you have probably reached the conclusion that the bird is a duck, whether he's wearing a label or not.[19]

Similarly, behaviors taken as representative of Communist leanings were attributed to Arbenz. Guatemala's decision not to sign the Rio Pact was interpreted as one sign despite the fact that Guatemala clearly stated that it abstained due to unsettled territorial disputes. This is also an example of the tendency to assume that actions are a result of some internal disposition rather than situational factors such as the wording of the Rio Treaty. The presence and legality of Communists in Guatemala was also taken as part of the "duck test." Eisenhower told Guatemala's representative in the United States in January 1954, that "we really couldn't help a government which was openly playing ball with Communists" despite their protestations that Guatemalan Communists were of slight political importance, had a right to exist, and were easily controlled.[20] Additional pieces of "evidence" included Guatemala's acceptance of the "ridiculous contention" that the United States used germ warfare in Korea and the minute of silence observed upon Stalin's death in the Guatemalan Congress (despite their protestations that Stalin, Churchill, and Roosevelt were World War II heroes and all deserved a minute of silence).[21] More important than these indicators were the nationalization of United Fruit Company properties, a labor strike in Honduras which Guatemala was accused of masterminding, and the purchase of arms from Czechoslovakia in May 1954. Again there was ample evidence that could have been interpreted to indicate that these were separate issues and did not indicate that Guatemala was racing toward communism. The conflict with the United Fruit Company had been explained repeatedly as a result of long years of exploitation. U.S. officials disparaged these arguments, deriding Guatemalan officials for continuing to "harp" on this issue. Instead, they asserted, communism was the real problem.[22] Labor strikes in Honduras were said to be controlled by Guatemala because three representatives of the Guatemalan government arrived in that area of Honduras at the time the strikes broke out, not because of centuries of labor exploitation in Honduras. Finally, arms purchases from Czechoslovakia were a clear indication of Communist influence, not a result of a U.S. boycott and increasing internal instability. Other evidence, such as Guatemala's "votes with the free world" at the UN, are noted in the diplomatic records but not attended to.[23]

The most complex image of Guatemala can be seen in the National Intelligence Estimate reports on Guatemala for 1952 and 1953. These reports describe the revolution accurately as a nationalistic response to military dictatorship and economic "colonialism." Arbenz is said to derive his strength from his association with the goals and values of that revolution. The army, while anti-Communist, is seen as supporting Arbenz and the opposition as disorganized and weak. That is the extent of the complexity. Arbenz is further described as "essentially an opportunist whose politics are largely a matter of historical accident."[24] He is described as allied with the Communists but not under their control. Communists are seeking to subvert the entire country, including every major political organization and the army. Their strength is derived from their ability to dupe the people into believing that they represent the principles of the revolution. Their goal is not to take over but to neutralize the country. There are odd contradictions in the 1952 NIE. On one hand it is argued that the anti-Communist forces are "potentially powerful" but lacking in leadership and organization. On the other, it is predicted that these forces and the army would move to prevent a Communist take-over. In the 1953 report, the evaluation of the anti-Communist elements is the same: they are not expected to organize "for effective counteraction."[25] Much of the opposition is described as nationalistic and opposed to U.S. domination but went by individualistic interests and loyalty to the revolution of 1944. The army is again described as personally loyal to Arbenz, unlikely to depose him unless the officers become convinced that: "[T]heir personal security and well-being were threatened by Communist infiltration and domination of the Government or unless the policies of the Government were to result in extreme social disorder and economic collapse."[26]

The evaluation of the army is interesting and important. These NIE reports appear to come closest to an effort to understand the political and institutional interests of the army and its probable behavior. As time rolled on toward June 1954, when Arbenz was overthrown, the view of Guatemalan politics and the military in particular is simplified. The military was described by some as political (an extraordinary depiction of the Guatemalan military) and the Arbenz government was increasingly described as Communist or pro-Communist. Threat perceptions grew as strong fears were expressed that Guatemala would attack or subvert its neighbors.

The Decision to Intervene

The decision to engage in covert paramilitary operations to overthrow Arbenz should be examined from two different angles; first, the decision by top-level policy makers to undertake the plan and second, the tactics used by operatives in the field to depose Arbenz. The quality of the decision making in these two phases varies directly with the complexity of the view of the Arbenz government.

The decision to approve the planning of a covert operation to overthrow Arbenz was made at the highest levels of government in late summer 1953, six months after Eisenhower entered office. The major decision makers were Eisenhower, Allen Dulles, John Foster Dulles, and a few other members of the State Department and the White House. The top-level CIA officials responsible for the operation other than Allen Dulles were Frank Wisner and J.C. King. The record concerning this decision is sketchy and likely to remain so since the major participants are all deceased. However, it is clear that Eisenhower and the Dulles brothers entered office advocating a tougher stand on "Communist subversion" and were less reticent to employ covert operations than Truman. Further, they had had initial success (in their view) in employing covert instruments in Iran, in 1953. Iran by all accounts is the lesson they drew upon when approving the development of a similar plot for Guatemala. In fact, Kermit Roosevelt, chief operative in the Iranian case, states with certainty that when he returned for a debriefing on the Iran adventure Dulles was delighted. Dulles reportedly proceeded to tell Roosevelt that he was planning another operation.[27] Schlesinger and Kinzer argue that Eisenhower gave tentative approval to go ahead with the planning in August 1953, leaving the ultimate decision to overthrow Arbenz for a later time.[28]

Two points are in order here. First, the individuals who decided upon the plot were people with extremely simplified views of Guatemala and Arbenz as described above. They apparently did not pause to evaluate the validity of their judgments that Arbenz was a Communist stooge, nor did they attend to the political complexities of Guatemala at the time. The opposition had no clear leader and was not unified but this did not give pause to the top-level decision makers. This lack of attention to Guatemalan politics disturbed Kermit Roosevelt so deeply that he turned down the offer to lead the Guatemalan coup project precisely because he did not believe the conditions in Guatemala were equivalent to those in Iran. He also claims that he tried to warn Dulles that "future coups wouldn't work unless the people and army in the country 'want what we want.' "[29] Dulles ignored this advice. Further, there is some evidence that these top-level decision makers did not evaluate the relative value of the risks associated with this operation and the gains to be made. In fact, the NSC report of August 19, 1953 argued *against* a covert operation in Guatemala because of the difficulty of keeping such an operation secret and the negative impact revelations of U.S. involvement would have on hemispheric relations.[30] A second important point is that despite the enthusiasm for the idea, Allen Dulles at least was aware of the chances of failure. He told Eisenhower that the odds were "better than 40 percent but less than even" that the coup would succeed.[31] Nevertheless, Eisenhower approved the idea. It was a plan approved with little examination of the political forces in Guatemala, their reaction to a coup led by an individual (later selected by the CIA) with little popular following if any, the characteristics of the Guatemalan military, the popularity of Arbenz, and the role of Guatemalan nationalism. Most importantly, there is little indication that they considered alternative policies for U.S.-Guatemalan relations. They simply wanted to get rid of Arbenz.

The second stage of the plot to overthrow Arbenz involves planning by CIA operatives in conjunction with the State Department and, in particular, the U.S. embassy in Guatemala. Here one finds slightly more complex evaluations of Guatemalan politics but again a willingness to take extraordinary risks that took the entire operation to the brink of disaster more than once. After the general plan for the overthrow was approved, responsibilities shifted to a lower official level. Frank Wisner, the

CIA Deputy Director for Operations, Deputy Tracy Barnes, J.C. King, (CIA Director for the Western Hemisphere) and a few others were the link between the field and Allen Dulles. Wisner chose a Colonel Albert Haney, at the time CIA station chief in South Korea, to direct operations in the field. Allen Dulles gave Haney "carte blanche authority" and told him to report directly to Wisner.[32] This removed Haney's operation from the influence of the Western Hemisphere division of the CIA and J.C. King. King turned out to be an internal critic of many of the operation's plans.

Two recent publications detail Haney's plan, *Bitter Fruit* by Schlesinger and Kinzer and *The CIA in Guatemala* by Immerman. Basically, he decided that the plot needed a Guatemalan figurehead and chose Castillo Armas as the "fake" leader of a paramilitary counterrevolutionary army, the Army of Liberation. However, the operation's success was to depend upon psychological warfare rather than military victory:

> Haney's approach was largely dictated by the belief that the CIA would be unable to muster sufficient military force for an invasion or an internal coup without vast outside pressure. There were too few exiles to mount a serious assault over the border, and Arbenz had too much support in Guatemala for the sort of "spontaneous" uprising the CIA had engineered in Iran. As Haney saw it, Arbenz's survival was dependent upon the loyalty of the Army so the objective must be to subvert that loyalty.[33]

Haney clearly had more insight into Arbenz's internal support and the political difficulties this coup would have to deal with. But he too ignored Guatemalan nationalism for he apparently believed any figurehead would do (as long as he looked Indian) and that, given the support for Arbenz, there would not be a civil war in response to the counterrevolution. Indeed, J.C. King warned against just such a possibility but was overruled by Allen Dulles who believed the plan to be "brilliant."[34]

Haney had a number of plans to achieve these goals including bribing Arbenz into resigning, a clear example of the patronizing view of Arbenz. It did not work. He planned to train exiles to form a fake band of revolutionaries, the Army of Liberation, and to give these forces credibility a tremendous propaganda campaign was designed to frighten the populace and, in particular, subvert Arbenz's support from the cities. In addition, the United States would supply airpower for bombing key targets within Guatemala, also with the purpose of frightening the public.

The most important and incredibly risky aspect of the plan was the reliance upon a fake counterrevolutionary force and propaganda. Briefly, the plan was for the Army of Liberation to cross the border and to engage in limited military action while the propaganda radio network broadcast reports that a major popular uprising was in process in support of Castillo

Armas. Meanwhile, the morale of the army was to be broken with the bombing raids and the prospect of possible U.S. intervention to support Castillo Armas. The question remains as to whether or not the CIA planners actually expected any popular uprising in support of Castillo Armas. Haney, according to Schlesinger and Kinzer, did not but it is possible that others at least hoped for such an event as will be seen below.

As the preparation for the coup was put into operation, John Foster Dulles pursued additional courses of action to try to undermine the Arbenz regime. At the tenth meeting of the OAS in Caracas in March 1954, Dulles ramrodded through a resolution condemning communism in the Western Hemisphere. It was a thinly disguised effort to isolate Guatemala and passed by virtue of U.S. ability to apply pressure to the Latin American governments. The administration also made an effort to rally congressional opinion against Guatemala with little difficulty.

The coup went into its operational phase after the Czech arms shipment of May 15, 1954 was discovered. However, anti-Arbenz broadcasts were already being transmitted from the CIA's propaganda radio, announcing that Castillo Armas had all the forces necessary to overthrow Arbenz. The U.S. government flew into something of a frenzy after the arms shipment was discovered. Top-level officials debated whether to invoke the Caracas Resolution and call an OAS meeting. They decided to search ships heading into Guatemala's ports, looking for arms, and tried a number of diplomatic maneuvers and threats to get the Europeans to permit this action. There were serious discussions as to what course of action should be taken if Guatemala aggressed against its neighbors and discussions concerning the possibility of sending U.S. troops into Honduras to quell strikes there.[35]

There has been some scholarly debate as to the ingenuousness of these discussions and plans to call an OAS meeting. Immerman, for example, seems to regard it all as a smokescreen since Dulles knew full well that the CIA plan was going ahead. However, an examination of the correspondence between U.S. officials could as easily lead to the conclusion that they were not relying solely on the CIA plan but in fact had little in the way of concerted strategy. They seemed to want the overthrow of Arbenz but were going to use any means available to achieve it. The administration actually operated in a chaotic state during this time as is indicated by Raymond Leddy's (Officer in Charge of Central America and Panama Affairs) memo to Ambassador Peurifoy wherein he explained U.S. actions regarding the OAS issue. He stated that the "rush of things here . . . surpasses all understanding" indicating the strain and tension felt by decision makers as they worked through their various tactics for overthrowing Arbenz. He further stated:

> There is one thing which I think you can be assured of and that is that we are on the road of settling this problem, either by the means now devised

or by some other means should these not succeed. There is 100 percent
determination here, from the top down, to get rid of this stinker [Arbenz]
and not to stop until that is done.[36]

Apparently Leddy was referring to at least two tactics, using the OAS to
isolate Guatemala and the CIA plan. In short, it appears that a number of
tactics were being tried with the hope that one would work. While
Washington appeared to be debating numerous alternatives, the invasion
plans proceeded. Castillo Armas's Liberation Army entered Guatemala
on June 18, 1954. Meanwhile, U.S.-piloted bombers hit a number of cities,
including Guatemala City, and the radio propaganda campaign proclaimed major victories for the rebels. The CIA radio jammed broadcasts
other than their own so that only propaganda got through to Guatemala
City. The broadcasts proclaimed that the time had come to rise up in rebellion and depose Arbenz but there was no uprising.

In the field things went badly for the Liberation Army. Despite the
CIA's belief that Arbenz's forces would be able to beat Castillo Armas, the
Liberation Army did have certain military operations planned. However,
the Guatemalan army successfully withstood the Liberation Army's 150
men. Consequently, when it became apparent that no popular uprising
would occur and that the Castillo Armas forces were as weak as feared
"the CIA ordered Castillo Armas and his men to stay put six miles inside
the frontier, avoid battles and await further instructions."[37] The truly
amazing aspect of this part of the story is that the success of the CIA plan
depended entirely upon its ability to present the *illusion* of rebel strength.
They believed that through radio propaganda and the impression of
power implied by the bombing raids that they could convince the people
and the Guatemalan army that the rebel forces were large and growing.
Unfortunately for the CIA and Castillo Armas two of "his" planes were
shot down. In a famous meeting between Allen Dulles, Eisenhower, and
others, Eisenhower was convinced to take the risk of exposing U.S. involvement in the operation by replacing the planes. At the time Allen
Dulles estimated that the Castillo Armas forces had only a 20 percent
chance with the planes, none without them.[38] The planes were replaced
and the bombing continued.

The end came for the presidency of Jacobo Arbenz on June 28, 1954. It
came as a result of several immediate events: Arbenz gave an order for the
military to arm worker-peasant militias for defense. This the military was
unwilling to do. Second, as Foreign Minister Toriello explained, the military could easily handle the ground conflict with the Liberation Army but
the air attacks were wreaking terrible damage and could not be stopped.[39]
Finally, the propaganda campaign was taking a toll not in provoking an
uprising against Arbenz but in dampening his support and creating
apathy among the urban dwellers. Ultimately, portions of the military de-

manded Arbenz's resignation on June 25, 1954. As the CIA had predicted, the army was indeed the key to the operation.

Evaluation

The fact that the CIA's plan worked does not mean that it was a brilliant, well-conceived plot. A number of factors argue otherwise. First, it was a tremendously risky plan, since it assumed that an army and a population could be convinced that a revolution was occurring when it was not. In fact, the Guatemalan military did fight successfully against the rebels. Additional information concerning the real weakness of the rebel forces was unavailable partly because the army decided not to go too close to the border, fearing a provocation of U.S. intervention. The CIA apparently had not predicted this restraint by the Guatemalan army. It is not clear how they expected to prevent the army from discovering the rebels' weakness. They did make an effort to prevent the Guatemalan military from using their planes to observe the condition of the rebel forces but how they expected the military to not figure out the rebels weakness from ground contact is a mystery. As mentioned earlier, the government believed that the ground war would be won.

A second peculiar aspect of this plan concerns expectations of a popular uprising. Richard Bissell, Dulles's aide, claims that no uprising was expected and it appears that Haney did not expect one either.[40] On the other hand, it is not so clear that others did not expect an uprising despite all the intelligence reports indicating that the opposition was unorganized and that Arbenz had support from labor and the peasants. There is evidence that an uprising was either expected or hoped for. Castillo Armas was ordered to halt his invasion after no uprising materialized and to wait for the air attacks to do their job. Further, Allen Dulles, in a memo to Eisenhower on June 20 seemed to believe that Castillo Armas could not achieve a military victory but that the question of a popular uprising was just that—a question:

> If the Guatemalan army should move . . . against the Arbenz regime, it is considered to have the capacity to overthrow it. On the other hand if it remains loyal and if most of the military elements commit themselves to vigorous action against the forces of Castillo Armas the latter will be defeated and a probability of uprisings from among other elements of the population is considered highly unlikely.[41]

In the same memo he states:

> The action of Colonel Castillo Armas is not in any sense a conventional military operation. He is dependent for his success not upon the size and strength of the military forces at his disposal but rather upon the possibility that his entry into action will touch off a general uprising against the Guatemalan regime.[42]

Thus it is simply not clear whether Dulles expected a popular uprising or not. The issue is important because it is only with an extraordinarily simplified view of Arbenz and Guatemalan politics that one would expect such an uprising. It also shows a remarkable failure to understand the importance of political support for the counterrevolutionary replacement of a popular president. Castillo Armas had no large base of support and there is no indication that serious attention was ever given to this as a potential problem. In general, the Guatemalan military, so crucial for this operation's outcome, was not carefully evaluated. Despite the fact that early evaluations of the Guatemalan military indicated that they were loyal to Arbenz and would be unless he aroused their anti-Communist passions, the decision makers did not ask why an anti-Communist military would continue to support Arbenz when U.S. officials had no doubt of his Communist inclinations. The strong nationalism of the military nearly prevented the final component of the operation from being completed—Castillo Armas's ascent to power. When the Guatemalan military finally deposed Arbenz, they explicitly promised to continue fighting against the invaders. It was only after the bombing continued and Peurifoy, revolver strapped to his shoulder, made clear threats to the military command that they bowed to the will of the United States.

In the long run, the key to the success of this operation was luck and sheer brute force—the bombing. That neither the CIA nor top-level officials understood the reasons for its success can be seen in the lessons they drew from this operation. They applied those lessons to the Bay of Pigs. This plan revolved once more around the idea that an exile force could be trained and sent into a revolutionary situation and that a popular uprising would follow in support of the counterrevolutionaries, overthrowing a "Communist dictator." They apparently did not learn the importance of air power for when Kennedy rejected the air support for the Bay of Pigs invaders, the plan was not called off. In order to disguise U.S. involvement, the idea was propagated by the Eisenhower administration that Arbenz was overthrown by a popular uprising in support of Castillo Armas. Oddly, by the time of the Bay of Pigs, the memory that this was fiction seems to have disappeared and the same expectations were applied to Castro's Cuba.[43]

Chile, 1970–73

Background

The second case of "successful" intervention is the Nixon administration's interference in Chile's peaceful road to revolution from 1970–73. There are striking analytical similarities between the cases of Guatemala and Chile although the nations and the interventions are quite different. As in the Guatemalan case, some preliminary background information is necessary to set the context for this intervention.

Chile was a remarkable and extraordinarily complex nation with a long history of democracy. The political system functioned on the basis of the 1925 Constitution and the Chilean military had abstained from political interference since the 1930s. Chile had a multiparty political system that operated through delicate coalitions. The parties included those from the far right through the far left. Among the most important during the 1960s were the Socialists, the Communists, the Christian Democrats, the Radicals, and the Liberal and Conservative parties. Economically, Chile was highly dependent upon the export of copper for its foreign exchange earnings. The copper industry was dominated by U.S.-based corporations including the giants, Kennecott and Anaconda.

During the period from 1958–70, Chileans elected three presidents of very different political principles. In 1958, Jorge Alessandri was elected, a conservative independent supported by the Liberal and Conservative parties with portions of the Radical party. In 1964, the Christian Democrat, Eduardo Frei, became president and in 1970, the Socialist Salvador Allende was elected under the banner of the Popular Unity Coalition.

Chile's relationship with the United States swung as dramatically during this era. During the Frei administration they were quite close. Chile was designated as an outstanding example of the accomplishments of the Alliance for Progress. This produced economic assistance from the United States that was "among the highest in the world on a per capita basis."[44] Frei had no problem in complying with U.S. requisites for Alliance aid since his own principles were the same as those pronounced by John Kennedy when he introduced the Alliance. Indeed, Frei began many reforms in Chile, most notably the "Chileanization" of the copper industry wherein the state began to acquire a percentage of the copper industry. Other programs included land reform and social welfare. The United States approved:

> Since Frei appears to have set out deliberately not to pose a major threat to U.S. interests, public or private, it is not surprising that the U.S. response was, in the main, sympathetic and cooperative. . . . United States policy toward the Frei government in the Johnson Administration became a kind of legacy of Kennedy's reformist aspirations.[45]

There were a few conflicts between the two states during the Frei period. These included disagreements about the U.S. invasion of the Dominican Republic, the admission of the People's Republic of China to the UN, the rapid recognition given by the United States of the military government in Brazil in 1964, and certain revelations concerning U.S. Army sponsorship of Project Camelot.[46]

Allende, like Arbenz, continued some of his predecessor's reforms and added his own. He had spent a career in the Chilean political arena, running for the presidency four times during those years. In 1970, Allende won a plurality of the vote and, in accordance with the constitution, the Congress had to decide which of the two finalists would assume the presidency. Traditionally, the candidate with the largest popular vote was selected and tradition was upheld in 1970. Allende, a Marxist parliamentarian, was chosen over his closest rival, Jorge Alessandri. Allende's program for Chile promised to follow a "via Chilena"—a Chilean path to socialism. His policies included the nationalization of major portions of Chilean industry and banking, agrarian reform, income redistribution, and social welfare. Most important from the standpoint of the United States was Allende's expropriation of the U.S.-based business' investments and holdings.[47] U.S. officials were also alarmed at Allende's ties with socialist countries.[48] The Nixon administration opposed Allende even before he took office. Three different covert operations were undertaken in 1970 in an effort to prevent Allende's election and ascent to the presidency. After Allende's election the United States followed an overt policy of economic sanctions and a multipronged covert operation designed to support Allende's opposition and promote conditions conducive to his demise.

Two points should be made in concluding this introduction to the case. First, close interaction between the United States and Chile during the 1960s resulted in extensive knowledge on the part of many U.S. officials about Chile, its political system and the channels through which influence could be exerted. Second, intervention in Chile was actually a series of interventions with several key decision points. This intervention is usually regarded as a "success," that is, the Nixon administration got what it wanted in the end. But when the intervention is examined in terms of its incremental parts, there were clearly as many failures as successes. As will be seen, the complexity and viability of the efforts to depose Allende tended to vary with the complexity of the image of Chile and Allende held by those individuals who made the decisions to intervene and formulated the plans for doing so.

Images of Allende and Chile

As in the case of Guatemala, there existed a set of government officials in the United States with an extremely simplified image of Chile and Allende. There were also two other groups with different images. One group saw Chile and its political system in a fairly complex fashion but saw Allende as the classic Communist: evil, antidemocratic, and scheming. The final group tended to see both Chile and Allende in a complex picture. Different policy combinations were preferred by each of these groups.

The first group, those with the most simplified and stereotyped views of Chile and Allende, was composed of Nixon and Kissinger. According to one account, the U.S. ambassador to Chile from 1967–71, Edward Korry, reported that Nixon had not liked Frei, whom he regarded as too far Left and "a Kennedy man."[49] More revealing is Kissinger's behavior. He not only knew very little about Chile, but also about Latin America as a whole. It was to the Chilean ambassador that Kissinger showed his contempt for Latin America when he said:

> Mr. Minister, you made a strange speech. You come here speaking of Latin America, but this is not important. Nothing important can come from the South. History has never been produced in the South. The axis of history starts in Moscow, goes to Bonn, crosses over to Washington, and then goes to Tokyo. What happens in the South is of no importance.[50]

When the minister protested that Kissinger knew nothing about the South, Kissinger responded by saying "No . . . and I don't care." Hersh describes the White House image of Latin America as that of a child, an image typical of those with a "dependent" stereotype of another state.[51]

The specific image of Allende held by the White House elite was quite simply that he was a Communist who would deliver Chile into the arms of the Soviet Union. Kissinger's position is clear from a press briefing given on September 16, 1970:

> The election in Chile brought about a result in which the man backed by the Communists and probably a Communist himself, had the largest number of votes.
>
> The two non-Communist parties between them had, of course, 64 percent of the votes, so there is a non-Communist majority, but a Communist plurality. I say that just to get the picture straight.
>
> According to the Chilean election law, when nobody gets a majority, the two highest candidates go to the Congress. Congress then votes in a secret ballot and elects the President. . . . In Chilean history, there is nothing to prevent it, and it would not be at all illogical for the Congress there to say, "Sixty-four per cent of the people did not want a Communist government. A Communist government tends to be irreversible. Therefore, we are going to vote for the No. 2 man."
>
> This problem is compounded by the fact that the non-Communist parties in Chile have been very divided among themselves, and you have the unusual phenomenon of people arguing, "Well, maybe Allende won't be so bad. Maybe he will run a democratic system." And it is the usual revolutionary dilemma that, with a revolutionary seeking power, those who represent the non-revolutionary side do not all at the same time clearly understand what is happening.[52]

Kissinger also stated that he had "yet to meet somebody who firmly believes that if Allende wins there is likely to be another free election in Chile."[53] He was convinced that Allende's election would affect Chile's neighbors in a leftward direction as well.[54] Thus the judgment was that Allende was a Communist and would do what Communists are wont to do. His history as a parliamentarian devoted to democratic procedure was disregarded as was the fact that he was a member of the Socialist party, not the Communist party, and as was his proclamation of the "via Chilena." This was important information that should have been part of a careful analysis of a new and peculiar government in Chile. It was discounted due to the power of the stereotyped image of a Communist. As will be seen in the next section, Nixon and Kissinger supported policies that conformed to this simplified view of Chile and Allende.

The second group of policy advocates is a curious one composed of Ambassador Korry and at least some members of the CIA. This group had a complex view of the Chilean political system but a simplistic image of Allende similar to Kissinger's. Korry's image of Chile is clearly expressed in an interview with William Buckley:

> [Chile was] the freest democracy in South America, a democracy which was of a totally different profile than any other country in all of Latin America. Ninety percent of all Chileans are literate, were literate. Eighty-five percent of those eligible voted in elections, which is better than in this country. Seventy percent of them were urban, very few landholders. There were practically no great fortune in the sense that you had them in Peru or Colombia. . . . You had a huge middle class in Chile. You had social democracy.[55]

Allende, on the other hand, was regarded as very dangerous, a man who would destroy Chilean democracy and who should be prevented from attaining office if possible. The CIA was also intimately familiar with the complexities of Chilean party politics, having had six years of experience in influencing Chilean elections by 1970. This group tended to support covert efforts to manipulate Chile's political system but was hesitant about or opposed to efforts to foment a coup in 1970.

The final group, composed of members of the State Department tended to see Chile's political system, and Allende as well, as complex. State Department representatives reportedly did not believe Allende's election heralded a Communist government in Chile and the department was not supportive of proposals to prevent Allende from taking office.[56] The evaluation of Allende was put forth in late 1969 and early 1970 but lost the policy debate by March 1970. The State Department role in the post-1970 operations was less important than that of other departments.[57]

The next issue that must be examined concerns the making of the decisions to intervene and the planning of those interventions. Particular attention will be devoted to the quality of the decision making (as defined above), and to the impact of images and the lessons of history on the quality of the decision making. Attention will be devoted to the covert operations since the overt policy evolved from the covert decision making of 1970.

The Decision to Intervene

The intervention in Chile took place in three stages: First, an anti-Allende campaign designed to prevent him from winning the election (March 1970–September 4, 1970); second, a two-track plan to prevent Allende from taking office (September–October 1970); and third, an effort to destabilize his administration (1970–73). The quality of the decision making in each stage varied considerably.

The decision making in stage one was fairly sophisticated and of high quality. Discussions began in the 40 Committee (appointed by Nixon to oversee covert operations) in March 1969 concerning the coming year's elections in Chile. Considerable debate was undertaken regarding the question of whether the United States should attempt to influence those elections as it had the 1964 elections in Chile. A number of options were considered including a simple anti-Allende campaign and/or a campaign in support of one of the other candidates. Involvement in the campaign was opposed by the State Department but supported by Ambassador Korry and the CIA. The proinvolvement advocates favored an anti-Allende campaign rather than a campaign in support of one of the candidates. The CIA clearly understood the difficulties of this type of operation and believed it could not successfully back either of Allende's two major opponents. There was a clear and concise evaluation of alternatives and the costs and benefits of those alternatives. Most importantly, the CIA was aware of the poor prospects for success and was cautious in engaging in the operation. They had warned the 40 Committee in April 1969 that this type of operation needed a long lead time and they had learned important lessons from their success in Chile in the massive campaign in support of Frei in 1964. The agency had maintained its liaisons with members of the Chilean security and intelligence agencies and made use of the influence mechanisms established in 1964. The operation was approved in March 1970. Six covert projects were used which "were focused into an intensive propaganda campaign which made use of virtually all media within Chile and which placed and replayed items in the international press as well."[58] This was a "spoiling" campaign, describing Allende as Stalin reincarnated. Despite the careful plans, Allende was not defeated. The effort did contribute to heightened political polarization and financial panic, however.[59]

The more interesting decision-making procedures occur in stage two. After the election, top-level U.S. policy makers met to devise methods to prevent Allende from becoming president. Track 1 was approved on September 14 by the 40 Committee and supported by Korry and the CIA. It included "political, economic and propaganda . . . activities."[60] The political portion of Track 1 consisted of support for Alessandri's bid to have Congress elect him, to be followed by his resignation. This would permit Frei to run for office again since he could not constitutionally succeed himself. The CIA attempted to "induce President Frei at least to consent to the gambit or, better yet, assist in its implementation" by trying to get individuals whose opinion he valued to pressure him. This did not succeed, for Frei refused to consider the idea. At the same time the CIA launched a propaganda campaign designed to illustrate the dreadful consequences for Chile should Allende be selected. This campaign was "designed to influence Frei, the Chilean elite, and the Chilean military."[61] The campaign was waged through the Chilean and international press and through CIA "resources" throughout Chile. Finally, in hopes of provoking a military response to Allende's pending victory, the 40 Committee decided to implement economic pressures including cutting-off credits and encouraging other countries to do the same. These actions could not prevent Congress from selecting Allende but they were continued after his appointment in October.

Track 1 decision-making procedures were less cautious and well planned than those of the "spoiling" campaign. One can see in this effort the dual image of Chile and Allende. The decision makers understood Chilean politics well enough to know that the political system would have to be manipulated, influenced, and because they had a complex view of that system they knew where to go and who to attempt to influence. However, their stereotyped view of Allende led them to believe they could convince Chilean politicians that Allende threatened the state and that the constitution and tradition should be bypassed in order to prevent his ascent to office. The argument was not effective on individuals who had competed with Allende and his coalition's parties for many years and who were devoted constitutionalists. While the Track 1 operation was in full swing, the Christian Democratic party had been engaged in long negotiations with each other and with Allende and Popular Unity to create an agreement providing measures to ensure Chile's democratic practices. This permitted the Christian Democrats to support Allende. Many of Allende's opponents had concerns about his policies, but they did not see him as Korry and the CIA saw him.

Track 2 was an operation reminiscent of the Guatemalan case. The decision-making procedures were very poor. The operation was decided upon by Richard Nixon on September 15, 1970 in a meeting with a few others including Kissinger and CIA Director Richard Helms. Nixon essentially ordered Helms to have the CIA make contact with the Chilean military and encourage any members willing to initiate a coup. The 40

Committee and the ambassador were not to know of this operation. Further:

> Between October 5 and October 20, 1970, the CIA made 21 contacts with key military and Carabinero (police) officials in Chile. Those Chileans who were inclined to stage a coup were given assurances of strong support at the highest levels of the U.S. Government both before and after a coup.[62]

Nixon's command was given despite the fact that the CIA had already reported that a coup was not likely to occur, as had Ambassador Korry. Nixon acknowledged that the chances of success were few but, according to Helms's notes, was not concerned with the risks involved. Nixon ordered the CIA to "make the economy scream" and use its best men to carry out the operation. Great pressure was applied to the CIA to succeed in this endeavor and the CIA chief in Chile, Henry Hecksher, reported that Nixon and Kissinger were "not too interested in continuously being told by me that certain proposals which had been made could not be executed or would be counterproductive."[63] In short, Nixon and Kissinger refused to listen to information that was not what they wanted to hear, consulted with no critics of the plan, and applied tremendous pressure to CIA agents who did not think the plan would work. It was a plan that reflected the exceptionally simplified view of Chile. According to the classic stereotype of Latin American states, military strongmen really control the polity and all one needs to do is find the right plotters. Those with a different image, such as Korry, believed that the military simply was not an alternative to Allende.[64]

Indeed, the CIA did find some plotters, and contact was made with two generals (one retired), Valenzuela and Viaux. This operation ended in the murder of a constitutionalist general, Rene Schneider, by the Viaux group while attempting his kidnap. After that incident the coup plotting collapsed. The plan cost the CIA as well. After the collapse of Track 2 the CIA lost all its "assets," that is, contacts, within the Chilean military. It took 10 months to rebuild those contacts.

After Allende's ascent to the Chilean presidency, the White House announced (in early November) the official policy that would be accompanied by covert actions and that would endure until 1973. National Security Memorandum 93 pronounced the "cool but correct" policy through which the United States sought to avoid becoming "a handy foreign enemy to use as a domestic and international rallying point" for the Allende government.[65] Meanwhile, overt economic pressure was continued and increased as did covert operations. Approval of spending for covert operations returned to the 40 Committee and during the next three years over $6 million were spent doing what the CIA did well, manipulating the Chilean political system. Briefly, the techniques used after 1970 included support for opposition parties in Chile and efforts to break the Popular Unity Coalition; propaganda campaigns and large amounts of money ($1.5 million) for support for the opposition media; support for private organizations; and continued penetration of the Chilean military in a successful effort to gather information on potential coups. It was the conclusion of the Senate investigating committee report that the Chilean military was well aware that the United States would have no objection to a coup to depose Allende.[66]

Evaluation

Evaluating the Chilean case is a difficult task in the end because it will never be certain how important the covert activities of the United States were in causing Allende's downfall. Clearly, the covert activities alone did not bring him down for the economic sanctions contributed as well. It is difficult to accept the argument put forth by Sigmund that Allende would have been overthrown with or without U.S. activities for the covert operations were massive, they were clever, and Chile's economy and polity did become unstable. One can come to some conclusions, however: It is quite clear that the operation based upon poor decision-making procedures, Track 2, was a failure and that the other operations, the spoiling campaign, Track 1 and the third stage had incremental failures but the desired effect in the end. The covert operations that utilized years of knowledge within the CIA about the Chilean polity, society, and military were results of careful evaluations of options and short-run costs.

The importance of the image of the target state can be seen in several respects in this case. Those with a simplified image, when left to their own devices, produced disastrous plots. Those with more complex images did the opposite but were also crippled by their simplified image of Allende himself. There were clear lines of policy disagreement in this case that conformed to differences in image.

Images of Allende also affected information processing. Those with the view of Allende as a stereotyped Communist tended to ignore vast amounts of information indicating that Allende posed no threat, that there was no significant threat of Soviet influence, that Allende did not intend to subvert his neighbors, and that Chile did not offer a model for other states. The Senate report cited so often concluded that National Intelligence Estimates providing numerous, sometimes conflicting, evaluations of Allende were not used:

> It appears that the Chile NIEs were either, at best, selectively used or, at worst, disregarded by policy makers when the time came to make decisions regarding U.S. covert involvement in Chile. 40 Committee decisions regarding Chile reflected greater concern about the internal and in-

ternational consequences of an Allende government than was reflected in the intelligence estimates. At the same time as the Chile NIEs were becoming less shrill, the 40 Committee authorized greater amounts of money.[67]

In fact, the policy makers tended to select information that supported their stereotyped view of Allende.

Finally, there is the issue of the lessons of history. In this case the CIA and Korry as well drew upon two lessons: the Bay of Pigs (to be avoided at all costs), and the successful interference in the 1964 elections in Chile. Korry argued repeatedly against direct or indirect intervention by the United States to prevent Allende from assuming office.[68] In other words, he did not want the United States to use obvious, highly coercive means to prevent Allende's presidency. The lessons drawn from 1964 were clearly appropriately instructive. The same country was involved, the mechanisms for influence were still in place, a short period of time had lapsed, and many of the actors were the same in 1970 as in 1964.

In general, therefore, one can see poor decision making leading to failure but good decision making leading to both success and failure from the standpoint of those creating the plans. The larger policy of opposition of Allende with his demise as a goal was based upon a stereotyped image of him, his country, a failure to evaluate all information carefully, and, as will be argued below, a failure to assess adequately U.S. goals and alternative means for achieving them.

Conclusions

Several conclusions are in order after examining the decision-making processes in these two cases. First, many of the limitations on optimal decision making were evident in these cases. Policy makers tended to use simplified images of the target state to interpret information and develop policy options. They relied upon a crude representativeness heuristic to evaluate Arbenz and Allende and in the process ignored crucial information that indicated the mistaken nature of their conclusions. In addition, in each case the more simplified the image of the target state, the poorer the quality of the decision-making practices. In short, interventions are not always the result of optimal decision making and are not likely to be so.

A second conclusion is a theoretical one. An examination of the decision-making procedures alone cannot adequately explain the success or failure of an intervention. In the cases observed here poor decision making was followed by both success (Guatemala 1954) and failure (Track 2, 1970). Good decision making was followed by both failure (the spoiling campaign) and success (Allende's downfall). Analyses of images and other psychological properties can explain why policy makers chose the options they selected, but the success or failure of the intervention in the end requires a larger analytical focus. In particular, much as the policy maker is well advised to analyze the internal dynamics of the target state, so is the scholar in explaining the outcome of an intervention. In some cases, most particularly Guatemala, but Chile as well, the sheer physical and economic power of the intervening state can, with time and in combination with internal factors, produce the desired outcome. Guatemala is the clearest case in this regard because it was the weakest and most vulnerable when confronted with massive U.S. pressures on all levels. This is not to say that the analysis of decision making is unimportant. Not only can it explain why the intervention was undertaken and formulated as it was, it can explain certain portions of the outcome, such as the imposition of a thoroughly unpopular president in Guatemala.

Perhaps most important is the pattern of strategy formation and goal selection that is revealed in a decision-making analysis of interventions. In both cases examined here policy makers had no real long-run strategy and they completely failed to analyze the impact of possible outcomes of their short-run tactics and methods on national goals and values. In each case the goal was simple—get rid of an undesirable government. In neither case did policy makers ask themselves what kind of political system would reemerge in these two countries when the current one was destroyed using the methods advocated and employed. In Guatemala they pushed into office a figurehead exile whose main attribute from the U.S. standpoint was his Indian appearance. In the case of Chile, there is no indication that Nixon or Kissinger or other top-level policy makers asked themselves what kind of government would follow Allende's demise. In the end this is why one must refer to these interventions as "successes" only in light of the short-run goals of the U.S. government at the time, for it is difficult to label participation in the establishment of two of the most brutal dictatorships in the Western Hemisphere a "success" just as it is difficult to see how it has served U.S. interests for the rest of Latin America to have watched us do so. Rather than ask the crucial questions and make the difficult decisions, with a blind eye U.S. policy makers chose to destroy democracy to save it.

Notes

1. Ideally the study should include a comparison case of decision making in an unsuccessful intervention. However, the Chilean case involves a number of policy selections, some resulting in "success" and others in failure. Hence that case provides opportunities for comparison.

2. See Richard Cottam, *Foreign Policy Motivation* (Pittsburgh: University of Pittsburgh Press, 1977); Alexander George, "The 'Operational Code': A Neglected Approach to the Study of Political Leaders and Decision-Making," *International Studies Quarterly* 13 (1969): 190–222; Ole Holsti, "Cognitive Dynamics and Images of the Enemy," *Journal of International Affairs* 21 (1967): 16–39; and Robert Jervis, *Perception and Misperception in International Politics* (Princeton: University of Princeton Press, 1976).

3. Irving Janis and Leon Mann, *Decision Making* (New York: Free Press, 1977), p. 11.

4. Walter LaFeber, *Inevitable Revolutions* (New York: Norton, 1983), p. 112.

5. Stephen Schlesinger and Stephen Kinzer, *Bitter Fruit* (Garden City, NY: Anchor Books, 1982), p. 37.

6. Cole Blasier, *The Hovering Giant* (Pittsburgh: University of Pittsburgh Press, 1976), p. 153.

7. Ibid., p. 157.

8. Michael Gordon, "A Case History of U.S. Subversion: Guatemala, 1954," in *Guatemala in Rebellion,* ed. Jonathan Freid, Marvin Gettleman, and Daniel Levenson (New York: Grove Press, 1983), p. 53.

9. See chapter 6 in Schlesinger and Kinzer, *Bitter Fruit,* for details on the United Fruit Company campaign against Arbenz.

10. Richard Immerman, *The CIA in Guatemala* (Austin: University of Texas Press, 1982), p. 74.

11. Ibid., p. 84.

12. Ibid., p. 86.

13. Dwight Eisenhower, *The White House Years. Vol. I: Mandate for Change, 1953–56* (Garden City, NY: Doubleday, 1963), p. 83.

14. Allen Dulles, *The Craft of Intelligence* (New York: Harper and Row, 1963), p. 221.

15. John Peurifoy, "Telegram to the Department of State," *Foreign Relations of the United States, 1952–1954, IV* (Washington, DC: U.S. Government Printing Office, 1983), p. 1,093.

16. Schlesinger and Kinzer, *Bitter Fruit,* p. 141.

17. John Cabot, "Memorandum of Conversation," *Foreign Relations of the United States, 1952–1954, IV* (Washington, DC: U.S. Government Printing Office, 1983), pp. 1,096–97.

18. Eisenhower, *White House Years,* p. 425.

19. Quoted in Immerman, *CIA in Guatemala,* p. 102.

20. Cabot, "Memorandum of Conversation," p. 1,096.

21. Eisenhower, *White House Years,* p. 422.

22. Cabot, "Memorandum of Conversation," p. 1,096; and Peurifoy, "Telegram to the Department of State," p. 1,094.

23. U.S. National Security Council, "Draft Policy Paper," *Foreign Relations of the United States, 1952–1954, IV* (Washington, DC: U.S. Government Printing Office, 1983), p. 1,082.

24. U.S. Central Intelligence Agency, "National Intelligence Estimate, 1952," *Foreign Relations of the United States, 1952–1954, IV* (Washington, DC: U.S. Government Printing Office, 1983), p. 1,033.

25. Central Intelligence Agency, "National Intelligence Ēstimate, 1952," p. 1,031; and U.S. Central Intelligence Agency, "National Intelligence Estimate, 1953," *Foreign Relations of the United States, 1952–1954, IV* (Washington, DC: U.S. Government Printing Office, 1983), p. 1,066.

26. Ibid., "National Intelligence Estimate, 1953," p. 1,070.

27. Kermit Roosevelt, *Countercoup: The Struggle for the Control of Iran* (New York: McGraw-Hill, 1979), p. 210.

28. Schlesinger and Kinzer, *Bitter Fruit,* p. 102.

29. Quoted in ibid., p. 101.

30. National Security Council, "Draft Policy Paper," p. 1,083.

31. Schlesinger and Kinzer, *Bitter Fruit,* p. 108.

32. Ibid., p. 109.

33. Ibid., p. 110.

34. Ibid., p. 112.

35. U.S. Department of State–Joint Chiefs of Staff, "Substance of Discussion," *Foreign Relations of the United States, 1952–1954, IV* (Washington, DC: U.S. Government Printing Office, 1983), p. 1,119–20.

36. Raymond Leddy, "Memo to Peurifoy," *Foreign Relations of the United States, 1952–1954, IV* (Washington, DC: U.S. Government Printing Office, 1983), p. 1,157.

37. Schlesinger and Kinzer, *Bitter Fruit,* p. 171.

38. Eisenhower, *White House Years,* p. 425.

39. Peurifoy, "Telegram to the Department of State," p. 1,181.

40. Immerman, *CIA in Guatemala,* p. 163.

41. Allen Dulles, "Memorandum by the Director of Central Intelligence (Dulles) to the President," *Foreign Relations of the United States, 1952–1954, IV* (Washington, DC: U.S. Government Printing Office, 1983), p. 1,175.

42. Ibid., p. 1,176.

43. Joseph Smith, *Portrait of a Cold Warrior* (New York: Putnam's and Sons, 1976).

44. Blasier, *The Hovering Giant,* p. 256.

45. Ibid.

46. Paul Sigmund, *The Overthrow of Allende and the Politics of Chile, 1964–1976* (Pittsburgh: University of Pittsburgh Press, 1977), p. 41.

47. Blasier, *The Hovering Giant,* p. 262.

48. U.S. Senate, *Intelligence Activities: Hearings before the Select Committee to Study Governmental Operations with Respect to Intelligence Activities of the United States,* 94th Cong., 1st sess., December 4 and 5, 1975 (Washington, DC: U.S. Government Printing Office, 1975).

49. Seymour Hersh, *The Price of Power* (New York: Summit Books, 1983), p. 263.

50. Quoted in ibid.

51. Ibid.

52. Henry Kissinger, "Background Briefing at the White House, September 16, 1970," in U.S. Senate, *Multinational Corporations and United States Foreign Policy: Hearings Before the Subcommittee on Multinational Corporations of the Committee on Foreign Relations,* 93rd Cong., March 20, 21, 22, 27, 29, and April 2, 1973 (Washington, DC: U.S. Government Printing Office, 1973), pp. 542–43.

53. Quoted in Hersh, *The Price of Power*, p. 270.

54. Sigmund, *Overthrow of Allende*, p. 116.

55. Edward Korry, "U.S. Policies in Chile Under the Allende Government: An Interview to Former Ambassador Edward Korry," in *Chile: The Balanced View*, ed. Francisco Orrego Vicuna (Santiago: University of Chile Press, 1975), p. 292.

56. U.S. Senate, *Intelligence Activities*, p. 190.

57. U.S. Senate, *Multinational Corporations*, p. 45.

58. U.S. Senate, *Intelligence Activities*, p. 168.

59. Ibid., pp. 166–70.

60. Ibid., p. 170.

61. Ibid., p. 171.

62. Ibid., p. 173.

63. Quoted in Hersh, *The Price of Power*, p. 282.

64. U.S. Senate, *Intelligence Activities*, p. 173.

65. Ibid., p. 174.

66. Ibid., p. 176.

67. Ibid., p. 195.

68. Korry, "U.S. Policies in Chile," p. 288.

8   VIETNAM: THE DECISIONS TO INTERVENE

Roger Hilsman

In the early years of its history, the United States was an advocate of revolution. Monarchies, especially, viewed it with fear and suspicion. In later years, the United States began to think of revolution as a threat, especially after the rise of Communist Russia. On occasion, as in the civil war in China, the United States sent aid and advisers to help the threatened government. But it was not until Vietnam that it intervened in a country seized by revolution with full-scale military forces of its own.

The primary reason that Vietnam came to the top of the U.S. agenda was that many Americans viewed it as directed by Moscow and Peking for the purposes of "world communism." Just before the inauguration of John F. Kennedy as president, on January 6, 1961, Nikita Khrushchev, chairman of the Communist party of the Soviet Union, made what was viewed as a declaration of war by means of "wars of national liberation." And in his meeting that same year with President Kennedy at Vienna, it was on Soviet encouragement and support for such wars that Khrushchev was harshest and most intransigent, even more so than on the question of Berlin and Germany. The Chinese, for their part, not only took a similar position but were the principal architects of the doctrine and strategy of "people's" or "revolutionary" warfare. This envisioned revolutions in which peasants played the central role rather than the urban proletariat—turning Marx and Lenin upside down.

Mao's first principle was the famous phrase that guerrillas were fish swimming in the sea of the people: "Guerrillas are fish, and the people are the water in which they swim. If the temperature of the water is right, the fish will thrive and multiply." One familiar comment is that revolutionary warfare is guerrilla tactics plus political action.

Mao has a great deal to say about tactics, but the gist of the difference between mere tactics and "revolutionary warfare" itself is contained in his description of the three phases of a revolutionary war. The first stage is almost purely political, with the activist cadres building support among the people, propagandizing and recruiting. The second stage is active guerrilla warfare, with bands of guerrillas ambushing government forces, raiding and harassing, but avoiding pitched battles. All this is combined with highly discriminating terrorism, sabotage, and assassination of government officials, especially unpopular government officials. The second stage is a systematic effort to destroy the people's confidence in the government's ability to function and to protect them. Its purpose is to make the government suspicious of the people and the people distrustful of the government—turning government and people against each other. It may be that power can be seized in the turmoil that follows this second stage. If not, the third and final stage is to establish "liberated areas." These are base areas, in which not only can supplies and recruits be obtained but in which the efforts of the people can be directed to the support of the revolution. In these base areas, the guerrillas can be transformed into regular forces and so turn guerrilla terrorism and harassment into a civil war in which the government troops can be engaged directly in conventional combat and destroyed. In the first stage food, money, and supplies can be obtained from the people, and the fact of their making a contribution commits them to the cause. Even in the second stage, outside help is not really essential. Money and supplies come from the people; weapons and ammunition can be taken from the government forces through ambush or surprise attack. It is only in the third and final stage that outside help might make a decisive difference, after the struggle has been transformed into a regular civil war. At that time, two conventional armies are locked in sustained combat, and the need for ammunition, weapons, and supplies assumes really large-scale proportions.

The Initial U.S. Reaction

The U.S. response was slow in coming, mainly because of differences within the U.S. government about the seriousness of the threat and about what the response should be. The U.S. military aid mission to Vietnam, for example, believed that their task was to help the South Vietnamese build a conventional army that could fight a Korea-type aggression from the North, and they resisted any change toward developing counterguerrilla forces. After Mao's speech following the Soviet Sputnik success declaring that the "East Wind prevails over the West Wind" in November 1957, the North Vietnamese reactivated the Communist cadres who had remained in South Vietnam after the 1954 Geneva agreements and began to use the old Ho Chi Minh trails through Laos to send down new cadres, selected from among the 90,000 southerners who had gone North in 1954.

By mid-1961, the Vietcong were estimated to have about 12,000 mainline guerrilla troops, and they more or less controlled as much as a third of the countryside in South Vietnam. Over 1,400 civilians, mainly village officials, had been assassinated in the previous 12 months and over 2,000 kidnapped.

In the late spring of 1961, Vice-President Lyndon B. Johnson visited Vietnam, and he returned to recommend a fundamental decision to "move forward with a major effort to help these countries defend themselves." He stated the choice in dramatic terms: The United States had either to pull its defenses back to San Francisco or go ahead with a full, "forward strategy."

The Taylor-Rostow Mission

By the fall of 1961, President Ngo Dinh Diem and the Vietnamese government were calling for help. On October 11, 1961, President Kennedy announced that he was sending General Maxwell D. Taylor and Walt W. Rostow to Vietnam to investigate and make recommendations. The final report of the Taylor-Rostow mission contained three sets of recommendations. The first was in effect a series of demands for political, governmental, and administrative reforms on the part of the government of President Diem. The second set of recommendations was that the United States should provide material aid and the technical advisers required for a broad-gauge counter-guerrilla program—economic measures; village-level civic, social, and political action; arms and equipment for a self-defense corps; and the specialized equipment, helicopters, and so on, to free the Vietnamese military from static defense and to give them the mobility to seek out the guerrillas in their own territory. The program would include helicopter pilots, mechanics, and other highly trained technicians who would operate the equipment while training Vietnamese to take over. In addition, the report also recommended sending to Vietnam two special Air Force squadrons—with the code name "Farmgate"—of slow-flying, propeller-driven B–26s and T–28s. These were Air Force units specially designed and put together for the purposes of small-scale guerrilla warfare. They were to be operated on a semicovert basis—Americans would do the actual flying but they would always be accompanied by a Vietnamese "observer," and the marking on the planes would also be Vietnamese. With the exception of these semicovert units, all this was merely more of the same kind of assistance that had been given in the past.

The third set of recommendations was for a qualitative change in the nature of the U.S. commitment in the direction that Vice-President Johnson had recommended. For the Taylor-Rostow report also recommended that 10,000 U.S. ground troops be introduced into Vietnam immediately and that the possibility be accepted that as many as six full divisions might eventually be required, which would total about half a million men.

President Kennedy approved the recommendations designed to bring about reforms in the Diem government and the step-up in military and economic aid and an increase in the number of U.S. advisers, technicians, and helicopter pilots, including the introduction of the "Farmgate" B–26s and T–28s with their pilots and mechanics. But he turned down the recommendation for committing U.S. troops.

President Kennedy's View

In 1951, when President Kennedy was a young congressman he and his brother Robert had visited Vietnam, and he had been dismayed at the French military and strategic situation. As Robert said later, as a result President Kennedy "determined early that we would never get into that position."[1] Nevertheless, Kennedy was shaken by the briefing Eisenhower gave him just before the inauguration. At the time, Laos was the crisis spot, not Vietnam. In spite of the Geneva agreements of 1954 which were supposed to end the fighting in all Southeast Asia and which created an independent Laos, the Communist forces had continued the war against the Lao government. Eisenhower, who had demonstrated over and over again during his administration an extreme reluctance to intervene anywhere with U.S. troops, "considered Laos of such importance that if it reached the stage where we could not persuade others to act with us, then he would be willing, *as a desperate last hope, to intervene unilaterally.*"[2] In the first two months of Kennedy's administration the Communist forces continued their advance until they controlled the whole eastern half of the country. On March 23, 1961, standing before three maps that showed the Communist advances in Laos from the time of the Geneva agreements in 1954 up to the time he was speaking, Kennedy said: "If these attacks do not stop, those who support a truly neutral Laos will have to consider their response. The shape of this necessary response will, of course, be carefully considered, not only here in Washington, but in the SEATO Conference with our allies. . . ." In spite of Kennedy's "early determination" not to get U.S. troops in the position the French had put themselves, the implication of this statement was clearly military intervention.

Then came the Bay of Pigs debacle. From it Kennedy felt he learned at least three lessons.[3] One was not to trust the experts—a lesson he thought he already knew. When he was a senator one of the favorite quotes among his staff was that "experts should be on tap and not on top." Yet this time he had let himself be ruled by them. Another lesson was never again to let the advocates of a policy deny him the views of others, even on the grounds of secrecy. The third was that the American people were not enthusiastic about intervening abroad. "The American people do not want to use troops to remove a Communist regime only 90 miles away," he said, "How can I ask them to use troops to remove one 9,000 miles away?"[4] As Robert Kennedy noted:

> I don't think that there is any question that if it hadn't been for Cuba, we would have sent troops to Laos. We probably would have had them destroyed. Jack has said so himself. . . . It was after Cuba that he began inquiring intimately into the situation in Laos. It was then that he found out that the Communists could send five men into Laos for every one that we sent in. That they could destroy the airports and therefore cut off our people after getting only a thousand or several thousand into Laos and that the only way really that we could win in Laos was drop the atomic bomb. . . . Therefore, in order to preserve Laos, for instance, we had to be prepared to engage in a major atomic war both with China and with Russia.[5]

Shortly afterwards Kennedy sent W. Averell Harriman to Geneva to take charge of the negotiations that led to the neutralization of Laos. Harriman was fond of saying that he got the instructions for six months of negotiations in a five-minute telephone conversation.[6] "All these people want me to go for a military solution in Laos," Kennedy told Harriman, "but that is impossible. What I want you to do is find a political solution."

When the situation in Vietnam worsened, Kennedy considered seeking the neutralization in Vietnam as well. But the neutralization of Laos had been possible because one of the major political leaders of the country, Souvanna Phouma, was a neutralist, and the Lao peoples preferred a neutralist solution under Souvanna to fighting. There was no prominent neutralist leader in Vietnam, and President Diem and his government seemed determined to fight. As related above, when General Taylor and Walt Rostow returned from their mission to Vietnam, they had urged sending U.S. troops. Although they were joined in this recommendation by many others, Kennedy compromised by increasing aid and sending 500 advisers in addition to the 685 authorized by the Geneva agreements, while refusing to send troops. According to Roswell Gilpatric, the deputy secretary of defense, even sending advisers was done reluctantly: "Even so small an increase was greeted by the President with a great deal of impatience. He showed at the very outset an aversion to sending more people out there."[7]

Kennedy's reluctance to send troops to Southeast Asia was reinforced by the views of General Douglas MacArthur. As Arthur Schlesinger, Jr., relates, Kennedy brought MacArthur to Washington to have lunch with a group of "bellicose" members of Congress:

He [MacArthur] said, noted the Attorney General, who was also invited, that he would be foolish to fight on the Asiatic continent and that the future of Southeast Asia should be determined on the diplomatic table. Alexis Johnson of the State Department, present too, thought MacArthur's argument made a very deep impression on the President. . . . I think that for the rest of the time he was in office this view of General MacArthur's . . . tended to dominate very much the thinking of President Kennedy with respect to Southeast Asia. It made, said Maxwell Taylor, a hell of an impression on the President . . . so that whenever he'd get this military advice from the Joint Chiefs or from me or anyone else, he'd say, "Well, now, you gentlemen, you go back and convince General MacArthur, then I'll be convinced." But none of us undertook the task.[8]

Taylor has in fact reported on President Kennedy's reluctance to send U.S. troops to Vietnam in great detail. When asked about the recommendation he and Rostow made to send troops, Taylor said: "The last thing he [Kennedy] wanted was to put in our ground forces. . . . I don't recall anyone who was strongly against [the recommendation], except one man and that was the President. The President just didn't want to be convinced that this was the right thing to do. . . . It was really the President's personal conviction that U.S. ground forces shouldn't go in."[9]

During this same period Kennedy also expressed his opposition to the use of combat forces to several other people. One was J. Kenneth Galbraith, to whom he also mentioned his worry about how many more defeats he could suffer after the Bay of Pigs and his pulling out of Laos.[10] Another was Arthur Schlesinger. "The troops will march in;" he said, "the crowds will cheer; and in four days everyone will have forgotten. Then we will be told that we have to send in more troops. It is like taking a drink. The effect wears off, and you have to take another."[11] Still another was George Ball. Ball reports that when he mentioned his similar fears that sending even a few advisers might eventually lead to sending as many as 300,000 troops, Kennedy said that if Ball thought that would happen he was "crazy as hell," that it couldn't happen—not so long as he was president.[12]

The Search for a Strategic Concept

While refusing suggestions about using U.S. troops, President Kennedy continued to hammer away on the point that guerrilla warfare was different from any other kind and that it required new tactics and doctrines. Events underlined his point and much of Washington became engaged in searching for a strategic concept for dealing with "revolutionary" warfare. As it turned out, the search resulted not in one, but two strategic concepts.[13]

One was the descendant of the thinking embodied in Vice-President Johnson's recommendations calling for a "forward strategy," in the Taylor-Rostow report, and in the thinking of the Joint Chiefs of Staff and the top levels of the Pentagon, including Robert S. McNamara, the secretary of defense.

The other strategic concept had a more diverse ancestry. Some of the ideas came from the American OSS experiences with guerrilla operations in World War II; some from the Special Forces effort at Fort Bragg; some from work in the universities on Chinese military thought and the guerrilla struggles in Greece, the Philippines, Malaya, and Algeria; and some from similar work on the problems of political development in the emerging countries. The main support for this second strategic concept came from the Special Forces and their supporters just below the top levels in the Pentagon, from the State Department, and from the White House, including Robert F. Kennedy.

The Johnson-Taylor-Rostow view tended to see the main source of revolutionary warfare as aggression from outside the country and in general believed that the principal means for dealing with it must be military. The White House-State Department view tended to see the principal source as internal to the country afflicted with insurgency and in general believed that the principal means for dealing with it must be political. In reality, of course, the two strategic concepts were neither so clear-cut nor so mutually exclusive as they seemed to be—or as it is necessary in this chapter to make them appear to be for the purposes of analysis. In addition, there were people in the Pentagon who adhered to the "political" approach and people in the White House and the State Department who adhered to the "military" approach. And even the people clearly associated with one or the other view were not always either consistent or convinced that the position they were associated with was completely right. The adherents to the "military" approach understood that the conditions for insurgency had to exist inside a country if the outside stimulus was to work, and they also believed that military measures had to be supplemented by political measures. The adherents to the "political" concept recognized that there was a very large military component in dealing with insurgency and that military measures were necessary. They also recognized that the insurgency probably would not have started without the aggressive stimulus from outside and that the measures for dealing with insurgency had to be placed in an international framework that included a policy toward the source of the outside stimulus. But in spite of all these qualifications, there was a fundamental difference between the two positions, as well as a serious political struggle between their adherents. McGeorge Bundy once said that Vietnam was the most divisive issue in the Kennedy administration. Indeed, it was, and the split came over these two essentially rival strategic concepts. The fundamental difference between them was whether revolutionary warfare should be met with a military program to which political measures were subordinate or with a political program to which military measures were subordinate.

The "Military" Approach

Among intellectuals, Walt W. Rostow was the main spokesman for the "military" approach in both the Kennedy and Johnson administrations. Rostow saw the modernization process as true revolution, containing its own dynamics. Like all revolutions, modernization was disruptive, upsetting the old ways and producing extreme vulnerabilities during the transition on which the Communists could prey. The Communists, Rostow said, were the "scavengers" of the modernization process."

Rostow saw the task for the United States as twofold—first, to hasten the modernization process past the vulnerable period of transition, and, second, to protect the country and preserve its independence during that vulnerable period. And it was because the vulnerabilities of transition were so awesomely great that Rostow was led in the end to put his emphasis on military means for dealing with a guerrilla war that had already begun. He called the "sending of men and arms across international boundaries and the direction of guerrilla war from outside a sovereign nation" a new form of aggression.

Applied to Vietnam this was, of course, an argument for attacking the North. A high enough level of punishment on the state that was the ultimate source of a guerrilla attack could theoretically make it cease its support and exercise whatever control it had over the guerrillas to make them stop fighting. If the level of punishment were high enough, the only alternative to ceasing its support to the guerrillas would be complete destruction.[14] International political considerations, on the other hand, might make it desirable to limit the punishment. Although many people argued that neither the Chinese nor the Soviets would intervene if the United States carried its punishment of North Vietnam through to complete destruction, if necessary by actual invasion, the advocates of the "military" approach in general agreed that political considerations made it desirable to keep the attack on the source of aggression limited. Even so, in the case of North Vietnam the lower levels of punishment to be inflicted by the proposed limited bombing program were severe, designed to destroy the transportation system in the North and a significant proportion of the industry on which the North had based its hopes for economic development. There seemed to be a good possibility that at some point the North would prefer to call off the guerrilla warfare rather than face continued punishment. If not, the argument for the "military" approach concluded, the punishment would at least impose a substantial cost on the country that was continuing to support the guerrilla warfare, and cut down on the flow of infiltrating men and supplies. So the army of the victim of the aggression, in this case the army of South Vietnam, would have a much greater chance of defeating the guerrilla aggression even if the aggressor could not be persuaded to quit.

As it was developed in the Pentagon, however, the strategy of the "military" approach was twofold—not only to punish and wear down the source of the aggression outside the country under attack, but to seek out and destroy the guerrilla units inside. The idea was to make maximum use of superior U.S. technology and of American abundance. U.S. wealth was sufficient to meet the supply needs not only of the government forces but of the civilian population, too, if that became necessary. Superior U.S. equipment could give the counter-guerrilla forces fantastic mobility and overwhelming firepower. In the case of Vietnam, there was a lack of manpower and especially of combat units with the necessary training and aggressiveness, but if no other way could be found this lack could be made up by using troops from the United States itself. With complete and total command of the air and with vast fleets of helicopters, the government forces could maintain the offensive and could seek out the guerrilla in his own jungle and mountain terrain. If mobility and aggressiveness were maintained, the argument continued, the kill-rate on the guerrillas could be kept at a level that would become unbearable. A high rate of casualties, difficulties of supply, and continued harassment from both ground and air would collapse the morale of many guerrilla units and simply destroy the others.

Inevitably this "military" strategic concept had corollary implications for the U.S. attitude toward the internal politics of the country under attack. Everyone concerned recognized the importance of winning the people, of political, economic, and governmental reform. But if the "military" approach was to succeed, both the government and the armed forces had to concentrate on maintaining a highly aggressive offensive against the guerrilla units. They could not afford to be distracted by political or social unrest. Inevitably as a consequence, and for perfectly sound reasons, the result was a bias toward somewhat authoritarian rule and toward postponement of political and social measures that might create social and political instability in the short run even though such measures would develop popular support in the long run.

The "Political" Approach

In the State Department, work on guerrilla warfare had been centered in the Bureau of Intelligence and Research as well as in the Policy Planning Staff.[15] The State Department view agreed that the "United

States must be prepared to become deeply involved," but differed about the methods. In State, the basic premise was that a successful counter-insurgency program depended on winning the support of the mass of the people. This meant that military measures had to be very carefully circumscribed. The danger of large-scale military operations was that their very destructiveness would alienate the people. What is more, the argument ran, regular forces—although essential for the task of deterring conventional aggression—were unsuited by both training and equipment for the task of fighting guerrillas. Regular forces were road-bound, unwieldy, and cumbersome, inevitably telegraphing their movements to the elusive guerrilla. Pointing to our historical experiences as a young nation in Indian fighting, the jungle experiences during the Philippine insurrection at the turn of the century, and OSS experiences in World War II, the State Department argument was that the way to fight the guerrilla was to adopt the tactics of the guerrilla. Small bands should be spotted at intervals throughout the area to be pacified. Using guerrilla tactics they would harass and ambush, while central reserves would be used to reinforce and themselves to ambush on escape trails leading from the point of contact. As the guerrillas in an area were slowly worn down, government control could be extended and the people given the means to protect themselves. And when the area was cleared and secured, the security forces could move on to the next. On the political side of the equation the approach was toward rapid change:

> We may find ourselves encouraging reformers to organize mass parties. . . . We are seriously interested in broadening the will and capacity of friendly governments to augment social and political reform programs as a basis for modernization. . . . We must foster the growth and use of international organizations as sources of help . . .—help that can be on the scene and in action before the crisis reaches its peak.[16]

But having stressed the vital importance of gaining popular support, the argument went on to contend that "it would be mistaken to think that guerrillas cannot thrive where governments are popular and where modernization, economic development, and reform are going forward." The point was that the existence of a guerrilla movement did not mean that a government was either popular or unpopular, and that modernization, reform, and measures to make the government popular could not alone defeat an established guerrilla movement. The people might like their government, but if they did not have physical security they could not resist the guerrillas' demands for food, money, and even recruits. Thus measures to make the government popular had to be combined with military and police measures to give the people physical security.

R.K.G. Thompson

It turned out that parallel work of a more detailed and specific kind was well advanced in Saigon itself, carried on principally by the head of the British Advisory Mission, Robert K. G. Thompson. Thompson was a career officer of the British colonial service who had spent most of his life in Malaya. He had played an important role in the defeat of the Communist guerrilla terrorism in Malaya, where he had served as deputy secretary and then secretary for defence. At first, the British had dealt with the guerrilla terrorism in Malaya as if it were a purely military problem, relying on large-scale military operations, bombing jungle hideouts, and so on, but after two years they were worse off than when they started. It was then that the British developed the "new village" program that finally defeated the Communist guerrillas. Applying this experience to Vietnam, Thompson had come up with what he called the "strategic hamlet" plan.[17] Thompson pointed out that the Vietcong's main effort was not in fighting the government's regular troops—they could have done more of that than they were actually doing at the time—but in attempting to gain administrative control over the 16,000 hamlets in South Vietnam. Winning battles against regular Vietcong units in the field would not really affect the struggle for the villages either way, whereas administrative control of the villages would give the guerrillas a base for supplies, taxation, and recruits. Thompson argued that it was a classic axiom that guerrillas could maintain themselves indefinitely so long as they had support from the population in the area where they operated. The support could be voluntary, motivated by, say, patriotism, as was the support given the French maquis effort against the German occupation in World War II. Or it could be given reluctantly, because the guerrillas so ruthlessly dominated the population that the forces of law and order could not give the people protection from terroristic retaliation on those who helped the government. More often, support is mixed, with some coming from loyalty and some from terror. When a guerrilla force enjoys support from the people, whether willingly, forced, or mixed, it can never be defeated by military means, however much it is harassed and attacked, shelled, mortared, and bombed by superior forces of infantry, artillery, air, and sea power.

The only way to defeat a guerrilla force operating in this way, Thompson believed, was systematically to cut it off from its true base of support—the people. To do this, the first step has to be to find a way to give the people physical security. For if they are not protected from the marauding bands of guerrillas and from their retaliation, the people cannot exercise a free choice between supporting the guerrillas and supporting the government. What Thompson proposed as the instrument to provide this physical security was the "strategic hamlet."

Strategic Hamlets

The strategic hamlet program was simply a way of arming the villagers of South Vietnam so that they could defend themselves if they were attacked by a small band of marauding guerrillas and at least hold out until reinforcements came if they were attacked by a large band. Setting up a strategic hamlet, however, would require political skill, care, and time. Civic action teams would have to be trained to go into each village to provide simple government services, agricultural extension loans, schools, teachers, and effective police protection, as well as training in the use of weapons for self-defense. The role of the police, of course, would be vital—for they would have to win enough people over to the government side to identify the Communist agents before it would be safe to distribute arms to a village militia. And during the weeks and months that all this was going on, regular military forces would have to be stationed in the region to protect both the civic action teams and the villagers until the hamlet was ready to defend itself.

The essence of the program was that it had to be a program—one lone strategic hamlet could not effectively defend itself. There had to be a hedgerow of hamlets, spreading out like an oil blot from the sea toward the mountains and jungle. Plastic identity cards had to be issued, curfews established, and provincial forces trained to set up checkpoints and ambushes during the curfew hours—an iron grid of security had to be established to control the movement of both goods and people, of rice and recruits. A solid bloc of these strategic hamlets, firmly established and consolidated, extending outward to make a zone of security, armed for their own protection and supported by military and paramilitary forces serving as reinforcements and ensuring the security of their rear areas and their lateral communication with each other, Thompson argued, could create the physical security the villagers must have before they could make a free choice between the Vietcong and the government.

The primary role of the strategic hamlet was to provide that free choice. But even though security is the first requirement in an effective counter-insurgency program, it would not be enough by itself to make the villagers choose the government side. They could only be brought to choose the government side if the government could show them that what it had to offer was something better than what the enemy could offer. And this, Thompson said, was the second role of the strategic hamlet. He saw the hamlet scheme and the bureaucratic apparatus that would be created to run it as the means for bringing about a revolutionary change in the lot of the peasants—economically, politically, socially, and culturally. The election of village officials, which President Diem had abolished, should be reinstituted. Land reform should be pushed forward, better medical services should be provided, and so should schools, teachers, and agricultural credit and extension work. A governmental structure should be set up in which information about villagers' needs would go up the ladder and simple government services would go down for the first time in the history of Vietnam. All this, Thompson argued, should be looked upon as a war measure more important than defeating the Vietcong in actual battle. If the program was successful, if the peasants in the strategic hamlets really did come to see that they were better off than under the Vietcong and if they were also free of the fear of retaliation, then they would finally commit themselves to the government's side. They would give the government forces information about the location and movement of Vietcong units and individuals; they would deny the Vietcong food and funds and supplies; they would fight against the guerrillas' raids on their villages and deny the guerrillas the opportunity to acquire recruits, whether by persuasion or impressment. The peasants, in effect, would be the ones who defeated the Vietcong, not so much by killing them as by reducing them to hungry, marauding bands of outlaws devoting all their energies to remaining alive. It would take years of slow, painstaking work, but once this turning point was reached, as Thompson saw it, once the majority of the population had taken the vital decision to throw in their lot with the government, the struggle against the guerrillas would be won. From there on only mopping up operations would remain.

Reaction in Washington

Thompson's ideas fitted in well with the thinking that was going on in Washington. Together, these ideas added up to a persuasive alternative to a military approach. Interestingly, they were based on the same premise as Mao's theories. If guerrillas were fish swimming in the sea of the people, so were the government forces. The key in either case was winning the support of the people. The guerrillas were trying to demonstrate that the government could not protect the people and that the people would be better off under the revolutionary government. The government had to demonstrate that it could protect the people and that they would in fact be better off under the government.

In the State Department's Bureau of Intelligence and Research, an analysis of past guerrilla wars seemed to indicate that guerrilla techniques were successful in only two sets of circumstances. One was when the main body of the enemy forces was fully engaged. The French maquis, for example, enjoyed the support of virtually the entire population, they were well supplied by air drops from the United Kingdom, and they were well organized. Yet they were not successful until after D-day, when the main body of the enemy was tied down in Normandy. The other set of circumstances was that to be found in Southeast Asia, as well as parts of Africa and Latin America. In Southeast Asia most peasants lived in villages, in a village culture that turns each village inward on itself. The people have little or no identification with the national government. The government is remote and little felt, except at tax collection time, and it is in any case incapable of giving the villagers day-by-day protection. The villagers are politically and psychologically isolated, by distance and lack of modern transportation systems. In such circumstances, it is not difficult for a trained and organized cadre to recruit an effective guerrilla force. In Burma in World War II, for example, several hundred officers and noncommissioned officers of the American OSS succeeded in building a guerrilla force of 30,000 men behind the Japanese lines—and they did it with white faces.

The State Department analysis also argued that the idea that government existed for the benefit of the people, that a government could really care, was as revolutionary in most of Asia as anything the Communists had to offer. In the State Department's view the program had at least a chance to win the allegiance of the people—if they could be given physical security for a long enough period of time for the appeal to begin to work.

Practice: 1962 to 1965

The Kennedy administration's initial policy decision on Vietnam, made following the return of the Taylor-Rostow mission in 1961 and reiterated early in 1962 adopted the political approach. But the implementation was never clear-cut. In general, the military representatives in Saigon continued to recommend essentially the "military" approach to the Vietnamese; the representatives of the State Department and the Agency for International Development (AID) continued to press for the political approach; and the U.S. mission lacked any clear line of authority and command that could control and coordinate the representatives of the often rival U.S. departments and agencies. Partly for this reason and partly because of purely Vietnamese rivalries, the result was frustration for the advocates of both the military and the political approaches.

The advocates of the military point of view felt that the "shooting war," as they called the military side of the effort, was hampered by the lack of aggressiveness among the commanding officers of the Vietnamese forces, by the inefficiencies of the highly centralized Diem regime, and by the regime's tendency to appoint officers for reasons of political loyalty rather than military efficiency. They found it particularly irksome to try to insure the vigorous implementation of military operations while playing the role of advisers, with no direct control or command. In general, however, the greatest frustration was the limitations on the war, both the strict rules about bombing in the South and the immunity from bombing enjoyed by the North.

The advocates of the political approach were equally frustrated. They felt that a sound strategic doctrine had been developed around the strategic hamlet program but that it was simply not being carried out. They felt that even though the U.S. military supported the idea, they did not really understand it. This meant that the U.S. military thought that the military measures were separate and distinct and so did not take care to subordinate military measures to the political. The U.S. advisers, to give a crude example, did not understand that if snipers fired at the government troops from a village the government troops should not fire back, according to the political doctrine, but bypass the village until political measures had time to work.

But bad as all this seemed, for the advocates of the political approach the greatest frustration was the Vietnamese government. President Diem stubbornly refused to broaden his political base or institute the social and political reforms the advocates of the political approach had recommended. Even when an appropriate policy was ordered, the failure to provide overall coordination at the center left huge gaps. An example was police work, which was as important to the political approach as social, economic, and political reforms. Most importantly, the military effort was not coordinated with the strategic hamlet program. Military operations proceeded independently, emphasizing "search and destroy" missions, although the very heart of the political approach was to concentrate the military effort on "clear and hold" missions that would provide both physical security and time for the political and social effort to win the people's allegiance.

The culminating frustration was the growing evidence that Ngo Dinh Nhu, Diem's brother and principal adviser who headed the strategic hamlet program, had corrupted the program to his own neo-Fascist purposes. Rather than following a carefully phased, oil-blot plan of priorities, in which the loyalties of each area were assured and all Vietcong agents eliminated before the troops and civic action teams moved on to the next, Nhu had thrown up so-called strategic hamlets all over Vietnam. When President Kennedy sent two of his advisers to check on the strategic hamlet program, they reported back that under Nhu it was "a sham, a fraud."[18] Most of the strategic hamlets were nothing more than a string of barbed wire around a village and a blast of propaganda, while Vietcong agents remained in place and the village continued to be under their control.

The Buddhist Crisis and the Coup Against Diem

Then came the Buddhist crisis, which culminated in the coup against President Diem. The origin of the crisis is ironical. In the spring of 1963, Diem attended the twenty-fifth anniversary of the appointment of his older brother as bishop of Hué. The celebration included a parade with a profusion of Catholic flags, and when Diem saw them he forcefully reminded the province chief of a long-standing ordinance, intended to foster patriotism, forbidding the flying of any but the national flag. He directed that thereafter the ordinance should be strictly enforced. The Buddhists chose to protest the order and other grievances a few days later on the 2,527th anniversary of Buddha's birth. They massed in front of the radio station and refused to disperse. Government troops in armored cars were then brought in. What happened next is confused. The Buddhists claim the troops opened fire without provocation. The troop commander claimed he heard a grenade explosion and feared a Vietcong attack. In any case the troops opened fire and nine people were killed.

Militant Buddhists staged demonstrations throughout Vietnam. World opinion was outraged. The Buddhists had bitten on an issue not so much of religious persecution as political discrimination. When they bit, they tasted political blood, and then they bit even harder. For a time they became the rallying point for all kinds of discontent in what was already a discontented society.

In time, the Buddhists hit on a form of protest that was as dramatically effective, especially on TV, as it was gruesome. After notifying the American television crews to be at a certain place at a certain time, a Buddhist bonze (monk) would appear at the place, drench himself with gasoline, and immolate himself in a towering column of flame.

As the Buddhist crisis continued, President Diem became increasingly isolated and more and more under the influence of his brother Nhu and his wife, Madame Nhu. Nhu's neo-Fascist philosophy led him to very harsh policies, and he was known to have begun using opium regularly. Madame Nhu, whose views earned her the nickname of "Dragon Lady," was if anything even more hard-line. She scornfully described the immolations as "Buddhist barbecues," for example, and offered to donate gasoline to any bonzes who wanted to follow the example.

The culmination of the Buddhist crisis came on August 21, 1963. Units of the Vietnamese Special Forces, which were under the command of Nhu, disguised in Army uniforms attacked Buddhist pagodas in all the major cities of South Vietnam killing and mutilating priests and nuns and desecrating religious relics. The U.S. government publicly condemned the action. Although Washington realized that condemnation would encourage coup plotting, neither hawks nor doves believed that the United States could honorably remain silent.

Coup plotting had been a way of life in South Vietnam for some time. After the attack on the pagodas, however, it seemed to be everywhere. It continued during the remainder of August and throughout September and October. Various groups of Vietnamese generals became convinced that Diem would have to be removed, and on two occasions plotters approached the U.S. embassy to ask what the attitude of the U.S. government would be if they staged a coup. The U.S. government was divided. The advocates of a political approach had become convinced that Diem could not now successfully lead the country. How could a president who ordered an attack on Buddhist pagodas win the political support of the people, they asked, in a country that was 95 percent Buddhist? The advocates of a military approach admitted that Diem had seriously damaged his changes but saw no possible successor with the prestige and ability needed.

In the end, the U.S. government did not actually engage in plotting a coup with the generals. Although no effort was made to hide U.S. disapproval of Diem's policies, the official answer to the generals was that the decision would have to be Vietnamese and that the United States could have no part in the decision. In fact, the solution that Washington desired above all others was that Diem remain but that he change his policy toward the Buddhists and that he send his brother Nhu as ambassador to Paris. It was this course of action—changing his policy toward the Buddhists and sending Nhu to Paris—that Washington urged on Diem. However, few in Washington believed that Diem would actually follow this advice, and the advocates of a political approach, at least, believed that a coup offered the only other chance for South Vietnam to win.

Even though the United States did not participate in the decision to launch a coup, there can be no doubt that U.S. disapproval of Diem's policies encouraged coup plotting. As mentioned above, no one believed that the United States could remain silent about the attack on the pagodas. However, disapproval was expressed in a number of other ways than condemning that attack. First, it was communicated by the private reaction of U.S. officials in the days that followed. Second, there were two additional public expressions of official disapproval. First, aid to the Vietnamese Special Forces was cut off, although not to the military, in accordance with a public statement made by President Kennedy himself that "What helps to win the war, we support; what interferes with the war effort, we oppose."[19] Second, on TV in response to a question about whether he thought South Vietnam could still win its struggle, Kennedy said that he did not think that the war could be won unless the Vietnamese government made a greater effort to win popular support:

> We are prepared to continue to assist them, but I don't think the war can be won unless the people support the effort and, in my opinion, in the last two months, the government has gotten out of touch with the people.

The next question was whether the Diem government had time to regain the support of the people, and the president said that he thought it did:

With changes in policy and perhaps with personnel I think it can. If it doesn't make those changes, I would think that the chances of winning it would not be very good.[20]

Kennedy was referring to the hope within the U.S. government that Diem would reverse his policy against the Buddhists and that he would send his brother Nhu as ambassador to Paris, but there is little doubt that the statement also encouraged the coup plotters.

The U.S. government had no advance knowledge of the coup, and many individuals among both hawks and doves doubted that the generals would in the end actually do anything.[21] Getting the Vietnamese generals to move, a Washington wit remarked, was like trying to push a piece of cooked spaghetti. But because there had been so much plotting, when Diem was finally overthrown on November 1, 1963, most Washington officials were surprised only by the timing.

Postcoup Reaction

The drawn-out Buddhist crisis and the coup removing Diem enormously widened the rift between the supporters of the military and political approaches in both Saigon and Washington. The advocates of the military approach tended to sympathize with Diem's policy of dealing ruthlessly with the Buddhists and were increasingly unhappy as the schism widened between the U.S. government and Diem. For a short period following Diem's overthrow, their hopes ran a little higher. But when the Vietnamese military junta failed to produce a unified government and a natural leader, and coup began to follow coup in rapid succession, the advocates of the military approach regretted the fall of Diem more and more and were confirmed in their conviction that the best hope for the vigorous military effort they desired lay not in broadening the government but in a single strong man, even though his government was authoritarian.

The advocates of a political approach were also frustrated by the failure of the military junta to produce a unified government. But they were even more frustrated by the Vietnamese failure to make the most of this "second chance" to carry out the political strategic concept.

The Buddhist crisis also affected President Kennedy's attitude toward Vietnam. At the beginning of the administration he told a number of his aides that he thought the United States was overcommitted in Southeast Asia but that since we were already there he was willing to send aid and advisers if the South Vietnamese government could rally its own people and use the aid effectively.[22] The Geneva agreements of 1954 had authorized 685 U.S. military advisers to South Vietnam to train its army. The first increase Kennedy approved added another 500. There were repeated requests for additional advisers, but Kennedy authorized only a few—the total when he was assassinated was 16,500. And on each occasion he expressed his reluctance more sharply. As Roswell Gilpatric, McNamara's deputy, said, "Resistance was encountered from the President at every stage as this total amount of U.S. personnel deployment increased."[23]

As for combat troops, organized military units as opposed to individuals serving as advisers, Kennedy made his position very public, in a press conference in March 1962. Sending combat troops would be, he said, "a basic change . . . which calls for a constitutional decision, [and] of course I would go to the Congress."

Schlesinger believes that Kennedy "was vaguely searching for a non-military solution—vaguely because Vietnam was still a sideshow."[24] As Schlesinger reports, Kennedy was disturbed at any statement by an administration official that appeared to increase our commitment in Southeast Asia or Vietnam or to put up an obstacle to a political settlement. In July 1962, Kennedy ordered McNamara to start planning for the phased withdrawal of U.S. military personnel from Vietnam, although it was not until May 1963 that the Pentagon produced a plan that was satisfactory.[25] Some people in the Pentagon apparently viewed the plan as a way of putting pressure on Ngo Dinh Diem, but McNamara did not understand it that way. "McNamara indicated to me," said his deputy, Roswell Gilpatric, "that this was part of a plan the President asked him to develop to unwind the whole thing."[26] Before his tragic death in an airplane crash, John McNaughton, who was assistant secretary of defense for international affairs, told Daniel Ellsberg "that Robert McNamara had told him of an understanding with President Kennedy that they would close out Vietnam by '65, whether it was in good shape or bad."[27]

In separate conversations with Senator Mike Mansfield, Kenneth O'Donnell, and Henry Brandon, Kennedy talked about his worries that the United States was being sucked into Vietnam little by little and about his desire to find a way out.[28] Kennedy also seems to have talked with his brother Robert about getting out as well. At an NSC meeting on September 6, 1963, Robert said that the fundamental issue was what we thought we were doing in Vietnam, what our goal was. "The first question is whether a Communist take-over could be resisted with any government. If it could not, now was the time to get out of Vietnam entirely, rather than waiting."[29]

Publicly, Kennedy hewed to the hard line: "For us to withdraw . . . would mean a collapse not only of South Vietnam, but Southeast Asia. So we are going to stay there." "I don't agree with those who say we should withdraw. That would be a great mistake."[30]

But privately Kennedy continued to search for a way out. He asked the prime minister of Canada, Lester Pearson, what the United States should do. "Get out," was the reply. "That's a stupid answer," Kennedy said (Pearson was a good friend with whom Kennedy could be frank),

"Everybody knows that. The question is: How do we get out?"[31] On one occasion he told Mansfield that he had been right, that the United States should totally withdraw from Vietnam. Referring to this conversation, Mansfield later told the columnist Jack Anderson that Kennedy "was going to order a gradual withdrawal. . . . [He] had definitely and unequivocally made that decision . . . but he never had the chance to put the plan into effect."[32] After Mansfield left the room, Kennedy remarked to O'Donnell that his political position was too weak to get away with withdrawal right away, that it would have to wait until after the election.[33] O'Donnell asked Kennedy how he could pull out without damaging U.S. prestige. "Easy," Kennedy said, "Put a government in there that will ask us to leave."[34]

From the beginning of the Vietnam problem Kennedy had never wavered, publicly or privately, in his opposition to the use of U.S. troops. As for the strategy that the United States should advise the Vietnamese to follow, he also consistently opposed a military approach in favor of a political approach that tried to win the allegiance of the Vietnamese people. But even though he preferred the political approach to the military, he had always been skeptical of it.[35] His doubts were not so much about the strategy itself as about the capacity of the South Vietnamese to carry it out. Such a political strategy had worked in Malaya and in the Philippines under Magsaysay. The central question to Kennedy, and the point that most of his advisers who advocated the political approach overlooked, was whether not just Diem but any possible South Vietnamese government leaders had either the power or the will to do what was necessary to reform their society and to embark on a program of protecting the people and winning their allegiance. Later, Robert Kennedy made the point poignantly as a self-criticism. "Our failure," he said of those who advocated the political approach, "was that we did not understand the difficulties of reform—we did not realize how thick the crust of Vietnamese culture really was."[36]

But it was crucial in President Kennedy's view that no matter what strategy was followed, the central role simply had to be played by the Vietnamese. And he reiterated on every occasion this point that no matter what strategy was pursued the struggle had to be won by the Vietnamese, that Americans could not win it for them:

> In the final analysis, it is their war. They are the ones who have to win it or lose it. We can help them, we can give them equipment, we can send our men out there as advisers, but they have to win it, the people of Viet-Nam, against the Communists.[37]

As the Buddhist crisis progressed Kennedy became more and more convinced that the Vietnamese could *not* win it. On several occasions he telephoned Assistant Secretary of State for Far Eastern Affairs Roger Hilsman, who was the action officer for Vietnam, to make sure that everything possible was being done to keep the U.S. profile low. "Remember Laos," was his most frequent admonition. By that he meant that the U.S. profile should be kept low, so as to avoid creating an obstacle to any opportunity, such as a negotiated settlement, that would permit an American withdrawal.[38] On one occasion, for example, when the South Vietnamese forces lost an engagement, the *New York Times,* clearly with a purpose of its own, put the opening paragraph of this story in one half of a little box on the middle of page one. In the other half of the box they put the opening paragraph of another story relating that a U.S. general had just arrived in Saigon for an inspection visit. The president called Hilsman before he had had breakfast and turned the air blue—angry at the fact that the general's visit "inevitably increased the United States commitment—contrary to my repeated orders to you." When Hilsman finally got a word in, he pointed out that he had not been informed of the general's visit and that he had no authority to prevent it even if he had been informed. That very afternoon, Kennedy ordered a National Security Action Memorandum issued saying that no officer or general or flag rank would visit Vietnam without the written permission of the assistant secretary for far eastern affairs.

The U.S. advisers in Vietnam now numbered 16,500, and as a concrete step Kennedy ordered the withdrawal of the first 1,000.

The Debate Shifts: Escalation or Negotiation?

Shortly after Kennedy's death, Walt W. Rostow again submitted a memo raising the question of bombing the North.[39] The memo also proposed bombing the infiltration routes in Laos and removing many of the restrictions on bombing and other military measures in the South.

The advocates of a political approach opposed all three proposals. Bombing the South, they argued, violated the most fundamental principle of the strategic hamlet concept and the idea of winning the allegiance of the people.

As for the infiltration routes, they doubted that bombing would have much effect. The routes were jungle trails. The men coming down them were on foot. The supplies were carried by reinforced bicycles. How could bombing stop this kind of infiltration? Also, most of the Vietcong's supplies and recruits came from inside the South. Cutting off the infiltration routes, even if bombing could in fact accomplish it, would have only a marginal effect. Furthermore, so far the men coming down the trails were southerners who had gone North in 1952. If the United States raised the ante by bombing the infiltration routes, the North Vietnamese would respond by including northerners. The United States and South Vietnam would be no better off than before and perhaps worse, and they would be paying the international political cost for nothing.

As for bombing the North, the advocates of a political strategy argued that although the United States and North Vietnam had never actually communicated with each other on the question, they were in fact both adhering to a tacit agreement.[40] So far the Viet Cong consisted solely of southerners, as mentioned above. By its own self-restraint the North maintained the fiction that the struggle was purely internal to the South, rather than being an international war or even a civil war between North Vietnam and South Vietnam. North Vietnam had 10 regular divisions that they had refrained from sending South. The tacit agreement was that if these divisions were committed, the United States would be justified in bombing North Vietnam. By the same token, if the United States bombed North Vietnam, the North would be justified in sending their regular divisions South.

President Johnson decided to postpone a decision and in the meantime appointed a committee to study just what targets might be included in bombing the North and what the effects would be.

The Debate Shifts

As the year wore on, the situation in Vietnam steadily worsened. President Johnson gradually increased the number of military advisers until, by the beginning of 1965, they numbered over 25,000. At the same time, the debate between the military and political schools of thought changed fundamentally. The advocates of a military approach took up Rostow's argument that the United States must attack the source of the aggression. So the central focus of the debate became the question of whether the struggle in Vietnam was a global Communist aggression or an anticolonialist nationalist movement whose leaders just happened to be Communists. In the process, the debate shifted from the question of whether a political or military strategy should be used to deal with the guerrillas to whether the next step should be to escalate the struggle or to seek negotiations. The composition of the two groups also changed, and from this time on the contending groups began to be labeled "hawks" and "doves."

The Hawks' Strategic Rationale

The hawks conceded that local, purely Vietnamese issues were also involved. But they insisted that the Viet Cong movement was ultimately inspired by Moscow and Peking and that a Communist victory would redound to their benefit strategically, economically, and politically.

The first of the strategic arguments in favor of U.S. intervention was that Vietnam constituted a strategic route and base for the penetration and domination of all of Southeast Asia. By the same token, Vietnam itself constituted an avenue into Southeast Asia for the Communist Chinese.

The second argument was President Dwight D. Eisenhower's "falling domino" theory enunciated in a press conference in 1954. The theory was concerned with internal, Communist-led, guerrilla insurgency and not with invasion by either Vietnam or China. The notion was that if Indochina fell to a native Communist insurgency, then the Communist parties of all the other Southeast Asian states would be encouraged to rebel, the Soviet Union and China would be encouraged to aid them. Implicit in the domino theory was the assumption that Southeast Asia was strategically crucial if the United States was to maintain its position in Asia and hence protect its own security.

One of the most sophisticated strategic, geopolitical arguments for U.S. intervention was offered by President Lyndon B. Johnson himself in a reflective mood at a meeting of the National Security Council.[41] He said that the fabric of what international peace and stability we had in the world was made up of sets of expectations by all the nations of the world—enemies, allies, and neutrals—about how each of the others will behave in a crisis. If the United States let South Vietnam "go down the drain," then every country in the world will have to go back to the drawing board, every nation will have to reexamine its assumptions about its security position. Japan will have to ask itself whether or not it was a wise decision to place itself under the U.S. nuclear shield and become an ally of the United States. Germany will have to rethink its position about the NATO alliance. All of our friends and allies will have to think hard about their friendship with the United States. One thing is certain, he went on to say, and that is if we let Vietnam go down the drain many, many more nations will decide that they have to build their own nuclear weapons. Nuclear proliferation will become rampant.

The policy implications flowing from this analysis were twofold. The first conclusion was that such an aggression could be met successfully only by military force. The second conclusion was that it *must* be met if the vital interests of the United States were to be preserved. Even failure, as Secretary of State Dean Rusk said, would at least teach the Communist world that such aggression would be very costly.

The Doves' Rationale

The rival view did not deny that the leaders of the insurgency were bona fide Communists and that Moscow and Peking gave it full support. But they argued that the insurgency was more accurately described as an anticolonialist and essentially nationalist movement, feeding on social discontent in the South, whose leaders just happened to be members of the Communist party through an accident of history. The leaders, this school asserted, were nationalists first and Communists only second. This school of thought conceded that a Communist Vietnam would be troublesome politically to U.S. interests in Southeast Asia, but its proponents insisted that it would be no more than troublesome. The economic implications were minuscule. Strategically, Vietnam was of little intrinsic importance. The Soviets would undoubtedly be given permission to use the port facilities as a base, but, the proponents argued, Hanoi's demonstrated determination to remain independent of both Moscow and Peking assured that the use would be limited.

On the strategic issues, the doves reached the opposite conclusion on every point. Consider a topographical map of Southeast Asia. The border between Laos and Vietnam is the spine of a mountain range, with subsidiary ridges coming off that spine perpendicular to the line from China south. The road and rail networks from China south in Vietnam must at places pass within a very few miles of the sea which makes them extraordinarily vulnerable to interdiction by both air and naval power. Thus it seems obvious that Vietnam has little strategic value as an invasion route from China into Southeast Asia. It was worth noting, the argument went on, that the Eisenhower administration implicitly acknowledged that Vietnam had little strategic importance by its refusal to intervene in the then-Indochina at the time of Dienbienphu.

The only feasible route for a strategic entree from China into Southeast Asia is through Laos. The route is well inland, screened by many miles of mountain ranges, and it ends up in Thailand, at the very heart of Southeast Asia, where it connects with both road and rail networks. The conclusion seems inescapable, the argument continued, that if any country has any strategic importance as a route into Southeast Asia it is Laos and not Vietnam. The Chinese actually built such a road from China across Laos linking up to the roads to Thailand as part of their aid program to Laos in the latter part of the Eisenhower administration and the early part of the Kennedy administration. The Eisenhower administration did in fact consider intervening in Laos in 1960, partly because of the road building and partly because of Soviet support to the Communist guerrillas in both Laos and Vietnam, but finally decided against it. The Kennedy administration also decided against intervention in favor of negotiating the neutralization of Laos, which was done by the Geneva Accords of 1962. If Laos is strategically more important than Vietnam, the argument concluded, then why should the United States fight for Vietnam when it did not fight for Laos?

As for the domino argument, the opponents of escalation conceded that if the Communists controlled all of Vietnam both Cambodia and Laos had only a small chance of maintaining a neutral status but would most probably come under the domination of Vietnam. The population of Laos was about 2 million and the population of Cambodia no more than 6 million, while the populations of North and South Vietnam together were about 38 million. But the probability that Laos and Cambodia would come under the domination of Vietnam would make Thailand, Burma, Malaysia, and Indonesia even more determined to deal swiftly and ruthlessly with any foreign-stimulated insurgency. Thus the probability that Laos and Cambodia would become dominoes, the opponents of escalation argued, made it sharply less likely that the rest of Southeast Asia would.

As for President Johnson's argument that if the United States permitted Vietnam to go "down the drain," the fabric of international politics would be ripped apart, the opponents argued that on the contrary if anything would rip apart the fabric of international politics it would be for the United States to intervene in Vietnam. None of the other nations of the world, the opponents argued, could see any strategic, political, or economic importance to Vietnam. If the United States turned the struggle in Vietnam into a major war, the rest of the world would think it had gone mad. It is bad enough for your friends to think you mad, the argument concluded, but if your enemies do the world will become a much more dangerous place.

Thus the opponents of escalating the struggle in Vietnam reached exactly the opposite conclusion: that the mistake would be not in letting Vietnam go "down the drain" but for the United States to intervene to try to prevent it.

The policy that flowed from this analysis was fundamentally different. If the insurgency was a nationalist, anticolonialist movement, then sending foreign troops of any kind would be self-defeating. Foreign troops would recruit more peasants for the Vietcong than they could possibly kill. And Americans would probably recruit more than those of almost any other nation. In Korea, the hated colonialists were Japanese, and when the peasants looked up at Americans marching by they saw the liberators. But U.S. troops in Vietnam would look quite different to the peasants. Americans are white and black—exactly the same as the French and their Senegalese colonial forces.

The Crisis of 1964–65

As the debate continued the situation in Vietnam continued to worsen. In mid-1964, the Vietcong shifted the focus of their military operations to the central and northern highlands, seizing outlying villages and military outposts. The Vietcong were very close to controlling Route 19 from Pleiku to the sea, and in the view of the hawks this would "cut the country in half" and so supplies and replacements coming down the infiltration routes would meet no line of defense until they reached the provinces bordering Saigon and the delta itself.

It is a measure of the difference between the two views that what was a crisis to the hawks was not necessarily a crisis to the doves. Starting with a different set of assumptions, the doves did not see the mountainous, sparsely populated highlands as the strategic key to the war but the population centers. To the doves the important routes for supplies and recruits were not the ones leading from North Vietnam but the ones leading from the concentrations of population around Hué, Saigon, and the delta. Once the loyalty of the population was secured, in the dove view, even a much greater flow down the infiltration routes could be dealt with at the government's leisure. In their view the only crisis was the continuing failure to concentrate on protecting the population and winning their allegiance.

There seems to be no doubt that President Johnson did not plan in advance to escalate the war. But there also seems to be no doubt that he was determined not to lose the war even if winning it required escalation. As mentioned earlier President Kennedy used to say that it was their war, the South Vietnamese, that they had to win it or lose it. What seemed clear in the days following Kennedy's assassination was that President Johnson had dropped the last three words. Where Kennedy had telephoned action officers to ensure that the U.S. profile was kept low and no opportunity for withdrawal was overlooked, President Johnson telephoned to ensure that nothing was overlooked that would help win the war. He did not want to escalate the war if it could be won without escalating. But he gave the impression that if escalation was necessary for victory, he did not shrink from it.

Throughout the summer and fall of 1964, President Johnson was involved with the election, but following it he turned his full attention to Vietnam. The arguments in favor of bombing the North did not focus so much on the strategic issues as on the more narrow issue of how it might benefit the war in the South.[42] Those officials who favored bombing did so for a variety of reasons. Some thought it would so punish Hanoi as to cause it to end the struggle. Others doubted this but favored bombing on the grounds that it would cut off the flow of supplies and infiltrators or severely reduce it. Still others favored the bombing on the grounds that it would make the whole North Vietnamese effort more costly and painful, even if it failed to stop the flow of supplies, and that this would improve morale in South Vietnam. President Johnson made a tentative decision to bomb the North some time in December or early January.

It is sometimes suggested that the decision to escalate the war was taken in retaliation for attacks on Americans and U.S. installations, such as the attack on the American barracks at Pleiku. Other suggestions have been that the bombing was in retaliation for an increased use of the infiltration routes or for a change in the type of infiltrators to include individual North Vietnamese in large numbers as well as ex-southerners. Still another suggestion has been that the bombing was in retaliation for a North Vietnamese decision to escalate by sending in the North Vietnamese regular divisions, mentioned above.

The historical record does not support any of these suggestions. First, there had been attacks on Americans and U.S. installations all along—a grenade was thrown at the U.S. ambassador as early as 1961; there was an attack on the U.S. Special Forces camp at Plei Mrong in July 1962; and so on. In any case, the attack on Pleiku came after the tentative decision, not before, although as described below the Pleiku attack does seem to have convinced at least one policy maker that the bombing was justified. Second, according to the official U.S. estimates of the time, the number of people coming over the infiltration routes remained fairly steady, ranging from 5,400 to 12,400 per year, from 1961 until after the bombing of North Vietnam in 1965. When all the intelligence was in, in fact, it turned out that fewer infiltrators came over the trails in 1964 than in 1962. Third, the evidence available at the time of infiltration by individual North Vietnamese is unconvincing.

All the evidence available was assembled in the Department of State's White Paper, "Aggression from the North, The Record of North Vietnam's Campaign to Conquer South Vietnam," which was issued in 1965 to support the case for bombing. No captured documents, equipment, or materiel were presented that indicate the presence of individual North Vietnamese in significant numbers. The White Paper was able to present the case studies on only four captured infiltrators who were ethnic North Vietnamese.

Neither was evidence presented of the presence of regular North Vietnamese units except the allegations of two of these and of two other captured Vietcong of southern origin.

Later evidence permits two conclusions. First, one battalion of North Vietnamese regulars had indeed already entered South Vietnam at the time the bombing began in February 1965. Second, the U.S. government did not know this at that time. In December 1964, and in January 1965, the first of a new family of Soviet small arms were recovered after clashes with a disciplined and uniformed military unit. This aroused suspicion, but it was not until the Highway 19 campaign in February and March of 1965 that evidence was obtained of the presence of significant numbers of North Vietnamese members of a march unit. Hard evidence then began to accumulate that regular North Vietnamese units had definitely been introduced into South Vietnam. But it was not until the enemy summer monsoon campaign in the central highlands that it was established that the infiltration of North Vietnamese regulars had begun in late 1964 and was of substantial size.[43]

The Political Groundwork

Even though the tentative decision to bomb North Vietnam did not come until December 1964, and January 1965, and the final decision did not come until after the attack on Pleiku, President Johnson had laid the political groundwork for the decision much earlier. As vice-president, Johnson was very familiar with the individuals and organizations involved in decision making on Vietnam and their views. Kennedy's decision to negotiate the neutralization of Laos indicated his position. The White House staff, principally McGeorge Bundy, the national security adviser, and Michael V. Forrestal, his staff specialist on Asia, were very skeptical of military intervention. In the State Department, Dean Rusk was "hawkish." George W. Ball, the undersecretary, W. Averell Harriman, the undersecretary for political affairs, and Roger Hilsman, the assistant secretary for far eastern affairs, were decidedly "dovish." The secretary of defense, Robert S. McNamara was "hawkish." The director of central intelligence, John A. McCone, was "hawkish." And the attorney general, Robert F. Kennedy, was very "dovish."

The members of the Joint Chiefs of Staff were a special case. After the Korean War, the military in general felt that they should never again be required to fight a limited, land war in Asia. Their feelings were so strong that around Washington they were jokingly dubbed the "never again club." Their position was that if a decision was ever again made to fight in a place like Korea the war should not be limited. In its extreme form the position was that before being sent into such a war the military should be guaranteed permission to do whatever was necessary to win, including the use of nuclear weapons.

In the Congress, both the Senate and the House, the members of the committees dealing with foreign affairs tended to be "dovish" while the members of the Armed Services committees tended to be "hawkish."

Thus President Johnson found himself in a position that whichever path he chose would be opposed by powerful groupings. As mentioned above, he preferred to win the war without escalating it, but he was determined to win even if it had to be escalated. Given this determination, the clever course for Johnson would be to ease out any "dovish" opposition in advance, since it was important for political reasons that he not appear to be departing too radically from the policy of previous administrations, especially the Kennedy administration. This he proceeded to do with consummate political skill. His first target was the assistant secretary for far eastern affairs, Roger Hilsman, who was offered an ambassadorship but chose to resign.[44] In the case of W. Averell Harriman, the president shifted him from undersecretary to roving ambassador with particular responsibility for African affairs, which took him out of policy making on Vietnam. Harriman remarked privately that if he had been 20 years younger, he too would have resigned.[45] He also went on to predict that Johnson would escalate the Vietnam War, that the escalation would fail, that the United States would have to negotiate, and that the president would have to choose him, Harriman, to be the negotiator because of his past record of negotiating with the Soviets—a remarkably prescient set of predictions, all of which came true.

In the case of George W. Ball, the president made him feel as if he were the only spokesperson for the dove position who would be permitted to remain. For almost two years Ball was content at this job of being the "house dove," but he then came to feel that he was being used and left for private life.

Members of the White House staff could not exercise independent power, so Michael V. Forrestal was not a serious problem. He was encouraged to stay on, presumably to ensure that he could not enter the public debate, but eventually he returned to private life. McGeorge Bundy's position as national security adviser did make him a problem. Bundy was the sole remaining Kennedy man who might offer serious opposition to bombing the North, and it was essential that he at least be neutralized. For reasons known only to himself, Johnson seems to have felt that Bundy could be tempted to go along with the policy. In any event, after Johnson had tentatively decided to bomb North Vietnam, he persuaded Bundy to go to Vietnam for a final check and recommendation. Bundy was reluctant, but he finally did go. During his visit the Vietcong attacked the U.S. base at Pleiku, and Bundy was persuaded by the attack to acquiesce in the decision to bomb the North, which effectively accomplished Johnson's purpose.

Robert F. Kennedy was a much more formidable political problem. What President Johnson did first was to announce to the public that for the election of 1964 he would not choose as his vice-presidential running mate anyone serving in his present cabinet, which was a roundabout way of saying that he would not choose Robert F. Kennedy. It had already become clear that Kennedy as attorney general was not going to be allowed to play a very important role in the Johnson administration. Privately Johnson suggested that the wisest course for Kennedy would be to resign and run for the governorship of Massachusetts or for the Senate from New York. In the end, Kennedy decided on the latter course, running for the Senate from New York.

The most formidable obstacle of all, however, was the Joint Chiefs of Staff. The way that Johnson dealt with the JCS was to divide them. During the period between the two world wars the doctrine of air power had been developed. The theory was that strategic bombing alone could win wars without the bloody attrition of battlefield combat. Bombing factories would destroy an enemy's capacity to build weapons and war materiel. Bombing cities, including workers' housing, would destroy civilian morale and so support for the war. Interdiction bombing, striking the road and rail networks leading from the home areas to the war zone, would prevent any war supplies that were produced in spite of the bombing from getting to the front. It was this strategy that the United States followed against both Germany and Japan in World War II.

Following the war the United States mounted a huge research effort to assess the effectiveness of the bombing. To the despair of the Air Force, the report, "The Strategic Bombing Survey," concluded that strategic bombing was not decisive and that the resources that had gone into strategic bombing would have been better spent in close support for the ground forces.

The Korean War gave the doctrine of air power one more chance. The United States Air Force had almost total air superiority over Korea and bombed the factories and towns of North Korea and the road and rail networks virtually at will.

But again, after the war the conclusion was that strategic bombing was not in fact decisive. There was no doubt that the bombing had slowed down the enemy in building up for an offensive. Bombing also made a buildup more costly. In effect, the enemy had to put three tons of supplies into the logistical pipeline to get one through to the front. But again it was clear that bombing did not win wars by itself.

What President Johnson did was in effect to hold out to the Air Force the prospect of one more chance to prove that strategic bombing was effective, that it could by itself win wars. So the initial proposal for escalation was not for making the struggle an American war, but only for bombing North Vietnam. This proposal, code-named Rolling Thunder, divided the JCS and nullified their resistance to anything that seemed likely to lead to another limited war in Asia.

Then in February 1965, the United States began bombing North Vietnam and the supply routes leading to South Vietnam. A few weeks later some regular combat ground forces were introduced to defend the airfields. The situation continued to deteriorate in spite of the bombing of North Vietnam, and in July the United States began to introduce ground forces on a large scale, with the total eventually reaching over half a million men.

Notes

1. As reported by Daniel Ellsberg, see Jann Wenner's interview with Daniel Ellsberg, *Rolling Stone,* December 6, 1973. The fullest account of President Kennedy's attitude toward Vietnam is given by Arthur M. Schlesinger, Jr., in his *Robert F. Kennedy and His Times* (London, 1978), chap. 31. Here I have followed that account and added my own personal knowledge from the official positions

that I held in the Kennedy administration first as the director of intelligence and research of the State Department and later as assistant secretary of state for far eastern affairs, in which position I was Kennedy's action officer for Vietnam. Documentation and additional details can be found in Roger Hilsman, *To Move A Nation*, (Garden City, N.Y.: Doubleday, 1967), in my personal papers in the Kennedy library, and in my oral histories in the Kennedy library, the Lyndon B. Johnson library, the Columbia University Oral History Project, the Congressional Research Service, Library of Congress, and in the Historical Office of the Department of State.

2. Clark Clifford, "Memorandum on Conference between President Eisenhower and President-elected Kennedy and Their Chief Advisers on January 19, 1961," 3 (Emphasis in the original).

3. Arthur M. Schlesinger, Jr., *A Thousand Days, John F. Kennedy in the White House* (Boston: A. Deutsch, 1965), pp. 296ff.

4. Notes on NSC Meetings, Hilsman Papers. President Kennedy made a similar statement to Richard M. Nixon: "In any event, I don't see how we can make any move in Laos, which is 5,000 miles away, if we don't make a move in Cuba, which is only 90 miles away." (Richard M. Nixon, "Cuba, Castro and John F. Kennedy," *Reader's Digest* (November 1964).

5. RFK, memorandum dictated June 1, 1961, 3, RFK Papers.

6. Personal communication from Harriman to Roger Hilsman, Hilsman Papers.

7. Roswell Gilpatric in a recorded interview by D.J. O'Brien, May 5, 1970, 19, JFK Oral History Program.

8. Schlesinger, *Robert Kennedy and His Times,* p. 704. Schlesinger's footnote 13 reads: "RFK, memorandum dictated August 1, 1961, 1, RFK Papers." Footnote 14 reads: "Alexis Johnson, in recorded interview by William Brubeck, n.d. [1964], 33–34, JFK Oral History Program." Footnote 15 reads: "Maxwell Taylor, in recorded interview by L.J. Hackman, November 13, 1969, 47."

9. Maxwell D. Taylor, in a recorded interview by L.J. Hackman, November 13, 1969, 43.

10. J.K. Galbraith, in an interview by Arthur M. Schlesinger, Jr., June 23, 1977.

11. Arthur M. Schlesinger's journal as cited in his *Robert Kennedy and His Times,* p. 1,000, footnote 21.

12. George Ball, in an interview by Arthur M. Schlesinger, Jr., June 15, 1977.

13. No matter how hard the participants in historical decisions may try to be fair to all sides of the policy debates in which they took part, they cannot avoid being somewhat more eloquent in describing the arguments their own side espoused than in their attempt to describe the arguments of their opponents. This chapter has this same failing. As a consequence, two things need to be said. The first is that in the debate described here there were reasonable arguments on both sides, and anyone's ultimate judgment, no matter which side it comes down on, must rest on a fine balancing of pros and cons. The second is that although the debates were sometimes heated, it would be wrong to deduce from the high level of passion a doubt as to anyone's motive. The participants on both sides were high-minded, patriotic, and intelligent people, wrestling manfully with stubbornly intransigent problems that were awesome in their complexity.

14. On this point General Matthew Ridgway's criticism of both Rostow and the author is one of the wiser things that has been said. The occasion was a conference at Bermuda sponsored by the Carnegie Endowment for International Peace in early 1968. The author had been arguing against Rostow's theory that our higher technological and industrial development would permit us to go up the ladder of escalation step by step until the North Vietnamese finally were forced to quit. The trouble with Rostow's theory, the argument went, was that the United States would run out of rungs in its ladder because of domestic and world opinion before the North Vietnamese would run out of rungs in their ladder. General Ridgway observed that we were both wrong. The trouble with U.S. strategy in Vietnam was that it was trying to use military force to achieve goals that military force was incapable of achieving. Force could kill people, and the United States enjoyed a sufficient technical and industrial superiority that it could indeed kill all the Vietnamese in the world if it were immoral enough to do so. But military force could not change people's political attitudes—and that was what the U.S. strategy was trying to do with military force in Vietnam. It was a totally inappropriate use of military force.

15. See Roger Hilsman, "Internal War: The New Communist Tactic," in his *Foreign Policy in the Sixties* (Baltimore: Johns Hopkins University Press, 1963).

16. Ibid.

17. Ironically, after the escalation of the war, Thompson also became an important adviser to the Johnson administration and a theoretician for the hawk strategy, which was the successor to the military approach.

18. Roger Hilsman and Michael V. Forrestal, "A Report on South Vietnam" n.d. [January 1963] Hilsman Papers. A copy is also in the RFK Papers.

19. CBS interview with Walter Cronkite, September 2, 1963.

20. Press conference, September 12, 1985.

21. Hilsman, *To Move a Nation*, pp. 511–12; 519.

22. Again the fullest account of Kennedy's attitude is Schlesinger's in *Robert Kennedy and His Times*, on which I have drawn here.

23. Roswell Gilpatric, in interview by D.J. O'Brien, August 12, 1970, 1, RFK Oral History Program.

24. Schlesinger, *Robert Kennedy and His Times*, p. 709.

25. U.S. Department of Defense, *The Pentagon Papers*, Senator Gravel edition (Boston, MA: Beacon Press, 1971) vol. 2, pp. 670–71.

26. Gilpatric, in O'Brien interview, August 12, 1970.

27. Ellsberg, *Rolling Stone.*

28. Henry Brandon, *Anatomy of Error* (London: A. Deutsch 1970), p. 30; Kenneth O'Donnell and David F. Powers, "Johnny, We Hardly Knew Ye" (Boston, 1972).

29. Hilsman, *To Move a Nation*, p. 501.

30. Press Conference, July 17, 1963, and CBS interview with Walter Cronkite, September 2, 1963.

31. As related by *Washington Post* diplomatic correspondent Chalmers M. Roberts, *First Rough Draft* (New York: Praeger Publishers, 1973), pp. 195–96.

32. *Washington Post*, August 3, 1970; Jack Anderson, "The Roots of Our Vietnam Involvement," *Washington Post*, May 4, 1975.

33. O'Donnell and Powers, "Johnny, We Hardly Knew Ye", p. 16.

34. Ibid., p. 18.

35. On this point see Schlesinger, *Robert Kennedy and His Times,* pp. 708ff.

36. Personal communication from Robert F. Kennedy to Roger Hilsman, Hilsman Papers.

37. CBS interview with Walter Cronkite, September 2, 1963.

38. Roger Hilsman, in a recorded interview by D.J. O'Brien, August 14, 1970, 20; letter to the *New York Times,* August 8, 1970; Hilsman, *To Move a Nation,* p. 536; and Hilsman Papers.

39. For a fuller description of these events see Hilsman, *To Move a Nation,* pp. 527ff.

40. Ibid., pp. 534ff.; and Hilsman Papers.

41. Notes on NSC meetings, Hilsman Papers.

42. For a fuller account of what follows see Hilsman, *To Move a Nation,* (Garden City, N.Y.: Doubleday), p. 531fn, and the same page and fn in the paperback edition, which includes information not available when the hardcover was published.

43. One final comment should be made. William P. Bundy, the assistant secretary of state for east Asian and Pacific affairs, who was the action officer for Vietnam in the Johnson administration, in a speech on August 15, 1967, described the 1964–65 infiltration of North Vietnamese regulars as "moving in for the kill." Agreed that we now know that they were beginning to move in, even if the U.S. government did not know it at the time, why for the kill? What is puzzling is why the North Vietnamese would take the chance of provoking U.S. retaliation, either by bombing or an invasion of North Vietnam (which Secretary of State Dean Rusk advocated at one point) if they were winning? The administration believed they were winning, as Bunday himself testifies, and the fact that they were winning was the reason for bombing the North. The administration also believed that the North Vietnamese believed that they were winning, again as Bunday testifies. So why should the North escalate and risk retaliation?

A more likely hypothesis seems to be that the fact that the United States was seriously considering bombing, which had spilled over into the newspapers, convinced the North Vietnamese that an escalation was coming and that they were simply preparing their response, including sending the first battalion the U.S. forces met on Highway 19, as an advance party to conduct reconnaissance.

44. Hilsman, *To Move a Nation,* pp. 534 ff., and Hilsman Papers.

45. Personal communication from Harriman to Roger Hilsman, Hilsman Papers.

9 IRAN'S REVOLUTION AND U.S. POLICY

Barry Rubin

Coping with revolutions has been one of the central problems for U.S. foreign policy. Given the great power and wide-ranging interests of the United States, changes of government abroad may be deemed threats to strategic assets, allies or investments. Given the worldwide U.S.-Soviet rivalry, Washington closely watches elections, coups, and political upheavals to assess whether they are likely to deliver "prizes" to Moscow's influence.

These considerations have repeatedly shaped U.S. foreign policy behavior. When U.S. governments concluded that developments offered dangers to allies or opportunities to eliminate antagonistic regimes, they frequently tried to foment or forestall instability in Third World countries. Washington has often provided aid or even troops to shore up friendly regimes facing subversion by neighbors or political opposition at home.

The 1978–79 Iranian revolution does not fit easily into this framework. The "exceptional" nature of Washington's apparently passive policy in the crisis plus the tremendous impact of Iran's upheaval on regional politics and U.S. international posture has stirred a great deal of controversy. One can well argue that the overthrow of the Shah and the ensuing hostage crisis were the most important events shaping U.S. foreign policy since the Vietnam War.

Two clear positions have emerged in assessing the errors of pre-Khomeini American policy. Liberals criticize an overly close association with the Shah's "disreputable" government. They accept—and sometimes exaggerate—the Shah's misdeeds and U.S. responsibility for them. Arguing that there should have been greater U.S. pressure for reform in Iran, they blame President Nixon and Secretary of State Kissinger for having tried to use the Shah as a surrogate for protecting U.S. interests in the Persian Gulf.

The conservative stand is one of almost uncritical acceptance of U.S. support for the Shah on the basis that there were no alternatives. Washington's mistake, they claim, was to betray the Shah at the critical moment despite his long record of assistance to U.S. interests. They blame President Carter's human rights program and alleged pressure for reform for precipitating the Shah's downfall.

Ironically, both schools share an essential premise with Khomeini and the Iranians who took over the U.S. embassy in Tehran. All agree that for better or worse, the United States had tremendous influence, even control, over events in Iran. The liberals see the Shah's cooperation with the United States as dispensable and believe that a determined Washington might have wrung reforms out of him. The conservatives assure us that a word from Washington would have sufficed to stop a mass revolution by—to paraphrase Winston Churchill's proposed solution to an earlier Iran crisis—"a splutter of musketry."

U.S. observers with long experience in U.S.-Iranian relations can be less sanguine. Thirty years of effort taught how difficult it was to ever convince the Shah of anything. Far from being an American puppet, the Shah faced his Bastille Day at a time when U.S. policy placed a high value on his strength and decisiveness.

Restraining the Shah

From the 1940s until 1972, U.S. policy sought to restrain the Shah from pursuing his military and strategic ambitions. In recognition of the Shah's shaky political base, Washington also made periodic attempts to encourage social reform and democratization in Iran. U.S. retrenchment during the Vietnam War, along with the Shah's spiraling oil wealth, rendered that traditional approach useless.

Moreover, this policy combining support and restraint did not lead to smooth relations between the two countries. The Shah resented and rejected U.S. pressures as thoroughly as his successors had; attempts to promote "good" causes, such as human rights, were no more popular than any other U.S. demands. Those liberal policy makers whose analysis made them most eager for peaceful change in Iran were cautious and unwilling to risk antagonizing or destabilizing the Shah.

The State Department never had any illusions about the Shah's obsession with military power, although his attitude had rational roots. The Shah's father was unseated by an Anglo-Soviet invasion in 1941 and he himself had been helpless to force the Soviets out again after World War II. Iran needed U.S. assistance to gain Soviet evacuation. The Shah had had ample experience with the consequences of military weakness.

The Truman administration's attitudes toward the Shah were typical of what was to follow and many of the State Department reports of those years could easily have been written a few months before the Shah's fall. During the Shah's first visit to the United States, Secretary of State Dean Acheson ridiculed his military ambitions. Chiang Kai-shek was collapsing in China at that very moment, Acheson told the Shah, because he failed to make reforms and depended instead on a large but vulnerable army. Reforms were all very well, replied the Shah, but military security always came first. Besides, the Nationalist Chinese lost because of their corruption, a problem that would never occur in Iran. U.S. policy makers were also well aware of the Shah's personal shortcomings—a dangerous combination of stubbornness and weakness alongside a mixture of blindness and arrogance.

The Shah's desire for a large army did not spring merely from the requirements for personal glory or of internal repression. Rather, nationalist sentiment made him unwilling to accept U.S. military protection as his sole assurance against any Soviet invasion. Like his successors, he wanted a strong, independent Iran beholden to no one. When the Kennedy and Johnson administrations tried to cut back military supplies to encourage a shift in spending priorities, the Shah publicly complained that Iran was being treated "like a colony." And he meant it. The dream was ultimately self-destructive, but it was hardly unpatriotic.

The Roots of Hatred

The victorious revolutionaries in Iran have painted U.S. policy in the deepest hues of evil reaction, but on numerous occasions Washington supported attempts at political reform in Iran. The most illustrative incident was Washington's relationship with the 1951–53 nationalist regime of Muhammad Mossadegh and even today, these events are of the greatest importance in shaping Iranians' perceptions of the United States. Yet again the lesson is different from what might be expected. U.S. behavior was not based so much on innate U.S. interests as it was on contention between different political and ideological camps within the United States.

Mossadegh was one of the most fascinating personalities of twentieth-century politics. A Swiss-educated nationalist and a charismatic feudal landlord, Mossadegh projected his emotions with an actor's skill. He made his health the barometer of the Iranian cause—fainting during his speeches to win sympathy, suffering from mysterious, undetectable illnesses at critical moments. When he first arrived in Washington, he emerged from the train hanging on his son's arm and bent weakly over a walking stick. Within moments, he tossed the cane away and skipped down the platform like a schoolboy.

Such antics, amusing to his Western interlocutors, were no mere eccentricities. Like Khomeini, and unlike the Shah, Mossadegh understood well the romantic drama that Iranians loved to find in their politics. He was a politician first and a statesman second, knowing that his image in the Tehran bazaar was far more important than his image in the salons of London or Washington. In contrast, the shy Shah saw himself as a hardheaded realist, carefully weighing and measuring every factor. Despite his splendid uniforms, the Shah was a gray figure, proud of his stern and aloof image. Thus, he was adept at building mighty edifices, but neglected to secure their foundations. He sought to overwhelm unpopularity with success.

But Mossadegh's populist approach also had its pitfalls. His great effort—to take the control of Iran's oil production and marketing away from the Anglo-Iranian Oil Company—failed because of British stubbornness and that of his own nationalist supporters. The masses supported Mossadegh, but would turn on him as a traitor if he made small concessions in order to consolidate larger prizes.

Washington preferred a compromise on the dispute to meet Iran's main grievances, to maintain the supply of petroleum, and provide Iran with political stability. Of course, there were limits to the Truman administration's willingness to side with Iran against Britain, but for almost two years every attempt was made to encourage a reasonable settlement.

Acheson recognized Mossadegh's domestic dilemma. A more moderate policy would endanger his position, the secretary of state believed. Iranian political culture has not changed very much since then, as Prime Ministers Shapur Baktiar and Mehdi Bazargan discovered in their dealings with Khomeini.

While the Truman-Acheson policy was sympathetic toward non-Communist Third World reformers, their Eisenhower-Dulles successors adopted a strong stance in favor of the status quo. While the Democrats refused repeated British suggestions for a joint coup, the new administration fell in with such plans almost immediately after Eisenhower's inauguration. Their CIA Director Allen Dulles was eager to demonstrate how his agency could solve such problems. While Iranians cannot be expected to make such distinctions, U.S. involvement in the anti-Mossadegh coup was simply the signal of a factional triumph in U.S. policy debate.

This new orientation was fatalistically summarized by Secretary of State John Foster Dulles in recently declassified testimony to the Senate Foreign Relations Committee. Obviously, he explained, social problems and political unrest would exist without communism, but the Marxists were so superior at capturing the forces of change that their influence over nationalist revolutions in the Third World could scarcely be challenged.

And so the increasing chaos in Iran and the growing strength of the local Communist party served as rationale for the August 1953 coup, in which the CIA helped overthrow Mossadegh and bring back the Shah. Soon, Eisenhower was portraying the action as having saved Iran from a Communist takeover; even the hapless Mossadegh was sometimes reinterpreted as a minion of Moscow. Iranians today regard this step as the beginning of U.S. satanic domination of their political life.

Matters were far more complex. First, CIA bribes to a few Tehran gang leaders could not have brought down Mossadegh unless his regime had already proven its domestic incompetence and its loss of control over the country. The maximalism of his supporters had made it impossible for Mossadegh to win a partial victory in the oil dispute. When he ran into difficulties, many members of his coalition abandoned him. There was little resistance—and a good deal of popular welcome—to the Shah's return.

If Mossadegh had only fallen of his own weight Iranians would have had to face their own responsibility in the fiasco and might have learned something about political flexibility from it. Instead, CIA involvement provided a foreign scapegoat for all their problems.

The impact on the CIA itself was also negative. Since the coup makers were pushing on an already open door, the CIA—and its superiors in the administration—were persuaded that the task could be easily repeated. Several later disasters can be traced to this misunderstanding over the ease and profitability of such covert destabilizations.

Finally, U.S. intervention revitalized the myth of foreign control over Iranian politics at a time when it was being banished. Having helped create the new order, Washington, like Doctor Frankenstein, found definite limits to its further influence over events. The old limits on the Shah's power by Majlis (parliament), prime minister, and middle-class nationalist opposition were shattered. Far from giving the United States power over the Shah, the coup freed him, allowing him to become a true dictator, guided only by his own will.

Guilt by Association

It did not take long for even the Eisenhower administration to discover the Shah's lack of legitimacy in Iran and this knowledge was never entirely forgotten. Already, however, long before Washington gave him carte blanche on arms' purchases and while it was still urging democratization, Iranians' image of the United States was determined.

The snag was not merely the Shah's dictatorial practices, of course, since most Third World countries live under that form of government today; far bloodier regimes have won a large measure of legitimacy. His difficulty was a stilted manner, an inability to cultivate the illusion of mass participation and a failure to fully utilize the modern totalitarian techniques of ideological regimentation in a single-party state.

Still, year after year the Shah defied the prophets of doom, the journalists and diplomats who predicted apocalyptic revolution if he did not change his ways. Those contemporary Galileos were forced to acknowledge that, in spite of their models and measurements, Iran still moved. The economy did well and the standard of living climbed steadily upward even before the 1973 oil price pole-vaults. The Shah seemed to defy political gravity. Who could question such success?

When the Kennedy administration pressed for a smaller army and for more economic and social spending, the Shah launched his own "White Revolution" from above. Washington was impressed with his land reform, but the CIA noted the neglect of planning and long-term development. The peasants would only benefit, the agency noted, if cooperatives and rural credit were properly organized, a step that was never taken.

But if the United States was unhappy with the Shah, the Shah was equally dismayed by Washington's treatment. He complained of being taken for granted. The massacre of the monarchy in neighboring Iraq, the rise of Nasser's influence and of radical Arab nationalism, and U.S. failure to back Pakistan in its 1965 war with India, all convinced him of the need to build Iran's forces and to keep his distance from the United States. In the 1960s the Shah moved toward détente with Moscow as he saw the main threat to the South—the Persian Gulf—rather than the northern front.

When British withdrawal from the Gulf left a strategic vacuum after 1971, the Shah did not need to be convinced that he was the one to fill it. He campaigned for the job as if it were a presidential primary. Washington, having wisely decided against direct involvement in the gulf, judged that steady aid to Iran and Saudi Arabia would make them the region's two pillars of stability. This idea, institutionalized in the June 1969 Nixon Doctrine, only reinforced the Shah's new doctrine.

The following events all strengthened Tehran's hand: the 1972 Nixon-Kissinger decision to sell the Shah all the arms he wanted, the Shah's March 1973 nationalization of oil production, and OPEC's price increases. The Shah was well aware of new leverage. When Khomeini's close ally, Ayatollah Montazeri, tells Iranians, "You have the resources and mines. You do not need the United States. The United States needs you," he is scarcely in conflict with the Shah's political discoveries.

If the United States needed Iran and the Shah controlled Iran, U.S. policy was consequently predicated on a calculated risk that the Shah would remain in power. This view became official creed. Studying modernization's social strains or remembering the hatred of politically conscious Iranians for the Shah was a task relegated to academics.

A Failure of Intelligence?

The rest is well known. Economic mismanagement and waste damaged Iran, but huge oil revenues almost covered the multitude of fiscal sins. U.S. arms companies scrambled to make sales for strategic reasons and as a way of recycling petrodollars, but if their marketing skills exceeded Iran's short-run absorptive capacity, it was the Shah himself who demanded that speed and volume. Taking direct control of the program, the monarch planned his purchases over breakfast, using copies of *Aviation Week and Space Technology* as if they were mail-order catalogs.

Meanwhile, massive revenues and economic development brought social upheaval. The migration of millions of peasants into the cities undermined the Shah as surely as the march of Great Burnam wood undid Macbeth. These demographic shifts upset the traditional domination of nationalist politics by the liberal middle class. Newly arrived villagers looked instead to their habitual source of political wisdom, the clergy. Their culture shock and mistrust of perceived Westernization coupled with the growing gap between rich and poor and an economic downturn in 1978, combined to produce the Iranian revolution.

The Shah simply lost control, ruined by his indecision and weakness and misinformed by his growing isolation. The carefully groomed army was incapable of coping with the crisis, given its docile, "yes-men" officers and unreliable peasant conscripts who were vulnerable to the ayatollahs' appeals. In the end, few were willing to fight for the Shah's continued rule.

Since the Shah collected all the threads of power in his own hands only he could save himself. Yet who could retain hope after reading the Shah's August 31, 1978 interview with the West German magazine *Stern*? Against all evidence to the contrary, he still maintained that his opponents were only a handful of terrorists. The *Stern* correspondent informed him that corruption was so rife in Tehran that even garbagemen had to be bribed to make their pickups and that "many humble people could not even make a living if they refused to take bribes."

"Do you really have to bribe people?" asked the Shah with disbelief.

"What should I do if the garbage piles up in front of the house? And believe me, Your Majesty," the reporter added, "everybody among the people knows that this is so."

Did the U.S. know better? Long prediction of an event may not prevent paralysis when it finally arrives. The Carter administration had inherited a policy that did not welcome warnings or criticisms about Iran's domestic situation. As in Vietnam, those charged with intelligence gathering were given incentives for bringing their conclusions into line with what their superiors wanted to hear. In the words of the House of Representatives Select Committee on Intelligence, "Long-standing U.S.

attitudes toward the Shah inhibited intelligence collection, dampened policymakers' appetite for analysis of the Shah's position and deafened policymakers to the warning implicit in available current intelligence."

How much might Washington have done differently? The Shah, of course, blames the United States for his downfall, but his case is far from persuasive. Did Iranians rise up because President Carter made speeches in favor of human rights? Was the Shah, who resisted far stronger U.S. pressures on a half dozen occasions, really paralyzed for six months awaiting Washington's permission to put down the demonstrations?

Certainly, the most important single factor for understanding U.S. policy was the Carter administration's failure to see that a revolution was going on until it was almost over. Consequently, the U.S. government had no coherent policy of action toward events in Iran until late December 1978, almost a year after the upheaval had begun.

During all this time, the administration had a choice among four types of responses to the revolution:

1. Sympathy or even covert support for the anti-Shah forces;
2. Support for the Shah within the context of limited U.S. ability to affect events within Iran;
3. An active attempt to abort any threat to the Shah's power and to defeat the opposition;
4. Acceptance of the Shah's likely downfall and an active U.S. plan to mediate a transition to a new regime.

Only the Shah, some Iranian exiles, and bizarre conspiracy theorists believe that the United States desired or actively conspired in the Shah's overthrow. No real evidence has come to light to point toward such a conclusion.

A milder view of this type has been presented by some conservative or neoconservative critics of the Carter administration. They argue that some middle-level State Department officials were so disposed against the Shah's regime that they were pleased to see him fall. They argue that career officers overstated the likelihood of the Shah's defeat, did not support strong enough measures to keep him in power, and underestimated the opposition's extremism.

In fact, career officials at State were slow and reluctant to predict the Shah's collapse or any need for a new regime there. Indeed, if they had done so earlier in 1978 it might have helped the administration properly estimate the crisis in time to affect events. But actually they only began to sound the alarm in the summer of 1978 when the situation was already far gone.

The second option, to support the Shah's own efforts to defeat the revolution, was the de facto policy of the United States from January until December 1978. Washington did not abandon its alliance with the Shah, it simply allowed him to deal with his own internal problems. Several public statements of support for him were issued, responding to calls from U.S. Ambassador William Sullivan in Tehran (who relayed the Shah's requests) and Iranian Ambassador Ardeshir Zahedi in Washington.

Ironically, the belief that the Shah did not need active assistance was the product of past U.S. confidence in the monarch. In the early 1970s, after all, President Richard Nixon and National Security Adviser Henry Kissinger had designated the Shah a pillar for the U.S.'s Middle East position and a regional power in his own right. Over the following years, Washington had filled Iran's orders for billions of dollars in military equipment.

The Nixon-Kissinger policy had projected the Shah as a powerful, decisive figure commanding tremendous armed might and acting as a major force for regional political stability. Even critics of the policy accepted its premises. Their concern was not of a Shah who was too weak but of a ruler who might be too strong. From 1974 on, particularly in Congress and the media, arguments were raised about the dangers of an overly ambitious, excessively determined Iran.

Among the questions that dominated the debate were: Would Iran's growing power frighten Saudi Arabia? Could the Shah's military might tempt him toward overreaching himself in the Gulf? Might the United States be pulled into some local war started by Iran? In short, the entire psychological preparation of the Carter administration was for an expansive and aggressive Shah, not a kitten-weak, indecisive monarch.

But did the United States undermine the Shah before the revolution and give him inadequate support during it? This view is presented by critics who advocated the third option: a clear, determined U.S. policy favoring the smashing of opposition. These critics point to the Carter administration's human rights policy as a major factor encouraging dissent in Iran and vitiating the Shah's self-confidence.

It is difficult to analyze the extent of the human rights policy's psychological effect on the internal Iranian situation, but it can be easily shown that the policy's substance has been vastly overestimated. Both internal and published administration human rights reports were quite soft on Iran and the Shah. Equally, it is hard to find any criticisms, quiet or publicized, of the Shah by leading U.S. officials. Finally, on the most important material area of bilateral relations—arms sales—the Carter administration did not deny Iran anything.

When, during his December 1977 visit to Tehran, President Carter called his host a rock of strength in a sea of instability, this hardly reflected a lack of confidence in the Shah's ability to survive politically. The Shah's own views of his future were, if anything, less sanguine. Knowing, as U.S. leaders did not, of his illness, the Shah slightly loosened the reins to bequeath his son popularity and a stable throne.

At the bottom of the U.S. debate over the Iranian crisis is an important, unspoken error about U.S. centrality in the causes and solutions for international problems. U.S. politicians, policy makers, commentators, and journalists generally know far more about the United States than about ideology and politics in foreign countries. Having grown up and lived most of their lives in a situation of U.S. world primacy, they overstate U.S. influence and potential for controlling events.

Both factors—relative ignorance about the situation abroad and hubris over the U.S. role on any given issue—make Americans take too much credit or too much blame on any given issue and undervalue internal Iranian causes for the revolution's victory. The situation is only made more difficult by the complementary, mirror-image complex of most Iranians. Refusing to take responsibility for tough decisions proved fatal for the Shah and his supporters in 1978 and 1979. Ayatollah Khomeini and his followers, like their hated enemies, blame Iran's problems on the United States.

Such a world view also explains why, in retrospect, the Shah felt betrayed by an administration that would not literally tell him what to do. Yet the Shah had never been an American puppet before. His own toughness had discouraged U.S. leaders from trying to shape Iranian policies. Consequently, after the revolution began, he never asked for U.S. intervention and the Carter administration felt that none was required. Requests for general reassurance and statements of support were met privately on numerous occasions and several times in public as well.

While the administration followed option two, however, a debate developed, beginning around August 1978, on whether to proceed to option three or option four. The U.S. perception that the crisis was getting out of Tehran's control resulted from some clear turning points, beginning with the Jaleh Square massacre of demonstrations on September 8 and ending with the Shah's appointment of a military government on November 6. Only in late September did the State Department even form a working group which spent most of its time debating whether more public statements supporting the Shah would be helpful or harmful to the situation.

Once the situation in Iran was seen to be serious and the Shah's survival in question, top policy makers began to focus on the problem. Should the United States escalate antirevolutionary efforts or should it conclude that the Shah was politically finished and try to broker a transition to a new, moderate regime?

Before discussing this conflict, it is important to stress why the Carter administration took so long to decide that a more concerted policy was needed. There are three types of factors involved: the unusual nature of the events in Iran, weaknesses in the reporting and analysis of information, and shortcomings at the top of the policy-making process. In international affairs, as in daily life, terrible accidents usually happen only when a number of things go wrong at the same time.

First of all, there was the complex situation in Iran itself. The revolution developed slowly, with demonstrations peaking around the mourning period following each earlier round of street marches and killings. There were few armed actions and no direct assault on the government or military. Policy makers found it difficult to understand the nature and appeal of Islamic fundamentalism and were equally mystified by the Middle East's first mass, popular revolution. After all, the chronic instability of regional states had always arisen from military coups or underground terrorist groups. Mass popular revolutions have been rare, to say the least.

How could the Shah's enormous army and secret police melt away so easily? Although the Shah's Pahlavi dynasty was only a little over a half-century old, centuries of monarchy rule had made a king appear indispensable. Even the opposition leaders, including Islamic fundamentalists, did not seem to believe before August 1978 that they would be able to overthrow the regime.

What bound the diverse opposition together was the remarkable popularity developed by the exiled Ayatollah Ruhollah Khomeini, particularly after August or September. Earlier, however, internal Islamic leaders like Ayatollah Shariat-Madari, spoke of a constitutional monarchy rather than an Islamic revolution. Given all these factors, the difficulty for analysts predicting what happened later is quite understandable.

Responsibility for failing to comprehend the depth of the problem early enough must be divided between the embassy and Washington. The key issue was not intelligence—the gathering of information—but analysis, the determination of what the data means. The reports sent by the U.S. embassy during the revolution consistently gave a detailed account of demonstrations, violence, statements of government and opposition leaders, etc. A great deal of such information was even available in the news media.

The U.S. foreign policy system is proficient at producing quantities of facts. Sometimes the amount of paper generated within the system threatens to strangle it. Yet no statement of facts verifiable by direct intelligence could tell decision makers whether or not the revolution would succeed or who would end up in control of it. Only individual observers using their understanding of Iran and political dynamics could make such a determination and seek to convince superiors of them.

The objective problem of predicting what would happen in a unique and complex political situation joined with the human failure to understand and warn about the developing crisis. The analytic shortcoming was reinforced by other factors:

• A bureaucratic fear of prophesying the revolution's victory should that conclusion prove wrong. Since such an outcome was contrary to existing policy and the Shah's presumed strength, lower and middle officials correctly suspected such news would be unwelcome to superiors. In fact, those quickest to predict the

Shah's downfall found themselves criticized for alleged wishful thinking, for being anti-Shah.

 • Legitimate concern that any conclusion that the Shah was doomed would become a self-fulfilling prophecy by undermining U.S. support the regime. If such estimates leaked into the press the result would be particularly damaging.

 • The distraction of the highest officials, involved in the Camp David Israel-Egypt negotiations and other matters, thus leaving people with less authority in charge of the seemingly lower-priority developments in Iran.

 • The Carter administration's ideological aversion to intervene in foreign internal conflicts, support dictators, or advocate repression. This point is often wrongly elevated, however, into the main or even sole shaper of U.S. policy.

The objective and analytical factors joined with a third problem: the administration's flawed policy-making process. Henry Kissinger's domination of U.S. foreign policy during the Nixon-Ford administration had presented presidents with both an opportunity and a challenge. The alternative was the possibility of centralizing control of foreign policy through the national security adviser. But much of the style and substance of the politics emerging from this monolithic structure was repugnant to the system's many critics.

President Carter chose to reject a Kissinger-style system in favor of a more pluralistic model. Carter's direct involvement in foreign policy decision making and concentration on detail brought him success at Camp David but meant that other issues would be neglected. His refusal to designate a single lieutenant on foreign policy prevented the formation of a clear chain of command and permitted an ongoing conflict between Secretary of State Cyrus Vance and National Security Adviser Zbigniew Brzezinski.

Consequently, even when the administration did begin to deal seriously with the Iran crisis, in the fall of 1979, internal bickering and indecisiveness delayed the formation of a clear policy. Vance and the State Department tended to support a policy favoring concessions by the Shah or even the transition to another regime. Brzezinski advocated strong support for the Shah and a call for a repressive response to the revolutionary threat.

This battle between options three and four developed only after option two—depending on a U.S.-backed Shah to resolve the crisis—had clearly failed. Carter certainly leaned toward Vance's interpretation of events but he never actually accepted this as a strategy. Rather, he vacillated for several months and avoided making a rapid decision by calling in an outside third party, former Undersecretary of State George Ball. Ball had to study the situation, which took additional time, before he finally, and predictably, sided with the State Department.

So at the end of December 1978, after meeting with Vance, Carter decided to seize on the Shah's acceptance of a cabinet headed by Shahpour Bakhtiar, a long-time oppositionist and leader of the moderate National Front. This was not a bad decision given its timing but by then U.S. options had become very narrow: it was too late for either concessions or repression.

The entire country was in revolt and saw no need to cooperate with an obviously collapsing government. The military was no longer reliable. Khomeini's domination of the opposition and his intransigent revolutionary objective should have been clear to everyone. Carter's strategy of backing a regime supported by neither the rulers nor the opposition was doomed to failure.

Does this mean that Brzezinski and those advocating an "iron fist" were correct? Kissinger and other realpolitik advocates insisted that concessions would never moderate the opposition and that reforms should only follow the establishment of order. While urging the Shah to repress demonstrations might have been better than doing nothing at all, it is not clear what such a policy implied other than more exhortations to the Shah and his generals. Sending U.S. forces would have been counterproductive and unacceptable at home; the regime certainly did not need more weapons.

Obviously, authoritarian regimes cannot retain power while changing their nature. This is beside the point. During the first months of crisis, relatively small modifications of the Shah's rule would have satisfied most opposition leaders. The small number of radicals could have been dealt with more easily. Even after opposition mounted, a constitutional monarchy and power for moderate anti-Shah forces would have taken the situation in quite a different direction. The regime's intransigence promoted the leadership of the most radical forces on the other side.

Advocates of a tough, repressive approach were better versed in the theory of power politics than about the real situation in Iran. A weak, hesitant Shah could not be mobilized into action. The army (dependent on draftees and technicians of doubtful loyalty) was not a simple machine that could be blithely ordered to shoot down thousands of fellow countrymen. An attempt at all-out repression might have produced a bloody civil war, the country's fragmentation, and opportunities for a leftist takeover or Soviet influence.

Iran's large size and population, proximity to the USSR, the politicization of the masses with Islamic and nationalist ideas, and modern communications, all made Iran a different country from what it had been in 1953 when the CIA could secretly buy enough demonstrators to change a regime. U.S. willingness to go into battle and advocate—or suffer— thousands of people killed was also reduced in the aftermath of Vietnam. In Iran, as in China 30 years earlier, the size, dangers, and difficulties of counterrevolutionary intervention were too risky to take.

Finally, by the time Brzezinski was advocating a hardline response, the military had already disintegrated and the opposition had consolidated to a point where his proposal was a fantasy. As late as January-February 1979, Brzezinski continued to speak of a military coup when many of the generals had already fled the country or made separate deals with Khomeini.

The last act of the drama was also the most farcical. Having decided to back Bakhtiar, Carter dispatched General Robert Huyser to Iran in January 1979. Huyser, like Ball, was dropped into the middle of an unfamiliar crisis to investigate the state of the Iranian army and to urge the generals to support Bakhtiar's already mythical regime. The Shah was pressed to leave the country to give Bakhtiar's transitional government an opportunity to reconcile the opposition with a continued moderate, pro-U.S. authority.

Naturally, the Iranian generals told Huyser what he wanted to hear, while either incapable or unwilling to risk themselves on Bakhtiar's behalf. Naturally, the already anti-U.S. opposition saw this effort as a final attempt to deny them power. On these points, Ambassador William Sullivan was quite correct in criticizing Huyser's optimism. But the ambassador's errors the previous year had destroyed his credibility in Washington.

Sullivan later suggested that talks with Khomeini's aides might have led to a deal in which the Shah and top generals would have left the country in exchange for the preservation of the army's chain of command. But why would Khomeini ever agree to preserving a pro-U.S. armed force dedicated to destroying his authority? Now Khomeini held all the cards of organization and legitimacy. In February 1979 he easily swept away Bakhtiar, the officer corps, the establishment politicians, and the remnants of U.S. influence.

The Shah's fall was due primarily to internal Iranian causes, factors that could not be erased by changes in U.S. policy at the very last minute. During 1978 Washington faced limited and unpalatable options. Nevertheless, the failure to understand events in Iran at a point where the threat had become reasonably clear paralyzed any U.S. response.

The conservative policy toward Iran represented by the Eisenhower policy in 1953 and by the Nixon-Ford buildup of Iran in the early 1970s traded off the risk of high involvement with the Shah's regime for considerable stakes in terms of security interests. Continuity seemed safer than risky social experiments and the Shah's durability became a basic premise of U.S. policy. The forces of opposition were ceded to the anti-U.S. camp.

This approach, of course, was not so arbitrary as hindsight implies. U.S. nervousness about keeping oil or the ability to block its transport out of Soviet or radical hands and Washington's determination to reinforce regional stability necessitated a good relationship with the incumbent regime in Iran. It was a regime that would not, and could not, change on its own.

Yet this U.S. policy also contributed to the trends of overheated economic development, overidentification with foreigners, importation of alien cultural influences, and high levels of military spending which helped fuel the anti-Shah revolution.

The liberal positions advocated by Truman, Kennedy, and Carter argued that governments respecting human rights and allowing more democracy would make stronger allies. Yet how could such goals be implemented? Pressures on such allies produced friction on the government level without necessarily winning popular sympathy for the United States. The very liberal sensitivities and political constraints that motivated such policies also prevented the intensity of intervention needed to produce progress. Ultimately, Washington could not substitute itself for the shortcomings of leadership in Tehran.

The U.S. failure to cope with the Iranian revolution thus had long- and short-range causes. The former was the policy of intense involvement and encouragement of the Shah to follow what proved to be a self-destructive course. The latter was a blindness to the immediate crisis of 1978 and a failure to take decisive action promoting either reform or repression at a time when it might have changed the course of events.

First and foremost, however, one must remember that the framework of events was *Iranian.* When U.S. leaders refuse to deal with the context of foreign revolutions, their policies fail; when foreign rulers are blind to their own countries they are doomed to defeat. If observers ignore this context of events they will draw the wrong lessons for the future.

Notes

This analytic chapter draws on the large amount of material already published on U.S. policy and on the Iranian revolution. First-hand accounts include Jimmy Carter, *Keeping Faith* (New York: Bantam Books, 1982); Hamilton Jordan, *Crisis: The Last Year of the Carter Presidency* (New York: Putnam, 1982); Zbigniew Brzezinski, *Power and Principle* (New York: Farrar, Straus, Giroux, 1983); Cyrus Vance, *Hard Choices* (New York: Simon and Schuster, 1983); John Stempel, *Inside the Iranian Revolution* (Bloomington, Ind.: Indiana University Press, 1981); William Sullivan, *Mission to Iran* (New York: Norton, 1981); and Gary Sick, *All Fall Down* (New York, 1985). The author's views are presented in *Paved With Good Intentions: The American Experience and Iran* (New York: Oxford University Press, 1980) and *Secrets of State: The State Department and the Struggle Over U.S. Foreign Policy* (New York, 1985). Of special value are the dozens of volumes of classified documents published by the "Students Following the Imam's Line" in Iran.

III: THE SOVIET UNION AND REVOLUTION

10 SOVIET INTERVENTIONISM

Jonathan R. Adelman

The Soviet approach to intervention against revolutionary movements that threaten its interests has been strongly colored by history, ideology, and geopolitics. The irony of Soviet leaders contemplating or using covert or overt force to crush revolutions is of course manifest. Few countries in the world today owe the very nature of their existence more to a revolutionary impulse than the Soviet Union, which was formed through the February and October revolutions of 1917 and transformed by Stalin's "third revolution from above" of the 1930s. For almost a century before 1917 Russian radicals had looked to revolution as the only hope of deliverance from Tsarism. From the 1890s the growing Russian socialist movement had strongly identified itself with international revolutionary currents and the Second International dedicated itself (at least on paper) to the destruction of the international order.

Nor did this strong identification with international revolution evaporate immediately after the taking of power in the October Revolution. Especially in its early years the Soviet leaders strongly promoted international revolution and tended to view events in the prism of Marxism and French revolutionary history. The creation of the Third International in Moscow in 1919 and convocation of a Congress of the Toilers of the East in Baku in 1920 was especially indicative of this trend. During the 1920s and early 1930s the Soviet Union actively intervened to foster the development of revolutionary Communist forces in a number of countries, most notably Germany (1919, 1920, 1923) and China (1927).

The failure of these efforts, the rise of Stalin, and the elevation of the Soviet Union to superpower status during World War II led to a Soviet reappraisal of its encouragement of revolution abroad. This was epitomized by the dissolution of the Comintern in 1943 and Stalin's advice to Tito, Mao, and French and Italian Communist leaders not to attempt to seize power in the aftermath of World War II.

Furthermore, after 1945, the Soviet Union, which heretofore had been predominant only in Mongolia, found itself with a vast sphere of influence in Eastern Europe encompassing 110 million people. Apart from Czechoslovakia and Bulgaria, the peoples of these countries—especially Poland and East Germany—were notably hostile to both the USSR and Soviet-style communism. To leave these countries essentially as they had been before 1939 seemed certain to create a permanent security threat to the Soviet Union. But to attempt to transform these countries from above without an internal revolutionary base, while ensuring security concerns, also guaranteed that any indigenous revolutionary movement would be aimed against Moscow and possibly be led by local Communists. This, then, was the paradox confronting the Soviet leadership—that by their actions they had created the base for anti-Soviet revolutionary sentiment. A second paradox also emerged on their southern flank. While pro-Western regimes as Turkey and Iran were largely inimical to their interests, the emergence of Islamic fundamentalism ensured that a revolutionary overthrow of regimes in countries as Iran and Afghanistan would not necessarily benefit the Soviet Union. A third paradox developed, primarily in the East but also in Yugoslavia. Communist parties that came to power largely on their own initiative but without Moscow's help tended over time to split away from Moscow and ultimately move toward the West. This was ultimately the case with Yugoslavia (1948) and China (1972 +). Thus the Soviet Union, which once hailed the triumph of the Yugoslav and Chinese revolutions, found itself denouncing Tito and Mao. In short, in the postwar world the question of how to deal with revolutionary movements has become vastly more complex for the newly powerful Soviet Union than it was for the isolated prewar Soviet leadership.

Interestingly, no comprehensive work has attempted to deal with the issue in a systematic way, either with intervention in general or with the interplay between the Soviet Union and revolution in particular. There have been some fine synthetic essays on the general topic, as those by Bialer and Dallin.[1] There have been some case studies of Soviet intervention decisions, both essays and books, dealing with such crises as Berlin 1948 (Adomeit), Hungary 1956 (Rice/Fry), Czechoslovakia 1968 (Valenta and Dawisha), Middle East 1973 (Golan), and Afghanistan 1979 (Valenta and Golan).[2] But there have been no overall attempts, as in this volume, to look at a series of case studies over time in comparative framework.

To initiate this process, I have reviewed four cases of Soviet intervention decision making under Brezhnev—Czechoslovakia (1968), China (1969), Middle East (1973), and Afghanistan (1979). While force was contemplated in all four cases, it was used only twice. Although our analysis is hampered by limited information, enough is available to draw some broad overall conclusions.

Several important conclusions arise from our study. First is the continuing central importance of relations with the United States for the Soviet leaders. The Soviet-U.S. axis has been the central axis of international relations. When the United States has been indifferent to a country's fate (Czechoslovakia in 1968) or lost its ability to maintain leverage on the Soviet Union through the death of détente and incapacity to intervene (Afghanistan in 1979), this has removed a major barrier to intervention. Similarly when the United States had indicated a strong interest and capacity to intervene at a time when it maintained leverage on the Soviet Union through détente (China in 1969, Middle East in 1973), this has been a major barrier to intervention. At all times the Soviet leadership sought to avoid direct military confrontation with the United States, preferring proxies whenever possible.

Second, there has been a cautious attitude toward risk-taking in crises, with a marked preference for low-risk operations. Despite temptation, the Soviet Union refrained from intervening in either China or the Middle East. In Czechoslovakia it hesitated and vacillated for months. Even in August it authorized the meeting of the two Politburos at Cierna in order to find a political solution to the crisis. Only when this failed did the politburo order the intervention. In Afghanistan the Soviets first tried hard to work with Amin. After this failed, they backed the Taraki coup against Amin which led to Taraki's death. Again, as in Czechoslovakia, they intervened only when they had exhausted the possible political and covert solutions.

A third related point has been a distinct unwillingness to deploy the armed forces unless the putative battlefield can be largely isolated and the correlation of forces is overwhelmingly favorable. In both China in 1969 and Israel in 1973 neither of these conditions held. Neither battlefield could be isolated from Western help. While the Soviets might have been able to ultimately win in both cases, the costs could have been very high. The Chinese army possessed some second-strike nuclear capability, a nearly two to one manpower superiority, and high morale. The victorious Israelis, having encircled the Third Army in the Sinai and moved to within 60 miles of Cairo, had good military equipment, strong leadership, high morale, and tested battlefield effectiveness. By contrast the Warsaw Pact forces invaded Czechoslovakia with strong numerical and material superiority and knowledge that the Czechs would very probably remain passive. Too there was no danger of Western intervention. Similarly in Afghanistan the Soviets felt they could isolate the battlefield and bring to bear overwhelming military superiority. They counted on rebuilding a strong Afghan army.

This may explain as well why the Soviet Union in general has not used force to bring the "deviant" Communist states (Rumania, Yugoslavia, and China) back into the fold. All three countries, in the wake of the Czech invasion and proclamation of the Brezhnev Doctrine, have strengthened their armed forces and fostered nationalist support for their military. All three, too, have created decentralized structures to carry out guerrilla warfare by a mobilized population. Moscow has gotten the message—invasion would be extremely costly in these three cases. Too, the "deviants" have fostered ties with the West, at least in part to strengthen their positions and add to the cost of any invasion.

The military factor, then, has been important. Although Soviet military power has grown notably, especially in airlift, naval, and missile capabilities, there has not been a corresponding increase in the aggressive use of military power. Moscow has tended to see military power as only one element in its foreign policy. It sees itself as having attained at best parity with the United States whose allies (Western Europe, Japan, China, and Latin America) are vastly stronger than Soviet allies (Eastern Europe). Alexander Dallin has aptly summarized the changes since Stalin:

> The quarter century since Stalin's death has seen a substantial increase in Soviet power—economic, military and political—along with evidence of serious strains and failures; considerably heightened professionalization and competence in the conduct of public policy, but also pockets of serious and disfunctional rigidities and bureaucratic irrationality; international assertiveness and involvement but also a measure of restraint in Soviet conduct abroad.[3]

Finally, our analysis shows that in both cases where the Soviet Union intervened, it seriously misjudged the extent and nature of the opposition to the invasion. Relying on information from the KGB and conservative elements inside Czechoslovakia, the Soviet leaders expected the Czech Politburo to oust Dubcek and install a pro-Soviet Indra government with popular support. All these expectations soon proved wrong. After the invasion, the party rallied around Dubcek and showed widespread passive resistance to the Soviet forces. Thus, after having arrested Dubcek and telling him that he would have to stand trial for treason, the Soviets then had to release him and reinstate him in power until April 1969. Similarly in Afghanistan the Soviets expected the Khalqs and Parchamites to fuse into one party, Karmal to unify the army behind him, and moderate reform measure (together with scapegoating Amin) to undercut the Moslem rebels. But none of this materialized. The Khalqs and Parchamites continued to feud, the army disintegrated, and reforms failed to gain support for the Karmal regime. And, more importantly, the Soviet army failed to crush the rebels. Indeed, much of its weaponry—as T–72 tanks and SAM missile batteries—proved singularly irrelevant and had to be withdrawn.

Interestingly, the threat of intervention seemed to be as efficacious as intervention itself. Under threat of intervention, the Chinese in 1969 agreed to start serious border negotiations with the Soviets and the Israelis in 1973 agreed to a cease-fire. While the Czech invasion in 1968 achieved its aims (but at a higher cost than anticipated), the Soviet invasion of Afghanistan is still bogged down.

From our case studies we can deduce the basic priorities of Soviet decision makers. Apart from the obvious need to defend the homeland from attack, the highest priority is given to the maintenance of Soviet control of Eastern Europe. Conceded by the West to be in the Soviet sphere of influence, Eastern Europe formed the German invasion corridor to Russia in two world wars. The security of Eastern Europe is seen as close to identical with the security of the Soviet Union. Given the inauthenticity of Communist regimes in the area, the Soviet Union will permit only limited deviations from Soviet domestic and foreign policy. This formed the justification for Soviet invasions of Hungary in 1956 and Czechoslovakia in 1968 and pressure on General Jaruzelski to declare martial law in Poland in 1981.

A second high priority has been to avoid military confrontation with the West, and especially the United States. The Soviet Union has a healthy respect for Western technology and U.S. military power. It strongly wishes to avoid military confrontations which could trigger a nuclear holocaust that would wipe out massive Soviet gains at home and abroad in the 69 years since the October Revolution. The invasions of Afghanistan and Czechoslovakia could safely be carried out without fear of Western military response. The same could not be said of actions against China or Israel. Interestingly, Western European reactions count for far less than U.S. reaction.

A third key priority has been the pursuit of benefits from East-West cooperation. Détente promised to provide tangible economic benefits for the Soviet economy through capital and high technology transfers. Militarily there was the promise of SALT treaties to cap the arms races and provide recognition of equality between the two superpowers. Politically there would be recognition of 1945 borders and the centrality of Soviet-U.S. relations. The achievement of these benefits would limit Soviet risk-taking in China and the Middle East. The demise of detente would help promote intervention in Afghanistan.

Our projected feasibility studies on the possible invasions showed a consistent conservative pattern of intervention only in cases with high benefits and low costs. In Czechoslovakia the analysis projected a viable conservative regime under Indra, low economic costs of occupation, and an easy military conquest with the help of a passive Czech army. In Afghanistan the analysis foresaw a popular Karmal regime, low economic costs, and swift military conquest of small, divided, and primitively armed rebel groups. By contrast, in China the predictions for a nuclear strike or ground assault involved very high economic costs, sizable military losses, and no possible puppet regime. In the Middle East, too, the analysis foresaw high economic costs, low political costs, and very considerable military risk. Overall, then, the Soviets displayed a highly rational and conservative style of decision making.

We now turn to an analysis of six Soviet intervention decisions with regard to revolutionary movements in or on the periphery of their sphere of influence. These decisions, which resulted in three positive and three negative decisions, should help clarify answers to the basic questions posed in the introductory chapter.

Notes

1. See the article by Seweryn Bialer and Alexander Dallin in Bialer's edited work, *The Domestic Context of Soviet Foreign Policy* (Boulder, CO: Westview Press, 1979).

2. For books see Hannes Adomeit, *Soviet Risk Taking and Crisis Behavior* (London: Allen and Unwin, 1982); Jiri Valenta, *Soviet Intervention in Czechoslovakia 1968* (Baltimore: Johns Hopkins University Press, 1979); and Karen Dawisha, *The Kremlin and the Prague Spring* (Berkeley: University of California Press, 1984).

3. See Alexander Dallin, "The Domestic Sources of Soviet Foreign Policy," in *The Domestic Context of Soviet Foreign Policy,* ed. Seweryn Bialer (Boulder, CO: Westview Press, 1979), pp. 335–408.

11　THE SOVIET-YUGOSLAV CONFLICT

Alex N. Dragnich

As we approach the fortieth anniversary of the Stalin-Tito break, we can say that we know a great deal about it. While the Soviet documents (apart from those published by Yugoslavia) are not available, documents for that period have been declassified. The Yugoslavs, including some of the participants, have written much about the subject. Yet one of Tito's close associates at the time, Milovan Djilas, who devotes a large part of his latest book to the confrontation with the Soviet Union, asserts that it "has not yet been properly described or explained. Numerous mysteries remain, not so much factual as psychological and ideological."[1] Consequently, those of us who are convinced of the adequacy of our knowledge concerning the matter, should take heed. At the same time, it is possible to say that Djilas has provided us with some additional information and new insights.

Prelude to the Break

Prior to the actual break in June 1948, no one seems to have thought that such an event was even possible. No less a Marxist theoretician than the Soviet oracle Nikolai Bukharin declared in 1936 that rivalry between Communist states was "by definition an impossibility." Capitalist society, he said, was "made up of selfish and competing national units and therefore is by definition a world at war. Communist society will be made up of unselfish and harmonious units and therefore will be by definition a world at peace."[2]

I am grateful for a short-term grant from the Kennan Institute of the Woodrow Wilson International Center that enabled me to consult sources in the Washington, D.C., area.

The creation of other Communist-ruled states after World War II, however, represented a new situation. The Comintern had been abolished in 1943, but in 1947 a new organization, the Cominform, was created, whose presumed purpose was the exchange of information among Communist parties. Stalin viewed it more as an instrument that would deliver directives from Moscow. Belgrade was chosen as the headquarters of the Cominform. In the wake of the Stalin-Tito split, some speculated that the choice of Belgrade was a way of effectively watching over Tito, although Djilas does not believe this to have been the motive.[3]

To be sure, Stalin had experienced troubles with Yugoslav Communists, and many of them perished in his Great Purges, including General Secretaries Sima Markovic and Milan Gorkic (party name of Josip Cizinski). For a time Stalin even seriously considered dissolving the Yugoslav party. In 1937, Josip Broz-Tito ("Walter") was sent to Yugoslavia by Stalin as general secretary of the Yugoslav Communist Party. Although Tito's role in the purge of his comrades in the Soviet Union is unclear there is little doubt that he had Stalin's confidence.

And in early 1948, to the outside world at least, it seemed that Stalin had not made a mistake. Domestically, Tito had set about organizing Yugoslavia on the Soviet model, politically, economically, socially, and culturally. Similarly, in foreign policy, in Eastern Europe Yugoslavia was the most vocal defender of the Soviet Union and a bitter critic of the West. At sessions of the United Nations General Assembly Yugoslav delegates were more vicious than Moscow representatives in their attacks on the United States.

Tito's Crimes

But Stalin wanted to dominate Yugoslav domestic and foreign policy. He wanted to engage in an advance review of Yugoslavia's proposed domestic and foreign policy actions. When the Yugoslav leaders resisted and showed their determination to follow some independent paths, Stalin addressed a number of critical letters to them in early 1948. When the answers to these were deemed unsatisfactory, Tito and his colleagues were asked to appear at a meeting of Cominform leaders, who would discuss the Yugoslavs' heresy. Tito's refusal to heed the summons forced Stalin's hand. Consequently, on June 28, 1948, the famous Cominform Resolution, denouncing the Yugoslav leaders and in fact excommunicating them from the "Communist family," was made public.[4]

What were Tito's crimes and how did Stalin seek to punish him? The Cominform Resolution heavily accented ideological issues. It charged that the Yugoslav party had relinquished its leadership role by dissolving itself into the Peoples' Front, that it had taken the road of nationalism, that it had failed to collectivize agriculture, and that its leaders were conceited and immodest, unwilling to admit their mistakes and engage in self-criticism. The Yugoslavs denied all.

In reality, however, Tito's crimes were not ideological, but political and economic. Stalin wanted to exploit Yugoslavia and keep it a producer of raw materials. Vladimir Dedijer argues that Stalin wanted to control all Yugoslav institutions—army, party, economy, transport, and the Yugoslav secret police—"in short everything." Moreover, he says that Stalin was prepared to subjugate Yugoslavia as early as 1944.[5]

Another of Tito's crimes, although less specifically spelled out by the Soviets, was in the international arena. First, Tito sought to make himself a second center of communism (perhaps even more after the eventual death of Stalin). Certainly, Tito was shooting for primacy among Balkan Communists, which Stalin was not willing to tolerate. Second, Tito became an embarrassment to Stalin, in view of the latter's agreement with Churchill about spheres of influence in the Balkans, including the 50–50 deal with respect to Yugoslavia. Stalin may have even tolerated Tito's independent actions in the Balkans so long as he worked for Moscow, but when Stalin realized that Tito was working for himself he (Tito) had to go. It could be argued that Tito's sins in the international field were more offensive to Stalin than Tito's resistance to attempted Soviet domination inside Yugoslavia.

In the years since 1948 various Yugoslav writers have pointed out that the Yugoslav Communists had experienced difficulties with the Soviets during World War II. Soon after attaining power, the Yugoslavs discovered that a Soviet film crew that came to Yugoslavia to make a movie of Tito's wartime Partisan struggle was used to recruit Yugoslavs into Soviet intelligence and to infiltrate the art world. Parenthetically, it might be noted that the film crew produced a movie that placed Tito in a subordinate role both in the plot and in history.[6]

Frictions between the Soviets and the Yugoslavs first arose, says Milovan Djilas, between the two secret services and the two propaganda services. Soviet recruiting of Yugoslavs, "especially Communists in sensitive positions, became aggressive and systematic," he says, and quotes Tito as saying: "A spy network is something we will not tolerate." Djilas also reports that Russian brides of Yugoslav officers and officials almost invariably turned out to be Soviet intelligence agents.[7] And he says that the Soviets went about recruiting agents among the Russians who had come to Yugoslavia after the Bolshevik seizure of power, and even among the children who had been born and reared in Yugoslavia.

Reflecting on the conflict, Milovan Djilas has said that the roots of the conflict lay in the Yugoslav leaders feeling of "being an independent power . . . a distinct political entity," while the roots of Soviet policy toward Yugoslavia "lay deep in the dictatorial structure of the Soviet state. . . .[8] Elsewhere he has written that the Soviet-Yugoslav conflict was one of a "small country with an expansionist world power."[9] In his view of Stalin, Djilas went through an extraordinary transformation, from looking upon Stalin as "infallible and sinless" to "the greatest criminal in history."[10]

Soviet Actions Against Tito

In the months following the Moscow-Belgrade break, the Soviets launched a many-pronged attack on Titoist Yugoslavia. Stalin's first move, expressed in the Cominform Resolution, was to call upon the "healthy" elements in the Yugoslav party to compel the leaders to recognize their mistake and to rectify them. In the past Stalin had been able to purge leaders of Communist parties. His confidence can perhaps be best exemplified by his statement to Nikita Khrushchev: "I will shake my little finger and there will be no more Tito. He will fall."[11] Stalin simply forgot that the Communist party leaders he had purged in the past lacked the power base possessed by Tito.

The second of Stalin's many-pronged attacks involved unsuccessful efforts to eliminate Tito and his close comrades. He was slow in launching this part of his campaign. Before much real damage could be done, the Yugoslavs had ousted and arrested the two members of their Politburo who had Soviet sympathies—Sretan Zujovic and Andrija Hebrang—as well as a number of lesser figures. They were merciless with pro-Stalin elements. The bulk of the known or suspected Stalinists, numbering perhaps 12,000 people, ended up on an island in the northern Adriatic known as Goli Otok (naked island). Others escaped abroad while a few were killed.[12]

Moreover, not all went smoothly for "the top leadership was unclear as to how far the Soviet government and its vassal states would carry their attacks," "slow to recognize Moscow's intentions," and "the confusion and hesitation of prominent officials had a disastrous impact on the stunned and uncertain lower functionaries and regular party members." Moreover, "pro-Soviet naivete and ideological blindness lulled our vigilance. . . . Even we at the top did not immediately grasp what dark, unpredictable dangers lay in wait for us and our nation."[13]

The aforementioned Moscow film crew had recruited Tito's bodyguard, who remained in that post until 1950. Djilas believes that Soviet intelligence was unable to induce him to commit murder, perhaps because he was not convinced that Tito was abandoning communism.[14] Vladimir Dedijer reports that in the East European Department of the Yugoslav Foreign Office "more than 20 [Soviet] agents were discovered during the first two years of the struggle," and "all confessed."[15]

More serious, which Djilas reports in his latest book, is that "even in Tito's proximity, among the employees who worked with him daily, there were Soviet agents, whom we had to remove gradually, without attracting attention." What is more, they discovered among Tito's bodyguards "officers who planned to wipe out the Politburo with automatic rifles as they were relaxing over billiards in Tito's villa" in Belgrade. Djilas does not say when the would-be assassins were discovered or what happened to them. He does say that this discovery was not publicized even among the inner party circle, "lest it create a sense of insecurity and . . . undermine the leadership's cult of invulnerability."[16]

The third of Stalin's actions against Yugoslavia was a type of economic blockade. Titoist Yugoslavia had oriented its trade to the East. The Soviet Union and the other Eastern European countries reneged on their trade commitments, and the treaties of friendship and mutual assistance were canceled. Interestingly enough this was not done until more than a year after the formal break. Perhaps because only then did the Soviets realize that the initial measures were not succeeding. Moreover, not long after the denunciation of these treaties came a new Cominform Resolution, condemning Tito as a Fascist spy in the pay of and controlled by the Western imperialist bloc. It was also in late 1949 that the two Soviet-Yugoslav joint companies (Danube navigation and civil air service) were liquidated. It was also late in 1949 that there was a mutual expulsion of many diplomats, but there were no breaks in diplomatic relations.

Traditionally, the countries of Western Europe had been Yugoslavia's normal trading partners, which under the circumstances was fortunate, but nevertheless a time of adjustment was needed. There were instances of economic sabotage by Cominform states, some of which were reported in the Yugoslav press and privately admitted by no less a person than Tito. After the initial shock, Yugoslavia was able to adjust. The quick action of the United States in unfreezing some $30 million in gold, which the prewar Yugoslav government had managed to move to New York in 1939 in the belief that an Axis attack was a distinct possibility, was of considerable assistance.

Too, Tito received additional U.S. economic aid, directly and through facilitating loans from the World Bank. In January 1949 the United States modified the application of export controls as they affected Yugoslavia, and in June limits on civil aviation were lifted. In July, the United States approved the export of a steel mill, even though the U.S. military establishment was opposed. In September, the Export-Import Bank gave Yugoslavia a $20 million credit and in December an agreement between Yugoslavia and the United States on reciprocal exchange of civil aviation rights was signed.[17]

It should be noted in passing that some Yugoslavs, notably Dedijer, have charged that the West (United States especially) used the Stalin-Tito quarrel to force a settlement of property claims and in other ways sought to lay down such conditions as would actually continue the plunder of Yugoslavia. Such allegations are manifestly untrue. The general outlines of the agreement on property settlements had been agreed upon on June 11, 1948, that is, before the Cominform Resolution.

Another aspect of Stalin's campaign against Yugoslavia was psychological warfare. Various pro-Soviet Yugoslav organizations sprang up in Eastern Europe, engaging in a propaganda war, border incidents, and terrorist incursions inside Yugoslavia. Dedijer says that in the years 1948–50, there were 5,000 border incidents.[18] Moscow constituted a new leadership for the Communist party of Yugoslavia, along with publishing large numbers of anti-Tito newspapers. There were also military troop movements near Yugoslavia's borders. By the end of 1949, the U.S. embassy in Belgrade was convinced that neither these actions nor the economic ones would succeed.[19]

A fifth part of Stalin's many-pronged campaign against Yugoslavia was a series of purge trials of Communist leaders in Eastern Europe, so as to prevent defections similar to Tito's. The most important of these, organized in Moscow, were the ones in Sofia, Budapest, and Prague, as well as lesser ones in Tirana, Warsaw, and Bucharest.

A final part of Stalin's campaign against Titoist Yugoslavia, a military invasion, was apparently called off after extensive planning. According to Hungarian General Bela K. Kiraly, the Soviets had designed a plan to invade Yugoslavia. He reports that in the summer of 1949 he was designated supreme commander of the troops Hungary would field against Yugoslavia at a time to be decided by the Soviet Union. He says that they war-gamed the plan in Budapest in January 1951, and that they were told that Albanian, Bulgarian, and Rumanian forces would attack Yugoslavia from their territories, and that Polish and Czechoslovak contingents would also participate.[20]

Kiraly asserts that their war games demonstrated that the military preparations to attack and eliminate Titoist Yugoslavia were ready. The question remains why the attack was never launched. Kiraly maintains that two factors were decisive. First, there was a purging of the Hungarian strategic leadership, charged with being Tito's stooges and promptly executed. Kiraly himself was imprisoned. Second, he says, North Korea launched the war against South Korea exactly when the Soviet bloc in Europe was ready to initiate the aggression against Yugoslavia. Kiraly is convinced that had not the United States and the United Nations intervened in Korea, the attack on Yugoslavia would have begun in the fall of 1950 or the spring of 1951 at the latest.[21] It should be noted also that the United States supported the Yugoslav-sponsored UN resolution that criticized the Soviet campaign against Yugoslavia. Also important, in the opinion of Djilas, were the September 1949 statements of the United

States and British foreign secretaries that put Moscow on notice that an attack on Yugoslavia would have serious consequences.[22]

Vladimir Dedijer says that Moscow had made a decision in principle to invade Yugoslavia, but that differences among Kremlin leaders as to the strategic and political consequences of a determined Yugoslav resistance resulted in inaction.[23] It is interesting to note that the United States, while aware of Soviet bloc troop movements on Yugoslavia's borders, concluded in September 1949 that such moves were in the nature of psychological warfare. The considered U.S. judgment was that "the Soviet Government is not likely to risk a direct military attack on Yugoslavia. . . ." Even should Soviet military action take place, the United States was convinced that it would not be of brief duration.[24]

In the long run the impact of the decision not to intervene militarily in Yugoslavia was seemingly to develop contingency plans for decisive intervention in certain Communist-ruled countries if Moscow believed that the Communist order was threatened. The cases of Hungary in 1956, Czechoslovakia in 1968, and Afghanistan in 1979 would seem to bear this out. Had General Jaruzelski failed to cope with the threat to the Communist order in Poland, Soviet intervention would probably have followed. On the other hand, intervention in China and Albania seems to have been excluded, but there was no real threat to the Communist order in either one of them.

It bears repeating that Communist rule was not threatened in Yugoslavia either. Tito held himself to be a faithful Communist. But even he thought that Communist rule was threatened in Hungary in 1956. According to what Vladimir Dedijer told Cyrus Sulzberger of the *New York Times*, "Tito had failed to help the Hungarians . . . because he feared a successful revolt in Budapest might have spread into Yugoslavia," which "would either have threatened to overthrow the entrenched, privileged class now ruling Yugoslavia or have doomed it to a new subservience to Russia. . . ."[25]

Additional Factors in Tito's Success

The astuteness of U.S. policy (supported by the British) needs emphasis. First of all the United States was convinced from the outset that the split with Moscow was real. Second, while U.S. policy makers would have preferred the overthrow of communism in Yugoslavia, they concluded that under existing circumstances there were only two possible outcomes: victory of pro-Moscow elements or Tito's success in staying in power. Consequently, the United States preferred the second alternative, despite its unhappiness with the oppressive nature of the Tito regime. Therefore, the main question was how to assist Tito in his struggle for independence from Moscow. The way chosen was a patient receptiveness to Yugoslav request for aid, without any seeming eagerness to embrace Tito, because such an eagerness would have provided the Soviets a propaganda peg, while at the same time possibly adding to Tito's difficulties within his own party.

Moreover, the U.S. embassy in Belgrade was convinced that Tito's prospects for success were good, and that "nothing short of Soviet-supported armed insurrection or open invasion can presently dislodge Tito . . . Stalin cannot oust him quickly without war."[26]

Milovan Djilas is simply wrong when he writes that Western diplomatic sources anticipated the swift fall of the Yugoslav regime, and the victory of a pro-Soviet team, at least insofar as the U.S. embassy was concerned.[27] The U.S. embassy in Moscow, while less optimistic about the prospects for Tito's survival than its counterpart in Belgrade, nevertheless believed that there was very little likelihood at this time of direct overt Soviet action.[28]

Consequently, the U.S. position meant that the West stood ready to provide assistance to Tito, including military aid, should he request it. Moreover, the U.S. embassy in Belgrade was convinced that evidence of Western readiness to support Yugoslavia as a United Nations member would influence the Soviets.[29]

At the same time, the United States hoped that in the long run the Yugoslav regime would evolve in the direction of democracy. Yet U.S. policy makers concluded that any effort in the short run to impose political conditions on aid would be futile. While following a policy of seeking to keep Tito afloat, however, the United States did not attempt to conceal the fact that the Tito regime was a Communist dictatorship. On the other hand the

> character of the regime would . . . stand in the way of a normal development of economic relations between Yugoslavia and this country. . . . If the Yugoslavs should demonstrate a wish to establish better relations with the West, this Government would not stand in the way.[30]

In the more than a year that elapsed following the break, the United States did not observe any appreciable rise in Tito's popularity at home or in the acceptance of the Communist system. There were "no illusions as to the nature of the present regime . . . which is both totalitarian and Communist." And "the best that we can hope from Tito is crafty self interest in playing both sides. . . . " Moreover, "Yugoslavia is still a totalitarian dictatorship led by men who have constantly followed, and so far continue to follow, an anti-U.S. policy."[31]

Another factor operating in Tito's favor was that the Soviet Union in 1948 was beset with numerous problems. The war had weakened the country seriously, and Lend-Lease aid had stopped abruptly when President Truman realized that Stalin was not going to abide by the wartime agreements concerning Eastern Europe. Moreover, U.S. aid to Greece and Turkey and the Marshall Plan to insure recovery of Western Europe were launched before the Stalin-Tito break, clear evidence that the United States was determined to resist Soviet expansionism. In addition, the United States possessed the atom bomb and the Soviet Union did not.

Still another factor that enabled Tito to survive was his command of the party membership for the most part recently recruited and little informed about Marxism. Except for Zujovic and Hebrang, and some lesser figures, there was continuity in the leadership of the party. Moreover, the knowledge of Soviet economic exploitative tactics, as well as efforts to recruit Moscow spies, were known to a significant degree among party and government workers.

In addition, Tito profited from support—some would say nonopposition—among the non-Communist masses. As in the popular mind, the Tito regime was identified with the Russians, any trouble in the Soviet camp was gleefully welcome. In those days, many anti-Communist Yugoslavs greeted me with "Long Live Tito!" But they hastened to add that they believed the break would speed the end of world communism. Red Army soldiers, by their behavior in Yugoslavia in 1944–45, nullified most of the historic pro-Russian feelings of the Yugoslavs, especially among the Serbs. According to Vladimir Dedijer, there were 1,219 rapes, 359 attempted rapes, 111 rapes with murder.[32]

Some have argued that Tito's success could be attributed to the fact that Tito and his comrades won power by themselves. The Yugoslav regime certainly sought to exploit this contention, but there is a danger in overestimating this as a reason. A persistent Soviet criticism of the Yugoslav leaders has been that they failed to acknowledge Soviet assistance in their path to power. Additionally, a Soviet historian has written that when Soviet troops first crossed into Yugoslavia they met not Tito's Partisans but the troops of Drazha Mihailovich, the leader of the other resistance movement in Yugoslavia.[33] Milovan Djilas now admits that the role of the Red Army was crucial as the Partisans could not have liberated Serbia and Belgrade without the Red Army, even with the 100 tanks that the Soviets had given them.[34] At the same time, Djilas writes: ". . . right up to the end of the war the Russians had been so far away that their agents could not even be brought in by plane."[35]

Finally, some analysts would argue that although he survived, Tito really failed, in the sense that no other Eastern European country (aside possibly from Albania's later actions) followed his example. In short, the "Titoist disease" did not spread. Moreover, these analysts would contend that subsequent developments in Hungary, Czechoslovakia, and Poland should not be viewed as Titoist, because these regimes were never pro-

Soviet in the way that Yugoslavia was. To a degree it could be said that they were precursors of Eurocommunism, a concept Tito never favored. In addition, Tito's harsh treatment of the Cominformists demonstrated that basically he was another ruthless Stalin. Be that as it may, it can be argued that Tito also failed in that he disappointed those who expected him to democratize Yugoslavia.

Conclusion

The foregoing is based on the sources available to me, but we cannot tell what additional materials may be forthcoming in the future, especially if Soviet archives ever see the light of day. It is fascinating to go back to another Djilas statement: "It is very difficult—impossible, in my opinion—to date the outbreak and list the causes of the Soviet-Yugoslav confrontation. Divergences began during the war. But our sense of intimate association with Moscow also stemmed from that period. . . ."[36]

Elsewhere he has written that "from our very first contact with Soviet officials and the Red Army in 1944—I had entertained doubts about Stalin and the Soviet system and wondered whether action can ever really coincide with principle."[37] Yet, as if to go back to their "not guilty" pleas of 1948, Djilas asserts "that not a single party leader was anti-Soviet—not before the war, not during, not after."[38] Even so, it seems reasonable to believe that the broad outlines of the conflict, as well as much of the detail, are not fairly evident. The only remaining question, it seems to me, is one of emphasis.

Finally, the available evidence concerning Soviet decision making with respect to Yugoslavia in the period under consideration suggests that Stalin was the decision maker. In retrospect it is interesting to note the views of Rumania's Ana Pauker soon after the break, when she said that if Stalin had known that he would meet defiance he would not have uttered the criticism against the Yugoslav leaders, but "would have done the business in another way."[39] But she did not hint what this would have been. It may also be instructive to cite the observation of Veljko Micunovic, like Djilas a one-time worshipper of Stalin, after twice serving as Yugoslavia's ambassador to Moscow: "The Russians regard Eastern Europe as their own internal affair and, to judge from all the evidence, they will not need anybody's approval, and certainly not the Yugoslavs', for any solutions they may decide on."[40]

Notes

1. Milovan Djilas, *Rise and Fall* (New York: Harcourt Brace Jovanovich, 1985), p. 234. This book was originally published in Serbo-Croatian in 1983 in Lon-

don under the title *Vlast* (power). This book is heavily cited in this chapter since he was a participant in these events and because in his latest book he reports a number of items about Soviet-Yugoslav relations that have not been reported elsewhere.

2. In an interview with Hamilton Fish Armstrong, *Tito and Goliath* (New York: Macmillan, 1951), p. ix.

3. Djilas, *Rise and Fall*, p. 138. A cogent summary of the main Yugoslav developments, from the inauguration of Stalinism to the post-Tito crisis, is to be found in Milorad M. Drachkovitch, ed., *East Central Europe; Yesterday, Today, Tomorrow* (Stanford, Ca.: Hoover Institution Press, 1982), pp. 349–98. The first two books dealing with the Stalin-Tito split are: Armstrong, *Tito and Goliath,* and Adam B. Ulam, *Titoism and the Cominform* (Cambridge, Mass.: Harvard University Press, 1952). For a more recent Yugoslav study, see Cedomir Strbac, *Judoslavija i odnosi izmedju socijalisickih zemalja: Sukob KPJ sa Informbiroom* (Belgrade, 1975). See also my article, "Tito withstands Russian Domination," *Current History* 23 (July 1952), pp. 23–27.

4. The texts of the pertinent documents may be found in *The Soviet-Yugoslav Dispute* (London: Royal Institute of International Affairs, 1948). For an excellent and vivid account of the circumstances surrounding the U.S. Belgrade embassy's prediction of the break, by one of the participants, see Charles G. Stefan, "The Emergence of the Soviet-Yugoslav Break: A Personal View from the Belgrade Embassy," *Diplomatic History* 6 (Fall 1982), pp. 387–404.

5. Vladimir Dedijer, *Novi prilozi za biografiju Josipa Broz Tita* (Zagreb, 1980), I, pp. 407, 409.

6. Djilas, *Rise and Fall*, pp. 78–79.

7. See ibid., pp. 83–85, 226.

8. Ibid., pp. 83–89 and 186.

9. Milovan Djilas, "Nacionalni problemi Jugoslavije danas," *Nasa rec* (London) (March 1985), p. 709.

10. Milovan Djilas, *Conversations with Stalin* (New York: Harcourt, Brace and World, 1962), pp. 57 and 187.

11. Nikita S. Khrushchev, *Khrushchev Remembers* (Boston: Little, Brown, 1970), p. 600.

12. Djilas, *Rise and Fall*, p. 245. He adds that Goli Otak "was the darkest and most shameful fact of the history of Yugoslav communism . . . worse than that, it was an unimaginable humiliation."

13. Ibid., pp. 209–10, 226–27.

14. Ibid., pp. 80–81.

15. Vladimir Dedijer, *The Battle Stalin Lost* (New York: Viking Press, 1971), p. 199.

16. Djilas, *Rise and Fall*, pp. 227–33.

17. See *Foreign Relations of the United States, 1949,* vol. 5, pp. 75–76; 209–20; 863–68; 905; 914; 946.

18. Dedijer, *The Battle Stalin Lost,* p. 278.

19. *Foreign Relations of the United States,* 1949, vol. 5, p. 982.

20. See his chapter in Wayne S. Vucinich, ed., *At the Brink of War and Peace: The Tito-Stalin Split in a Historic Perspective* (New York: Brooklyn College Press, 1982), pp. 273–88. See also map of supposed Soviet operational plan against Yugoslavia (1949–51), ibid., p. xii.

21. Ibid., pp. 285, 286.

22. Djilas, *Rise and Fall*, p. 259.

23. Dedijer, *The Battle Stalin Lost*, p. 279.

24. *Foreign Relations of the United States, 1949*, vol. 5, 945–48.

25. Cyrus Sulzberger, *The Resistantialists* (New York: Harper and Brothers, 1962), p. 106. This book was withdrawn before formal publication, but some copies are available. Ten years later the book was published under the title, *Unconquered Souls: The Resistantialists* (Woodstock, N.Y.: Overlook Press, 1973), p. 182. In the latter edition, the author explains that legal problems with letters from Ernest Hemingway and Dedijer's protests and fears prompted him to suspend publication of the book in 1962. In the 1973 version a number of direct quotes from Dedijer have been dropped, and now appear as Sulzberger's own interpretations of Dedijer's positions!

26. *Foreign Relations of the United States, 1948*, vol. 4, pp. 1078–84.

27. Djilas, *Rise and Fall*, p. 204.

28. *Foreign Relations of the United States, 1948*, vol. 4, pp. 1082–84.

29. Top secret cable, July 1, 1948, Decimal Files, Department of State, National Archives, 860h.00/3048.

30. Circular telegram, June 30, 1948, from the Secretary of State to diplomatic missions, Decimal Files, Department of State, National Archives, 860h.00/6–3048.

31. See *Foreign Relations of the United States, 1949*, vol. 5 (Secretary Acheson to Secretary of Defense Johnson), p. 916; (President Truman to National Security Council, December 8, 1949), p. 49; (Department of State Policy Statement, September 1, 1949), p. 942.

32. Dedijer, *Novi prilozi az biografiju Josipa Broz Tita*, I, pp. 410–11.

33. I.S. Girenko, *Sovietsko-Jugoslavskie otnoshenia* (Moscow, 1983), p. 93.

34. Milovan Djilas, *Wartime* (New York: Harcourt Brace Jovanovich, 1977), p. 406.

35. Djilas, *Rise and Fall*, p. 78.

36. Ibid., p. 82.

37. Ibid., p. 69.

38. Ibid.

39. Conversation between Pauker and British ambassador to Belgrade, Charles Peake (Peake's letter to Charles Bohlen, 10 August 1948). Decimal Files, Department of State, National Archives, 760h.61/8–2448.

40. *Moscow Diary* (New York: Doubleday, 1980), p. 32.

12 THE HUNGARIAN CRISIS OF 1956: THE SOVIET DECISION

Condoleezza Rice and Michael Fry

The 1956 Hungarian crisis provides a rich body of data for the study of political, economic, and military phenomena within the Soviet bloc. In the political sphere, the crisis was a test of Soviet foreign policy, a case of possible bloc dissolution, and an exercise in client-sponsor state relations. Hungarian government policy in the crisis was a testimony both to the need to legitimize itself and to secure the economic and political regeneration of a Communist system. Issues of civil-military interaction permeated the crisis. These problems are perennially important given the frequent upheavals which the Soviet bloc has experienced, and continues to witness. Some of these themes have been examined in the substantial body of literature on the crisis but others merit further examination. This study will analyze the Soviet decision as a discrete problem, and thereby contribute also both to the literature on the Hungarian crisis itself and on the nature of Soviet crisis decision making.[1]

The leadership in Moscow took decisions in circumstances of acute strain, over a limited period of time from October to November 1956, and under considerable pressure. The Soviet leadership had to decide if and how to involve itself in the Hungarian revolt, in the immediate wake of the Polish crisis. The actual stability of the Soviet bloc was involved; the stakes were thus very high. Furthermore, decisions were taken during a period of collective leadership, historically a period of high tension in Soviet domestic politics, when the tribulations of the elite were more in evidence and even exposed. Yet a fundamental analytical problem remains. Soviet decisions, not unlike those of the British Commonwealth,

Previously published as "The Hungarian Crisis of 1956: The Soviet Decision" by Michael Fry and Condoleezza Rice, *Studies in Comparative Communism, 16,* no. 12 (Spring-Summer, 1983). Reprinted by permission.

are presented to the world with a common voice and united front. Doctrinal insistence upon monolithic unity, in the Soviet case, masks divisions of opinion. Consequently, there is little evidence that options are considered, that coalitions form around issues, that certain leaders actually waiver, and others fervently oppose the course of action ultimately preferred. Only after leaders are deposed, and even then rarely, does evidence of a certain kind emerge on dissent. Memoranda and minutes, reports and ripostes, are unavailable.

During periods of collective leadership, however, one can more certainly document the existence of factions and coalitions, even if one is unable definitively to identify membership. Several studies of collective leadership suggest that relatively thinly veiled struggles between coalitions of individuals, reaching, in a pyramidal fashion, for the power of the deposed or deceased leader, regularly occur. In the Soviet case, the loss of a central, dominant person results in the process, which itself indicates possible identification with errant options can be disastrous for individuals or coalitions.

Finally, Soviet decision making took place in an international environment of great fluidity and extraordinary tension; the second postwar Middle Eastern crisis coincided exactly with the Hungarian revolt. Clearly, the coincidence of the two crises is important and provides not only an opportunity to examine the connections between them, but also provides additional evidence from which to evaluate Soviet decisions. For those who acknowledge that examinations of Soviet decision making are of necessity exercises as much in extrapolation and deduction as in textual analysis, this is a welcome situation.

The Setting

The Soviet invasion of Hungary on 4 November 1956 was a dramatic and drastic step, the ultimate form of interference in the affairs of a bloc-member state. Military invasion against a ruling Communist party was an option to which Stalin had never resorted and one which the Soviet leadership had shunned in Poland only a few months earlier. The context of this decision is therefore not without its significance.

In the wake of the death of Stalin, Georgii Malenkov's New Course and Nikita Khrushchev's secret speech of February 1956 had thrown the Soviet bloc into a state of turmoil. The changing political fortunes within the Kremlin oligarchy and the resultant gyrations in Soviet bloc policy set in motion forces within the satellite countries which East European leaders could not control. Malenkov's New Course prompted the reemergence of many of the victims of the postwar purges, most notably, Imre Nagy in Hungary and Wladyslaw Gomulka in Poland. Power struggles within the East European Communist parties resulted. The sudden presence of the victims of the old system, in combination with discussion of the economic and political excesses of earlier times, threatened the very bases of the power of the Stalinists. While the Soviets watched and in most cases acquiesced, they were forced to allow the political resurgence of their domestic enemies, and permit a reassessment of political and economic policies. Then, Malenkov's fall in the USSR weakened the leaders of the New Course in Eastern Europe, and initiated a renewed struggle for control of the respective Communist parties.

The situation was complicated further by attempts to legalize and reinforce Soviet-East European bloc relations. A system of multilateral organizations, most importantly COMECON and the Warsaw Pact, replaced the long-standing, bilateral Soviet-East European treaties. Soviet dominance and even terror were to be replaced, at least oratorically, by a brotherhood of socialist states joined in equality and harmony.

By 1956, this new Soviet policy bred serious complications, first in Poland and then in Hungary. The Soviet Union eventually acquiesced in the Polish course of action, under Gomulka. The Poles gained considerable freedom in domestic affairs, while leaving the matter of foreign and defense policy firmly under Soviet control. Konstantin Rokossovsky, the Soviet military leader acting as Poland's defense minister, was, however, recalled.

Events in Hungary took an entirely different course. On 4 July 1953, Matyas Rakosi had given up the premiership to Imre Nagy, but retained the position of first secretary of the Communist party. Rakosi had suffered from the political results of the death of Stalin and continued to be undermined by the attacks on Stalinism. Nagy instituted a broad reform program out of conviction: a change of emphasis from heavy industry to the production of consumer goods; attempts to reduce the economic strain and privation, and restrict the use of forced labor; agricultural policies with less emphasis on collectivization; a curtailing of repression and the powers of the secret police; the release of political prisoners; and attempts to foster a freer artistic, educational, and cultural atmosphere. These policies apparently did not offend Moscow. In February 1955, however, on the heels of Malenkov's fall in the Soviet Union, Nagy was expelled from the Politburo and the Central Committee, replaced by Andras Hegedus, and eventually thrown out of the party. The charge against him, as against Malenkov, was the neglect of heavy industry.

Rakosi could not, however, whatever his personal preferences, restore the status quo before Nagy. A return to Stalinist economic policies, to a police state, to censorship, and to a confrontation with the church, was not possible. Nor was it desired by Khrushchev in the light of his speech of February 1956 to the Twentieth Party Congress. The Nagy program, moreover, evolving toward a form of national communism, had popular support. In fact, Nagy had left an imprint not easily eased. He had laid down a concept of alternative economic, political, and cultural policies within the parameters set by Communist ideology and the seeming permanent reality of a Communist state. Moreover, his disagreement with Rakosi had spread out from elite circles into schools, universities, factories, and intellectual circles. Nagy had simulated an authentic politicization process which was not in essence a form of anticommunism, but a discussion of the nature and goals of the Communist system and of how to secure a purer and more virtuous form of communism. Nagy remained a Communist throughout the debate.

Rakosi, therefore, faced neither an easy situation, nor one which he understood fully. Solutions would not come easily—he could not simply crush dissent as he might have preferred. It became necessary, for example, to find scapegoats for the 1949 execution of Lazslo Rajk, charged with being an agent of the United States. The Rajk affair became something of a cause celebre, culminating in the state funeral of 6 October 1956. In the aftermath of the Poznan disturbances in June, Rakosi attempted to arrest Nagy and his associates and to reinstitute repressive measures, only to be opposed successfully by the Central Committee. In July, Khrushchev summoned Rakosi to Moscow. On his return, he confessed to errors, to being guilty of practicing the cult of personality. On 18 July, Rakosi resigned as first secretary of the party and was succeeded by Erno Gero.

The vital trends in Hungary were not reversed. Events in Poland seemed to stimulate greater unrest in Hungary, providing examples of and demonstrating the need for, an alliance between intellectuals and workers. A growing feeling of nationalism developed, focusing on the Nagy reforms. Destabilizing events in Hungary in effect cumulated and reached a climax late in October. On 14 October unrest rocked the universities; on 19 October the news of Gomulka's defiance of Khrushchev reverberated throughout Hungary.

The critical period lasted from 21 October to 4 November. Unrest and fighting in Budapest, particularly from 23 October, led Gero to call for Soviet military aid which was promptly rendered on 24 October. The presence of foreign troops, however, stirred anti-Soviet sentiment, worsened the unrest, and rapidly led, with Soviet agreement, to Gero's fall and the ascendancy from 24 October of Nagy and Janos Kadar. The Nagy government, calling for a cease-fire, from 24–28 October, promoted the withdrawal of Soviet troops, amnesty for freedom fighters, and far-reaching domestic political forms. On the morning of 29 October, following the armistice of the previous day, Soviet units began to leave Budapest, although the withdrawal was never completed and fighting continued on 30 October. Nagy formed a coalition government and offered a return to a multiparty system and free elections. Furthermore, steps were taken to create a military high command purged of Soviet influence and loyal to the revolution. Colonel Pal Maleter, a leader in the revolt, ultimately became defense minister. On 30 October the Soviet leadership dispatched Anastas Mikoyan and Mikhail Suslov for the second time in the crisis to Budapest[2] to begin negotiations on normalization, but Nagy's policy, seeking the neutralization of Hungary, began to gain momentum.[3] During the negotiations on the withdrawal of Soviet troops, between the Hungarian high command and the Soviet military delegation which lasted until 3 November, the Hungarian defense minister and delegation were arrested. Kadar, now head of the party in Hungary, who had defected on the night of 1 November and had broken with Nagy, returned to Hungary from Moscow on 3 November. A few hours later, at dawn on 4 November, Soviet troops attacked Budapest in strength; a full-scale invasion had begun.

Several important questions follows. Who made the decision to invade? Why did the Soviet Union forsake the "Polish option" and undertake such drastic measures? Was the Soviet leadership planning to invade Hungary as early as 23 October, or were they playing a waiting game, undecided, hoping that events would take a moderate turn? Was the leadership divided or united throughout the crisis on the proper course to be pursued in Hungary? In effect, how can one explain Soviet behavior?

Various approaches are possible. One can, for instance, suggest patterns of input and communication to the executive bodies which should have determined policy. Their role was probably diminished, however, in the critical days of the crisis, for responsibility for assessing the options open to the Soviet Union in the Hungarian situation gravitated to the highest levels of the oligarchy. This trend is neither surprising nor inexplicable. Crisis decisions are often taken by small groups, and frequently the normal policy-making hierarchy does not operate fully in such circumstances. The decision-making process circumvents that hierarchy in times of extreme emergency, leaving it responsible merely for collecting and filtering the information which reaches the executive group, and for establishing the context in which evidence is presented.

As the crisis worsened, the situation was probably handled by the Politburo,[4] its full members, or perhaps by a smaller group within it. Khrushchev himself stated that the Politburo deliberated and handled the question of Hungary at the behest of the entire Central Committee.[5] Further, two different groups had visited Yugoslavia with an eye to establishing policy toward the Soviet bloc as a whole. On 1 October, Khrushchev had appeared with "comrades" Nikolai Bulganin and Aleksei Kirichenko;[6] with Tito at Yalta, around 18 October, Mikoyan, Mikhail Pervukhin, and Georgii Zhukov were pictured together.[7] In any case, even Khrushchev was not yet firmly enough in control to hand it to a rump group to manage the crisis.

If one assumes that the responsibility for decision making in the

Hungarian crisis gravitated to the Politburo one must explore the question of its cohesion and unity. Can one assume, for example, that the policies explored and ultimately employed toward the Hungarian situation were handled by a Politburo that was essentially united and consistent; that unanimity and cohesion were departed from but rarely and only over marginal issues? Or is there evidence of deep division, fundamental disagreement, and fluctuating posture over time? The fact that the Soviet hierarchy was in a state of some disarray in 1956 over a wide range of issues, and that the Politburo was laboring with the politics of collective leadership, would at the very least seem to indicate disagreement, unless the Hungarian crisis, in its seriousness, actually produced unity.

Hierarchical factors were also important. Malenkov, Stalin's heir apparent, had been in eclipse since 1955 when his New Course was publicly criticized for its neglect of heavy industry. After Malenkov's fall, Khrushchev emerged as the strongest leader and, at the time of the Hungarian crisis, wielded considerable power. In the international sphere Khrushchev had been at the forefront of Soviet Union-NATO activity in the final months of 1955. Within the bloc he was initially responsible for the attempt to secure a rapprochement with Yugoslavia. Domestically, Khrushchev was selected to deliver the de-Stalinization speech at the Twentieth Party Congress. On the other hand, he had only recently been heavily involved in the Polish situation, the outcome of which, and his role in that affair, had not placed him above criticism. Undoubtedly, when Hungary exploded, he received some of the blame from those who had favored a less conciliatory course in Poland. The idea that what could be regarded as a retreat in Poland might have encouraged Nagy undoubtedly was not lost on Khrushchev's enemies. This uncertainty about Khrushchev might in part explain his absence from the Soviet delegation sent to negotiate with the Hungarians. Finally, in 1957, he had opposed several critical decisions in 1956, one of which may have been the policy followed toward Hungary. Khrushchev defeated this group in the Central Committee but the very fact of the struggle points to the prevalent limits on his authority.

Mikoyan and Suslov, as full members of the Politburo, played major roles in the Hungarian situation.[8] The former was identified as a supporter of Khrushchev, as were Dmitrii Shepilov, minister of foreign affairs and member of the Party Secretariat; Bulganin, the prime minister; Zhukov, minister of defense; and Lazar Kaganovich, deputy chairman of the Politburo and later a member of the antiparty group. Khrushchev's critics were Viacheslav Mototov, former foreign minister, closely associated with Stalin and brought under suspicion by Khrushchev's anti-Stalinist campaign, and Malenkov, Khrushchev's rival, who held him responsible for his own demise. Suslov remains something of an enigma. He was actually senior to Khrushchev and survived on the Politburo until his death in February 1982. Michel Tatu, in his study of the Politburo members, contends that Suslov always provided a check on the man in power. Further, Tatu argues that Suslov maintained, in 1956, at least tenuous ties with the members of the antiparty group.[9]

Some who were not Politburo members probably played important informational roles. They included Marshal Konstantin Rokossovsky, just returned from Poland; Marshal Ivan Konev, senior first deputy minister of defense, head of the Warsaw Pact High Command and a rival of Zhukov's; and Marshal Rodion Malinovsky, first deputy minister and chief of the ground forces. Police and internal security advice were no doubt sought from Ivan Serov, formerly Beria's assistant and the then KGB head. The secret police network, however, was in decline after Beria's demise. The Politburo was determined to assert control over the secret police and had subjected it to pronounced reorganization and extensive purges. Reports from Czechoslovakia in 1968 indicate that Beria's men in Eastern Europe were recalled between 1953 and 1954. The two responsible for Czech affairs were executed upon returning to Moscow.[10] It is probable that Beria's operatives in Hungary suffered the same fate. The point is that, with a new KGB group in Hungary and with perhaps a partial dismantling of the network, the secret police system was weakened. The efficiency of this very important source of information was undermined at a critical time. This probably bred confusion over the seriousness of the situation, as critical but conflicting reports arrived in Moscow. Serov personally, however, did enjoy sufficient political favor to accompany a group of regular and candidate Politburo members to Yugoslavia during October.[11]

One other source of information deserves attention—the Soviet embassy in Budapest. The embassy was, until and between the visits of Suslov and Mikoyan, the Politburo's most direct source of information on events in Hungary. Yuri Andropov, ambassador to Hungary from 1953 to 1956 (with a brief recall to Moscow in 1955–56), was an important link. Later appointed head of the secret police and a member of the Politburo, Andropov became general secretary after the death of Brezhnev in November 1982. Throughout the crisis Andropov handled the bulk of negotiations with the Hungarian leaders, including a critical meeting with the Hungarian Council of Ministers on 1 November. In all probability Andropov was responsible for informing the Politburo of crucial changes in the posture of the Hungarian government. Given his later position as head of the secret police, one might assume that he was, in these earlier stages of his career, also involved in the post-Beria secret police network, and may have reported directly to Serov or independently of him. That would not have been an uncommon function for any Soviet ambassador in a satellite country and seems particularly relevant in Andropov's case. Another intelligence source could have been Georgii

Tikhonov, the chief of military counterintelligence operations in
Budapest. He is, however, never mentioned in any account of the negotiations with Nagy.

Soviet Options and Decision-Making Scenarios

In the abstract there were four options at the disposal of the Soviet
leadership, forming a continuum of escalation. Nonintervention and the
avoidance of involvement would allow the Hungarians to work out their
own future. Such a response, however, was incompatible with the theme
of responsible bloc adaptation and had not been permitted even to the
Poles that same year. To permit, with due consultation, reform and
liberalization would be consultation with bloc adaptation and would provide that acceptable degree of national communism that went to but not
beyond the point where such changes threatened Communist rule, bloc
solidarity, and Russian influence. What constituted the critical threshold
was probably the key to the debate in Moscow. The Soviet Union, as a
third option, could seek to influence decisively the debate in Hungary by
a flexible response, using both direct pressure, by way of high-level visits
and a variety of propaganda means, and indirect influence exercised
through other bloc members. The Soviet leaders had a battery of ideological, political, economic, and financial means at their disposal; their response could be plural and change over time. Finally, the Soviet Union
could intervene by military force and impose a solution on Hungary.

Analytically, the task is not merely to explore these options but to
view them as part of Soviet decision making in crisis and in a period of collective leadership when process and outcome are at issue. One helpful
analytic tool is to construct scenarios and then to examine the available
evidence in support of them. Four scenarios merit consideration. A
united elite may have, throughout the whole crisis, preferred and ultimately enacted a consistent policy. Alternatively, a united elite may have
initially favored a particular policy, only to change that policy in the light
of fresh circumstances and new evidence, while retaining its essential
cohesion. The idea of a divided elite holding firmly to a single policy is
possible to contemplate in the abstract but seems unworthy of lengthy development in this case. It would defy the logic of collective leadership and
require what was absent in this case, that is either the presence of a single
and omnipotent leader or group, or the isolation and subversion of competitive factors. Finally, a divided elite might, after favoring an alternative
course of action, ultimately accept or reconcile themselves to a final decision, in this case military intervention.

The military option, the cold war scenario would suggest that a
united and consistent Politburo was determined from the outset, and

planned accordingly, to prevent by military action any significant changes in the Hungarian political system. The elite in Moscow was not divided on this question. The Polish example served to stiffen them and to convince them that they could not afford a repetition in Hungary. Only the erection of a puppet government could save Hungary from invasion. The Politburo, in effect, intended to make an example of Hungary. Indeed it may have wished to establish a precedent, as the Brezhnev Doctrine would later do explicitly.

The evidence supporting this scenario is at best slim. One might argue that the reinforcement of the various Soviet garrisons in Hungary between 19 and 22 October, the prompt response to Gero's request for aid on 23–24 October, and the description in *Pravda* on 25 October of events in Hungary as "counter-revolutionary activity" is evidence not only of Soviet willingness but also of a preference to use force against Hungary.[12] However, there was no commentary on the reported change of government in Hungary, and Nagy himself was not termed counterrevolutionary. Further, the 28 October statement that the "Anti-People's Venture" had collapsed would have to be seen as a smokescreen,[13] and neither an expression of Moscow's perception of the situation nor a gesture to Nagy. It would follow that the partial Soviet evacuation from Budapest on 29–30 October and the negotiations between the Soviet military mission and Hungarian high command must be viewed as fraudulent acts, as mere stalling tactics to enable the preparations for actual invasion to be completed. Moreover, the troop movements within Hungary, supposedly to be the preface to a Soviet evacuation, must be regarded as a tactical regrouping and reorganizing maneuver, in preparation for the final invasion. Finally, the 30 October declaration on the equality of states in the *Pravda* editorial "On Friendship and Cooperation Between the USSR and Other Socialist States"[14] must be seen as a trap and a provocation, calculated to drive Nagy toward extreme moves and thoroughly compromising responses. This scenario posits elite unity and a single policy option.

Alternatively, as a second scenario, it is clearly reasonable to argue that the very gravity of the Hungarian situation must have sponsored, however reluctantly and hesitatingly, fresh levels of cohesion. A consensus, however fragile, must have developed because of the life-and-death nature of the problem, involving as it seemed to do the national security of the Soviet Union. There were, in all likelihood, inner reservations and vigorous debate, but following Poland, the Hungarian affair dictated closing of ranks. The Politburo, guided by Khrushchev, agreed that Poland was a model for bloc adaptation and, up to 31 October, decided to treat Nagy like Gomulka. It agreed to live with the revolt, accept its consequences, however reluctantly, welcome reform, and make peace with change. Then, from October 31, this united elite, swayed by fresh and disturbing evidence, changed its collective mind and agreed on the need to crush Nagy and the revolt, and to work with and through Kadar. These decisions had broad support but required improvised military response which was mounted between 1 and 3 November.

Those who support this scenario must assume that Khrushchev had already secured a near or actual preeminent position and could control, via the Secretariat, the Politburo's sources of information, agenda, and the nature of the advice it received. Moreover, he must have secured, over the Polish question, a considerable degree of agreement on the new formula for bloc unity and evolution and support for national roads to communism. The Politburo must have regarded this solution as working in Poland and anticipated a similar outcome in Hungary. When it became clear that this was not the case, by 31 October, they decided to act with military means. The *volte-face* was based on Hungarian folly, not Soviet preference.

An alternative explanation focuses on the functioning of a divided elite in Moscow in 1956. The Soviet response to the Hungarian revolt reflected deep divisions within a Politburo that was caught by surprise and riddled with uncertainty. Its members were divided on ideological, policy, and personal grounds and reacted in an indecisive and unsure manner. These divisions were in the nature and essence of the post-Stalin succession, for at least two factions, led by Khrushchev and Malenkov respectively, confronted each other. Khrushchev and his followers were hard-liners on domestic policy but moderates in matters of bloc cohesion and development. Malenkov, a professed moderate in domestic policy, teamed with the Stalinist Molotov, and took a position antithetical to Khrushchev's bloc policy. They had differed in their response to the Polish crisis and drew different conclusions about its lessons and meaning for the future of bloc adaptation. The military was also divided with Zhukov's group facing its detractors. In sum, a majority led by Khrushchev initially opposed intervening militarily, but after a certain point a fresh majority coalition emerged which preferred the military option. In this scenario the cohesion of the elite fluctuates and the policy option changes decisively. It is important here to emphasize the irony of a Malenkov-Molotov coalition. Malenkov should have, by all accounts, been a soft-liner on bloc policy. This new course brought Nagy and Gomulka to the fore and they were identified with him. But in the power struggle in the Kremlin, Malenkov found himself in the company of the arch-Stalinist Molotov. These coalitions are not rare in Soviet power struggles (note the odd coalitions that the Lenin succession created). Obviously the Molotov-Malenkov association was really an anti-Khrushchev alliance, rather than an ideological one. This supports the contention that in times of succession, important decisions, even on critical matters like Hungary, take on a highly political character.

In the presence of a power struggle it seems reasonable to suggest also that there was little initial agreement over the course to be followed in Hungary. Malenkov's group, those outside the range of power, and including Molotov, Malenkov, and Kaganovich, would not cooperate readily with Khrushchev's supporters, who wielded the greater power. Perhaps three factions evolved: a severely militant group which, in light of recent events in Poland, and perhaps even in the Polish situation itself, favored invasion; a moderate group led by Khrushchev which favored invasion only after considerable provocation by Nagy; and those who, even then, in Khrushchev's words, "thought that the lending of aid might be misunderstood."[15]

Finally, it is difficult to believe that Zhukov and the more militant Konev were not drawn ultimately into the debate. They were doubtless unwilling to see the reliability of another satellite army threatened. The recall of Rokossovsky had left the military establishment in the USSR uncertain about the course of civil-military relations in Poland. While Zhukov supported Khrushchev in most matters, Konev would have been able to argue, perhaps persuasively, that Hungary's moves of 31 October and 1 November, especially the de-Sovietization of the Hungarian high command and the rise of Maleter, were completely unacceptable. The security of the Warsaw Pact was at issue. This indeed might have finally united the military behind the invasion option and deprived those still opposing invasion of any military support.

The bulk of the evidence would seem to support this scenario. Khrushchev was committed to bloc adaptation and transformation. He was convinced that they must devise a new formula to preserve the unity of the bloc and to secure a community of states led by the USSR. This policy, however, was not necessarily accepted fully by the whole Politburo. There were those who feared the decline of Soviet leadership and believed that too rapid and drastic reform would lead to crisis within and even disintegration of the bloc. Khrushchev's formula in Poland had, in the eyes of some, actually invited and precipitated the events in Hungary. In turn, Hungary could lead to unrest and revolution in other Communist satellites.

Khrushchev himself admitted that the Soviet elite was divided on how to respond to the Hungarian revolt. The statement is elaborated in his memoirs.[16] Khrushchev claimed that the Politburo adopted the invasion strategy with great uncertainty and concern and only after the most agonizing discussion. He admitted further that there were those who were against the invasion even after the step was taken. Again that would suggest the presence of three groups: those who favored invasion from the beginning, those who were later convinced of its necessity, and those who never favored that option. This admission underscores the seriousness of the decision to invade. The invasion option presented grave risks. The new conciliatory line and emphasis on equality in the bloc was bound to be affected and, more importantly, the vigorously sought rapprochement with Tito would have been endangered by hasty action.

Both the "Chinese" and "Yugoslav" versions suggest that the Soviet elite was seriously divided and felt it necessary to sound out external opinion. The Chinese claimed that the Politburo was in total confusion and that only their intervention enabled the Politburo to make decisions in 1956, not only to invade Hungary but also not to invade Poland. While it is difficult to fathom the extent of Chinese involvement, Khrushchev's own account acknowledges that he consulted Liu Shao-chi on the range of options under discussion, before the Politburo arrived at any decision. Liu was about to leave Moscow and was less than firm in his views. He seemed to prefer, however, that the Soviet Union should not intervene, and understood that Khrushchev himself did not at that time favor an invasion. Undoubtedly, consulting the second ranking member of the Chinese government was necessary in order to avoid the appearance and future charge of unilateral Soviet action. After the Politburo decided to invade, its members hurried to the Moscow airport to inform Liu of the decision. Liu did not dissent.[17] In all probability, it had seemed necessary, internally, to convince certain members of the Politburo that military invasion of Hungary would not cause problems with other Communist allies, and indeed, might be welcomed in some quarters. Tito was also consulted, apparently, and gave tacit support after the fact to the Soviet decision to invade.[18]

Finally, men who were not above exploiting errors and applying labels were prone to use a decision as critical as Hungary to discredit their enemies. The real divisions of the recent past clearly dictated that the Soviet elite could not have joined the debate over Hungary in any but a divided frame of mind.

If the Politburo was indeed divided, it is still very difficult to identify clear divisions and lines of demarcation between individuals by a process of extrapolation. In the debate on defense spending in 1954, Malenkov and Pervukhin had opposed Khrushchev, Bulganin, Molotov, and Kaganovich. The latter group demanded large increases and carried the day. In 1955, those who favored heavy industrial growth, led by Khrushchev, had succeeded in diminishing the power of Malenkov's New Course group. But it is dangerous to extrapolate too freely across issue areas and from the domestic to the international field. That is to say, because a Stalinist and an anti-Stalinist group opposed each other over agricultural, industrial, or cultural policies, because defense policies created other alignments, and because individuals had taken identifiable and apparently unyielding position on celebrated occasions, did such division necessarily occur in the debate over Hungary? Most observers agree that, over Hungary, Malenkov, Molotov, Kaganovich, and Konev opposed Khrushchev, Bulganin, Mikoyan, Shepilov, and Zhukov. The position of Suslov remains ambiguous. Moreover, it has been argued persuasively that rather than a homogeneous fact-finding duo, Mikoyan and Suslov might have represented opposite factions. Since it is known that Mikoyan was a Khrushchev supporter, Suslov might, therefore, have been in opposition to Mikoyan's position. Much like the mission to Warsaw, which had harnessed the enemies Kaganovich and Khrushchev, the Hungarian mission might have reflected the fact that division in the Politburo were severe enough to require that any such enterprise must represent opposing factions.

Both the second and third scenarios can accommodate the probability of contingency planning. On 4 November 1956 the Soviet forces were able to deliver a devastating blow at Budapest and other key areas and centers. There was little doubt within 24 hours about the outcome in Budapest. This assault probably could not have been mounted in three days, between 1 and 3 November. It involved minimally the movement of certain divisions, equipment and materials, some of which came from the Central Ukraine. Moreover, there were Soviet troop movements to the Hungarian border by 30 October. Khrushchev admitted that he asked Marshal Konev to ready an invasion force but claimed that this was done only after the decision to invade was made.[19] In any case, one would have to assume that contingency plans always existed to make possible a decisive and rapid operation should it be necessary.

There is a good deal of evidence to suggest that the Politburo decided on 31 October to 1 November that military intervention in Hungary was unavoidable and that preparations should be put into high gear immediately. The second visit of Mikoyan and Suslov to Budapest, on 30 October, if primarily to negotiate normalization, was also one of evaluation. They returned to Moscow on 1 November. That day, Andropov met with the Hungarian Council of Ministers. Doubtless he reported Nagy's intransigence immediately to Moscow. Nagy had attempted to reorganize the Hungarian armed forces, to de-Sovietize them, and to appoint a general staff loyal to the new policies. He had been, for a number of years, a proponent of a more neutralist stance for Hungary. One account even claims that on 1 November Nagy abruptly dismissed Ambassador Andropov when he asked about the possibility of retaining Soviet rocket bases in Hungary after neutralization had been implemented.[20]

One must conclude, therefore, that, after receiving the reports of Mikoyan and Suslov, from Budapest on 31 October and in person on 1 November, and after Andropov had reported on the final negotiations with the Hungarian Council of Ministers, the Politburo decided, perhaps reluctantly, that military intervention was necessary. Preparations and penetration of Hungary were made in earnest as relations deteriorated. Kadar formed a new government, cooperated with the Soviet Union, and called for Soviet intervention at the appropriate time. Presumably, other bloc leaders urged the Soviets to move against Nagy.

Nagy had violated the accepted canons of satellite behavior, going much further than even moderates could possibly allow. The situation in Hungary now presented a quadruple threat; to the Communist party dominance, to the reliability of the army, to the stability of the Eastern bloc, and to the Soviet security system. Khrushchev's policy of concession and peaceful bloc adaptation was not working in Hungary. The Politburo was not willing to see Hungary defect. Khrushchev could not risk being charged with errors which might bring about that eventuality, and, indeed, spread further. While there may have been those who never preferred an invasion, as Khrushchev claimed, most probably an overwhelming majority of the Politburo now agreed that there was no alternative to military force. Following Nagy's defiance, there was no longer a choice, and in the early hours of 4 November, the Soviet Union invaded Hungary.

On 2 November, as preparations were being made for military intervention, the Soviet leaders learned that the United States was seeking a cease-fire in the United Nations to halt Anglo-French operations. The split in the Western camp was now obvious. The international situation was therefore distinctly favorable. It should be noted that *Pravda* took full advantage of the divided world attention, focusing heavily on the Suez crisis.

How, in fact, were the two crises linked? What is the evidence concerning the role of Suez in the calculations of the Soviet elite over Hungary? There are at least two possibilities. The first posits that the Suez debacle was a most convenient occurrence, and perhaps even an unexpected one, for a Politburo which had already decided on invasion. It drew international attention away from Hungary, splintered global indignation, distracted the nonaligned states and, dividing the Western bloc, turned U.S. wrath against its own allies. But no more than that. The second possibility is that Suez was ultimately the key to the Soviet decision to invade. In this reasoning, the principle concern of the Politburo over invading Hungary was the fear that the West might intervene. With John Foster Dulles in office the Soviet Union considered Western intervention a real possibility. Suez altered the situation decisively. It allowed the Soviet Union a free hand to invade Hungary without fear of denunciation from the Afro-Asian bloc, let alone reprisals from the West.

The evidence favors the former interpretation. The critical point in the Hungarian situation antedated the crucial point in the Suez crisis. The decision to invade Hungary was made on 1 November; military preparations in earnest and the dispatch of reinforcements to Hungary began then, and possibly a little earlier, as a result of Khrushchev's directives to Konev. The deep and apparently unbridgeable division between the United States and its allies became clear only on 2 November with the introduction of the cease-fire resolution in the United Nations. No doubt Soviet intelligence warned of possible U.S. action against Britain and

France; a serious rift in the Western camp was obviously likely. One could argue, therefore, that the Soviet Union began its military preparations, waited for Suez to devastate Western harmony, decided to invade Hungary because of western disarray, and time the military move accordingly. Other factors were, however, involved.

On 31 October and 1 November, Nagy took the steps that finally made him quite unacceptable to the Soviet leadership. He had gone far beyond Gomulka's liberalization in Poland, incidentally, far beyond the reforms that Alexander Dubcek would undertake in Czechoslovakia. The Soviet leadership must have assumed either that Nagy was a nationalist demagogue, actually hostile to both the Soviet Union and to communism, or that he had lost control of the situation in Hungary and could no longer steer the country on a moderate and acceptable course. In either case, the Soviets could not allow the defection of Hungary; they had to risk the possibility of Western action. The actual ramifications of Dulles's policies were not clear, and it seems unwise to assume that the Soviet Union would risk dissolution of the bloc in deference to speculation about U.S. reactions. The Suez crisis was, therefore, very convenient and significant, but not decisive. It comforted the hesitant in Moscow and gave the Soviet press an issue which could force the Hungarian situation off the front pages between 1 and 3 November. It deprived Nagy of a monopoly of international concern and a more devoted forum in which to embarrass the USSR and make the case against Soviet aggression. The Politburo would, however, have put down the Hungarian revolt without the Suez affair.[21]

Conclusions

Certain conclusions seem valid. First, the Soviet leadership of 1956 was not united. Individual differences, ideological and policy divisions, and the struggle for power made unified response to almost any issue impossible, not excluding the Hungarian challenge. The Soviet missions to Budapest contained representatives of different groups. However, when Suslov, Mikoyan, and presumably Andropov reported that the most drastic measures were necessary, the majority of the Politburo acquiesced. The Soviet elite, understandably, depended heavily on these first-hand accounts of the situation.

Second, the majority of the Politburo backed the initial involvement of Soviet troops but preferred, after 26 October, a response similar to that made toward Poland. This resulted in the conciliatory initiatives of 28 and 31 October. The decree of 30 October, Suslov and Mikoyan's negotiations with Nagy, and the agreement to negotiate a Soviet troop withdrawal undermined the view that military invasion was always the preferred option. Rather, it appears that, as Khrushchev claimed, the decision to invade was made after lengthy deliberation and the prolonged weighing of options. The decision was too momentous to be taken either lightly or hurriedly. Logically, the events between 31 October and 1 November in Hungary, Nagy's apparent domestic and foreign policy preferences, coupled with the reports of Andropov, Suslov, and Mikoyan, brought the moderate group to the side of those favoring invasion.

Third, it is unlikely that the Suez crisis was the critical factor in the Soviet decision. Serious preparations for the invasion were undertaken and the invasion was ordered because the Soviet leadership felt that the Hungarian situation had become a serious threat to Soviet security and bloc solidarity.

Fourth, the Soviet decision in the 1956 crisis was made much as the crisis decision literature would lead one to expect. There was rational debate about options, under pressure, by a relatively small group which was no monolith. *Homo sovieticus* debated and waivered just like his Western counterpart. Sources of information varied and conflicting evidence surfaced, necessitating reports at first hand by members of the leadership themselves. In a sense and up to a critical point Nagy held the initiative as much as Khrushchev, if not the resources and the power. Pathos and villainy were both present and the former property surely outweighed the latter in 1956.

Finally, the relationships between the Hungarian crisis and events in Czechoslovakia in 1968, and Poland in 1980, require consideration. A divided Politburo had, in 1956, both established a process and provided an example of how to handle a crisis of this nature. The model would largely hold whether or not a succession crisis was in progress in the Soviet Union. The invasion of Hungary was the first such case of this kind;[22] it created a precedent for an additional policy option that was open to the Soviet Union in bloc managements. As the Politburo contemplated this highly dangerous and controversial option in 1956, it searched for a justification; the existence of counterrevolutionary elements in a fraternal state provided the necessary legitimization. Invasion by invitation also went some way to explain the action both within and outside the bloc. Clearly, the concept of "limited sovereignty" did not emerge first in the Czechoslovak crisis of 1968 when it became formalized in the so-called Brezhnev Doctrine. Moreover, the practice of interbloc consultation prior to intervention was first established in 1956. The existence of the mature machinery of the Warsaw Pact has made consultation a more potent and sophisticated step, but in an informal way the Hungarian crisis set the precedent. The Soviet leadership learned the triple value of consultation with its allies. It increased bloc solidarity, masked Soviet unilateral behavior, and provided a justification for history. From the alternative but equally critical perspective, the Hungarian crisis should have laid down the ground rules for and the boundaries of client-state behavior. Deviations from the ground rules would not be tolerated. An attempt to introduce political pluralism domestically or to reach for internal control of the armed forces were the critical thresholds. Crossing those thresholds would invite invasion.

Notes

1. Several general works exist on the Hungarian crisis. Among these Endre Maront's *Forbidden Sky* (Boston: Little, Brown, 1971) and Ribor Meray's *That Day in Budapest* (New York: Funk and Wagnalls, 1969) are interesting and helpful accounts. Paul E. Zinner's *National Communism and Popular Revolt* (New York: Columbia University Press, 1956) is an excellent documentary account of the events of 1956 in both Poland and Hungary. Zbigniew Brzezinski's *Soviet Bloc: Unity and Conflict,* rev. and enl. ed. (Cambridge: Harvard University Press, 1967) places the conflict within the general framework of changes in Soviet bloc policy after the death of Stalin. Two recent works on the Hungarian crisis are also helpful. These are N.F. Dresziger, ed., *The Hungarian Revolution Twenty Years After* (Kingston, Ont.: Brown and Martin, 1976) and David Pryce-Jones, *The Hungarian Revolution* (New York: Harrison, 1970). On the question of the Soviet decision, Ernest A. Nagy's *Crisis Decision Setting and Response: The Hungarian Revolution* (Washington, D.C.: National Defense University Research Directorate, 1978) offers conclusions that are not supportable. There is an excellent work on Soviet crisis decision making by Jiri Valenta entitled, *Soviet Intervention in Czechoslovakia* (Baltimore: Johns Hopkins University Press, 1979). An interesting and invaluable Communist account used in the preparation of this essay is *Dvadtasat' piat' let Svovodnoi Vengrii* (Moscow: Politizdat, 1971).

2. Mikoyan and Suslov had visited Budapest on 24 October, presumably to report on the use of Soviet troops in response to Gero's request.

3. The historical record on Nagy's "neutralization" is clouded at best. Clearly he took the ultimate step, publicly announcing withdrawal from the Warsaw Pact, in response to Soviet pressure (1 November). It is not possible to argue that it was this public statement which led the Soviets to full-scale invasion (troop movements were begun on 29 October). But the published record is presumably only one part of the story. The possibility of private conversations between Nagy and the Soviets, espionage by high-placed Hungarians or to other private communications could have led the Soviets to conclude that neutralization was imminent. It should be noted that Nagy's foreign policy (enunciated in his *On Communism*) was decidedly neutralist, praising the nonaligned movement of the Bandung Conference. See Brzezinski, *The Soviet Bloc* (p. 219) who dates these foreign policy theses at January 1956, and the Soviets were undoubtedly aware of these statements. A chronology that does not take into account these possibilities is flawed.

4. The terms *Politburo* and *Presidium* are often used interchangeably to denote Presidium of the Central Committee of the Communist Party of the Soviet Union. In this study the more common term (and the one preferred by Khrushchev), Politburo, will be used.

5. Nikita S. Khrushchev, *Khrushchev Remembers,* trans. by Strobe Talbot (Boston, Mass.: Little, Brown, 1970). Khrushchev's memoirs must be used with appropriate caution. However, there seems to be no reason to be especially skeptical about them simply because they are Soviet.

6. Pictured in *Pravda,* 2 October 1956, p. 3.

7. Pictured in *Pravda,* 18 October 1956, p. 2.

8. Khrushchev makes a point of insisting that Mikoyan and Suslov were in Budapest, not in Moscow, when the decision was reached to invade. There are grounds to question his memory on this point, however (Khrushchev, *Khrushchev Remembers,* p. 417).

9. Michel Tatu, *Power in the Kremlin* (New York: Viking, 1967), p. 29.

10. Karel Kaplan, "Thoughts on the Political Trials," *Nova Mysal,* 6 July 1968.

11. Pictured in *Pravda,* 6 October 1956, p. 3.

12. *Pravda,* 25 October 1956. Actually this unsigned report was buried among the coverage of the October Revolution celebration. The mention was brief and only in reference to difficulties in Hungary.

13. *Pravda,* 28 October 1956, unsigned editorial, p. 3.

14. *Pravda,* 31 October 1956, unsigned report of the declaration, p. 1.

15. Khrushchev, *Khrushchev Remembers,* p. 408.

16. Ibid.

17. Khrushchev, *Khrushchev Remembers,* p. 421, and "The Origin and Development of the Difference Between the Leadership of the CPSU and the PRC," *Jin-min jih-pao,* 6 September 1964 (Peking: Foreign Languages Press, 1963). Certainly after the invasion, the Chinese wholeheartedly gave their support. The hard-line that the PRC adopted in the 1950s, however, led the Chinese to charge the USSR with vacillation and revisionism in its policies toward Tito and the bloc. The Chinese claim that they advocated invasion and that their advocacy was decisive in 1956. Both the Khrushchev and Chinese account were written after the Sino-Soviet break, and it is possible that Khrushchev did not want to concede the point. Ernest Nagy's view, that China "opposed" the invasion, is impossible to sustain (Nagy, *Crisis Decision,* p. 14.

18. Brzezinski, *The Soviet Bloc,* p. 234.

19. *Khrushchev Remembers,* p. 418.

20. *Pravda's* coverage of the Western aggression escalated from front-page coverage on page 5 (*Pravda,* 1 November 1956) including signed "letters" and a signed editorial by V. Brovskii, to page one stories and lead editorials (unsigned) on 2 and 3 November. On 4 November, the Hungarian intervention (page 1) was finally reported, but on the very next page, there was full-page coverage of the Suez crisis. The coverage again included letters, signed stories, and signed and unsigned editorials.

21. Khrushchev analyzed the connection between the Suez and East European crises, claiming that the West risked the Suez affair hoping that the USSR's

hands were tied because of events in Poland and Hungary. He did not, however, claim that Suez tied the hands of the West in dealing with the East European crisis (*Khrushchev Remembers,* p. 412).

22. The police action in the eastern zone of Germany in 1953 was not against a recalcitrant wing of a fraternal Communist party as was the case in Hungary 1956 or Czechoslovakia 1968.

13 THE BUREAUCRATIC POLITICS PARADIGM AND THE INVASION OF CZECHOSLOVAKIA

Jiri Valenta

On August 3, 1968, at the peak of the Czechoslovak crisis, Leonid Brezhnev and other members of the Soviet delegation to the Bratislava conference, together with the leaders of several Warsaw Pact countries—East Germany, Poland, Hungary, and Bulgaria—appeared to have reached a *modus vivendi* with Alexander Dubcek's leadership. Simultaneously, Warsaw Pact forces were ordered to cease their maneuvers on Czechoslovak territory. Many observers of Soviet politics interpreted these events as a victory for the Czechoslovak reformers. Yet only 17 days later the agreement was broken by the sudden military invasion of Czechoslovakia by these same countries—all partners of Czechoslovakia in the Bratislava agreement.

Among observers of Soviet politics, there were some skeptics who doubted that the Bratislava rapprochement would last for long, but few expected a military move so soon. Also, as former commander in chief of the U.S. Army in Europe, General James H. Polk, recently noted, both U.S. government and NATO officials considered a Soviet invasion to be highly unlikely.[1] Even Charles Bohlen, one of the most pessimistic U.S. officials, frankly admitted that he underestimated Soviet timing on the use of military force.[2]

Why did so many policy makers and analysts fail to predict the Soviet decision to intervene? Recent literature on U.S. foreign policy suggests that such failures often arise from a tendency to treat the state as a unitary actor, rather than analyzing bureaucratic conflict and consensus building

Previously published as "The Bureaucratic Politics Paradigm and the Soviet Invasion of Czechoslovakia" by Jiri Valenta, *Political Science Quarterly*, 1979. Reprinted by permission.

within that state. Thus, some analysts tend to see Soviet foreign policy making in the post-Stalin era through the conceptual "lenses" of what Graham Allison has christened the "rational policy paradigm."[3] Surprisingly, many explanations of why the Soviets intervened in Czechoslovakia seem to fit this characterization. Some observers such as Hans Morgenthau and Herman Kahn conclude that the invasion was aimed at preventing Czechoslovakia from shifting its orbit closer to West Germany.[4] Others, such as Boris Meissner, emphasize the importance of the so-called Brezhnev Doctrine, which stresses the "limited sovereignty" of socialist states in Soviet decision making.[5]

Can a better explanation of the Soviet decision to invade Czechoslovakia be found by applying the bureaucratic politics paradigm? Who were the central figures in Soviet decision making? What were the interests of these decision makers and how did these interests affect their stands on the Czechoslovak issue? Who were the advocates of military intervention? Who were the skeptics? Did coalition politics evolve and how did various factors (for example, sources of information, external pressure) affect this evolution and the shaping of the final decision to invade Czechoslovakia? This chapter seeks to test the validity of the bureaucratic politics paradigm by placing these inquiries in perspective and applying the paradigm to Soviet management of the Czechoslovak crisis in 1968.

The Bureaucratic Politics Paradigm

The general argument of the bureaucratic politics paradigm can be summarized as follows: Soviet foreign policy actions do not result from a single actor, the Politburo, rationally maximizing national security. Instead, these actions result from a policy of political interaction ("pulling and hauling") among senior decision makers in the Politburo and the heads of several bureaucratic elites at the Central Committee level. The methodology of the bureaucratic politics approach used here does not suggest that purely abstract institutional and organizational interests motivate Soviet foreign policy actions. Bureaucratic politics is seen instead as based upon and reflecting the division of labor and responsibilities among Politburo members in various policy areas. This division arises from two conditions: a highly bureaucratic political system and a collective leadership in which no single decision maker possesses either sufficient power or sufficient wisdom to decide all important policy matters.

It is reasonable to assume that Soviet leaders, as their U.S. counterparts, share a certain set of images of national security.[6] This set of images conditions the answers to questions asked by key bureaucracies: Who are our friends and who are our enemies? With whom shall we ally and with whom shall we struggle? Undoubtedly the shared images of national security interests affect the attitudes and arguments of Soviet decision makers in internal debates. Despite these shared images, senior Soviet decision makers may differ as to how to approach and resolve various issues.

Organizational Actors

Foreign policy formulation among Soviet leaders proceeds within a conglomeration of organizations controlled and coordinated by the Politburo.

The main organizational participants in the decision-making process are the various departments of the Central Committee of the Communist Party of the Soviet Union (CPSU) and the national security ministerial bureaucracies: the Ministry of Foreign Affairs, the Soviet Committee for State Security (KGB), and the Ministry of Defense and its various branches.[7] Under circumstances that will be discussed further, departments dealing with internal affairs and regional party bureaucracies in the non-Russian national republics (particularly the more important ones, such as the Ukraine) may also become involved in the decision making.

The pursuit of various bureaucratic responsibilities with respect to constituencies leads to organization conflict—disagreements over budgetary allocations, organizational values, scope of authority, organizational sense of mission, and self-image. Organizations less concerned with budgetary implications of their organizational missions, such as the Central Committee's International Department and Department of Liaison with the Communist and Workers parties and the Ministry of Foreign Affairs, are interested mainly in their self-image and influence in the Soviet decision-making process. For example, the International Department tends to assess foreign policy decisions on the basis of their effect on its mission abroad, notably in the maintenance of ties with such constituencies as the Communist parties and the pro-Communist trade unions in the West and the "progressive forces" in the Third World. In contrast, the subdivisions of the Soviet military establishment—ground forces, strategic rocket forces, air defense forces, naval forces, air forces, and rear services—themselves organizations with extensive proclivities, are greatly concerned with budgetary implications of policy decisions.[8]

Some Soviet bureaucracies are assigned missions that can be accomplished mainly at home. Examples of such bureaucracies are the Central Committee's Department for Propaganda, the Party Control Commission, the Department of Science and Higher Education, and party bureaucracies in the Soviet national republics; all are charged with domestic and ideological supervision, indoctrination, and "party discipline." International developments and Soviet foreign policy actions are generally viewed by these departments in terms of the effect on their stated missions. As one source has observed, segments of the foreign policy establishment, such as the International Department and the divisions of the Ministry of Foreign Affairs responsible for relations with the Western countries, are likely to be more interested in good relations with Western countries than the bureaucracies charged with ideological supervision or with political stability in the various Soviet national republics, such as the Ukraine and the Baltic republics. The latter departments tend to view detente with suspicion, for it makes their organizational mission of ideological supervision and indoctrination more difficult.[9]

Uncommitted Thinking

Most Soviet decision makers do not head organizations with homogenous constituencies. Some run organizations with clearly defined missions or formal organizational goals. Many have broad responsibilities and sometimes overlapping foreign and domestic interests. Although there are Soviet bureaucrats who seek organizational interdependence, the pattern of overlap somewhat invalidates Allison's notion: "Where you stand depends on where you sit." The decisions of some senior decision makers who are less influenced by organizational parochialism are characterized by *uncommitted thinking*. Personal interests, varying backgrounds, and previous political career experience provide additional clues to a given Soviet decision maker's position on a given political issue. For example, those Soviet decision makers who, as leaders of party bureaucracies in non-Russian republics, had to deal with the volatile "nationalism" issue share a background experience that can affect their political stand. Finally, each participant's position on an important issue is undoubtedly influenced by other personal factors—prestige within the Politburo, personal idiosyncracies, and the still unresolved question of succession.

Domestic interests of Soviet decision makers likewise affect their stand on issues. In Soviet decision making, the challenges of internal politics are much more real and forceful than alleged threats of "U.S. imperialism," "German revanchism," "Czechoslovak revisionism," or "Chinese adventurism." Domestic political constraints in Soviet foreign policy making have grown in importance in the past two decades. Particularly under the more stable leadership of Brezhnev, Soviet decision makers are more susceptible than ever to domestic pressures.

The Nature of the Czechoslovak Crisis

The political crisis in Czechoslovakia, which initially appeared to be only a power struggle, shaped up in several months as a struggle for a more pluralistic concept of socialism.[10] Subsequent events in Prague—the resignation of Antonin Novotny's Moscow-oriented supporters, the reformist orientation of Dubcek's leadership, the revival of freedom of the press—created from the Soviet point of view a dangerous political situation in one of the most important Warsaw Pact countries with a potential impact on neighboring East European countries and the Soviet Union itself. "Prague spring," however, differed significantly from the kind of revolt that the Soviet leaders had experienced in Budapest in 1956. Dubcek's leadership did not challenge the basic elements of Soviet national security interests; it did not, for example, recommend revising Czechoslovakia's foreign policy orientation. Czechoslovakia would retain its membership in the Warsaw Pact and COMECON. Nor did Dubcek proclaim that a limited pluralism would signify loss of overall control by the Communist party; power, although somewhat diffused, would remain in the hands of the reformist party leadership. Nevertheless, from the Soviet point of view, the developments in Czechoslovakia were problematic and potentially dangerous.

Still, any threat to the Soviet Union's dominant influence in Eastern Europe was only potential and not imminent, and would have been incremental at that. For a long time, Soviet decision makers were unsure of their policy options with respect to Czechoslovakia. Should they reverse or merely limit the post-January changes in Czechoslovakia? What means should they use to contain Czechoslovakia's influence?

Parochial Priorities, Perceptions, and Stands

All senior Soviet decision makers must have been disturbed by Czechoslovak reformism. They evidently agreed that the political situation in Czechoslovakia had to be stabilized and they seem to have recognized that the situation might require the use of military force. Thus covert preparations for military action and possible intervention probably began in the early stages of the crisis—February to March 1968. This military build-up during the crisis served not only as a logistic preparation for the invasion but also as an instrument of psychological pressure against Czechoslovakia. In fact, the military build-up had been accomplished by late June or early July; but the political decision to invade Czechoslovakia was taken only in late August after a long process of pulling and hauling among the senior decision makers. Each player, depending on his bureaucratic position, domestic interests, personal background, and idiosyncracies, gave a somewhat different reading (or several readings) of the Czechoslovak issue. Consequently, the players took contrasting stands on the issue and disagreed on the means that should be used in its stabilization.[11]

The decision makers responsible for domestic affairs were especially concerned about the effect Prague reformism might have on the Soviet Union. In the perception of the Ukrainian party bureaucracy and its head P.E. Shelest,[12] as well as of other party bureaucrats in the Soviet Union's non-Russian republics (Belorussian leader P.M. Masherov and Lithuanian leader A.Iv. Snechkus, among others), "deviant" ideas of reformism and federalism could spill over from Czechoslovakia to encourage nationalism in their own republics.[13]

To the party bureaucrats charged with ideological supervision and indoctrination, such as A.Ya. Pelshe of the Department of Party Control Committee, S.N. Trapenznikov of the Department of Science and Education, and officials from the major cities (including Moscow's City First Secretary V.V. Grishin),[14] the Czechoslovak "disease" posed a threat to the containment of domestic affairs. This was especially true among the intellectual, scientific, and literary communities where Prague reformism was seen as reinforcing ideas among the members of the Soviet establishment (such as academician A.D. Sakharov), who hoped to see in their own society the same conditions then materializing in Czechoslovakia.

Another group of decision makers with strong organizational ties feared that Czechoslovak reformism would galvanize Soviet dissidents and reformists. To the KGB,[15] and also to the Warsaw Pact Command, reformism was a threat to organizational mission and authority in Eastern Europe. To General A.A. Epishev's Department of Political Administration of the Soviet Army and Navy (concerned with ideological and political supervision of the Soviet armed forces), Prague reformism and the weakening of morale observed in the Czechoslovak military posed serious threats to discipline in the Warsaw Pact. Thus, it is not surprising that early in April 1968 General Epishev expressed the willingness of the Soviet military to respond to an appeal from "healthy forces" (that is, antireformists) in Czechoslovakia "to safeguard socialism."[16] Chairman of the Supreme Soviet N.V. Podgorny, who was probably among the uncommitted players, signaled a hard-line stand on the Czechoslovak issue.[17] His position was probably influenced by his own experience with "nationalism" as the head of the Ukrainian party apparatus, where he was Shelest's predecessor.

Decision makers with responsibilities for foreign affairs appear to have taken a somewhat different reading of the Czechoslovak issue, concluding that intervention would be too costly. What was primarily a domestic issue to officials responsible for domestic affairs was primarily an issue of external relations and ties with constituencies in the West to officials responsible for foreign affairs. M.A. Suslov, chief coordinator of Soviet policies in the international Communist movement, and B.N. Ponomarev and his deputy V.V. Zagladin, leading bureaucrats in the International Department, were concerned with the impact of the events in Czechoslovakia. A military intervention would undermine their organizational mission, their personal prestige, and the maintenance of good ties with their constituencies—the Communist parties and trade organizations in the West and the "progressive" forces in the Third World. Moreover, it would threaten the coming world Communist conference scheduled for November 1968.[18] And, they warned, the intervention would push the Chinese into the U.S. camp.[19]

Premier A.N. Kosygin, who at that time was responsible for governmental diplomacy and was an advocate of the Nonproliferation Treaty (NPT) and an early start to SALT talks with the United States, probably also feared the harmful effects of intervention.[20] Bureaucrats at the International Department and the Ministry of Foreign Affairs seemed to feel that intervention would be detrimental to ongoing foreign policy strategies, would strengthen U.S. opposition to SALT, and would enhance the electoral prospects of Richard M. Nixon—the presidential candidate who at the time was perceived as a staunch anti-Communist and an advocate of U.S. strategic "superiority."[21]

The Secretary General

In contrast to a U.S. president's capacity to accept or reject the views of the National Security Council and to alter the composition of the government, the secretary general of the CPSU must have the support of most of his colleagues in the ruling elite. Even though the events surrounding Nixon's resignation have shown that a U.S. president can be removed from office by the threat of impeachment, the chief executive cannot be deposed by a mere coalition of National Security Council or cabinet members. In Soviet politics this outcome is quite possible, as Khrushchev's fall in October 1964 demonstrates. Whereas the U.S. president has come to exercise "the power to persuade," the secretary general in the Soviet Union acts as first among equals and thus is required not only to persuade but also to identify himself with, or better, to create, a winning coalition in the Politburo. (This was even more true in the late 1960s, when Brezhnev's personal influence as secretary general was relatively minor compared with that of the 1970s.) These constraints of the office could be observed in Secretary General Brezhnev's behavior during the Czechoslovak crisis. In trying to play the game according to the rules of first among equals, Brezhnev vacillated between the interventionist and noninterventionist coalitions during the several stages of the crisis in an attempt to identify himself with the prevailing one.[22] Brezhnev's indecisiveness became obvious when he apologized in June 1968 to one of the most outspoken Czechoslovak reformers, J. Smrkovsky, for attacks of Soviet "propaganda" against him, explaining that this had happened because of a lack of information.[23] Also, some shifting of stands by other players, particularly those with no organizational commitments, obviously took place during the protracted crisis. The continual changes in Soviet decisions, especially during the last strenuous phase of the crisis, indicate that some of the decision makers, including Brezhnev, altered their stands several times.

East European Players

As in the Soviet Union, there appear to have been two schools of thought among the East European elites regarding the Czechoslovak situation. One was represented by East German leader Walter Ulbricht and the Polish leader Wladyslaw Gomulka; the other by Hungarian leader Janos Kadar. Gomulka hated Dubcek and envied his popularity in Czechoslovakia. This animosity was fueled by the March 1968 student demonstration in Warsaw and the ongoing factional struggle in Poland, presumably influenced by Prague reformism.[24] Ulbricht feared the effects of the "cancer" of Dubcekism in his own country.[25] Whereas Ulbricht and Gomulka considered Czechoslovak reformism a threat to their bureaucratic positions and saw intervention as an opportunity to improve their domestic as well as interbloc postures, Czechoslovak reformism was a boon to Kadar's cautious pursuit of greater domestic flexibility in Hungary. Kadar's tolerance and benign neutrality toward Czechoslovakia[26] were probably motivated, in his perception, by the chance of a nonmilitary resolution, which would allow the continuation of Hungary's moderate domestic policy; for example, the experiment with economic reform begun early in 1968 known as the New Economic Mechanism (NEM).

Contrary to most reports of the situation, during the 1968 crisis the Czechoslovak leadership was divided into two competing coalitions—reformists and antireformists. The antireformist coalition was composed of heterogeneous elements, including those who in the early stages of the crisis supported Dubcek (D. Kolder and V. Bilak) but later, for a variety of reasons, began to fear loss of their power at the forthcoming Congress of the Czechoslovak party. After its defeat at the regional and district party conferences in June and July, the antireformist coalition intensified its effort to discredit the reformists in Dubcek's leadership and to secure Soviet "fraternal assistance"[27] by providing "proofs" to the Soviet Politburo of the presence of "counterrevolution" in Czechoslovakia.

Playing Coalition Politics

Politics in the Soviet Union, as in Western countries, makes strange bedfellows. As suggested by a survey of several cases, most notably Robert Tucker's and Stephen Cohen's analyses of Soviet politics in the 1920s, and Michael Tatu's study of Soviet politics in the 1960s,[28] coalitions in Soviet politics are loose, temporary, issue-oriented, heterogeneous alliances of convenience among different subgroups powerful enough to carry out their policies. Moreover, in the Soviet Union the prime motivating factors in the formation of coalitions are not necessarily ideological considerations but rather calculations of expected payoffs (including that of being on the winning side), or calculations of compatibility and conflicts of interest.[29] Although a winning coalition in Soviet politics at minimum is composed of a majority of senior Politburo members, it must also include influential Central Committee bureaucrats.

The opposition of such coalitions can change unexpectedly and dramatically. As stressed earlier, there was a diversity of opinion among senior decision makers on *how* to cope with the "Czechoslovakia threat." The decision makers favoring Soviet intervention, in building up an interventionist coalition, conceptualized the Czechoslovak situation as a zero-sum game—one side's gain was the other side's loss. Although some differences of opinion about the implementation of military intervention probably existed among members of this coalition, they probably perceived it as the only option available. Their aim was the removal of Dubcek and his supporters by military force. The payoff of such a policy, as seen by the various segments of this coalition, rested in excising the "cancer" of Czechoslovak reformism. Some members appear to have joined the interventionist coalition to obtain other kinds of payoffs, mainly bargaining leverage on other issues. Ideological bureaucrats like Trapeznikov may have hoped that the crushing of Czechoslovak reformism would strengthen their positions in dealing with dissidents and reformers at home.

On the other side, members of the noninterventionist coalition, citing the high risks of military intervention, conceptualized the Czechoslovak crisis as a non zero-sum game and thus recommended resolution of the crisis by political or economic means. Undoubtedly, a range of opinion existed among those Soviet officials who questioned the wisdom of military intervention, some advocating political bargaining, others perhaps political or economic coercion, or even actions aimed at "the destabilization" of Dubcek's regime. For example, in April 1968 Zagladin, one of the skeptics of the intervention, was reported by D. Voslensky, an eyewitness and adviser to the Central Committee of the CPSU, to have stated that the situation in Czechoslovakia "should not be dramatized" since "it cannot be compared with Hungary" (in 1956). Zagladin agreed with Voslensky that the USSR's policy should be politically supportive of Dubcek against both extremes in Czechoslovak politics: the discredited supporters of Novotny as well as the anti-Soviet forces.[30] What united these policy makers were perceptions of the high risks of military intervention; but they apparently differed among themselves as to the means for dealing with the "Czechoslovak threat." Thus they recommended resolving the crisis by a variety of means short of invasion, and at considerably less political cost.

These differences between coalitions were highlighted several times during the crisis. Whereas a Soviet military delegation (which included the interventionist Epishev) used pressure and coercion during its May visit to Czechoslovakia, Premier Kosygin used persuasion.[31] Whereas Kadar displayed a moderate stand toward Czechoslovakia at the Warsaw Conference in July, Ulbricht pressed for intervention.[32] Shelest tried to break up the bargaining during the negotiations between the Czechoslovak and Soviet leaderships at Cierna-on-Tisa by insulting the Czechoslovak reformists and accusing them of actively supporting separatist tendencies in the Transcarpathian Ukraine; Suslov, under pressure from several influential Communist parties (Italian, Spanish, Yugoslav, and Rumanian), and perhaps fearing for the forthcoming world Communist conference, argued in favor of a political resolution of the crisis.[33]

Consensus Building

During the crisis, a deadline imposed by circumstances, together with the requirements of consensus building, had an impact on coalition formation. The deadline, as projected by the interventionist coalition, was September 9, 1968, the date of the Fourteenth Extraordinary Party Congress in Czechoslovakia, during which most of the pro-Soviet Central Committee members would be expelled and a new pro-Dubcek slate would be elected, thus legitimizing his program. The interventionists argued that a decision must be made before the Congress took place. According to one interventionist, Ulbricht, the date of the Czechoslovak Congress set a deadline for the Warsaw Pact countries, because afterward "they would be faced with a completely new situation. . . . All the good Communists would lose their posts." Thus, "the Warsaw Pact must react before this Party Congress can take place."[34] In short, the Congress of the Czechoslovak Communist party provided the occasion for resolving the issue.

Various maneuvers took place in an effort to create a consensus on policy. The interventionist coalition evidently tried to enlarge the decision-making circle by bringing in new participants. For example, in April 1968, K.F. Katushev, a regional party official with no previous experience in foreign affairs, replaced an experienced, but not "hard enough," foreign policy bureaucrat, K.V. Rusakov, in the important post of party secretary in charge of the Department of Liaison with Ruling Communist Parties. Another regional bureaucrat, Y.V. Ilnitskii, who as party secretary from Transcarpathia was even more obscure than Katushev, participated with Katushev in postintervention diplomacy. Ilnitskii also spoke at the important July session of the Central Committee of the CPSU, which dealt exclusively with the Czechoslovak issue.[35] The very fact that the rules of the game were probably being readjusted and tuned to the interests of the interventionist coalition (both Ilnitskii and Voss, thought to be nonmembers of the Central Committee of the CPSU, spoke in this forum) suggests that the interventionists succeeded in expanding the circle to include participants who could dramatize the danger of Czechoslovakia's influence upon the non-Russian republics in the Soviet West. In general, bureaucrats from this part of the Soviet Union belonged to the interventionist coalition and constituted one of its most important factions. At the July session, almost half of the speakers were representatives of these republics. These officials, because of geographic proximity and cultural and social peculiarities of their republics, seem to have been much concerned about "contamination" from the Czechoslovak "disease."[36]

Maneuvers in Influencing the Decision

The maneuvering among Soviet decision makers during the Czechoslovak crisis took place within an organizational context. An illustration is the performance of the Warsaw Pact command and its commander in chief, Marshall I.I. Iakubovskii, during the June-July military exercises on Czechoslovak territory. According to a Kosygin-Dubcek understanding, the regular Warsaw Pact units originally were not scheduled to participate in these exercises. But Iakubovskii reportedly insisted on deploying Warsaw Pact troops in Czechoslovakia until September 20—the closing day of the Party Congress—and he was reluctant to order their withdrawal despite earlier assurances from Kosygin to Dubcek.[37]

The resignation of the chief of staff of the Warsaw Pact, General M.I. Kazakhov, signaled that even at the top of the Warsaw Pact command there were fears that military intervention against the only "natural ally" of the Soviet Union might have a detrimental effect on the Soviet Union's defense system in Eastern Europe. Moreover, for the Soviet military services, resolution of the Czechoslovak crisis probably had important budgetary implications. Perhaps it was not accidental that long-time advocates of the Soviet version of "flexible response and ground forces lobbyists, Generals Iakubovskii and S.M. Shtemenko[38] (who replaced the reclutant General Kazakhov shortly before the invasion),[39] were numbered among the interventionists, and that General I.G. Pavlovskii, the new commander in chief of the ground forces command reestablished in December 1967, was in charge of the invasion. Perhaps, the ground forces lobbyists within the armed forces saw in the crisis an opportunity to improve their organizational mission. There were also signs, however, that other branches of the armed forces, in particular Marshal N.I. Krylov's strategic forces, whose organizational mission was hardly affected by developments in Czechoslovakia, may have had doubts about the wisdom of military intervention.[40]

The Soviet Committee for State Security (KGB), particularly officials responsible for East European and domestic affairs, aligned itself with those bureaucracies whose organizational mission was adversely affected by Prague reformism. KGB men in Prague had been dismissed, their security surveillance system dismantled, and past KGB activities revealed. It is therefore not surprising that the KGB engaged in various maneuvers to influence the Soviet decision, including producing such "proofs of counterrevolution" and "Western subversion" in Czechoslovakia as fabricated leaflets threatening the people's militia, and the discovery of a "secret cache" of U.S.-made weapons (packed in Soviet-made bags) near the Czechoslovak-West German border.[41] Moreover, the KGB conducted covert actions against reformists (which entailed distributing anti-Dubcek leaflets) and probably produced resolutions, letters, and articles threatening and discrediting Czechoslovak Minister of the Interior J. Pavel and other Czechoslovak reformists.[42] All of these actions, which dramatized the situation in Czechoslovakia, served to build support among Soviet bureaucracies and the public for intervention.

The Role of Information

The collection and processing of information is an important function of several Soviet foreign policy bureaucracies. The fiercely competitive atmosphere of the bureaucracies could conceivably compel an agency to "manage" its information in the hope of enhancing its organizational or ideological mission or scoring an advantage over a rival agency.[43]

Soviet decision makers, as their Western counterparts, receive incomplete and distorted information from their agencies abroad. A case study relating to Czechoslovakia shows how information sent to Soviet decision makers can be manipulated. During the Novotny era, Soviet leaders received more or less accurate information from Czechoslovakia through established organizational channels of the information and communication systems. With the personnel changes made under Dubcek's leadership, they lost control over these channels and many times appeared not to have adequate or accurate information. Thus, Soviet decision makers were forced to seek alternative East German, Polish, and Czechoslovak antireformist sources of information on the critical Czechoslovak issue. Furthermore, they relied heavily on information and intelligence estimates of the KGB, which were affected by that organization's self-serving interests. Similarly, the reports of the Soviet ambassador to Czechoslovakia, Chervonenko, appear to have been influenced by his background experience as Soviet ambassador to China, by his relationship with Czechoslovak reformists, and by his possible fear of becoming the man who "lost Czechoslovakia." The reports may also have been influenced by Chervonenko's fear that if the intervention did not occur, Czechoslovak reformists would succeed in convincing the Soviet leadership (as Smrkovsky had attempted to do during negotiations with Brezhnev in June 1968) to recall him from Prague.[44]

The KGB and Ambassador Chervonenko were ill-prepared to assess correctly the configuration of the non-Communist forces in Czechoslovakia, the balance of forces between reformist and antireformist coalitions, and Dubcek's popularity; as a result, the picture they presented to the Soviet Politburo was a distorted one. Dubcek and other reformists were portrayed as a minority force in the Czechoslovak leadership who relied mainly on the support of "radical" pressure groups and who were potential agents of the "imperialist" powers. The antireformists in turn were characterized not as what they were—a small rival group fearing a loss of power—but as representatives of a widespread opposition among the healthy party cadres and as dedicated Communists opposed to the right-wing coup in Czechoslovakia.[45] The significance of certain developments during the Prague spring—for example, the emergence of various political clubs, and radical pronouncements such as the famous "Two Thousand Words"—was vastly overrated and presented as proof of the counterrevolution in Czechoslovakia.

The Bureaucratic Tug-of-War

The negotiations at Cierna-on-Tisa between the Czechoslovak and Soviet leaderships (where nine of the 11 members of the Soviet Politburo were present) brought about an uncertain *modus vivendi.* Although no written agreement materialized and only verbal promises were made by both sides, selected teams from the Soviet and Czechoslovak contingents pledged to defuse the crisis. Shortly afterward, on August 3, the conference of Warsaw Pact members (minus Rumania) took place in Bratislava. Here, despite the objections of Ulbricht and Gomulka, the ambiguous promises of the Cierna negotiations were incorporated in the loose ideological language of the Bratislava declaration. The provisional and ambiguous nature of the agreement was underscored by the fact that the Soviet leadership ordered the withdrawal of Warsaw Pact units from Czechoslovakia, but not those units concentrated around the Czechoslovak borders. The latter units did not return to home stations but remained in encampments along the Czechoslovak frontier.[46] The divided Politburo decided against intervention; but at the same time it did not order the dismantling of the military build-up. The outcome of the negotiations was perceived only as a provisional settlement that did not exclude intervention if the Czechoslovak reformists failed to implement the agreement.

The bureaucratic tug-of-war within the Soviet Politburo intensified after the negotiations. The Soviet leaders must have returned to the Soviet Union with differing expectations of the compromise—the noninterventionists hopeful that it would work, the interventionists convinced that it would not. Some elements of the noninterventionist coalition were satisfied with the results, particularly the removal of the direct threat to the world Communist conference[47] and of a possible indirect threat to the SALT negotiations. The interventionists, on the other hand, were disappointed because their strongly felt bureaucratic demands were not included in the Bratislava declaration. As before the Bratislava accord, the interventions sought to build a consensus for ending the temporary truce with Czechoslovakia.

At this crucial stage, elements of the interventionist coalition—the party establishment in the Soviet Union's Western non-Russian republics, the departments of the Central Committee of the CPSU concerned with ideological supervision and indoctrination, the interventionists in the KGB, and the interventionists in the armed forces—communicated to the Politburo their dissatisfaction with the sudden moderation of Soviet policy and intensified their efforts to reverse the trend. The bureaucrats responsible for ideological supervision and indoctrination used cryptic language to express their disapproval with the agreement, which did not call for reimposition of censorship in Czechoslovakia.[48] The interventionists in the non-Russian republics, particularly in the Ukraine, similarly communicated their disapproval of the policy of nonintervention.[49] Ukrainian party boss Shelest redoubled his efforts to mobilize the bureaucracies to undo the Cierna-Bratislava compromise, reportedly by supplying the Politburo with accounts of the alarming situation in Czechoslovakia and the stimulation of nationalist sentiment in the Ukraine.[50]

In not criticizing Czechoslovakia's dismissal of KGB agents from Prague (in whose behalf a high KGB official, Vinokurov, intervened unsuccessfully with the Czechoslovak Minister of Interior Pavel),[51] the Cierna-Bratislava agreement did not reinstate to its former prominence the KGB organizational mission in Czechoslovakia. This further angered the KGB leadership. Some Soviet generals who believed that during the Prague spring Czechoslovakia's defense capabilities were seriously shaken and weakened considered the Bratislava declaration provisions too ambiguous and were probably displeased with the Politburo's decision to withdraw Warsaw Pact troops from Czechoslovak territory.[52]

Pressure from East European Interventionists

Polish leader Gomulka, fearing that appeasement of the Czechoslovaks would intensify factional tension at home and possibly weaken his position at the November 1968 Congress of the Polish Communist party, probably signaled to the Soviet leadership that he could give no guarantee of political stability in his country unless the Soviet Union used military force to restore order in Czechoslovakia.[53] East German leader Ulbricht, who in June had tried to create a political crisis with West Germany over Berlin, in August (shortly after the conference at Bratislava) unexpectedly proposed an exchange of missions of economic cooperation with West Germany's "revanchists." He also undertook a visit to Karlovy Vary in Czechoslovakia for negotiations with Dubcek shortly before the invasion on August 12. Ulbricht's actions were aimed at convincing the coalition-ridden Soviet Politburo that the "soft" nature of the Cierna-Bratislava understanding might have unfavorable consequences for East Germany and that Dubcek's regime was not complying with the Cierna-Bratislava agreement and should be removed.[54] To the Czechoslovak antireformist coalition, the Cierna-Bratislava compromise was seen as contributing to a defeat at the forthcoming Extraordinary Party Congress in Czechoslovakia on September 9. Accordingly, shortly after Bratislava they apparently transmitted urgent reports to the Soviet Politburo, depicting the Congress as leading to disintegration of the Czechoslovak leadership and to the generally unstable political conditions in Czechoslovakia.

The Final Debate: Logistic and Rational Arguments, Shared Images, Costs, and Deterrence

The scattered evidence suggests that the Politburo's final decision was based on information and estimates provided by the KGB and Ambassador Chervonenko, and on "urgent" reports from Ulbricht, Gomulka, and the Czechoslovak antireformists, D. Kolder, A. Indra, and V. Bilak who forecasted a "right-wing" takeover at the Extraordinary Party Congress.[55] All these signals and pressures probably made it easier for interventionists in the Soviet Politburo to argue that military intervention after the Congress would be much more difficult and costly, and that dealing with the impact of Czechoslovak reformism on the Soviet Union and Eastern Europe, should it be validated at the Congress would be much more problematic. The argument that military intervention could not be delayed any longer was apparently reinforced by logistic considerations of the Soviet armed forces, particularly the rear service. Their commander in chief, General S.S. Mariakhim, in evaluating the so-called rear service exercise that took place in July (actually a preparation for a military build-up on the Czechoslovak borders), implied that if the Politburo were to decide to withdraw these troops, he could not guarantee the success of a military intervention in the future without disruption of the Soviet economy and its transportation system.[56] As it was, the rear service exercise, in which thousands of reservists were called up and thousands of motor transport vehicles were mobilized from civilian resources, was probably already detrimental to the collective harvest in the Soviet Union. Continuation of the exercise would be even more costly, and the command of the rear services apparently did not consider an indefinite military presence around Czechoslovakia to be a viable organizational option. In short, the "logistics" argument held that after Bratislava only two options were available: either dismantle the military build-up or intervene.

Meanwhile, the United States—caught up in Vietnam, racial disturbances, and presidential politics—was either unable or unwilling to do anything on behalf of embattled Czechoslovakia. This posture was implied by the public statements of Secretary of State Dean Rusk in July 1968, by the Johnson administration's continued interest in the SALT negotiations, and by the behavior of the U.S. armed forces in West Germany. (In July, strict orders were given to the U.S. command in West Germany forbidding all activity, including an increase of air or ground patrols, on Czechoslovak borders that might be interpreted by the Soviets as supportive of Dubcek's regime.) This state of affairs probably strengthened the case of the interventionist coalition.

Furthermore, Dubcek's dismissal of General V. Prchlik under pressure from the antireformist coalition shortly before the negotiations at Cierna and Bratislava signaled the possibility that Czechoslovakia would not use its military forces to resist an intervention. Prchlik, head of the Security Department of the Central Committee of the Czechoslovak Communist party, was perhaps the only military man in an important position who suggested military defense as a possible government option in case of a Soviet invasion.[57] Dubcek's naivete and indecisiveness and his inexperience in foreign affairs (which contrasted with his expertise in internal politics) were seen in his performance during the Cierna negotiations, when he apparently gave Brezhnev some awkward assurance about the composition of the Czechoslovak leadership.[58] His focus on intergovernmental games, while ignoring the mounting pressures on Czechoslovakia and the implications of intensified debate in the Soviet Politburo, hardly prepared him to expect or to deal with intervention.

Soviet decision makers increasingly came to share ideas propagated by certain bureaucracies that disposed them toward intervention. The view that the Soviet Union should prevent the spread of anticommunism and "the unnecessary shedding of the blood of Czechoslovak Communists,"[59] along with the analogy of Czechoslovakia as a "second" Yugoslavia or Rumania,[60] apparently struck a chord among uncommitted senior decision makers. Also, the one-sided characterization given in Czechoslovakia, in Eastern Europe (particularly Rumania and Albania), and in the West which portrayed the Cierna-Bratislava agreement as a Czechoslovak triumph and a Soviet defeat, while noting other signs of Soviet "weakness," probably moved Soviet decision makers in the direction of intervention.[61]

It is unlikely that in their arguments the interventionists invoked the threat of Western intervention in the near or foreseeable future in Czechoslovakia, for such an argument would not have been taken seriously by Soviet officials. It was clear to them, particularly after Bratislava, that the Dubcek government would not "deviate" in its foreign policy orientation,[62] and that NATO intervention in Czechoslovakia was highly unlikely. This is not to say that the argument of the "threat from the West" was not employed in the debate preceding the invasion in order to "move the bureaucracies" and create public support. However, for the most part, the interventionists probably based their arguments on the need for the Soviet Union to be in a position to cope with the unpredictability of internal developments in Czechoslovakia after the Czechoslovak Party Congress and to control the impact of these developments on the Soviet Union (primarily in the Ukraine), on Soviet dissidents and reformers, and on the unstable conditions in Poland and East Germany.

Anatomy of a Decision

In the face of the growing consensus emerging from Soviet bureaucratic politics and the pressures from Eastern Europe, the arguments of skeptics of the wisdom of the invasion grew less persuasive. Secretary General Brezhnev, in particular, was concerned with the domestic political effects of a policy of nonintervention. In the post-Bratislava period he apparently decided to join the interventionist coalition because of the various bureaucratic pressures that may have threatened to undermine his position in the Politburo. It seems that he assessed the Czechoslovak issue not only according to its national security implications but also according to the increasingly powerful influence of the interventionist coalition. The desire to be on the winning side might also explain how Brezhnev and other uncommitted players made their final decision.

Brezhnev's final stand on Czechoslovakia may also have been affected by his disappointment with Dubcek. Brezhnev in particular seems to have trusted Dubcek at the beginning of the crisis, but may have believed himself cheated by Dubcek during the negotiations at Cierna. Brezhnev could not afford to be seen as weak and indecisive, or "soft" on revisionism and anticommunism.[63] He was acutely aware that something had to be done about Czechoslovakia, and in the final bureaucratic conflict he was a member of the coalition that argued in favor of intervention rather than equivocation. While Hungarian leader Kadar was engaged in secret negotiations with Dubcek to find a political solution to the crisis, a new consensus with the Soviet leadership materialized on August 17–18, culminating in the reluctant decision to use military force. Still, some noninterventionists such as Kosygin may have felt that the effects of the intervention could be minimized in the realm of foreign policy, as implied by diplomatic notes to the Western powers regarding Czechoslovakia and by Kosygin's message of August 19 to President Johnson agreeing to a summit meeting and an early October start to the SALT negotiations in Leningrad. His message was an attempt to moderate the probable U.S. reaction to the invasion and a reassurance that arms control negotiations were expected to continue.

According to preintervention intelligence reports from the KGB and Ambassador Chervonenko on August 20, at the last session of the Czechoslovak presidium prior to the convening of the Slovak Party Congress (which was to take place on August 26), the reformist coalition would be defeated and the antireformists would stage a coup. They would then create a new "revolutionary" government and petition the Soviet Union for "fraternal assistance."[64] However, although they tried, the Czechoslovak antireformists succeeded neither in carrying out the coup nor in proclaiming a new government. This failure suggests that the Politburo was not properly aware of the enormous popularity of Dubcek's "right-wing opportunist" minority or of the weaknesses of the antireformists. This erroneous intelligence appears to have been the main cause of the initial political mismanagement of a militarily perfect intervention.

Conclusions

It is beyond the scope of this study to provide a general analysis of Soviet decision making in foreign policy. The bureaucratic politics paradigm is only one of several means of approaching the subject. The conclusions of the study must be tentative, for, although some data are available, the study depends greatly on the author's interpretation of cryptic and incompletely known communications among the Soviet decision makers. Nevertheless, application of the bureaucratic politics paradigm to the Czechoslovak case demonstrates that the early Soviet "soft" policy toward the Dubcek regime was not a ruse calculated to lull that regime into a false sense of security while plans for intervention were being perfected. The findings of the study generally support the arguments of writers who hold that the rational policy approach alone is inadequate in predicting Soviet foreign policy decision. The Soviet decision to intervene militarily in Czechoslovakia was not based on a uniform set of perceptions of national security (such as fears of a "West German threat"), but was shaped by many factors: the bureaucratic interests and perspectives of senior decision makers, manipulated information, East European political instability and pressures, intergovernmental games in Czechoslovakia, signals of U.S. noninvolvement, logistic considerations, and, finally, shaky compromises among various elements in the Politburo.

The prediction of Soviet actions is a venturesome exercise, and this study does not make the Soviet decision-making process any less mysterious. It does make the point that the failure of Dubcek's advisers and of many Western observers to understand the significance of the internal dynamics of Soviet decision making or of the signals among its members accounts in part for their being unable to anticipate the invasion of Czechoslovakia on August 20, 1968. Furthermore, Dubcek's advisers had not seriously researched Soviet politics; nor did they take seriously the signs of debate and the changing "bureaucratic mood" in the Soviet Politburo. These deficiencies proved fatal. The bureaucratic politics paradigm does not guarantee foresight. The demand that an analyst be able to predict precisely an upcoming invasion is unrealistic. But the bureaucratic politics paradigm can improve the chances of detecting signals of serious debate in the Soviet Politburo. Perhaps the Soviet press is so boring that we sometimes ignore it. But as the Czechoslovak case demonstrates, signs of bureaucratic conflict as reflected in the Soviet press can shed light on the politics of intervention. Judicious application of the bureaucratic politics paradigm, then, focusing upon the dynamics of the role played by the bureaucracies involved, can be useful in the analysis of Soviet national security and foreign policy decision making. The Czechoslovak case points to the possibility of usefully studying Soviet decision making from this perspective.

Notes

1. General James H. Polk, "Reflections on the Czechoslovakian Invasion 1968," *Strategic Review* 5 (1977): 36–37. The author of this article arrived at the same conclusion while discussing the issue with several former high officials in the Johnson administration.

2. Bohlen's memorandum to Secretary of State Dean Rusk, August 13, 1968 as quoted in Charles E. Bohlen, *Witness to History 1929–1969* (New York: Norton, 1973), pp. 530–31.

3. Graham T. Allison, *Essence of Decision: Explaining the Cuban Missile Crisis* (Boston: Little, Brown, 1971). Also see Morton H. Halperin, *Bureaucratic Politics and Foreign Policy* (Washington, D.C.: The Brookings Institution, 1974).

4. See for example, Hans Morgenthau, "Inquisition in Czechoslovakia," *New York Review of Books,* December 4, 1969, pp. 20–21; Herman Kahn, "How to Think about the Russians," *Fortune,* November 1968, pp. 231–32.

5. The document usually referred to as the locus of the Brezhnev Doctrine is an article by S. Kovalev, "Sovereignty and the International Obligations of Socialist Countries," *Pravda,* September 26, 1968. For a discussion see Boris Meissner, *The Brezhnev Doctrine,* East Europe Monograph 21 (Kansas City: Park College Governmental Research Bureau, 1970). Most published studies of the Czechoslovak crisis depend more or less upon a rational policy model.

6. On the "shared images" of national security interests held by U.S. leaders, see Halperin, *Bureaucratic Politics,* pp. 11–12.

7. For an examination of institutions involved in Soviet foreign policy decision making, see Vernon V. Aspaturian, "Soviet Foreign Policy," in *Foreign Policy in World Politics,* ed., Roy L. Macridis (Englewood Cliffs, N.J.: Prentice-Hall, 1962); Jan F. Triska and David D. Finley, *Soviet Foreign Policy* (New York: Macmillan, 1968); and Vladimir Petrov, "Soviet Foreign Policymaking," *Orbis* 17 (Fall 1973): 819–50.

8. For a discussion, see Roman Kolkowicz, "The Military," in *Interest Groups in Soviet Politics,* ed. H. Gordon Skilling and Franklyn Griffiths (Princeton: Princeton University Press, 1971), pp. 160–64; and Andrew W. Marshall, *Bureaucratic Behavior and the Strategic Arms Competition* (Santa Monica, CA: Southern California Arms Control and Foreign Policy Seminar, October 1971).

9. Dimitri Simes and Gordon Rocca, "Soviet Decision Making and National Security Affairs," Memorandum 20–KM–11–1, November 1973, Georgetown University Center for Strategic and International Studies, Washington, D.C., 1974, pp. 25–26.

10. For a detailed treatment of the origins of the Prague spring, see, in particular, H. Gordon Skilling, *Czechoslovakia's Interrupted Revolution* (Princeton: Princeton University Press, 1976) and Galia Golan, *The Czechoslovak Reform Movement: Communism in Crisis 1962–1968* (Cambridge: Cambridge University Press, 1971).

11. The differing perceptions of Soviet officials regarding the Czechoslovak crisis can be deciphered by an analysis of the contents of their speeches and public statements. Some officials consistently attacked the "nationalist" and "right-wing revisionist" elements, "various demagogues and renegades" and "degenerates," and their "models of democratic socialism" and policies of "limitless decentralism." They called for "revolutionary vigilance" in the USSR, and some of them began to hint at offers of "fraternal assistance" to the "healthy forces" of Czechoslovakia in their struggle "against imperialist intrigues." Meanwhile, other officials, who consistently refrained from cryptic assaults on the Czechoslovak leadership, pledged respect for "each other's views," the "right of autonomy" and "noninterference in the internal affairs" of other Communist parties, some of them occasionally expressing publicly their "confidence in the Czechoslovak party." During the crisis this group, instead of attacking the "right-wing revisionist," consistently assaulted the "left revisionism" or "left adventurist pervasion of Marxism" in the Chinese leadership as the main danger to the USSR. The former groups of officials, on the other hand, probably because of their preoccupation with the Czechoslovak issue, did not express any concern regarding the policies of the Chinese leadership.

Hereafter, in keeping with the purpose of this chapter, the public speeches and pronouncements of Soviet leaders will be referred to without going into lengthy analyses. For a detailed analysis, see Jiri Valenta, "Soviet Decision-making and the 1968 Czechoslovak Crisis," *Studies in Comparative Communism* 8 (Spring-Summer 1975): 147–73.

12. For Shelest's views of the Czechoslovak crisis, see his speeches in *Pravda Ukrainy,* February 17, 1968, and *Pravda,* July 5, 1968. See also an analysis by Grey Hodnett and Perter J. Potichny, *The Ukraines and the Czechoslovak Crisis* (Can-

berra: Australian National University, 1970).

13. For Masherov's views, see *Sovetskaia Belorussiia,* May 11, 1968. For Snechkus's views, see his article, "The April Session and Some of Our Tasks," in *Kommunist* (Journal of the Central Committee of Lithuania) 6 (June 1968): 3–7, and *Kummunist* 10 (October 1968): 9–10.

14. For Pelshe's stand, see *Neues Deutschland,* May 4, 1968, and *Tribuna* (Prague), March 26, 1969. Trapenznikov's militant view on the Czechoslovak issue is developed in his book *At the Turning Points of History* (Moscow: Progress, 1972), pp. 73–78. For Grishin's stand, see *Pravda,* April 23, 1968.

15. For KGB position on Czechoslovak reformism, see Ladislav Bittman, *The Deception Game: Czechoslovak Intelligence in Soviet Warfare* (Syracuse, N.Y.: Frolik Defection* (London: Leo Cooper, 1975), pp. 130–79.

16. As reported in *Le Monde,* May 5–6, 1968.

17. For Podgorny's views, see Radio Moscow, May 6, 1968, and *Pravda,* July 10, 1968.

18. For Suslov's views, see *Pravda,* February 28 and May 6, 1968. For Zagladin's views, see *Pravda,* April 29, 1968, and Radio Moscow, March 21, 1968.

19. Dimitri Simes, "The Soviet Invasion of Czechoslovakia and the Limits of Kremlinology," *Studies in Comparative Communism* 8 (Spring-Summer 1975): 178. See also hints in the "The Political Course of Mao Tse-tung on the International Scene," *Kommunist* (May 1968): 95–108.

20. For Kosygin's views, see his speeches in *Sovetskaia Belorussiia,* February 15, 1968; *Izvestiia,* July 2, 1968. As late as July, Kosygin expressed "confidence in Czechoslovak Communists," *Pravda,* July 15, 1968. For Kosygin's stand on SALT, see Lyndon B. Johnson, *The Vantage Point* (New York: Holt, Rinehart and Winston, 1971), pp. 484–85; John Newhouse, *Cold Dawn: The Story of SALT* (New York: Holt, Rinehart and Winston, 1973), pp. 91–94; and an interview with Dr. Walt W. Rostow, July 26, 1974, Austin, Texas.

21. Simes, "The Soviet Invasion," p. 178. See also A. Grigorysants and V. Rogov, "Leninist Ideas are Invincible: The Policy of Anticommunism Meets with Failure, Richard Nixon Again," *Trud,* August 13, 1968.

22. For Brezhnev's views, see Radio Leningrad, February 16, 1968, and *Pravda,* February 23, March 30, and July 4, 1968; E. Weit, *At the Red Summit: Interpreter behind the Iron Curtain* (New York: Macmillan, 1973), pp. 209–10.

23. An interview with Josef Smrkovsky published posthumously in *Listy* (Roma), no. 2 (March 1975): 11–12.

24. Weit, *At the Red Summit,* p. 205; Alexander Dubcek's letter to the Federal Assembly of Czechoslovakis and the Slovak National Council, October 1974 (hereafter referred to as Dubcek's letter) in *Listy,* no. 3 (April 1975): 14.

25. Dubcek's letter, p. 14.

26. For Kadar's views on Czechoslovakia, see his interview in C.L. Sulzberger, *An Age of Mediocrity: Memoirs and Diaries, 1963–1972* (New York: Macmillan, 1973), pp. 476–77.

27. Dubcek's letter to Comrade K. Smrkovsky, *Listy,* no. 2 (May 1974): 5; and an interview with Smrkovsky, *Listy,* no. 2 (May 1974): 15; and Zdenek Mylynar, *Ceskoslovensky pokus o reformu 1968* (Koln: Index-Listy, 1975), p. 233.

28. Robert Tucker, *Stalin as Revolutionary* (New York: Norton, 1973); Stephen F. Cohen, *Bukharin and the Bolshevik Revolution: A Political Biography,*

1888–1938 (New York: Knopf, 1973); and Michel Tatu, *Power in the Kremlin: From Khrushchev to Kosygin* (New York: Viking, 1969).

29. The concept of calculations of expected payoffs is developed in William H. Riker, *The Theory of Political Coalitions* (New Haven: Yale University Press, 1962). For an important modification of Riker's theory, see Robert Axelrod, *Conflict of Interest: A Theory of Divergent Goals with Application to Politics* (Chicago, Ill.: Markham, 1970), esp. pp. 165–85.

30. See exerpts from the diary of a Soviet eyewitness Professor M. Voslensky, a former arms control expert of the Central Committee of the CPSU, now living in Munich. "This Will Only Help Americans," *Der Spiegel* 34 (August 21, 1978): 126.

31. Kosygin's moderate behavior was reported on Prague television, May 22, 1968; and in *Zemedelske noviny,* May 22, 1968. Here I benefited from an interview with a former deputy prime minister of the Czechoslovak government, Ota Sik, June 5, 1974, St. Gallen.

32. Weit, *At the Red Summit,* pp. 201–2.

33. Pavel Tigrid, *Why Dubcek Fell* (London: MacDonald, 1971), pp. 86–87; and an interview with Smrkovky, *Listy,* p. 13.

34. Ulbricht quoted in Weit, *At the Red Summit,* pp. 202–3.

35. Ilnitskii wrote several articles at the time expressing his concern about the Czechoslovak influence on the inhabitants of his region. See *Pravda Ukrainy,* July 29, 1968; "Our Light: Internationalism," *Kommunist Ukrainy* 1 (1969): 85–93; and an analysis of Hodnett and Potichny, *The Ukraine and the Czechoslovak Crisis,* pp. 144–45.

36. For Voss's view, see "Some Questions of Ideological Work of the Party Organization," *Kommunist Sovetskoi Latvii* 10 (September 30, 1968): 7–15.

37. Tigrid, *Why Dubcek Fell,* p. 68.

38. For Shtemenko's and Iakubovski's views, see General Shtemenko, *Nedelia* 6 (January 31–February 6, 1965); and General Iakubovski, "Ground Forces," *Krasnai zvezda,* July 31, 1967, and his articles "Friendship Born in Battle," *Krasnai zvezda,* June 23, 1968, and "The Battle-ready Community of Armies of the Socialist Countries," *Kummunist* 5 (1970): 90–100.

39. John Thomas, *Soviet Foreign Policy and Conflict Within the Political and Military Leadership* (McLean, VA: Research Analysis Corporation, September 1970), p. 9.

40. John Erickson, "Towards a New Soviet High Command: 'Rejuvenation' Reviewed," *Royal United Service Institute Journal* (England) 9 (September 1969): 37–44.

41. An official Czechoslovak investigation of the "secret cache" of weapons concluded that this allegation was "a provocation." See an interview with Smrkovsky, *Listy,* p. 15.

42. For the activities of the KGB see Bittman, *The Deception Game,* p. 214; and Frolik, *The Frolik Defection,* p. 148.

43. See *The Penkovsky Papers* (New York: Doubleday, 1965), pp. 255–77, and a report in *Die Welt,* November 1, 1975.

44. Smrkovsky told Brezhnev that Chervonenko did not inform the Soviet leadership "accurately," and indicated that Czechoslovak reformists hoped that he would be recalled. See an interview with Smrkovsky, *Listy,* p. 15.

45. Tigrid, *Why Dubcek Fell*, p. 98. Soviet leader Ponomarev reportedly complained about the incompetence of Chervonenko" after the invasion, in ibid., p. 227.

46. Polk, "Reflections," p. 37.

47. See hints of this in the authoritative article "Strength in Unity," *Pravda,* August 5, 1968.

48. For example, see hints in "The Political Milk of *Literarni listy*," *Literaturnaia gazeta,* August 14, 1968; G. Kibets and A. Stepanov, "Dictatorship of the Proletariat: Its Content and Forms," *Sovetskaia Rossia,* August 9, 1968.

49. Pravda Ukrainy, August 1, 1968; "Fidelity to Marxism-Leninism: Source of the Strength of Socialist Cooperation," *Kommunist Ukrainy* 8 (August 1978): 3–13; *Sovetskaia Estoniia,* August 4–7, 1968.

50. See "The Removal of Shelest," *Listy,* no. 4 (July 1972): 33; "The Unexpected Soviet Initiative-Thaw in Prague," *Le Monde,* June 17–18, 1973.

51. Robert Little, ed., *The Czechoslovak Black Book* (New York: Praeger, 1979), pp. 80–81; Frolik, *The Frolik Defection,* p. 150.

52. Czechoslovak Prime Minister Cernik reported that this had been concluded by the Soviet general prior to the intervention. See Tigrid, *Why Dubcek Fell,* p. 95. For hints of military dissatisfaction with the Bratislava agreement, see *Krasnai zvezda,* August 18, 1968.

53. Jan B. Weydentahal, "Polish Politics and the Czechoslovak Crisis," *Canadian Slavonic Papers* 14 (January 1972); 46, and Weit, *At the Red Summit,* p. 205.

54. For an analysis see Melvin Croan, "Czechoslovakia, Ulbricht, and the German Problem," *Problems of Communism* 1 (January-February 1969): 1–5.

55. Dubcek, *Listy,* p. 5; and Mlynar, *Ceskoslovensky pokus,* p. 233; and Tigrid, *Why Dubcek Fell,* p. 98. Also see hints in "The Letter of Warning of the Soviet Politburo," of August 17, 1968, reported on Radio Prague, August 20, 1969.

56. An interview with General S.S. Mariakhin, *Krasnaia zvezda,* August 14, 1968; and Polk, "Reflections," p. 32.

57. Jiri Pelikan, "The Struggle for Socialism in Czechoslovakis," *New Left Review* (January-February 1972): 27. (Pelikan was the former chairman of the Czechoslovak Assembly's Foreign Affairs Committee). For an argument stressing the importance of the deterrence of East European countries facing Soviet intervention, see Christopher D. Jones, "Soviet Hegemony in Eastern Europe: The Dynamics of Political Autonomy and Military Intervention," *World Politics* 29 (January 1977): 216–41.

58. Tad Szulc, *Czechoslovakia Since World War II* (New York: Viking 1971), p. 374; and Dubcek's speech, September 26, 1969, as reported in *Svedectvi* (Paris), no. 38 (1970): 275–76.

59. Interview with Czechoslovak leader J. Piller, Prague Radio, September 17, 1969.

60. Brezhnev reportedly said that Czechoslovakia was not Rumania or Yugoslavia and that the Soviets would not let Czechoslovakia go. Reported by M. Vaculik in *The Secret Vysocany Congress,* ed. J. Pelikan (London: Allen-Lane, 1971), pp. 26–27.

61. See hints in "The Letter of Warning of the Soviet Politburo," reported by Radio Prague, August 20, 1979.

62. A. Snejdarek (a former foreign policy adviser to Dubcek's leadership) in Kusin, *The Czechoslovak Reform Movement,* p. 51. Even Soviet Ambassador Chervonenko never complained about Dubcek's foreign policy. See the interview with Czechoslovak Foreign Minister J. Hajek, *Reporter* (Prague) 3 (October 16–23, 1968): 45.

63. At the crucial Politburo session on August 17, 1968, several Politburo members reportedly were critical of the "hesitation and weakness in dealing with the Czech question," Tigrid, *Why Dubcek Fell,* p. 97.

64. An interview with Smrkovsky, *Listy,* pp. 16–19; Havlicek in Little, *The Czechoslovak Black Book,* pp. 23–29.

14 THE USSR AND KHOMEINI'S REVOLUTION

Carol R. Saivetz

The decade between 1969 and 1979 witnessed a period of increased Soviet military activity in the Third World. In the War of Attrition between Egypt and Israel, Soviet pilots flew intercept missions across the Suez Canal; during the 1973 Yom Kippur War, the Soviets threatened to introduce their troops unilaterally if the United States would not go along with a joint intervention to save the Egyptian Third Army; in 1976, and again in 1977–78, Moscow participated in cooperative interventions in Angola and Ethiopia by providing logistical and airlift support for Cuban troops; and finally in 1979, the USSR sent its own troops into Afghanistan to prop up a besieged Third World Communist ally. Although the circumstances surrounding each of these intrusions differ, taken together each instance seemed to portend greater Soviet propensity to intervene in the Third World.

It was during this period that the Iranian monarchy of Shah Muhammed Reza Pahlevi disintegrated under pressure from dissatisfied and disaffected elements across the Iranian political spectrum. The final fall of the Peacock Throne and its replacement by a militantly anti-U.S. regime proved a profound loss to U.S. strategic and political interests in the gulf. The USSR, with its long, common border with Iran, tried, of course, to take advantage of this unexpected opportunity through diplomatic, political, economic, and propagandistic means. And while Moscow proffered some military and security aid to the Khomeini regime, it has thus far not chosen military intervention as a foreign policy tool.

This chapter will explore the reasons why, coming as it did in a decade of significant Soviet military activity, the Iranian revolution did not evoke a direct Soviet military response. The first section of the chapter will examine both Soviet objectives in the gulf region and a likely calculus of decision making with regard to active involvement. In light of our analysis of Soviet decision making, we will explore Soviet perceptions of the Iranian revolution, and analyze probable reasons why the Soviets chose not to intervene. Finally, we will speculate on future Soviet policy toward Iran.

Soviet Regional Objectives and Soviet Decision Making

Explaining Soviet international behavior is a difficult endeavor and one on which there is no agreement. As scholars we are forced to extrapolate from policy statements, esoteric discussions in the Soviet academic journals, and from hindsight. We can, nonetheless, make educated guesses about both the apparent aims of Soviet-Third World relations and the probable decision-making calculus used by Soviet policy makers.

Any analyses of Soviet foreign policy in the Persian Gulf region must be made within the context of Soviet-Third World relations in general. While, of course, there are regional variations in both policy and objectives, the USSR seems to have become involved in the Third World with four goals in mind. First, the USSR (as would any state) operates with a clear concern for its security. In the context of our discussion, this means that Moscow's interest in contiguous regions is enhanced. The propinquity of the gulf makes the region one of the Soviet Union's top priorities in the Third World. In the words of one *Izvestiia* columnist: "We are not indifferent to what is happening in a region so close to our borders."[1]

This, indeed, is not a new phenomenon: Historically, Russia has long maintained an interest in Iran. Beginning in the 1800s, Russia's southward expansion brought the Tsarist empire not only to the Iranian border, but also to the point of direct involvement in Iranian domestic affairs. By the turn of the century, Iran became a pawn in the Anglo-Russian chess game then being played in Northwest Asia. The two rivals for regional power signed a convention in 1907 which divided the country into British and Tsarist spheres of influence and in 1908, Tsarist troops entered Iran.

The end of World War I and the disintegration of the Tsarist regime brought about changes in Soviet-Iranian relations. Condemning Tsarist secret treaties, the Bolshevik government proclaimed a new basis for its foreign relations: The Soviets appealed to the "Toiling Muslims of Russia and the East" and abrogated the agreement partitioning Iran. Following a short-lived attempt to establish the Soviet republic of Gilan in northern Iran, Lenin opted instead for a treaty with the central Iranian government. The treaty included mutual pledges not to join military alliances against the other and not to permit hostile forces to operate from the other's territory. And in a clause originally directed against Tsarist forces then still operating in Iran, Russia reserved the right to intervene in Iran "for the purposes of carrying out the military operations necessary for its defense."[2]

During World War II, the pro-German leanings of Reza Shah prompted almost a repeat performance of 1907 from both the USSR and Great Britain: They agreed to occupy Iran jointly for the duration of the war. At the same time, Reza Shah abdicated in favor of his son and the young Shah forced the USSR and Great Britain to sign a formal occupation agreement. In 1945, however, the British withdrew as stipulated in the agreement, while the Soviets remained entrenched in northern Iran. In addition, the Tudeh (Communist) party proclaimed the independence of Azerbaijan. When the United Nations Security Council urged both Iran and the USSR to negotiate, the Tehran government in effect sought to buy out the Soviets. In return for Soviet withdrawal, Iran agreed to establish a joint Soviet-Iranian oil company subject to the approval of the Majlis. The Soviets withdrew, Tehran crushed the rebellion in Azerbaijan, and in the end, the Majlis refused to grant Moscow the promised oil concessions.

Second, the Soviets have apparently acted with a clear view of the potential strategic and geopolitical advantages certain territories provide. From their first attempts to leapfrog the so-called northern tier to their recent search for ports to receive the Soviet navy, the Kremlin clearly understands that certain countries represent political and military bridgeheads into specific regions. The Soviets currently enjoy a significant presence in both the PDRY (The People's Democratic Republic of Yemen) and Ethiopia astride the Red Sea. And Iran would be a political and strategic prize.

As Moscow's power projection capabilities have grown, the Soviet Union sought to extend its military presence in ways that would enhance Soviet abilities to fight a war or assist an ally. In the words of one military adviser: "In some situations, the very knowledge of a Soviet military presence in an area in which a conflict situation is developing may serve to restrain the imperialists and local reaction."[3] Soviet cultivation of regional actors netted calling privileges in Umm Qasr in Iraq and facilities in Aden. This potential naval presence carries with it, in the Soviet view, a major political impact as well: "Official visits and the working calls of our ships to foreign ports make a substantial contribution to the improvement of mutual understanding between states and peoples and to the enhancement of the international authority of the Soviet Union."[4]

The assumption that the Soviets recognize both the geopolitical and strategic importance of the Persian Gulf region also carries with it the negative corollary of attempting to deny these advantages to the West. Thus, a third goal of Soviet policy in the Third World has been to counter Western influence positions around the globe. The Soviets have stepped into areas when and if the United States' relationship with a particular state became strained. Moreover, the Kremlin encourages and promotes anti-Westernism and anti-Americanism among nationalist Third World leaders. Moscow has in some cases merely played a balancing game, while in other instances this probing has led to the successful establishment of a strong Soviet presence.

In Iran, the Kremlin tried to use Khomeini's strident anti-Americanism to establish common ground between Moscow and the new regime in Tehran. The seizure of U.S. diplomatic personnel in the U.S. embassy in Tehran in November 1979 seemed to present the Soviets with a chance to solidify their ties with the Khomeini regime. At first, Soviet Farsi-language broadcasts beamed to Iran were stridently anti-American, but following a U.S. official protest, the broadcasts were toned down. Nonetheless, the official Soviet line was openly sympathetic to the Tehran government. As a correspondent wrote in *Pravda*:

> To be sure, the seizure of the American embassy in and of itself does not conform to the international convention concerning respect for diplomatic privileges and immunity. However, one cannot pull this act out of the overall context of American-Iranian relations.[5]

The USSR used its veto in the Security Council to prevent the council from implementing economic sanctions against Iran. At the same time, the Soviets began to warn Iran against possible U.S. invasions. When in fact the United States did attempt to rescue the hostages, the Soviets issued shrill propaganda attacks. Elsewhere in the gulf, the Soviets have concluded an arms deal with Kuwait (after a U.S. refusal to sell stingers), solidified their relations with the PDRY (after a more compliant leader was installed in 1978), sought to establish diplomatic relations with Saudi Arabia and other gulf states, and opposed the Gulf Cooperation Council.

The strategic value of the gulf and the Soviet desire to lessen Western influences there cannot be considered without mention of oil. The rich oil reserves of Iran, Iraq, and the Arabian Peninsula certainly enhance the region's strategic and political value. Over the past several years, instability in the gulf, Soviet proximity to the area, and speculation about Soviet oil reserves have provoked concern about possible Kremlin control of the supply of Mideast oil. In 1977, the CIA estimated that the USSR would become a net importer of oil by the mid-1980s. This prompted alarm that Moscow would drive toward the gulf in order to ensure its own supply. More recent studies, however, criticized the CIA estimates and argued that the Soviets would continue to have an adequate oil supply for years to come. That the Soviets do not need the oil does not preclude arguments regarding Soviet desires to control the spigot. Several Western analysts contend that Soviet interest in the Persian Gulf is dictated in large measure by the wish to choke off the West's supply of oil. Although such a possibility cannot be ruled out completely, access to oil would seem to be a by-product and not the prime motivation for Soviet intervention in the gulf. Moreover, as will be argued below, a Soviet invasion of Iran and/or the gulf does not appear to be imminent.

Fourth, the Soviets have been intent on securing for themselves superpower status; that is, a firm international recognition that they are indeed a coequal of the United States. In terms of policy, this has meant a Soviet push to obtain legitimacy for their activities in the Third World. Just as the United States has intervened repeatedly to change governments or merely to effect the course of policy, the Soviets too want to secure that right for themselves. In addition, in the Soviet view, superpower status means establishing diplomatic relations with as many states as will accept a Soviet embassy, regardless of ideological and political orientation.

Over the years as the USSR has pursued these goals, it has suffered reverses and generally learned about the volatility of Third World politics.[6] The Soviets' experiences have prompted them to move cautiously and to weigh several factors when deciding responses to specific Third World situations. Three of these factors will be discussed below.

1. The local environment. Soviet policymakers, like their Western counterparts, must assess the characteristics of the unfolding Third World situation. In a purely domestic squabble, Moscow would consider whether Soviet activity such as gun-running or political maneuvering would assist a Soviet client to achieve power. In a local conflict, the Kremlin must decide if it wants to take sides, fully cognizant that partisanship has its costs.

In either a domestic squabble or a local conflict the patron also needs to weigh the response of regional actors to its actions. Could Soviet involvement trigger regional political (and perhaps military) ramifications which are detrimental to Soviet foreign policy interests? For example, would Kremlin interventionism be accepted by other regional actors or would they soundly condemn the intrusion and perhaps turn to the West for protection?

The situations in which the Soviets have intervened cooperatively or by themselves are cases where the survival of Communist or quasi-Communist regimes have been in question. In the Third World context, the category of regimes might well be extended to include "socialist oriented" states.[7] As the USSR has demonstrated both in Eastern Europe and the Third World, intervention occurred to preserve loyal regimes: In many cases, the Soviet arrogated to themselves the intervention decision (the so-called Brezhnev Doctrine) while in others they ostensibly provided military aid by request and invitation. As will be discussed below, Iran in 1979 presented neither an example of a threatened Communist regime, nor a "host" to invite in the Soviet troops.

2. The international environment. No one would dispute that in the 1970s and 1980s, the USSR became far more capable in effecting political and military outcomes in the Third World than a decade earlier. With their increased power projection capabilities and their enhanced global naval presence, the Kremlin possesses the ability to challenge its rivals, the United States and China. Yet, the desire to reduce Western and Chinese influence is clearly not synonymous with a willingness to risk a major superpower confrontation. Indeed, Soviet behavior in the Third World demonstrates Soviet sensitivity to the security interests of the United States. The late Yuri Andropov, for example, not only emphasized Soviet interest in its southern flank, but conceded U.S. interests in Central America. He said in a somewhat sarcastic remark:

> It is, however, far from being a matter of indifference to us what is happening directly on our southern border. Washington even goes as far as arrogating for itself the right to judge what government must be there in Nicaragua since this allegedly affects U.S. vital interests.
> But Nicaragua is over a thousand kilometers away from the U.S.A. and we have a rather long common border with Afghanistan.[8]

Thus, a fundamental variable in any Soviet foreign policy decision would be the likelihood of a major U.S. response to Soviet initiatives. For example, even in the volatile Arab-Israeli dispute, the Soviets, although willing to provide Syria with sophisticated weapons and definitely hoping to perpetuate the conflict, have demonstrated their disinclination to escalate the conflict.[9] By the same token, they correctly perceived that the United States would not respond militarily to the cooperative interventions in Angola and Ethiopia or to their own invasion of Afghanistan. In the latter case, however, the Kremlin did apparently misjudge the political fallout from the invasion.

3. Success and failure. Finally, Kremlin policy makers will in all likelihood calculate the probability of success and the time required for a successful operation. Will the levels of assistance offered be adequate to propel the chosen contender for power into ascendancy or to ensure the recipient state's victory in a border war? Will Soviet or Cuban troops be necessary? For how long will they be engaged? Would the troops be able to maintain the government in power? It is clear that the Soviets miscalculated both the success and duration of the Afghan invasion. From the Soviet perspective, especially in light of events in Poland and the continuing struggle in Afghanistan, a quick, clean operation would clearly be most desirable.

Soviet objectives and Kremlin analyses of the risks and benefits of involvement all affect Moscow's policy toward Iran. In the next section we will examine Soviet perceptions of the Iranian revolution and Soviet activities in the postmonarchical period in light of the discussion of objectives and decision making.

The Soviet Union and the Iranian Revolution

In the period following the restoration of the Iranian monarchy in 1953, the Soviets pursued a double-tracked policy of criticizing the Shah's close military ties with the United States while establishing cordial and mutually beneficial economic relations with Iran. The Shah, for his part, seemed determined to find a niche between the two superpowers, periodically playing one off against the other. In the mid-sixties, Iran and the USSR signed a series of economic agreements which provided for a $300 million credit, a steel mill at Isfahan, and a natural gas pipeline. Two years later, Tehran bought armored personnel carriers and trucks from Moscow. During the seventies, economic relations between the two neighbors flourished. Iran became the largest Third World purchaser of Soviet equipment, and the two agreed to proceed with the construction of a second pipeline. Despite a major price dispute in the mid-seventies, economic relations continued. By all indications, the Soviets were as surprised as their U.S. counterparts with the weakness and eventual collapse of the monarchy.

Signs of the revolution that was to occur in Iran began to appear at least a year earlier, with massive demonstrations in several Iranian cities. The Soviets, at first, appeared discomfited by these early events and went to great lengths to explain what was occurring in Iran and to deny reports that "Marxists" or "Communists" were behind the unrest. By November 1978, the Soviet leadership seemed determined to make the best of what could be a difficult situation. The imminent collapse of the government in Tehran presented Moscow with an unknown variable. The Soviets, at this point, made no moves to intervene directly, although propaganda aimed at the West and at Tehran, itself, made it clear that Moscow felt its interests at stake. In a major address, Party Secretary Leonid Brezhnev warned against foreign intervention in Iran. Later, the Soviets could take credit for forestalling a U.S.-led intervention to prop up the ailing Shah and his crumbling regime.

Had the Soviets chosen armed intervention in Iran, the most propitious time would have been between February 1979 and December 1979. During these 11 months, between the Ayatollah Khomeini's arrival in Tehran and the invasion of Afghanistan, several factors might have facilitated a Soviet intrusion. First, it was a period in which the Khomeini forces had not yet completed their consolidation of power. Power was wielded by an ad hoc network of committees, not all of which were controlled by pro-Khomeini forces. Secular and leftist forces were still vying for political position and the conservative cast of the revolution was not yet set. Second, the Kremlin, at this point, hoped that a congruence of interests could be developed between itself and Khomeini. Moscow obviously tried to use the Ayatollah's vehement anti-Americanism for its own ends. The Soviets might have even hoped that the new regime in Tehran would request Soviet assistance against the United States. Third, ethnic uprisings and demands for national autonomy were prevalent during the early stages of the Iranian revolution. Moscow has found a variety of nationalisms in Iran which it alternately attempted to exploit and worked to overcome.[10] These nationalisms at the least prevented the immediate consolidation of the new regime and at the outset seemed to provide Moscow with ready opportunities. Fourth, the collapse of the Shah's regime created disarray and uncertainty in Washington. Unclear as to what Khomeini's ascension to power would portend, and divided over what kinds of policies to pursue, the Carter administration seemed unlikely to respond militarily to any Soviet action.

By November 1979, and certainly by December, the situation was far less clear cut. Once U.S. diplomatic personnel were seized by militant pro-Khomeini students in Tehran, the U.S. stake and hence probable response to Soviet intervention could be counted on to be greater. The United States would want to protect its hostages against any Soviet onslaught. Moreover, once Soviet troops invaded Afghanistan, some sort of U.S. reaction would be even more likely. The United States, under those circumstances, could not afford to sit back and permit a Soviet occupation of yet another Asian nation.

If the Soviets were to have intervened, they undoubtedly would have used the pretext of having been invited in by some political faction—either in power or close to achieving power. Yet, the situation in Iran did not present the Kremlin with a likely candidate. For the Soviets, the problem lay in the attitudes toward Khomeini adopted by potential "hosts." In the period immediately following Khomeini's arrival in Tehran, several political groupings across the ideological spectrum of Iranian politics cheered the fall of the Shah and many adopted a wait-and-see attitude toward the new regime. For example, the Fedayin i Khalq, a leftist group, was neither prepared to cooperate with the Tudeh nor was it willing to work with the Khomeini regime.

The Tudeh party, with its strong ties to the Kremlin, was of course the most likely candidate. Following the flight of the Shah from Tehran, many Tudeh activists, including Nuraddin Kianuri, the newly appointed party head, returned to Iran from their exile in Eastern Europe. Kianuri had replaced Iarj Iskandari who, although the long time leader of the party, was opposed to cooperating with the Khomeini regime. The party which operated legally during the first revolutionary phase proclaimed its fidelity to Marxism-Leninism while supporting the clerical regime.

   This Tudeh policy of support for Khomeini grew out of the party's desire not to repeat its mistakes of 1951–53. Then, a two-year crisis involving British oil interests and the shape and future of the monarchy provided the Tudeh and the Soviets with a major opportunity to influence events in Iran. In March 1951, Muhammad Mossadegh became prime minister and the Majlis nationalized the Anglo-Iranian Oil Company. The nationalization angered the West; in fact, the Truman administration refused to grant a loan to Iran in response to the nationalizations. The ensuing crisis in Tehran found the Shah and Mossadegh increasingly at odds. In mid-1952, the Shah dismissed Mossadegh, but popular demonstrations led by his National Front and by the Tudeh put him back in office. By 1953, both the British and the Americans plotted to overthrow the Mossadegh government. The plan collapsed, at first, when Mossadegh learned of the plot. As a result, the Shah fled from Tehran and antimonarchical rioting erupted in the streets. Mossadegh, apparently feeling that the riots were endangering some of his bases of support, moved to suppress the street demonstrations. Since many of the demonstrations had been organized by the Tudeh party, this provoked a split between Mossadegh and the Communist movement. By many accounts, the Tudeh controlled the streets and debated actually seizing power.

   During this period, the Soviets openly sided with the nationalist demonstrations and of course with the Tudeh's call for increased anti-imperialist activity. However, so soon after the signing of the Korean armistice, and just five months after Stalin's death, Moscow was not prepared to act to support a Tudeh coup in August 1953. For its part, the Tudeh miscalculated by not supporting Mossadegh at the appropriate time. On August 21, the CIA returned the Shah to power. In addition, the Tudeh bore the brunt of the post-1953 repression. The Shah's newly created secret police, Savak, hunted down Tudeh party members and destroyed their underground networks.

   In 1979, with its newly acquired legal status, the Tudeh opened offices in several cities and began semi-weekly publication of the party newspaper. In August the party ran into trouble with the Khomeini forces. When the party paper was shut down and the office of the party's Secretariat sealed off by revolutionary guards, the USSR and the Tudeh took a cautious approach. Moscow was still endeavoring to use indirect means to influence the course of the revolution and indeed continued to flatter Khomeini's revolution. The Tudeh saw its primary goal as the retention of its legal standing and for that reason continued to dissociate Khomeini from attacks on leftists. In fact, Kianuri claimed:

> It was Khomeini who urged calm when the Islamic right started burning books and attacking the offices of left-wing organizations. It is he who has renewed the call for unity. Our entire policy is aimed at preventing Khomeini from being relegated to the Islamic right.[11]

With or without a "host," Soviet policy makers considering a possible invasion of Iran in 1979 would also have had to take into account the situation in neighboring Afghanistan. The coup in Kabul in April 1978 brought to power the People's Democratic Party of Afghanistan (PDPA). With the accession of indigenous Communists to power, the Soviets stepped up their levels of assistance to and intensified their party-to-party ties with the new Afghan regime. In December 1978 the Soviets and Afghans signed a Friendship and Cooperation Treaty. By winter/spring 1979, Soviet commentaries included Kabul among the socialist-oriented states and listed Afghanistan among participants in a meeting of the "socialist community."[12] Simultaneously, rebel resistance stiffened: In mid-March, government authorities faced a major uprising in Herat. There, mobs running wild through the streets murdered representatives of the PDPA as well as Soviet advisers. According to most estimates, between 3,000 and 5,000 Afghanis were killed before order was restored. The Soviets responded by rushing increased military assistance, including far more sophisticated equipment than previously provided, to the Kabul government.

Certainly, by late spring, the Soviets were aware of the PDPA's deteriorating situation. The party was increasingly beset by internal strife and by the brazen resistance. Yet, from the Kremlin's perspective, with the Communist party in power and with the friendship treaty on the books, Afghanistan represented a major Soviet stake. In fact, in June 1979 Leonid Brezhnev appeared to signal the Soviet commitment to Afghanistan. He said: "We shall not leave in need our friends, the Afghan people, who have the right to build their lives the way they wish."[13]

Following Amin's assumption of complete control in September, the situation in Afghanistan deteriorated still further. Despite the antipathy between Amin and the Kremlin, the Soviet presence in Afghanistan was too large, and the Soviet stake too great to permit a divorce. Soviet doctrine does not permit the reversibility of a Communist revolution, especially one to which Soviet prestige was now linked. Like Iran, Afghanistan shares a common border with the USSR; but unlike the Iranian case, the fragility of the PDPA position presented a direct challenge to Moscow's self-proclaimed status as the super socialist. Thus, if any military action were going to occur (in the fall of 1979) its probable target would be Afghanistan, not Iran. Preparations for the invasion apparently began in October, and the actual assault occurred in December 1979.

In addition, the Soviets would have had to consider the response of the other states in the region. It would seem, in all likelihood, that a Soviet invasion force would trigger strong regional opposition. Except for Afghanistan, whose Communist government could be expected to support any Soviet moves, and the PDRY, whose vanguard party not only supports the USSR, but is supported by East German and Cuban advisers, the rest of the regional actors would clearly be alarmed. Iraq, the other state with ties, including a 1972 Friendship and Cooperation Treaty, with the Soviet Union, would not have wanted to see Soviet troops on its border. Although Moscow's relations with Baghdad date from the overthrow of the Iraqi monarchy in 1958, in the long run Iraq has proven to be a less than pliable client state. By 1978, it became clear that Baghdad wanted to maintain a foreign policy independent of Moscow on such issues as support for the Eritran rebels in Ethiopia and diversification of arms supplies. Symbolic of the deterioration of Iraqi-Soviet relations was the Baghdad government's arrest and execution of several prominent Communists. In all probability, the gulf states—despite their ambivalence about a U.S. presence in the region—would turn to the United States for assistance in the face of an invasion.

Finally, the Soviets would have had to consider the response of the Khomeini regime and of the Iranian armed forces. Faced with a foreign invasion, it seems likely that the charismatic Khomeini would have been able to mobilize popular support and perhaps convince politicians to put aside their political differences. Wars and outside threats frequently serve to galvanize local populations and to revive if not create patriotism. As for the military, in the period immediately following the Shah's exile many questions were raised about the status of the Iranian military. The morale of the troops was low, a result of having been used as the local police force to quell demonstrations. In the face of desertions and then purges, the serviceability of the equipment was also in doubt. Nonetheless, if we can extrapolate from the Iranian war effort against Iraq a year later, the military proved capable of stopping the Iraqi advance and indeed even of counterattacking and advancing onto Iraqi territory. Moreover, Khomeini has been able to instill a fanaticism in the young—a fanaticism demonstrated in the willingness of Iranian youth to die for the cause of the revolution.

Logistically, a Soviet invasion of Iran would proceed through treacherous mountainous terrain and then move either east toward Tehran or south toward the oil fields in Khuzistan. The invasion route has few roads, and limited rail service. It, therefore, presents many potential points of interdiction and few, if any, alternate routes. The combination of terrain and Iranian military force (however weak) would seem to mean that the Soviets would face military and guerrilla opposition. Any invasion, as the Soviets were to find out in Afghanistan would require a long-term commitment. Moreover, it would seem that the odds of long-term success would be very low.

Of course, with nearly six years hindsight, it is clear that the Soviets, throughout the first year or so of the Iranian revolution, continued to use indirect methods in their attempts to effect changes in Iranian policy. The Soviet Union could not help but be pleased to see the fall of the pro-U.S. regime in Tehran. Yet, the clear religious nature of the revolution proved troubling to Moscow. Both press commentary and academic analyses attempted to dissociate the religious elements from the initial success of the revolution: Calling Islam a "catalyst of nationalist attitudes," Soviet observers, at the time, went so far as to claim that the Iranian revolution was in no way a religious movement.[14] Pravda's political commentator stressed that the collapse of the monarchy created the favorable preconditions for the end of imperialist domination and for the "democratization" of the country, that is, the participation of leftist (including Communist) forces.[15] Even as the regime clamped down on leftist forces, the USSR did not condemn it, but urged moderation. As noted above, Soviet observers seemed to hope that anti-Americanism would provide the common ground.

Following the invasion of Afghanistan, the Iranians became much more suspicious of the USSR. Furthermore, Khomeini as well as other Islamic heads of state began providing limited aid to the Afghan rebels. Nonetheless the Soviets did not give up on Iran. When the Iran-Iraq war erupted in September 1980, the Soviets seemed to tilt toward Iran in yet another effort to cultivate the Khomeini regime. While holding up the shipment of spare parts to Iraq, the Soviets permitted both Syria and Libya to transship Soviet equipment to Tehran. (It should be noted, however, that the USSR hedged its bets. Although it refused to aid Iraq directly during the first six months of the war, Warsaw Pact countries picked up the slack.)

Despite all these efforts to cultivate the Khomeini regime, the aging cleric proved almost as anti-Soviet as anti-U.S. By early 1982, Soviet observers noted problems in the Soviet-Iranian relationship and began to express their frustration at the deteriorating situation. Pravda correspondent Pavel Demchenko, a veteran Middle East observer wrote:

> We know that the Shi'ite clergymen who hold the reins of government in Iran are not uniform in their political beliefs or social positions. There are various conservative factions . . . with extreme right wing views. It seems that it is these groups who want to put up obstacles to the expansion of Soviet-Iranian relations even though such action could harm the Iranian economy and Iran's ability to fight imperialist pressure.[16]

Others evidenced genuine contempt for Khomeini and his programs. Commentators claimed that Khomeini's social programs reminded them of the Middle Ages, while several journalists charged that the clergy gave priority to establishing their own monopoly on power rather than to the solution of pressing socioeconomic problems. With the arrest and trial of Tudeh party members in early 1983, and the expulsion of Soviet diplomats later that year, the Soviets resorted to outright name-calling. Many observers claimed that Khomeini has perverted the course of the revolution. Vladimir Volinskii, an Iranian specialist whose radio programs to

Iran were initiated in 1982 to "clear up misconceptions" criticized Khomeini's drive to become the arbiter of all Mideast revolutions. He said: "Islam has been declared as the only and most revolutionary teaching and this propaganda has reached the point of buffoonery."[17] And R.A. Ul'ianovskii, a prominent orientalist and deputy director of the International Department, wrote: "[the clergy used only] that part of their traditions which was reflected in the conservative, and at times reactionary, dogmas of Islam . . . the clergy did everything in its power to establish the *outdated* moral and ethical standards of the Koran and the Shari'a."[18]

Prospects

The current state of Soviet-Iranian relations is at best strained. The Soviets seem to alternate between calling Khomeini names, blasting the fundamentalism of the regime and praising the potential for economic and political cooperation between Tehran and Moscow. The Tudeh, although it survived longer than other independent political groups in Iran, is decimated. By the same token, the Kremlin appears to be keeping a finger in the Iranian pie. Not only are Syria and Libya continuing to transship military equipment to Tehran, but there are also reportedly East Germany security advisers within the country.[19]

Although the Soviets did not invade Iran in 1979, the possibility of a future Soviet invasion cannot be ruled out completely. Western scholars and military specialists are currently involved in a far-ranging debate over whether or not the United States possesses the ability to stop a Soviet attack.[20] On the Soviet side of the ledger, everyone concedes the Kremlin an advantage based on proximity: Geography means that Soviet response time will be quicker; Soviet troops have less distance to travel and Soviet pilots fewer miles to fly. According to recent estimates, there are 24 Soviet divisions proximate to the region, while the U.S. Rapid Deployment Force has far fewer. Moreover, the regional states, as noted above, are reluctant to permit a U.S. military presence within their borders.

The problem with all these analyses is that few—if any—question why Moscow would contemplate an invasion and whether or not the Kremlin chiefs would indeed initiate one. The Soviet Union certainly benefited from the collapse of a U.S. pillar of regional security. No longer does Washington enjoy a regional policeman or a listening post on the Soviet border. However, the Kremlin also suffered a loss: the much needed supply of natural gas and the relative security of a known, stable regional power on its borders. In fact, Soviet propaganda constantly stresses the long-standing beneficial economic ties between Moscow and Tehran. It is as if the USSR is advertising for a reinstitution of the gas deal. Furthermore, although many Western portraits of the Soviet fear of

Islamic fundamentalism are overdrawn, the Islamic revival has introduced a new factor into Soviet foreign policy calculations. In the period
following the Iranian revolution, the USSR suddenly found itself faced
with a series of events, each of which had an Islamic component: the tribal
and ethnic nature of the rebellion in Afghanistan which precipated the introduction of Soviet troops: the outbreak of the Persian Gulf war between
Shi'ite Iran and Sunni-led Iraq which seems to damage Soviet hopes for a
united anti-Israel, anti-U.S. front; the assassination of Anwar Sadat by an
Islamic group; and the activization of the Muslim Brotherhood in Syria
which clearly threatened the regime of a pro-Soviet Middle East ally.

But, what specifically would trigger a Soviet invasion? The argument
has been made that the Soviets would see as a threat a strong Iran that was
vehemently anti-Soviet or an Iran in renewed close alliance with the
United States.[21] Neither appears to be an imminent possibility. The pro-
longation of the Iran-Iraq war coupled with Iran's isolation would seem to
preclude Tehran from becoming a major military power in the region
from some time to come. As for Iranian-U.S. relations, Washington's long
association with the Shah makes it a convenient scapegoat and galvaniz-
ing force in Iranian society. Khomeini's revolution directed as it is against
westernization could not survive a reinvigoration of U.S.-Iranian relations. No future Iranian regime—and the clerical regime appears durable
for some time to come—could retain its legitimacy and accept the U.S.
presence *status quo ante*.

Just as in 1979, Soviet decision makers in the second half of the 1980s
would have to consider the probable U.S. and regional response to any intervention. In the intervening six years, the United States has created the
Rapid Deployment Force, sought regional basing rights, and generally
made it clear that the gulf is of vital security concern to us. Moreover, the
Iran-Iraq war has unleashed a dynamic in the region which is detrimental
to Soviet interests. At the outset of the war, Moscow publicly proclaimed
its neutrality, while alleging that the United States hoped to use the war
for its own ends. But Soviet desires to manipulate the war to the detri-
ment of the United States clearly backfired. If anything, U.S. alarm at the
increasing instability in the region and the potential threat to Western
oil supplies led to a marked increase in the U.S. military presence: U.S.
naval deployments have been coupled with the transfer of sophisticated
technology such as AWAC's and stingers to Saudi Arabia. As the U.S.
military presence in the region has been enhanced, the tone of Soviet
rhetoric has become shriller. For example, the Soviets accused
Washington of contravening international norms and of seeking "direct
control" over the Persian Gulf.[22] Moreover, *Pravda* and *Izvestiia* as well
as both Farsi and Arabic broadcasts all refer to the "massing" of U.S. military force in the region. Evgenii Primakov, the director of the Institute of
Oriental Studies argued in an *International Affairs* article that the United

States was preparing for a "tough confrontation" with the Soviet Union on global and regional levels simultaneously.[23] In the final analysis, Moscow seems increasingly alarmed that because of concerns over shipping lanes in the gulf a permanent U.S. presence might be accepted by regional powers.

Soviet foreign policy decision makers would also still need to assess regional reactions to any contemplated invasion. Within the last year, the Kremlin has intensified its diplomatic offensive in the gulf. For example, the USSR agreed to sell military equipment to Kuwait (following a U.S. refusal), signed a Friendship and Cooperation Treaty with the Yemen Arab Republic, and attempted to ameliorate its strained relations with Iraq. Yet, none of these ties would seem to guarantee acceptance of a Soviet invasion of Iran. Kuwait is a member of the Gulf Cooperation Council and remains decidedly neutral. The treaty with North Yemen, as compared to other friendship treaties, is weak: There is, for example, no military clause. Moreover, the Kremlin has had to make it clear to the PDRY that its new relationship with YAR is not directed against the former.[24] Finally, Iraq clearly desires to play an independent role. Not only has it diversified its arms supply, but it also recently reestablished diplomatic relations with the United States after 17 years.

In addition, the Soviet Union would have to keep in view the political fallout from Afghanistan. That invasion compromised the standing of the USSR as a champion of the nonaligned. It also served to attenuate ties between Moscow and many of the Muslim states. An invasion of yet another Muslim country—one which proclaims its anti-imperialism— would further alienate regional and Muslim support. Thus the ramifications of a second invasion would further complicate the long-term Soviet effort to establish a stake in the Middle East and to remain an active player there. The reaction of India, although not a Middle East country, would also have to be taken into consideration. The government of Indira Gandhi was returned to power just in time to prevent an anti-Soviet vote on Afghanistan in the Security Council. The cost of that vote has apparently been major new arms agreements, including the latest MIG fighters. The cost of an invasion of another Third World country might be even higher.

Recently, Western scholars concerned about Soviet encroachment in the gulf have argued that, at the very least, the USSR possesses the ability to intimidate regional actors. Many argue that by virtue of its proximity alone the Kremlin must be considered a player in the region. It would seem however that even if Soviet intimidation is a factor in regional politics, none of the states in the gulf would welcome a Soviet invasion of Iran. In all probabilities, the gulf states (with the exception of the PDRY) although clearly ambivalent about the U.S. presence in the region could not countenance a strong Soviet military presence. Most seem intent on regional security guaranteed without outside intervention. Their anti-imperialism extends to the USSR as well.

Notes

1. V. Matveev, Izvestiia, June 10, 1984, pp. 4–5 in *Foreign Broadcast Information Service* (hereafter *FBIS*) SOV–84–117, June 15, 1984, p. H2.

2. As cited in Alvin Z. Rubinstein, *Soviet Policy Toward Turkey, Iran, and Afghanistan* (New York: Praeger, 1982), p. 61.

3. V.M. Kulish, *Military Force and International Relations* (Moscow: International Relations, 1972) translated by the *Joint Publication Research Service* (hereafter JPRS) 48947, May 3, 1973, p. 103.

4. S.G. Gorshkov, *The Seapower of the State* (London: Pergamon Press, 1979), p. 251 as cited in Bryan Ranft and Geoffrey Till, *The Sea in Soviet Strategy* (Annapolis: Naval Institute Press, 1983), p. 195.

5. A. Petrov, "Display Prudence and Restraint," *Pravda*, December 5, 1979, p. 5.

6. For further discussion see Carol R. Saivetz and Sylvia Woodby, *Soviet-Third World Relations*, (Boulder, Colo.: Westview Press, 1985), especially chapters 4 and 7.

7. The Soviets describe a socialist-oriented state as one completing the non-capitalist transition to socialism. It is, essentially, a state whose pro-Soviet foreign policy is complemented by espousals of Marxism-Leninism and by the adoption of Soviet-style institutions.

8. Interview with Yuri Andropov, TASS, April 24, 1983 in *FBIS-SOV–83–80*, April 25, 1983, pp. AA9–10.

9. Carol R. Saivetz, "Moscow and Damascus: A Troubled Alliance," *Obozrenie*, February 1985.

10. Marvin G. Weinman, "Soviet Policy and the Constraints of Nationalism in Iran and Afghanistan," in Yaakov Ro'i, *The USSR and the Muslim World* (Winchester: George Allen and Unwin, 1984), pp. 226–61.

11. *L'Unita*, September 30, 1979, as cited in Aryeh Y. Yodfat, *The Soviet Union and Revolutionary Iran* (New York: St. Martin's Press, 1984), p. 62.

12. TASS from Ulan Bator, May 30, 1979, as cited in Henry S. Bradsher, *Afghanistan and the Soviet Union* (Durham: Duke University Press, 1983), p. 97.

13. Moscow Radio, June 11, 1979, *FBIS–SOV–79–116*, June 14, 1979, p. D1.

14. N. Prozhogin, "Stormy Time," *Pravda*, January 7, 1979, p. 4 in *Current Digest of the Soviet Press*, hereafter (*CDSP*) vol. 31, no. 1, January 31, 1979, p. 15.

15. V. Ovchinnikov, "Political Commentator's Notes," *Pravda*, February 13, 1979, p. 5, *CDSP*, vol. 31, no. 6, March 7, 1979, p. 15.

16. Pavel Demchenko, "USSR-Iran, In the Interests of Good Neighborliness," *Pravda*, March 9, 1982, p. 4.

17. In October 1982 the Soviets initiated a new Farsi language series designed to "clear up misconceptions" about the Soviet Union. This quotation is from a broadcast entitled "National Liberation Movement and their Friends," October 31, 1983 as translated in the *Joint Publication Research Service* (hereafter *JPRS*) 84861, December 2, 1983, p. 24.

18. R.A. Ul'ianovskii, "International Life: Moral Principles in Politics and Policy in the Sphere of Morals: Iran—What Next?" *Lituraturnaia Gazeta*, June 22, 1983, in *FBIS-SOV–33–127*, June 30, 1983, p. H3 (emphasis added).

19. In an article which appeared in *Foreign Affairs* in the spring of 1983, Shahram Chubin alleges that the Soviet Union and Iran signed a military agree-

ment, the provisions of which included the training of Iranians in the Soviet Union, technical assistance, and the loan of Soviet advisers to Iran. No other source mentions the existence of such a treaty. See: "The Soviet Union and Iran," *Foreign Affairs,* vol. 61, no. 4 (Spring 1983).

20. See for example the series run in *International Security,* W. Scott Thompson, "The Persian Gulf and the Correlation of Forces," vol. 7, no. 1 (Summer 1982); and Joshua M. Epstein "Soviet Vulnerabilities in Iran and the RDF Deterrent," vol. 6, no. 2 (Fall 1981).

21. See Dennis Ross, "Considering Soviet Threats to the Persian Gulf," *International Security,* vol. 6, no. 2 (Fall 1981).

22. *Sotsialisticheskaia Industriia,* "The Gendarme Prepares the Nightstick," March 24, 1984, p. 3 in *FBIS-SOV–84–060,* March 27, 1984, p. H5.

23. E.M. Primakov, "USA: Policy of Destabilization in the Middle East," *International Affairs,* March 1984, p. 39.

24. In his dinner speech honoring the president of North Yemen, Konstantin Chernenko said:

> Naturally, it (the treaty) does not contain a single clause infringing on anyone's interests or directed against third countries.
>
> During the past week, we have had good and *frank* conversations with the leaders of the two Yemen states.

As cited in TASS, October 9, 1984, in *FBIS-SOV–84–197,* October 10, 1984, p. H5.

15

THE SOVIET UNION AND THE TWO CRISES IN POLAND: 1956 AND 1980–81

Andrzej Korbonski and Lubov Fajfer

By the mid-1980s the study of international crises has become one of the most widely researched areas in the field of decision making in international relations. Conspicuously absent has been an attempt to analyze the crises involving the Soviet Union and a number of East European countries. While much has been written about the Soviet interventions in Hungary in 1956 and Czechoslovakia in 1968, and the Solidarity crisis in Poland in 1980–81, almost no study has tried to analyze these crises with the aid of theoretical frameworks developed by Western political scientists for the purpose of analyzing international crises in Western Europe or the Third World.

Two definitions of international crises are of particular interest. Michael Brecher, looking at a crisis from the vantage point of top policy makers, sees it as a situation characterized by three necessary and sufficient conditions: (1) a threat to basic values, accompanied or followed by (2) high probability of involvement in military hostilities and the recognition that there is (3) a finite time for response to the external value threat.[1] Ned Lebow defines an international crisis in terms of three "operational criteria": (1) Policy makers perceive that the actions or threatened actions of another international actor seriously impairs concrete national interests, the country's bargaining reputation or their own ability to remain in power; (2) Policy makers perceive that any action on their part designed to counter this threat (capitulation aside) will raise a significant prospect of war; (3) Policy makers perceive themselves to be acting under time constraint.[2]

The purpose of this chapter is to utilize the "necessary and sufficient" conditions and "operational criteria" for the analysis of two crisis situations involving the Soviet Union and Poland in 1956 and 1980–81. Poland experienced three additional political crises in 1968, 1970, and 1976 but as none of them involved a serious threat of Soviet military intervention, they are not included in our discussion.

What is wrong with traditional historical and analytic studies is the striking persistence of conventional wisdom, shaky assumptions, crude simplifications, and even faulty premises that seem to characterize Western understanding of Soviet policy toward Eastern Europe. Despite some progress in the last quarter century, there are still a number of empty or half-empty boxes to fill.

The Kremlin policy has traditionally been assumed to be concerned only with maintaining total hegemony and control over Poland and its people, without permitting even the slightest departure from the norm. Any relaxation of Soviet domination over its largest partner in the area could be expected to create a powerful demonstration effect, perhaps even a domino effect, in the rest of the region. Yet, as this chapter will attempt to show, the actual Soviet behavior toward Poland in both 1956 and 1980–81 turned out to be far more complex and unpredictable than anticipated on the basis of earlier experiences. Rather than being explainable by a single factor, Soviet behavior was the outcome of the interplay of many forces and influences, both external and internal, short term and long term.

Let us begin by reviewing what were the Soviet stakes in Poland in the mid-1950s and late 1970s, and how different they were from their stakes elsewhere in Eastern Europe. According to Zbigniew Brzezinski, the Soviet Union had four major objectives in aiding and abetting the Communist takeover of Eastern Europe, including Poland, after World War II: (1) denying the region to states hostile to the USSR and potentially threatening its security; (2) making sure that firm control over the individual countries remained in the hands of elements friendly to Moscow; (3) utilizing the region's resources for the purpose of supporting Soviet postwar economic recovery and development; and (4) taking advantage of Eastern Europe as a convenient jumping-off point for a possible offensive against the West.[3]

This implies that in both 1956 and 1980–81 the most important Soviet interest in Poland remained that of security. While this view is not without merit, it raises the question of what "security" meant to Moscow. Especially in the wake of the 1980–81 crisis, the Soviet concept of security was far broader than the conventional Western one. To the extent that neither in 1956 nor in 1980–81 was Poland about to leave the Warsaw Pact, developments there did not threaten Soviet security in the Western sense of the word, as developments in Hungary did in 1956 and possibly did in Czechoslovakia in 1968. Soviet security in the region requires Eastern Europe to act as two buffer zones: one narrowly defined in terms of physical or military security, and the other conceptualized more broadly in terms of Soviet political and ideological concerns.[4]

The fact that Poland lay astride the lines of transportation and communication linking the Soviet homeland with the Group of Soviet Forces in East Germany added an important dimension to Moscow's relationship to Warsaw. It was, ostensibly to protect these lines, that two Soviet divisions have been permanently stationed in Poland since 1945, except for East Germany the longest time that any Soviet troops have been stationed outside the borders of the USSR. Poland's strategic importance to the Soviet Union was further enhanced by its controlling some 300 miles of the Baltic coast. While the Baltic Sea has become a Soviet-dominated lake, the fact that Poland might, at least in theory, interfere with sea lanes between the Soviet ports such as Leningrad and Riga, and the North Sea, was clearly of some significance.

Poland's armed forces have traditionally been the strongest in the region. The most flagrant example of Soviet concern for establishng firm control over the Polish military was the unprecedented appointment in 1949 of Soviet Marshal Rokossovsky as minister of defense and commander in chief of the Polish armed forces. Given Poland's history, the traditional attitude toward Russia, critical geographical position, plus Stalin's paranoia, it was not unreasonable that the Soviet leader should have wanted to emasculate the Polish military, even though it showed no signs of disloyalty to Moscow.[5]

The second Soviet objective in Poland, as elsewhere in Eastern Europe, was to safeguard the Communist political system. The Communist seizure of power and subsequent Stalinization of the country, while differing in agricultural and religious policy, did not differ greatly from those taking place in most of the countries in the region.

Still, at the time of Stalin's death in 1953, communism appeared to be rather firmly rooted in Poland and the country itself could serve as a successful model of a faithful Soviet satellite. While Hungary, East Germany, and even Czechoslovakia took advantage of the Malenkovian "thaw," Poland, if anything, embarked on a get-tough policy vis-à-vis the Church and the peasants.

What were the Soviet economic stakes in Poland? Together with the rest of the region, throughout the Stalinist period the country was economically exploited and the size of Poland's contribution to Soviet economic recovery was well illustrated by the amount of the so-called "debt" owed by Poland to the USSR and cancelled by Moscow in November 1956.[6] Between 1956 and 1980 Poland represented less of an economic asset to Moscow than East Germany and Czechoslovakia which were the main suppliers of technologically advanced machinery and equipment. Although Poland specialized in the production of ships, rolling stock, and other specialized industrial equipment, from the Soviet point of view, Poland represented neither a major economic asset nor burden.[7]

Could Poland be viewed as a useful platform from which to launch a Soviet attack against Western Europe? Not having a common border with West Germany or any other NATO member, Poland's utility in this area was obviously not as high as that of East Germany, Czechoslovakia or, even, Bulgaria. On the other hand, the country's sheer size and its control over a portion of the Baltic coast and of the supply lines linking East Germany with the Soviet homeland made it one of the keystones of the Warsaw alliance. According to the WTO *ordre de bataille* of the mid-1960s in the event of a war the Polish army was to participate in a westward thrust along the Baltic coast and occupy Denmark.[8]

To sum up, it may be said that the Soviet stakes in Poland in the mid-1950s and late 1970s were high, especially from the military-strategic and political-ideological points of view. Prior to 1956 Poland gave relatively little cause for concern for the Soviet leaders: the ruling party appeared so secure as to allow some degree of domestic liberalization, and the country faithfully toed the line of Soviet foreign policy. Although the Polish population was dissatisfied with the lack of rapid material improvement, that dissatisfaction tended to be muted and created no major problems for the ruling oligarchy. There were no signs of a growing popular ferment that was to explode in October 1956 and bring down the Stalinist regime.

The 1956 Crisis: The Background

For the most part, the three years following the death of Stalin in March 1953 did not witness a major transformation in the relationship between the Soviet Union and its satellites in Eastern Europe. Yet important events were occurring in Eastern Europe and the Soviet Union. The arrest and execution of Beria, the downgrading of the Soviet secret police, and mass release of political prisoners was emulated by Moscow's junior partners. The division of Stalin's spoils between Nikita Khrushchev (party) and Georgi Malenkov (government) accompanied by growing calls for a return to "Leninist norms" with emphasis on collective leadership and leading role of the party, was echoed throughout Eastern Europe. The Korean War armistice, the 1954 Geneva conference, the proclamation of the principles of peaceful coexistence by the USSR, and the Geneva summit meeting of 1955, represented the major milestones on the road to East-West rapprochement and a thaw in the Cold War.

All these changes were warmly welcomed by the East European countries. The threat of the Cold War turning into a shooting war and possibly culminating in a victory for the West, automatically spelled the end of Communist rule in the region. As long as a danger of a United States-Soviet confrontation existed, the dependence of the three key East European countries—Czechoslovakia, East Germany, and Poland—on

Soviet military protection continued unabated. Any relaxation of international tension was bound to enhance the sense of security and ensure a rosier future for most of these countries.

The emergence of China as a coleader of the international Communist movement and the reconciliation between the Soviet Union and Yugoslavia in June 1955 were even more significant for Eastern Europe. Until the mid-1950s, China's influence in Eastern Europe was at best marginal; after 1953 it began to grow rapidly. The truce between Khrushchev and Tito could not help but to affect Eastern Europe to a very significant degree. After 1955 Titoism or national communism was implicitly accepted by the Kremlin as an alternative model of socialist construction and its repercussions proved far-reaching. It not only suggested the demise of the Stalinist doctrine of "one road to socialism" but also struck a heavy blow against the anti-Tito factions in the East European ruling oligarchies which were still very much in control in their respective countries.

Paradoxically enough, the death of Stalin in March 1953 and the beginning of the gradual dismantling of the Stalinist system, caused relatively few ripples in Poland. While Czechoslovakia, East Germany, and Hungary experienced a series of dramatic developments, the official policy in Poland not only appeared to toe the line identified with the late dictator, but even went beyond the limits associated with Stalinist practices. The violent attacks on the Catholic Church, including the trial of Bishop Kaczmarek and imprisonment of Cardinal Stefan Wyszynski in September 1953, demonstrated that the party was betting on Stalin rather than Malenkov.

The situation in Poland after the Second Party Congress in 1954 changed little from 1953. The "New Course" did not bring the expected results. The farm sector continued to lag; the standard of living showed hardly any improvement; the party *apparatchiki* were as confused as ever about policy changes; and the masses as stubborn and alienated and refusing to fall in line with the new policy. A new feeling of dissatisfaction was in the air in the months to come.

The keynote address at the Third Plenum in January 1955 was delivered by Bierut, back in his role as the general secretary of the Central Committee. Bierut enumerated the major "errors and deviations" committed by the security organs organizations, and then announced that after a thorough reorganization of the security *apparat* by the Politburo, persons unjustly imprisoned were freed and rehabilitated. The open acknowledgment that the rule of terror was to be replaced by the "power of persuasion" and the increased attention to the demands of the people could not fail to have serious repercussions. This belief was strengthened by the concluding part of Bierut's speech in which he promised much closer cooperation between the party and the nonparty masses, particularly the intelligentsia.[9]

The "second stage" of the "New Course" did not last very long. The leaders evidently decided they had gone too far in proclaiming the new era in the relations between the party and the people, possibly influenced by events in the Soviet Union and in the other countries in the bloc.

The whole situation was most confusing. Gomulka's secret release from a jail in December 1954 was a tacit acknowledgment that perhaps his views were not as heretical as the party would have liked to think. Nevertheless, the *aktiv* as well as the population at large were still led to believe that *gomulkovshchina* was as much of a heresy as ever. Moreover, Malenkov's ouster and Khrushchev's renewed insistence on the superiority of heavy industry over all other sectors, could only serve to compound the confusion in the minds of the Polish party leaders at all levels.

On the eve of the Twentieth Congress of the Soviet Communist Party, scheduled for February 1956, the Polish party was in a state of flux. The Six-Year Plan for agriculture was far from being fulfilled, with agricultural production growing only 19 percent as against the planned rate of 50 percent. Too, the working class was disillusioned by the fact that the real income of peasants had increased more than that of the working class.[10] Disarray in Poland was reflected by growing ferment among the intellectuals, the continuing release of political prisoners jailed in the Stalinist period, and the growing alienation of the youth, especially in the wake of the International Youth Festival, held in Warsaw in the summer of 1955.

The admission of the failure of economic policy and the lack of success in raising the country's standard of living removed one of the few remaining official claims to legitimacy. After 1955 the Polish government found itself on the defensive, probably for the first time since the Communist takeover, and the consequences of that largely unexpected development, were impossible to predict and calculate.

The 1956 Crisis: Escalation and Resolution

The eight month period between February and October 1956 witnessed a quasi revolution in Eastern Europe which made the year 1956 truly an *annus mirabilis* in the history of world communism and which largely transformed the political landscape in Eastern Europe. The key events included Khrushchev's "secret speech" at the Twentieth Congress of CPSU; continuing rapprochement between the USSR and Tito's Yugoslavia; and growing assertiveness of China.

Although in his denunciation of Stalin, Khrushchev, interestingly enough, did not criticize the post-1945 Soviet policy toward Eastern Europe, his wholesale condemnation of Stalinist methods was bound to have serious consequences in the region. The grudging acknowledgment of the bankruptcy of the doctrine of "one road to socialism" and of its replacement by the notion of "many roads to socialism," accompanied by the escalating flirtation between Khrushchev and Tito, convinced the East Europeans that they were being given a green light to de-Stalinize and to experiment with new forms of socialist construction. Finally, the slowly growing rift between Moscow and Beijing in the wake of the Twentieth CPSU Congress offered the East European countries additional room for maneuvers and new options of which some of the states, notably Albania and some extent Rumania, availed themselves in the early 1960s.

In his perceptive analysis of the consequences of de-Stalinization in Eastern Europe, Brzezinski examined its differential impact on the individual countries in the region in terms of four variables: the depth of the socioeconomic crisis caused by rapid industrialization; the rift between the rulers and ruled, and especially between the ruling oligarchy and the intellectual elite; the availability of alternative leadership; and the extent of anti-Titoist commitment on the part of the respective regimes. On the strength of his analysis, Brzezinski pointed to Hungary and Poland as the two logical candidates for a major upheaval.[11]

The situation in Eastern Europe in the aftermath of the Twentieth Congress was much more complex than its rather simplified image presented by the author of the *Soviet Bloc*. The Soviet-sponsored policy of *Gleichschaltung* carried the seeds of its own destruction: it meant that the layer of uniformity and conformity proved extremely thin and fragile and that given a chance, the traditional or historical attitudes, perceptions, and values began to reassert themselves in the individual countries of the region. The fact that the revival of national values differed from country to country was due primarily to the persistence of what is often called *differentio specifica* in the particular countries rather than to some common processes or phenomena throughout the region.

It is useful to divide the various developments between February and October 1956 into two broad categories, internal and external, which interacted with each other and contributed to the escalation of the crisis.[12]

The most important and unexpected event was the death of the general secretary of the Polish party, Bierut, who had been closely identified with Moscow and Stalinism in March 1956. The Kremlin also attached considerable importance to Bierut's succession, as illustrated by Khrushchev's personal participation in the selection of Edward Ochab. Ochab was a compromise candidate whose tasks were to keep a lid on the changes induced by the de-Stalinization decreed by Moscow, and to heal the rift within the party, caused by the same phenomenon.[13]

The next few months witnessed growing turmoil in the country fueled by two extraneous decisions originating in Moscow: the formal statement lifting the "unjust" dissolution of the prewar Communist party of Poland in 1938, accompanied by a posthumous rehabilitation of its leaders, and a resolution dissolving the nine-year-old Communist Information Bureau (Cominform).[14] The thaw spilling over from the East was followed by nationwide discussions of Khrushchev's "secret speech" delivered at the Twentieth CPSU Congress.

In April, Gomulka and a number of leaders, imprisoned during the Stalinist period, were officially freed and rehabilitated.[15] Several prominent Stalinists were dismissed from their government positions and some of them were put in jail. Finally, the Polish parliament, the *Sejm,* passed an amnesty law which resulted in a mass release of political prisoners.

While Ochab appeared to be in full control of the liberalization process, it was becoming obvious that he was mostly a transitional leader. The logical replacement was Gomulka who was clearly interested and who was approached by the Politburo in May to discuss the possibility of his returning to active work in the party. The ouster from the Politburo of Jakub Berman, a notorious Stalinist, an *eminence grise* in the Polish party since the mid-1940s and a person widely recognized as Moscow's man in Warsaw, showed the ascendancy of the liberal wing within the party.

The key event was the riots in the city of Poznan at the end of June.[16] The rioting, which resulted in a loss of lives and had to be suppressed by the military, was the first open and violent challenge against the established order in Eastern Europe, far more bloody and extensive than previous demonstrations and strikes in East Berlin and Plzen in 1953. The party leadership was taken by surprise. Instead of adopting the traditional hard-line policy vis-à-vis the strikers, Ochab called a meeting of the Central Committee in the middle of July. This "Seventh Plenum" became the longest Central Committee meeting in Poland's history (10 days) and reflected a sharp division within the party that showed no signs of being healed.[17]

The Kremlin undoubtedly watched events in Poland with considerable interest but there is no evidence of the Soviets trying to put a lid on the liberalization process. The Soviet Union was becoming increasingly involved in the Middle East crisis, trying to improve relations with Tito's Yugoslavia, and attempting to deal with the emerging Hungarian crisis. Unlike in Hungary, at least in Poland the top party leadership was apparently willing to let the events take their course and did not try to stop the demands for greater democratization.

Moscow's concern with Poland mounted after the Poznan riots. In early July the Kremlin granted Warsaw an emergency loan of 100 million rubles in gold, to prop up the faltering economy. On July 22, a high ranking Soviet delegation headed by Khrushchev's close allies, Prime Minister Nikolai Bulganin and Marshal Georgi Zhukov, arrived in Poland, ostensibly to celebrate Poland's national holiday. There is evidence that the Soviet leaders urged Ochab to adopt a tougher line toward the liberal faction and to slow down the process of liberalization.[18]

Soviet pressure only strengthened the determination of the liberal faction to push on with the reforms and even the conservative wing resented Moscow's interference. Warsaw defiantly approved the readmission of Gomulka and his close collaborators to the party, followed by continuing negotiations with him.

Moreover, Ochab apparently decided to seek support for his policy of incremental liberalization elsewhere in the Communist camp. In September, the Polish party held secret talks with the Yugoslavs and a Polish delegation, headed by Gierek, went to Beijing where Ochab received strong support from the Chinese leadership.[19] It became an open secret that the Eighth Plenum of the Central Committee in October would see the election of Gomulka to party leadership.

On the eve of the plenum, the Soviet ambassador notified Ochab that a delegation of the Presidium of the Soviet Communist Party, led by Khrushchev, would arrive in Warsaw on the opening day of the plenum. It was clearly a last ditch attempt by the Soviets to prevent Gomulka from assuming the leadership of the Polish party.

The details of Khrushchev's sudden visit and of his confrontation with Gomulka are still largely shrouded in secrecy.[20] Khrushchev applied considerable pressure on the Poles, including an order for the Soviet troops stationed in Poland, to move on Warsaw. Ultimately an armed confrontation never came to pass and Khrushchev left Warsaw apparently persuaded that Gomulka represented no major threat to Soviet hegemony and that he could be brought around in due course. Khrushchev was ready to grant Gomulka unprecedented concessions, such as the dissolution of collective farms and establishment of a *modus vivendi* with the Catholic Church, as a price to prevent an explosion in Poland, similar to the one that followed in Hungary.

The question immediately arises, why the Soviets did not invade Poland as they did Hungary? Khrushchev did not have a good excuse to do so; unlike Hungary, Poland did not declare its neutrality and its withdrawl from the Warsaw Pact which could have been perceived by Moscow as *casus belli*. Second, the Kremlin must have been impressed with the incremental character of liberalization process in Poland which proceeded, at least seemingly, under party's supervision. Third, the encounter with Gomulka must have convinced Khrushchev that Gomulka was indeed an orthodox Communist whose bark was worse than his bite. The fact that despite the removal of some diehard Stalinists such as Berman, Minc, the economic tsar of the Stalinist period, and Radkiewicz, the Polish Beria, the Gomulka team included several representatives of the "healthy forces" clearly acceptable to Moscow, and this fact alone guaranteed that the Polish liberalization would not go out of hand. Fourth, the changes in Poland appeared to have the support of both Tito and Mao, whom the Kremlin had to take seriously. Finally, the Kremlin's preoccupation with Hungary and the Middle East suggested cautious and careful treatment of the Polish changeover. By hindsight, Khrushchev's judgment proved correct and the initial confrontation with Gomulka became ultimately transformed into a seemingly close friendship and Poland's deviation came to an end about a year after it began.

Still, a Soviet military intervention appeared imminent and the fact that it did not take place as it did in Hungary, had to have additional reasons. As in the 1980–81 crisis, Khrushchev must have realized that a Soviet invasion would have been very costly. The role of the Polish military in the Poznan riots of June 1956 and its apparent readiness to defend the Gomulka regime against the advancing Soviet forces four months later, suggested that both the Polish officer corps and soldiers were caught up in the spirit of liberalization, despite the presence of high ranking Soviet military "advisers" headed by Marshal Rokossovsky. Especially worrisome was the attitude of the usually reliable Internal Security Forces, which were among the first to stop the Soviet troops outside Warsaw. A contemplated armed intervention would have been bloody and costly.

To conclude, from a perspective of 30 years, the events in October 1956 represented the most critical turning point in recent Polish history. Because of October 1956, Polish communism as a political and economic system, as an ideology and a way of life, has failed not only to acquire a modicum of legitimacy but also to generate some measure of popular support, similar to that existing in other countries in Eastern Europe. The seeds of future crises in Poland in 1968, 1970, 1976, and above all in 1980–81, were sown in October 1956. Had the events in 1956 turned out otherwise, the country might very well have been spared much of the trauma that has characterized the decades of the 1970s and 1980s.

The Crisis of 1980–81: The Background

By the middle of the 1970s some radical measures were necessary to improve the lagging economic performance. Given the total failure of the previous attempt at reforming retail prices which ended in Gomulka's downfall in December 1970, it was imperative for Edward Gierek to proceed with utmost caution. And yet, despite the relatively fresh memories of the debacle of December 1970, Gierek incredibly disregarded all the lessons supposedly learned from that experience and, without any official warning, announced a fairly radical reform of retail food prices at the end of June 1976. Predictably, the workers in several industrial centers rioted, forcing the regime to call off the reform within 24 hours. The Soviet leadership which worked hard to convene the Conference of European Communist Parties in East Berlin at the time of Gierek's announcement, must have been horrified, disgusted, and frustrated with the ineptitude of its strongest East European ally.[21]

By early fall the internal political situation in the country appeared once again to be stabilized. Gierek's increasingly inept domestic policy must have given Moscow serious concern. The Soviet options were deceptively simple: one was to get rid of Gierek and replace him, the other one was to keep him in power, at least for the time being. By November Moscow decided to keep the old regime in power and even to provide it with sizeable economic aid.[22] As in the case of Gomulka in 1968, the Kremlin apparently concluded that the benefits accruing from maintaining the status quo exceeded the potential cost of a prolonged and possibly controversial changeover at the top. The decision reflected Moscow's strong aversion to perpetuating internal instability in its client-states and its unwillingness to intervene directly in their domestic affairs, except when absolutely necessary.

Moscow's decision to continue its support of Gierek in both 1976 and 1980 is not very surprising. While the alternative leaders must have been perceived as wanting, Gierek after his near-collapse of June 1976 had exhibited considerable power of recovery and talent for political survival. Moreover, throughout the latter part of the 1970s, Gierek's stature and prestige as an international statesman continued to grow. Hailed as a major international figure by President Carter during the latter's visit to Warsaw in December 1977, Gierek also succeeded in developing a "special relationship" with both President Giscard and Chancellor Schmidt, which could not help but impress the Kremlin leaders.

In contrast to Rumania, Poland toed the Soviet line not only at the Helsinki Conference in 1975 but also at the follow-up meeting in Belgrade in 1977–78. Unlike Hungary, Poland steadfastly refused to associate itself with some tenets of Eurocommunism. Again, unlike Rumania, Poland showed no interest in cultivating its relations with China and the Third World. To be sure, Warsaw was taken by surprise by the Soviet intervention in Afghanistan and initially at least, its endorsement of the invasion appeared lukewarm. Nonetheless, it was Gierek who was chosen by Moscow to host the very important meeting in Warsaw between Brezhnev and Giscard in May 1980. Gierek's role as a valuable intermediary was to be further enhanced by his forthcoming trip to West Germany in August and Giscard's return visit to Warsaw in September, both later cancelled.

On the political arena the post-1976 period had witnessed the persistent growth of the opposition movement which although numerically small was actually becoming institutionalized and national in scope. The fact that the Polish regime had tolerated the dissent was a good testimony to the government's inherent weakness and lack of legitimacy. Gierek hoped perhaps that an improvement in the economic situation may reduce or neutralize the discontent. Whether the Polish regime received Soviet approval for its relatively mild antidissident policy is difficult to say; it may be speculated that having decided to support Gierek, the Kremlin was prepared to give him a free hand in handling the opposition, even at the risk of his appearing much more tolerant than his counterparts in Czechoslovakia, East Germany, and Rumania, not mentioning the USSR itself.

Gierek's domestic difficulties were compounded by the rising assertiveness of the Catholic Church after 1976. Although its undisputed leader, Cardinal Wyszynski, was unwilling openly to challenge the regime, the lower ranks of the clergy and some Catholic intellectuals were getting restless and impatient with the cautious policy of the episcopate. The authority and prestige of the church received a powerful boost with the election in October 1978 of Cardinal Karol Wojtyla, Archbishop of Krakow to papacy and the announcement that the new pope, John Paul II, would visit Poland in June 1979. These events represented a tremendous shot in the arm for an overwhelming majority of the Polish population at a time when the deteriorating economic and political situation had created a feeling of apathy and hopelessness. The choice of a Pole to ascend the papacy gave birth to an outburst of national pride and patriotism, comparable only to the heady days of October 1956 when the newly elected party leader Gomulka gained enormous popularity and the Communist system itself may have been said to become legitimate, albeit for only a short time. The triumphant tour of the pontiff, greeted by hundreds of thousands of his countrymen, was a most visible and convincing testimony of the church's ability to mobilize its followers.[23]

It may be assumed that the Kremlin had no major objections to the pope's visit. The second half of the 1970s had witnessed a number of visits to the Vatican paid by high ranking Soviet and East European officials, eager to build bridges between the Holy See and the European Communist countries. The Kremlin chose not to veto John Paul's return to his native land and once the visit was over, Moscow must have been largely pleased with its results. The visit itself was remarkably devoid of antigovernment demonstrations and within hours of the pontiff's departure the country appeared "normal" once again.

Moscow must have been greatly relieved by the rather benign character of the papal visitation although there was some evidence of considerable excitement generated by it in Lithuania, the only Soviet republic with a Catholic majority. Although there was a strong interest in the visit in nearly all the East European countries, the political effects were likely to be next to nil there. Too, the new pope appeared to be interested in continuing the *Ostpolitik* of his predecessor Paul VI.

For several months prior to the visit, the Gierek regime escalated its antidissident activity and several of the leading dissidents had been attacked, beaten, arrested, and generally harassed by the authorities. The question remained whether the Polish church, invigorated by the papal visit, would expand its collaboration with the dissidents or whether it would assume a more autonomous stance and, in fact, pre-empt and monopolize dissent.

The Polish regime's ability to defuse popular discontent clearly depended on its skill and determination in dealing with the persistent economic difficulties. The year 1979 witnessed continuing spillover of global economic problems into Poland which was now paying the heavy cost of the economic "opening to the West" in the form of inflation, especially in the energy and raw materials field. Its economic growth in 1979 was, in fact, negative and its national income in that year was 2 percent below 1978.[24]

There appeared to be no one capable of leading the country out of the political and economic morass. With the party divided, Gierek was unable to exercise whatever authority and prestige he had left. Moreover, he was afraid to enter into an alliance with the church or with the masses which he continued to accuse of betraying his trust in June 1976.

The reformist wing in the party was caught in a dilemma. Apart from a sheer risk of challenging the established regime, it was not fully agreed on the diagnosis of the economic ills plaguing the country and on the methods of recovery. Some felt that Gierek had made a monumental mistake in turning to the West for help in modernizing the Polish economy. They blamed the failure of that policy on lack of true Western support and advocated the abandonment of the "Western connection" in favor of returning to the Soviet fold. In the face of a growing energy crisis, the West was not likely to bail out Poland and the only country capable of doing it was the Soviet Union. The Soviet Union was well aware of the deteriorating economic situation and was perfectly ready and willing to watch Poland's economic situation worsen until the moment of imminent collapse when Moscow would step in and save Warsaw from disaster.[25]

Official statements delivered at the Polish Party Congress in February 1980 suggested that the Gierek regime, apparently strengthened by the purge of several key individuals, had finally decided to reform the Polish economy. That resolve must have received an additional boost from a group of Western bankers to whom Poland owed $20 billion, who visited Warsaw in April 1980, reaffirming their demand for economic reforms. The upward revision of retail meat prices announced on July 1, 1980, was seen as putting the price system on a more rational basis.

The 1980–81 Crisis: Escalation and Resolution

The political crisis in Poland that erupted in the wake of the above price reform was not entirely unexpected. It had been building up for a number of years and the only surprising thing about it was its intensity. The workers' frontal attack on the Polish Communist regime in August and September 1980 was the third in a series of similar challenges in the past decade, beginning with a bloody suppression of the demonstrations on the Baltic coast in December 1970 and continuing with the more limited strikes in June 1976.

The crisis in Poland caught the Gierek regime and the Kremlin by surprise. Moscow was probably misled by Gierek who, on his annual summer pilgrimage to the Soviet Union, did not bother to return to Poland until the middle of August. Prior to his departure he probably reassured his Soviet hosts that the situation on the Baltic coast was under control. This may explain the lack of Soviet reaction to the Polish events during July and most of August. The first official commentary which appeared on August 27 reflected a high degree of uncertainty and confusion about the true meaning of the strikes and the proper way of reporting them.[26]

The challenge to the established regime in Poland could not have come at a more inopportune time for Moscow. Bogged down in Afghanistan, keeping a wary eye on China, bent upon rebuilding détente and resuming friendly relations with France and West Germany, and economically more and more overextended, the Kremlin's room for maneuver was severely circumscribed. Moscow remained largely silent during the first two months or so of the strikes, except for sporadic attacks on "antisocialist elements" in Poland. Great pain was taken not to aggravate the situation. The Warsaw Pact maneuvers scheduled to take place in East Germany in early September were downplayed. The Kremlin granted Poland a substantial hard currency loan and persuaded Czechoslovakia and East Germany to provide additional economic aid to Warsaw.

Following the signing of the August 31 Gdansk agreement between the workers and the government, the Kremlin must have decided that Gierek had to go. In early September *Pravda* mentioned for the first time "the errors" committed by the Polish party leadership.[27] The effusive praise heaped by Brezhnev on Gierek's successor Stanislaw Kania, suggested that the Kremlin was hardly displeased with the changeover in Poland. Gierek's failure to learn any lessons from the events of June 1976 and his behavior during the critical days of August must have persuaded the Soviet leadership that he had lost all authority and credibility within the Polish party and society at large. In contrast, Kania's credentials looked impressive: by virtue of his position as one of the Central Committee secretaries he had had close contacts with the Polish military and security forces and he had also maintained good relations with another important actor on the political scene—the Catholic Church. He evidently was viewed by the Kremlin as a good if not ideal choice to stabilize the Polish situation.

Moscow may have decided to de-escalate its harsh criticisms to give

Kania a chance to restore normalcy and in light of the growing concern for the future of Poland manifested by the West, and especially by the United States, then in the final stages of the hard-fought election campaign. The threat of Soviet intervention in Poland was being mentioned prominently by both presidential candidates and the Soviet leadership.

Moscow rejoined the anti-Polish campaign in the second half of November, following the legalization of the statute of the new union, Solidarity, by Poland's Supreme Court and continuation of strikes in various parts of the country. The strike of railroad workers, including those manning the lines used by the Kremlin to supply its troops in East Germany, drew a sharp Soviet reaction that hinted darkly about the strike's threat to Soviet security interests. Shortly thereafter the Soviet Union started serious preparations for a military intervention in Poland, which appeared imminent in the first decade of December.

The Soviet leadership probably had given serious thought to a military intervention already in the second half of August. The upheaval in Poland in 1980 had gone well beyond the Czechoslovak crisis of 1968 which brought about a Warsaw Pact military intervention.

However, already at the end of August, on the eve of the Gdansk agreement, Brezhnev, following U.S.-Soviet meetings had publicly implied that the Soviet Union had no intention to interfere in Polish internal affairs.[28] The threat of intervention disappeared from the headlines for the next two months only to return with a vengeance at the end of November, and reached its apogee in the first half of December.

Shortly after Senator Percy, the incoming chairman of the Senate Foreign Relations, who visited Moscow at the end of November, warned the Soviet leaders against intervening in Poland, the Kremlin issued its own warning to Warsaw, strongly suggesting that a Soviet military action was being seriously considered. This was followed by media reports of increasing deployment of Soviet army reservists in the Subcarpathian military district. The growing tension was interrupted by the sudden summit meeting of Warsaw Pact leaders in Moscow who on December 5 issued a declaration expressing their hope that Poland would be able to overcome its difficulties and offered their help.[29]

Nonetheless, the Soviet military build-up alongside Polish frontiers continued and was completed a few days after the Moscow summit. It was accompanied by sharp Soviet attacks on the newly independent unions which were being accused of counter-revolutionary activities. The overall situation looked ominous when on December 12, the NATO Council meeting in Brussels issued a strong warning to the Kremlin not to intervene militarily in the Polish crisis. Moscow reacted angrily and soon indicated that it was prepared to let the Poles settle their problems alone. This position was reaffirmed a week later by Brezhnev who told the visiting Polish foreign minister that the Kremlin had full confidence in the

Polish party's ability to deal with the union.[30] The danger of intervention seemed over.

The first two months of 1981 were characterized by a definite lull in Soviet-Polish relations, and by the inability of the Polish government to establish a *modus vivendi* with the rapidly growing unions. On February 9, Prime Minister Jozef Pinkowski resigned and was replaced by the minister of defense, Jaruzelski, who became Poland's fourth premier in less than a year. Two days later, the new prime minister who contrary to expectations retained the Defense portfolio, appealed to the unions for a 90-day moratorium on strikes which was quickly accepted by Lech Walesa, the leader of the Solidarity movement. In the meantime, party leader Kania traveled to Prague and East Berlin in an obvious attempt to reassure Poland's harshest critics that the situation was under control. The belief that the worst was over was reinforced by both Brezhnev and Kania who in their respective addresses delivered at the end of February at the Twenty-sixth Congress of the Soviet Communist Party, suggested that with Soviet assistance the Polish party has been making progress in re-establishing its authority in the country.

The apparent honeymoon was unexpectedly interrupted a few days later by the announcement of a Soviet-Polish summit meeting in Moscow. The communique gave a lukewarm vote of confidence to the Polish party and the Kremlin again resurrected the "Brezhnev Doctrine." Moscow also repeated its readiness to help the Polish party in a "radical healing of the situation in the country."[31] Within 48 hours the Polish authorities detained or interrogated a number of leading dissidents who had been left alone by the authorities ever since early September. Too, large scale joint military maneuvers, code-named *Soyuz '81,* were announced for the second half of March with the participation of forces from the Soviet Union, Czechoslovakia, East Germany, and Poland.

The question of why by the summer of 1981 the Soviet Union had refrained from intervening militarily in Poland has been a favorite topic among the Western observers of the Polish scene.[32] The crisis in Poland represented a most serious challenge not only to the Soviet Union but also to the whole body of Marxist-Leninist doctrine, more serious perhaps than the Titoist heresy of 1948. Since the Soviet Union had in the past intervened militarily in Hungary and Czechoslovakia, both of which had committed lesser sins in the Soviet book, there was every expectation that an armed invasion of Poland was only a matter of time.

The fact that no such intervention had taken place as of the middle of 1981 provided a good testimony to the complex dilemma faced by the Kremlin leaders. In Moscow's eyes the estimated costs outweighed the benefits, with both sides of the equation changing all the time and hence the ultimate outcome highly indeterminate.

Having decided against armed intervention, the Soviets tried to prevent the reaching of a genuine agreement between the Polish party and Solidarity. The strategy consisted of cycles of confrontation-compromise-polemic. While the tension between Moscow and Warsaw eased with Brezhnev's address at the Czechoslovak Party Congress on April 7—in which the Soviet leader expressed his belief that "Polish Communists" themselves would be able to contain the crisis—his failure to give full support to Kania and Jaruzelski cast a shadow on future relations.[33]

Soon thereafter, Soviet concern shifted to the Extraordinary Congress which clearly raised fears of replicating the situation in Czechoslovakia in 1968 with its impending purge of hard-line elements in the party and wholesale approval of reforms aimed at democratization of the ruling party. Beginning in April, Moscow's top priority became to delay the Congress and, barring that, to manipulate the agenda in order to prevent the approval of liberal reforms. Act one was an unexpected, one-day visit in April to Warsaw of Mikhail Suslov, the well-known conservative Soviet watchdog of Communist orthodoxy. The visit was followed by a wave of sharp attacks on the Polish party which was accused, among others, of "revisionism," one of the gravest sins in the Communist vocabulary.[34] Act two was a June 5 letter of the Soviet Central Committee, to its Polish counterpart ominously stating that despite their commitment to contain the crisis, the Polish leadership allowed the situation to deteriorate still further.[35]

Although the Kremlin letter did not stop the Extraordinary Ninth Party Congress from being convoked on schedule, it clearly affected its outcome. Moscow dispatched Foreign Minister Andrei Gromyko to Warsaw 11 days before the opening of the Congress. The communique issued after Gromyko's visit reaffirmed Soviet decision to let the Congress take place, yet also stressed the continuing validity of the Brezhnev Doctrine.[36] The Congress itself, which met on July 14, was an anticlimax. The delegates elected a new Central Committee and Politburo and by defeating both the conservative and liberal candidates, it endorsed the centrist leadership of Kania and Jaruzelski.[37]

The victory of the centrists and the overwhelming approval of reforms that made the Polish party unique in the annals of international communism, could hardly be welcomed by the Kremlin. Yet the Congress not only reaffirmed Poland's close ties to the USSR but also kept the liberal faction in check. Things could have been worse and the official Soviet reaction reflected considerable ambivalence toward developments in Poland.

The expectations of further liberalization and economic reforms raised by the Congress were not fulfilled. The party and the government were neither able to cope with the escalating political and economic crises nor willing to reach a compromise with Solidarity. The latter began to challenge the government by presenting it with a series of radical demands which reached their height at the Solidarity Congress, held in September and October. The demands included a call for free elections, economic self-management, free access to media, and final legalization of free labor unions.

The Soviet reaction was not long in coming. On September 10, a message was delivered from Moscow complaining about the "mounting wave of anti-Sovietism in Poland" and warning that "further leniency shown to any manifestation of anti-Sovietism does immense harm to Polish-Soviet relations and is in direct contradiction to Poland's allied obligations and vital interests of the Polish nation."[38] The statement was considerably harsher than the Kremlin letter of June 5 which castigated Solidarity as a counter-revolutionary force without, however, invoking the specter of anti-Sovietism. The September message was followed by a barrage of attacks on just about every aspect of Polish "renewal" which continued unabated for the next two months.

The pressure from Moscow managed to intimidate the moderate faction within the Polish party and embolden the conservative wing, long dissatisfied with Kania's inability or unwillingness to suppress Solidarity and other opposition groups. Most likely with the encouragement of the Kremlin, the Central Committee elected at the July Congress ousted Kania on October 17, replacing him with General Jaruzelski who thus became the most powerful leader in the Communist world, combining party leadership with premiership and command of Poland's armed forces.

Those who expected the new party leader to deal with the mounting crisis in a resolute manner were soon disappointed. Like his predecessor, Jaruzelski was unable to reach a compromise with the opposition for the purpose of stabilizing the country and initiating the process of economic recovery. His attempt to bring Solidarity and the Catholic Church into some kind of a "united front" proved abortive when it became obvious that both the union and the church were to play a highly subordinate role in the new arrangement. Presumably on Moscow's insistence Jaruzelski subsequently declined to negotiate with Solidarity and also refused to proceed with the legislation on self-management, censorship, and independent labor unions which were of particular concern to Solidarity. The latter responded with a threat of general strike, a call for a referendum concerning the future Polish political system, and a demand for the ouster of the party from industrial enterprises. Solidarity designated December 17 as the day of national protest to coincide with the anniversary of the 1970 Baltic coast riots. Shortly before that date, on December 13, General Jaruzelski proclaimed the state of emergency, imposed martial law, and established a military council which was to rule the country until further notice.

The coup which was executed with remarkable precision, managed to decapitate Solidarity which put up a surprisingly mild resistance. Justifying the imposition of martial law as a last ditch effort to prevent a national catastrophe, the military regime arrested over 6,000 opposition members and abolished several concessions granted to Solidarity in the course of the previous 16 months. Within a few weeks all active resistance was broken and the military regime appeared to be in full control of the situation.

The Polish situation represented a synthesis of both the Hungarian revolt of 1956 and of the Czechoslovak reform movement of 1968. As in Hungary, the workers' rebellion soon acquired a mass character and overwhelming popular support, while the process of democratization with the ruling party strongly resembled the ideas put forward by the architects of "Prague spring." The combination of these two features made the Polish crisis of 1980–81 a most serious threat to Moscow and the rest of the Communist alliance.

The Kremlin must have greeted the imposition of martial law in December with mixed feelings. The coup succeeded in destroying Solidarity and in preventing the collapse of Poland's political system. Yet the fact that the Polish Communist party proved incapable of restoring order and had to be replaced by the military as the supreme authority in the country, reflected the total bankruptcy of the Communist system. Moscow's ambivalence was illustrated by the absence of official praise for the military rule, although Moscow was forced to grant Jaruzelski an additional substantial loan to save the Polish economy.[39]

In the middle of December 1981 the Polish crisis remained far from settled. Possible Soviet military intervention depended on the ability of the Polish military rulers to stabilize the country and to start the process of economic recovery. The prospect of an early political and economic stabilization was not bright. The Communist party appeared to be in serious disarray and was losing membership at a rapid rate. Deprived of certain key imports, the economy was limping along. The food situation remained perilous and passive resistance on a mass scale was making a quick recovery highly questionable.

Conclusions

The time has come to see whether our examination of Soviet-Polish relations in 1956 and 1980–81 has verified the original premise that perceived the Soviet policy vis-à-vis Poland as a synthesis of several distinct factors, forces, and processes, both permanent and transitional.

On the assumption that the Kremlin's policy toward Poland has been primarily, if not exclusively, motivated by Soviet national interest, the principal goal of that policy had to be the safeguarding of Soviet security.

Whatever tended to reduce that security—as perceived and interpreted by Soviet leadership—had to be resisted and ultimately eliminated.

Except for the crisis in 1980–81, developments in Poland have not threatened Soviet security. The successive political crises of October 1956, March 1968, December 1970, and June 1976 were generated by various internal processes and policies and have seriously challenged neither the supremacy of the Communist party nor Soviet hegemony in the region. The ruling oligarchy and military generally appeared loyal and obedient to Moscow. The sheer numerical size of the military made it an important component of the Warsaw Pact and a significant link in the Soviet security system, despite some doubts about its reliability.

The Polish ruling elite's devotion to the Soviet cause presumably had an impact on Moscow's attitude toward Warsaw. Since 1956, impressed by the unflinching loyalty of the Polish leaders, the Kremlin allowed them considerable attitude in their foreign policy. Although Poland, unlike East Germany and to some extent Czechoslovakia, has not been used as a Soviet proxy in the Third World, it has after 1970, performed a number of useful tasks for the USSR, especially in the context of Moscow's policy of rapprochement with the West.

Moscow between 1956 and 1980 had also granted Poland far more leeway in its domestic affairs than that allowed the other members of the alliance. This became particularly true in the second half of the 1970s which witnessed the birth of a dynamic movement and of a growing political mobilization of the Catholic Church. Poland was seen as a loyal and reliable member of the Warsaw alliance, and thus an important Soviet strategic and military asset.

Economically Poland was certainly less of a Soviet asset than Czechoslovakia and East Germany. Not that Poland was a burden: it was exporting to the Soviet Union considerable quantity of new materials and consumer goods as well as some capital goods. It was only toward the end of the 1970s that Poland has become an economic basket case and hardship to Moscow, which in 1976 was forced to provide emergency aid to the Gierek regime threatened with economic collapse. There is no evidence that Soviet policy toward Poland has been greatly influenced by economic considerations.

The attitudes of Soviet leaders toward Poland were likely shaped by their perceptions of Poland as a Soviet asset or burden, a reliable ally or a reluctant camp follower. Their perceptions, in turn, were formed by personal knowledge or information supplied by Moscow's sources in the country. None of the Soviet leaders had any first-hand knowledge or experience of Poland. Brezhnev never developed a warm personal relationship with Gomulka, if only because of the latter's widely rumored friendship with Khrushchev. During the 1970s Gierek apparently succeeded in convincing the Soviet leadership of his undying loyalty as well as of his popularity at home. Brezhnev evidently viewed Kania and Jaruzelski with considerable suspicion.

What about the impact of Russian history and traditions on Soviet attitude toward Poland? In contrast to Bulgaria or Czechoslovakia, Soviet leaders tended to view Poland if not as a traditional enemy then at least as a country which historically has held little love and much contempt for Moscow. The events of World War II and the process of postwar Communist takeover followed by Stalinization, did little to change that attitude. The awareness of historical sensitivities may have been at least partly responsible for a somewhat benign official policy toward Poland.

Soviet behavior has also been influenced by Moscow's policies and attitudes toward third countries as well as by the general state of East-West relations. Thus Soviet nonintervention in the 1956 crisis in Poland was most likely caused by Moscow's concern with the developments in Hungary and the Middle East. The obvious Soviet interest in improving relations with West Germany and France was responsible for making Poland a useful East-West intermediary. The tough anti-Soviet stance assumed not only by the United States but also, surprisingly enough, by its NATO allies, must have impacted Moscow's calculations, reducing the risk of military intervention.

Soviet policy toward Poland in both 1956 and 1980–81 has been characterized by an ambivalence caused by the complexity of influences affecting Moscow's perception of its strongest East European ally. That complexity has clearly increased since the 1980–81 crisis and if the various factors and processes continue changing at a rapid rate, they will force us to revise many of the assumptions and premises that underlay this study.

Did the Polish-Soviet crises of 1956 and 1980–81 fulfill the three "necessary and sufficient" conditions and "operational criteria" of an international crisis?[40] To Soviet policymakers, the assumption of power in Poland by the anti-Stalinist regime headed by Gomulka in 1956, might initially be perceived as representing a "threat to basic values." Khrushchev realized rather quickly that Gomulka was, by and large, an orthodox Communist and that granted some concessions on the domestic front, the new regime was hardly likely to present a major threat to Moscow's vital interests.

The creation of Solidarity in August 1980 represented a "threat to basic values." Ideologically, it challenged the Leninist conception of the "leading role of the Party." Militarily it threatened the lines of transportation and communication between the USSR and the Soviet forces in East Germany, and affected the Polish armed forces, a key component of the Northern Tier of the Warsaw Pact. Political unrest raised the threat of a spillover from Poland to its neighbors, Czechoslovakia and East Germany. Thus, the emergence and rapid growth of Solidarity was seriously impairing Soviet national interest, and failure on the part of Moscow to react would clearly compromise its position not only in Eastern Europe but also in the entire international Communist movement.

Did the events preceding the two crises in Poland take the Soviet leadership by surprise? Insofar as the 1956 crisis is concerned, surprise was largely absent, even though Soviet reaction to the crisis was slow. Events in Poland after August 1980 took the Kremlin by surprise and it took Moscow several weeks before it fully realized the potential threat to its interests. What followed was a sequence of interactions between Moscow and Warsaw which eventually resulted in a major conflict between the two countries.

A series of decisions reflected Moscow's perception of the growing threat of the Polish domestic crises in 1956 and 1980–81 getting out of control and endangering the unity of Soviet empire in Eastern Europe. The Soviet leadership seriously considered military intervention in October 1956 when Soviet troops began advancing on Warsaw and there were numerous signs in 1980–81 that an armed Soviet intervention was imminent. Interestingly enough, the danger of a Soviet intervention did not significantly affect the domestic situation in Poland. If anything, in 1956 it seemed to strengthen Gomulka's position in the party. In 1980–81, either the threat of an intervention was not perceived as credible by both the government and Solidarity, or both the Polish regime and workers realized that a surrender by one to the other would not significantly reduce the probability of a Soviet invasion, making a continuing stalemate a preferred outcome, at least until December 1981.

An interesting aspect of both crises was that neither side seemed to have operated under a time constraint. Although the Soviet leaders at some point became concerned with the course of events in Poland in the summer and fall of 1956, as illustrated by the sudden visit of Khrushchev to Warsaw in October 1956, there is no evidence of Moscow issuing an ultimatum with a specific deadline. The same was largely true for the situation in 1980–81. The only possible example of a time constraint was the fact that the Extraordinary Ninth Party Congress was scheduled to take place in Warsaw in July 1981 and that Moscow was clearly worried about its outcome.

In both crises Moscow behavior appeared clearly unpredictable, keeping the Polish leadership guessing about the Kremlin's intentions. The period of uncertainty lasted only a few months and came to an end with Khrushchev's giving his *imprimatur* to Gomulka's regime. The situation in 1980–81 was more unpredictable and the period of uncertainty lasted considerably longer. The high probability of an armed intervention in the winter of 1980 and spring of 1981, was followed by a more conventional pressure exerted on Poland at least until the July 1981 Congress. The decisions taken by the Congress very likely surprised the Soviet leaders and provided them with more time and additional room for maneuver. Soviet behavior between July and December 1981 can be described as unpredictable, thus raising questions about the validity of Bruce Russett's belief that in a crisis situation one power must make its actions more readily predictable to other powers and particularly to prospective opponents.[41] While the threat of a military intervention has not disappeared completely, it certainly has abated and other means of pressure have been applied in lieu of a direct armed intervention.

The 1956 crisis was terminated by the apparent agreement between Khrushchev and Gomulka which allowed the latter to assume the reins of power in Poland. The imposition of martial law in December 1981, often referred to as an "intervention by proxy," brought the 1980–81 crisis to an end, at least for the time being. However, the question still remains as to why the Soviet leadership decided against full-scale intervention in both 1956 and 1980–81. In both cases there were two key reasons: Moscow's perception of fierce Polish resistance to the intervention and the Kremlin's belief that an overt military action would harm Soviet relations not only with Western Europe, which the Soviet Union has been trying to decouple from the United States since the mid-1950s, but also with the United States and even the rest of the Communist camp. Soviet intervention in Hungary in 1956 angered Washington and delayed rapprochement with Moscow, eagerly pursued by Khrushchev. A similar move toward Poland in 1980–81 would have put the last nails in the coffin of U.S.-Soviet détente, something that apparently Moscow is not yet ready to do.

To conclude, the answer to one of our original questions regarding the validity of Western approaches to the study of international crises, as applied to the Polish-Soviet crises of 1956 and 1980–81, is generally an affirmative one. All the necessary ingredients, except one, were present with varying intensities: threat to basic values and interests, sharp conflict, and high probability of war. The only seeming exception was the absence of a perceived time constraint but even in this case there were strong indications that time was running out and that some drastic action would have to be taken sooner rather than later.

Notes

1. Michael Brecher, "State Behavior in International Crises," *Journal of Conflict Resolution,* vol. 23, no. 3 (September 1973), pp. 446–47.

2. Richard Ned Lebow, *Between Peace and War* (Baltimore and London: The Johns Hopkins University Press, 1981), pp. 10–11.

3. Zbigniew Brzezinski, *The Soviet Bloc* revised and enlarged ed. (Cambridge, Mass.: Harvard University Press, 1967), pp. 4–5.

4. For a discussion of a Soviet concept of security, see Andrzej Korbonski, "Eastern Europe," in *After Brezhnev: Sources of Soviet Conduct in the 1980s,* ed. Robert F. Byrnes (Bloomington, Ind.: Indiana University Press, 1983), pp. 304–5.

5. For details, see Andrzej Korbonski and Sarah M. Terry, "The Military as a Political Actor in Poland," in *Soldiers, Peasants and Bureaucrats,* ed. Roman Kolkowicz and Andrzej Korbonski (London: George Allen and Unwin, 1982), pp. 162–64.

6. In this regard Soviet exploitation of Poland paralleled that of Eastern Europe in general during the Stalin era.

7. For a discussion of Poland's participation in CMEA, see Andrzej Korbonski, "Poland and the CMEA: problems and Prospects," in *East European Integration and East-West Trade,* ed. Paul Marer and John Michael Montias (Bloomington, Ind.: Indiana University Press, 1980), pp. 355–81.

8. Personal interviews, Los Angeles, California, summer 1978.

9. Boleslaw Bierut, "Zadania Partii w walce o umacnianie codziennej wiezi z masami pracujacymi," *Trybuna Lubu,* January 26, 1955.

10. Hilary Minc, "Pierwsze wnioski," *Trybuna Ludu,* December 31, 1955.

11. Brzezinski, *The Soviet Bloc,* pp. 200–5.

12. For an excellent bibliographical essay on the events in 1956, see George Sakwa, "The Polish 'October': A Re-Appraisal Through Historiography," *The Polish Review,* vol. 23, no. 3 (1978) pp. 62–78.

13. For details, see Flora Lewis, *A Case History of Hope* (Garden City, N.Y.: Doubleday, 1958), pp. 101–7.

14. *Pravda,* February 21, 1956, and April 18, 1956. For an English translation, see Paul E. Zinner, ed., *National Communism and Popular Revolt in Eastern Europe* (New York: Columbia University Press, 1956), pp. 9–11 and 37–39.

15. For details, see "Kalendarium Kryzysow w PRL (Lata 1953–1980)," *Zeszyty Historyczne* (Paris), no. 66 (1983) pp. 146–47.

16. A most comprehensive account can be found in Jaroslaw Maciejewski and Zofia Trojanowiczowa, eds., *Poznanski Czerwiec 1956* (Poznan: Wydawnictwo Poznanskie, 1981). For Soviet reaction to the Poznan riots, see Veljko Micunovic, *Moscow Diary* (Garden City, N.Y.: Doubleday, 1980), pp. 76–77.

17. *Nowe Drogi,* vol. 10, no. 7–8 (July-August 1956) pp. 3–30 and 137–254. For an interesting account by a participant, see Jan Ptasinski, "Powrot Gomulki," *Polityka,* 16 February 1985, pp. 8–10.

18. Apparently Bulganin wanted to address the Seventh Plenum but was not allowed to do so by the Polish Politburo. Lewis, *A Case History of Hope,* pp. 165–66.

19. Ibid., pp. 182–84.

20. For Khrushchev's personal account of his meeting with Gomulka, see Strobe Talbott, ed., *Khrushchev Remembers: The Last Testament* (Boston: Little, Brown, 1974), pp. 200–5. See also, Lewis, *A Case History of Hope,* pp. 209–18.

21. "The East Berlin Communist Conference," Radio Free Europe Research, *Special Report Poland/23,* July 13, 1976.

22. For details of the Moscow visit of a Polish delegation see "Relations with the USSR: A New Stage," Radio Free Europe Research, *Situation Report Poland/ 39,* November 19, 1976. See also, N. Ponomaryov and V. Zhuravlev, "USSR-Poland: Fraternal Alliance of Peoples," *International Affairs* (Moscow), no. 1 (January 1977) pp. 86–91.

23. For an account of the pope's visit, see Radio Free Europe Research, *The Pope in Poland* (Munich: RFE/RL, 1979).

24. *Rocznik Statystyczny 1980,* p. 23.

25. Personal interviews, Warsaw, July 1979.

26. For an extensive coverage of the Soviet press reaction to the events in Poland in August and September, see Radio Free Europe, *August 1980: The Strikes in Poland* (Munich: Radio Free Europe Research, October 1980), pp. 237–54.

27. Article by Gus Hall in *Pravda,* August 31, 1980.

28. *Los Angeles Times,* August 30, 1980.

29. *New York Times,* December 6, 1980.

30. Ibid., December 27, 1980.

31. Ibid., March 5, 1981.

32. For a comprehensive analysis, see Seweryn Bialer, "Poland and the Soviet Imperium," *Foreign Affairs,* vol. 59, no. 3 (1980) pp. 522–30; Jiri Valenta, "Soviet Options in Poland," *Survival* (London), March 1981, pp. 50–59; and Richard D. Anderson, Jr., "Soviet Decision-Making and Poland," *Problems of Communism,* vol. 31, no. 2 (March-April 1982) pp. 22–36.

33. For excerpts from Brezhnev's speech, see *New York Times,* April 8, 1981.

34. John Darnton in *New York Times,* April 14, 1981.

35. The full text of the letter can be found in *New York Times,* June 11, 1981.

36. John F. Burns in *New York Times,* July 6, 1981.

37. Jerzy Urban, "Zmiany na szczycie," *Polityka,* 25 July 1981, pp. 1, 5.

38. The text of the message can be found in *New York Times,* September 13, 1981.

39. Actually, the total Soviet economic aid to Poland was not inconsiderable. According to Polish official sources, between July 1980 and July 1981 it amounted to $4.5 billion, *New York Times,* July 9, 1981. Following the imposition of martial law in December 1981, the USSR apparently granted Poland additional $3.9 billion in aid and credits, *Los Angeles Times,* January 7, 1982.

40. Questions may be raised regarding the idea of Poland being considered a sovereign state, and therefore the appropriateness of applying an international crisis model to the Soviet-Polish crisis. We feel, however, that the fact that the Solidarity movement did take place in Poland and that the Polish government appeared to be in control of its armed forces, suggests a high degree of sovereignty, at least in some crucial areas of state conduct.

41. Bruce M. Russett, "Cause, Surprise and No Escape," *Journal of Politics,* vol. 24, no. 1 (February 1962) p. 21.

16

THE SOVIET INVASION OF AFGHANISTAN: PURSUING STABILITY AND SECURITY

Cristann Lea Gibson

The Soviet invasion of Afghanistan in December 1979 has generated a number of diverse theories concerning the "expanded" role of the Soviet Union in world affairs. The USSR's apparent willingness and capability to project military power to enforce the survival of a "friendly" Communist regime outside of the Soviet bloc is viewed by some as a new breach in the well-perceived boundaries in regional and global relations. The Soviet decision to invade, however, demonstrates neither a new model of behavior nor a recently generated set of interests. In Afghanistan the Soviets have employed a well-tested, consistent, and largely successful methodology for securing and maintaining influence and control. The three-phased approach—work within and alignment with the national Communist party, covert extension of influence and control of key elements (military, police, pro-Soviet factions), and military intervention—has been used all or in part with respect to every client-nation in the Soviet orbit. The effectiveness of the first two phases has usually precluded the necessity for intervention, but Hungary, Czechoslovakia, and now Afghanistan are a testament to the commitment of the Soviet Union to the preservation of the security of its borders at all costs.

The purpose of this chapter will be to demonstrate the degree to which these three phases of Soviet control were present in Afghanistan and to show that these methods were consistent with those applied elsewhere and over time. In this sense there is very little that is new about Afghanistan. If Afghanistan's geostrategic position is analyzed with respect to the long-standing Russian and Soviet goal of preserving a *cordon sanitair* of politically reliable nations on its borders, Afghanistan is not an issue of sudden Soviet adventurism or methodical expansion into the Third World. The Soviets have intervened militarily in Afghanistan before (1925 and in 1929) and for many of the same reasons. Therefore, Afghanistan should not continue to be analyzed in terms of a new age of Soviet foreign policy but in terms of the consistency of the 1979 invasion with past actions and interests. It is obvious that the invasion of Afghanistan tragically surprised those within the Carter administration and was allowed to take on a new and largely erroneous meaning because of their collective naiveté. To those analysts who study the Soviet Union comparatively and over time, Afghanistan is remarkable only in its predictability. Afghanistan demonstrates a persistent and frequently costly goal of Soviet foreign policy and decision making.

The Afghan Background

The Soviet invasion of Afghanistan differed very little in cause or consequence from earlier invasions by the British Empire, the Russian Empire, or the Soviet state. The First and Second Afghan wars in 1839 and 1879 were initiated by British invasions in response to the threatened expansion of the Russian Empire's influence in Afghanistan and in the region. The ongoing British and Russian contention over using Afghanistan territory as a buffer between empires was eventually muted by the St. Petersburg Convention of 1907, but the continued internal unrest and the rising tide of Afghan nationalism, eventually resulted in the Third Afghan War in 1919. As a result of the conflict and despite their initial success, Britain was forced to recognize Afghanistan's independence and to renounce its protectionist policies. In 1919 the Soviet state took advantage of the British position and also affirmed its continued interest in Afghanistan and recognized Afghanistan's independent status in the region.

Freed from the possibility of overt conflict with Great Britain over its interests in Afghanistan, the Soviet Union proceeded to conclude a treaty of friendship with Amir Amanullah ostensibly to offset the loss of British trade and aid. The treaty formally established a Soviet-Afghan relationship that was dependent upon the extension of Soviet long-term economic assistance. Urged on by Moscow, Amanullah began a program of modernization that was financed by Soviet support during the early 1920s. His methods for secular reform and modernization rapidly incited rebellion by the conservative Muslim population. In 1924, in response to Amanullah's request for aid in putting down a local revolt, the Soviets first sent military advisers to Afghanistan.[1]

During the same period the Soviets were extending their economic and military interests in Afghanistan they were also consolidating their control over the Central Asian Republics. The majority of the resistance groups (*Basmachi*) operated in and were given refuge by common tribes and nationalities in Afghanistan. Many of these early anti-Soviet rebels later settled in Afghanistan and kept their hatred well fed by the Soviet actions in Central Asia. Some of these tribes were the first to fight the Soviets in 1979.[2] The first Soviet invasion of Afghanistan in 1925 was an attempt to eliminate the bands of *Basmachi* rebels based on the island of Urta Tagai in the Amudarya River. The Soviets needed very few troops to annex the island. They finally withdrew even that small contingent in 1926 after concluding a nonaggression treaty with Afghanistan. The expedient Soviet retreat was an effort to avoid further British and Afghan threats.[3]

The continuation of modernization and secular reforms in Afghanistan eventually resulted in a major revolt in 1929. Amanullah fled to Quandahar and was replaced by a band of Tadzhik, Uzbek, and Turkmen "bandits."[4] The Soviets wasted little time deciding to support Amanullah against the anti-Soviet bandits. They initiated an invasion made up of a mixed force of Afghans and Soviet Central Asian forces numbering 1,500. Despite their efforts Amanullah abdicated and fled to India. The Soviets then withdrew their forces.

Mohammad Nadir Khan was made king in 1929 and immediately began to reverse all reform programs and to limit severely Soviet influence. In 1933 Amanullah's son Mohammad Zahir succeeded Nadir Khan as king. Zahir ruled for the next 40 years maintaining a pro-British and varyingly anti-Soviet stance.[5] After World War II, when the British withdrew from the region in 1947, Zahir feared the Soviets would try to recoup the influence the British had lost. In an effort to forestall Soviet interests he appealed to the United States for aid and support.[6] From 1946 to 1955 the Afghans received a series of small loans from the United States. The strong U.S. commitment to Pakistan (created in 1947), the ongoing Afghan-Pakistan animosity, and the general U.S. perception that Afghanistan was of little strategic importance in the region contributed to the sporadic and limited nature of U.S. aid to Afghanistan. As a result of the United States' unwillingness to assume the role Britain had occupied in Afghan economic and military affairs and the limitations on regional trade because of the tribal dispute with Pakistan, the Afghans were forced to turn to the Soviets for aid in the early 1950s. Between 1950–55 Afghan-Soviet trade and economic and military aid grew by 50 percent.[7] As a part of their general expansion into the Third World that began in 1953, the Soviets extended a 100 million ruble line of credit to Afghanistan and agreed to build transport, communication, and trade networks and to help in the modernization effort. Although the United States continued to supply nominal aid during this same period it was vastly and apparently willingly allowed to be overshadowed by the Soviet effort.

During the majority of his reign King Zahir was an ineffectual leader whose dealings with the Soviets were left in the capable hands of his first cousin and Prime Minister Prince Daoud. After Daoud left the government in 1963, Zahir attempted to initiate a very cautious reform program that most significantly resulted in allowing freedom for political parties in opposition to the crown.

In 1965 the Communist-oriented party, the People's Democratic Party of Afghanistan (PDPA) was formed. By 1967 this volatile and tribally mixed party had split into several factions. The two dominant factions were the militant nationalist and anti-Soviet *Khalq* and the more urban, pro-Soviet *Parcham.*[8] Although Moscow retained ties with both factions it did not recognize the PDPA or its derivatives as representatives of the Soviet Union in the region.[9]

Despite the creation of parties and some limited parliamentary and constitutional reform, Zahir's rule did not move beyond the absolute power of a conservative monarchy. The unrest among the more modern urban elements, chiefly military officers led by Prince Daoud, had grown steadily since the late 1960s. In July of 1973 while Zahir was in Italy Daoud and his followers finally seized power in a bloodless coup. Daoud wasted little time in instituting a republican system. Although he initially included leftist members in his cabinet, when he had secured a broader power base he replaced them from 1974 to 1977 with more conservative appointments. In 1977 Daoud established a new constitution that allowed only one legal political party, his own National Revolutionary party. The net result of the new Constitution, the ouster of Parcham appointees, and the continued exclusion of the Khalq led to a reunification of the PDPA in 1977. The reforms led also to the erosion of the legitimacy of Daoud as he moved further away from traditional forms of government and support.

Phase One: Working with the Communist Factions

When the Khalq and Parcham factions reunited into the People's Democratic Party of Afghanistan (PDPA) in 1977 to plot the overthrow of Prince Mohammad Daoud Khan and to establish a "revolutionary" regime in Afghanistan, they did so at the urging of the Soviet Union.[10] Afghanistan was securely tied to the Soviets through long-term modernization efforts involving over 600 million rubles of aid since 1956 for the construction of highways, electrical plants, airports, communications equipment, and the initiation of extensive educational and training programs. In addition, the Soviets provided military and technical assistance, including the training of over 4,000 Afghan officers.[11] In the four years of Daoud's reign the Soviet-Afghan relationship had resulted in an enormous amount of Soviet military and economic assistance and was dependent upon the Soviets to extract and purchase most of Afghanistan's natural gas and other exports. Despite Daoud's Soviet learnings he began to pursue international and domestic goals that conflicted with Moscow in an effort to extend his circle of trade and to offset growing Soviet dependence. In the region Daoud pursued relations with India, Egypt, and China signaling a strong interest in their "nonaligned" status. Daoud also opened relations with U.S.-backed Pakistan, Saudi Arabia, and Iran and asked for additional economic aid. Negotiations were also opened to obtain military training from India, Egypt, and Pakistan. In 1974 the Shah of Iran committed long-term economic aid ($2 billion over 10 years) to modernize transportation and communication within Afghanistan and may have even encouraged Daoud to break away from Soviet influence.[12] This offer of regional assistance combined with an economic agreement with China would have radically shifted the balance of trade and influence in favor of the West within the region.

In 1978 Daoud culminated a policy of growing repression of opposition parties that had begun in 1975. In April, after a large funeral demonstration, he arrested a number of top PDPA members including faction leaders Nur M. Taraki, Hafizullah Amin, and Babrak Karmal. With the leadership incarcerated and identifiable factions under threats of imprisonment the party of only a few thousand was effectively dominated by a large contingent of Khalq, left-wing army and air force officers.[13] This military element, in anticipation of their own arrest and the enforced disintegration of the party, decided to push the coup ahead. On April 27 they surrounded the palace, captured and killed Daoud, his family and supporters, took over transportation and communication facilities, and freed the PDPA leaders. Although the Soviets were probably informed of the sudden necessity of the coup by their many advisers in Afghanistan and pro-Soviet factions led by Karmal, circumstances argue against any real complicity on the part of Moscow regarding the timing of the coup.[14]

With a successful revolution and the installation of a pro-Soviet, Marxist regime headed by Taraki (secretary general of the PDPA, president of the Revolutionary Council, and prime minister) and supported by an all-party cabinet, Moscow was confident of a renewed commitment to Soviet goals.[15] During July 1978 after a period of uneasy rule, the PDPA dissolved once again into opposing Khalq and Parcham factions. The pro-Soviet Parcham members of the cabinet were methodically removed and replaced by Khalq members. The remnants of the Parcham faction were subsequently repressed and eventually executed along with all other opposition parties.[16] Karmal and other pro-Soviets took refuge in the Soviet mission and eventually fled to the Soviet Union. Karmal spent his time in Moscow much like other exiled leaders had during World War II (for example, France's Thorez) being tutored in the workability of the Soviet model and the rewards of loyalty to the Soviet state. Soviet willingness to host these Afghan exiles leaves little doubt that they saw the potential for using Karmal should the government of Afghanistan again try to move outside the Soviet orbit.

Despite growing popular hostility to the government's Communist tactics, in December 1978 the Soviets and Afghans formalized their mutual goals and signed a Treaty of Friendship and Cooperation to extend aid and trade agreements and to provide exchanges in the fields of science, technology, education, and communication.[17] Aid projects included some 170 facilities built by the Soviets to advance the Afghan economy including factories, roads, irrigation systems, and power-generating plants.[18] This augmented form of capital and labor-intensive Soviet aid was typical of other client agreements (Cuba, North Korea, bloc countries) and could not be effectively countered in the short-term by Western sources. Article four of the treaty also provided for the parties by mutual consent to "undertake appropriate measures to insure the safety, security, independence and territorial integrity of both countries."[19] This section of the treaty formalized the place of Afghanistan in the Soviet sphere of influence. Because the United States did not make any attempt to offset Soviet aid either by extending additional trade agreements, or by signaling its disapproval by withdrawing minimal aid to a Communist Afghanistan (aid was finally suspended in February 1979), Soviet claims to Afghanistan had been tacitly approved.

Faced with little political opposition, Taraki and Deputy Prime Minister Amin began a period of heavy-handed reform that rapidly disturbed the very foundation of Afghan religious, cultural, economic, social, and tribal norms. The communization of land violated centuries of feudal relationships and nomadic life. It alienated the rural population and aroused the provincial warlords. The aggressive atheism of the Communists deeply offended the Muslim population (almost 95 percent of the Afghan population) and undermined the rule of the government in Kabul where the only form of political legitimization was rule through the guidance of Allah. Continual slaughter of the political opposition meant an ever-widening circle of tribal blood feud (life for a life) and revenge that became the sole commitment of hundreds of families and even whole tribes. The inexperience and ruthlessness with which these alien reforms were instituted virtually guaranteed a broad-based, long-term, and very virulent opposition.

By July 1978 opposition to the Taraki-Amin regime had stretched across all ethnic groups from Pushtuns to Uzbeks and permeated all of the rural provinces and smaller urban areas. The Khalq were able to maintain control only in the larger cities. By late 1978 a whole network of guerrilla bands had taken sanctuary in Pakistan and operated freely across the border in Afghanistan. In spite of Soviet efforts to curtail rebel activity the bands of guerrillas continued to significantly disrupt land supply routes.

Rebel factions held the countryside and claimed the allegiance of the majority of the population within the 28 provinces. The usual basis for governmental support, the Afghan army, was plagued with a high rate of desertion and large-scale mutiny. As anti-Communist and anti-Khalq sentiment grew so did animosity for the Soviet presence.

After a large uprising in the city of Herat in March 1979 that resulted in the wholesale slaughter of Soviet military advisers and their dependents, the Soviets sent in more military advisers, (about 1,500 added to the 2,500 already present), and increased the flow of arms.[20] Because of the brutality of the attacks, the remaining families of advisers were recalled to Moscow to avoid their becoming hostages. Initially the Soviets provided the air power (primarily assault helicopters able to negotiate the mountainous terrain) to subdue rebel strongholds and scatter resistance. This hit-and-run style of attack worked only for a limited time since the rebels could retreat across the borders into Pakistan and take refuge among tribal members living in these areas.

Phase Two: Covert Soviet Actions

Although Taraki was prime minister and head of the Revolutionary Council, Amin was actually in charge of the day-to-day administration of reform policy. He was responsible for both the rapidity and vehemence with which it was pursued. The Soviets had correctly identified Amin as the force behind the reforms and had moved as early as May for his ouster in an effort to limit the deterioration of Afghan internal affairs. U.S. intelligence memoranda suggest that by May the Soviets intended to replace Khalq leadership with Parcham (Karmal) reliability.[21]

In June the Soviets sent Vasily Safronchuk to Kabul as the second deputy to Ambassador Aleksandr Puzanov. He was to attempt to persuade Taraki and Amin to curtail the removal and replacement of all Parcham and progressive elements within the government, and to begin to broaden their base of support. He was also to attempt to slow down the pace or stop the reforms that had splintered the Taraki-Amin government's legitimacy.[22] As it became apparent that Taraki and especially Amin could not or would not soften their position despite internal disintegration and Soviet insistence, Safronchuk undertook the second part of his mission, to change the government itself. In July leaflets began to appear in Kabul attacking Amin as a "CIA agent" and as an enemy of the Soviet Union.[23] As a result of this leaflet campaign Safronchuk was identified by U.S. intelligence sources as the main Soviet architect of the internal movement for radical governmental change in Afghanistan. Sources felt his presence was indicative of the growing Soviet concern over the rapidly deteriorating situation, their "determination to save the revolution" and the need to install new leadership.[24]

In the midst of these events, after a trip to Cuba to attend a conference of the nonaligned nations, Taraki visited Moscow in September
1979. He was undoubtedly pressured to oust Amin and to allow the
Soviets to help him regain control. This plan failed before it had a chance
to be implemented, however, because three days after Taraki's return to
Kabul, Taraki's security guard attempted to kill Amin at a meeting
sanctioned by Soviet Ambassador Puzanov. When the plot failed Amin
imprisoned Taraki and later executed him. Given the number of plots
against Amin initiated by Moscow and his amazing ability to stay one step
ahead of assassins it is probable that Amin had informants within Taraki's
circle that warned him that the Soviets were backing Taraki against him
and planning to use his ouster as an excuse for slowing down the reform
process and thereby decreasing the growing resistance.[25] Since Puzanov
had implicated himself and the Soviet government in the attempt on
Amin's life, Amin could afford to accuse him openly of complicity and
have him declared *persona non grata.* Moscow was left with little choice
except to replace him with a more acceptable candidate, F.A. Tabeyev, a
Tartar Muslim. Although Moscow took its time in Puzanov's removal and
left Safronchuk in place there was very little that could be done to alter the
internal situation once Amin came to power. The covert side of Soviet operations in Afghanistan began to focus on fifth column military issues and
reconnaissance.

Although it is clear from Soviet troop deployments that the decision
to prepare to use military force was taken sometime in late November,
this did not prevent the Soviets from one last covert attempt to overthrow
Amin. On November 28 the Soviets sent Lt. General Viktor S. Paputin,
first deputy minister of Internal Affairs (MVD), to Kabul. Working with
the Ministry of Internal Affairs he was to help Amin reorganize the internal security police. It is probable his real mission was to organize the anti-
Amin elements of the police and army.[26] He also was in an ideal position
to supply current intelligence to supplement the growing network of
Soviet advisers and to help secure communications. After the assassination attempt on Amin failed on December 17 Amin entrenched himself in
a palace fortress in Kabul and tightened his hold over any political opposition making himself invulnerable to further attempts at overthrowing the
government. It is apparent that whatever Paputin's mission was it failed
and he died soon after the invasion. Because his official obituary appeared without the usual formalities of a picture or Brezhnev's signature,
the prevailing rumor suggests that he may have committed suicide.[27]

If All Else Fails: Preparing for Intervention

After Amin took power in September 1979 he continued to pursue
policies that proved to be as troublesome as Moscow suspected. Amin
was never pro-Soviet. He sought survival for himself and Afghanistan by

continuing to appeal to the West and to try to diversify his sources of aid and trade. Amin openly appealed to the United States for help and tried to press the issue of Afghanistan's nonalignment status in spite of continuing to accept the dominating influence of Soviet aid and military equipment. Although he promised a "softening" of the earlier reforms (religious freedom, constitution, repression), for which he was largely responsible, the rebellion was already too widespread to be contained by long-term, vague promises. Amin refused to take definite measures to broaden his political base by including members of Parcham and pro-Taraki Khalq in his government or to stop his bloody form of political repression. Given Amin's internal rigidity and mounting interest in the West the Soviets would have had growing reason to view Amin as unreliable and ineffectual. This Soviet perception of the unreliability of Amin was reminiscent of their assessment of Dubcek just prior to the invasion of Czechoslovakia in 1968.

With the Afghan government in control of less than one-third of the 28 provinces, and the army in a state of mutiny (the desertion rate was on the rise as rebel activity gained strength), the relentless continuation of the *jihad* (holy war) against the Communist regime led to the conclusion that the Amin regime would fall. If the regime fell it might be replaced by the brand of radical Muslim nationalism evident in Iran, and Soviet influence in the region would be severely jeopardized. In addition, the spread of fanatic Muslim nationalism so close to the Soviet Central Asian republics could compromise them internally, sowing unrest in an already alien population. This argument for the isolation and elimination of radical elements in Afghanistan to prevent their contamination of the Soviet Muslim population was virtually paralleled by arguments made by party leaders of the Soviet Western republics during the spring Czech crisis. They were convinced that economic and social reforms would corrupt the rest of the Eastern bloc if not stopped in Czechoslovakia. Along with Muslim Pakistan and Turkey, a non-Communist, Muslim Afghanistan could form a decidedly hostile group of nations close to the Soviet border. On the other hand, if the rebels did not succeed in toppling the regime, then Amin might finally be successful in obtaining help from the West. Any of these alternative outcomes would cancel Soviet influence and investment in Afghanistan.

As it became increasingly apparent that Amin could not be removed by covert measures and replaced with a more pro-Soviet leader, a Soviet decision to use military force became the only realistic option available to prevent the failure of the Afghan Communist "revolution" and the replacement with an anti-Soviet Islamic government. The Soviets could attest to the ultimate reliability of neighboring nations that had Soviet troops stationed on their soil such as East Germany, Czechoslovakia, Hungary, Outer Mongolia, and Poland. Less reliable in their "different roads to socialism" were those Communist neighbors free of the Soviet presence, China, Yugoslavia, and Rumania. Most threatening would be a border nation with a hostile, non-Communist government that had openly renounced Communist revolution. Not only would such a nation be a threat to the Soviet geostrategic concept of buffer states but it would appear as an open challenge to Soviet political and ideological hegemony in the region. A non-Communist Afghanistan would also suggest to the growing number of Marxist developing countries that the Soviets would allow a rollback of communism.

At the same time covert measures were being employed in Afghanistan the Soviet General Staff began preparing military contingency plans for invasion. As early as June 1979 plans were in operation for mobilizing and practicing airlift capabilities in the region. In April Moscow sent A.A. Yepishev, head of the MPA, to Afghanistan to survey the situation. In August he was followed by General I. Pavlovsky, deputy defense minister, and commander of the Soviet ground forces. Pavlovsky arrived in Kabul with a large delegation of general officers, ostensibly to "help organize" the Afghan forces, and stayed until October.[28] Both generals had performed the virtually same reconnaissance and preparation role in Czechoslovakia in 1968. This high-level reconnaissance yielded a very detailed picture of the problems associated with any plan for invasion. It is probable however, that the same military that counseled an overwhelming and rapid victory in Hungary and Czechoslovakia were much more cautious if not pessimistic in their assessment of the resistance and terrain in Afghanistan. Unlike Czechoslovakia, Afghanistan was not an industrialized country full of large cities linked by multiple forms of transport and communication. Afghanistan had only a few large population centers connected by dirt roads. There were no railroads and only one major highway linking the Soviet Union and the capital. The terrain was mountainous and forbidding and rebel bases throughout the countryside and in Pakistan made maintaining communications very difficult. In addition, the majority of Soviet troops were without combat experience or mountain training and were equipped with weapons more suited to the European theater. Despite the prevailing view of U.S. analysts, the opportunity to test new weapons and gain battlefield experience probably did not sway the Defense Ministry toward recommending invasion. The possibility of any long-term military commitment would strain limited resources and without a much larger commitment of troops (one estimate has suggested almost four times the 100,000 troops already engaged there) there could be no "winning" of Afghanistan. In light of these speculations, the Soviets were clearly hoping for a "surgical" solution to the Afghan problem.

From October on the Soviets made definite tactical arrangements for invasion. Throughout October and November the Soviets mobilized the reserves in the border areas and established a command headquarters in Termez at the Soviet end of the Salang highway.[29] The reservists were deployed in five motorized rifle divisions in order to bring them up to full strength (at least 50 percent were reserve forces). Those initially mobilized were mostly local MVD troops charged with guarding the border and as such were largely homogeneous units made up of Tadziks, Uzbeks, and Turkmenistans. Since these were the first troops employed in Afghanistan these were the first Soviet troops to be recalled. Although some analysts have maintained that they were removed because they proved ethnically and religiously unreliable, it is also true that their tour of duty (initially a few months) ended when they were replaced by regular army units.[30] These regular units were mobilized and deployed once it became clear that Afghanistan was a long-term military commitment. These troops, like all regular units in the Soviet military, were heterogeneous.[31] The Soviets also redeployed men and materiel from the western USSR and called up special technical classes (engineers, construction experts, and radar operators).

By late November tactical aircraft were moved to border areas in Central Asia and a theater C^{3}I network was deployed. The maintenance of the element of surprise (at least in Kabul) and the necessity for rapid military advance, as in the successful operation in Czechoslovakia in 1968, demanded that the Soviets deploy an initial force large enough to take and hold Kabul, Bagram airfield, and most land routes, especially the vital Salang highway. From November 29 to December 5 two battalions of the 105th Airborne were airlifted into Afghanistan to secure the Bagram airfield north of Kabul, the Kabul airport, and the Salang highway from Termez in the Soviet Union to Kabul. Air transport was assembled in mid-December in staging areas in Taskent and Moscow and two additional airborne divisions were put on alert. By the second week in December the majority of six divisions were stationed on or near the Soviet border with Afghanistan. The assemblage of such a large force for the invasion was due in part to the Soviet experience with the Hungarian intervention in 1956 when two divisions were overwhelmed and had to be supplemented by the deployment of 10 additional divisions.

Phase Three: The Invasion Begins

The movements of Soviet divisions (approximately six) and the number of troops deployed made Soviet intentions to intervene quite clear to U.S. intelligence sources. The United States issued both public and private warnings to the Soviets on March 23, November 1, and on December 28 after the invasion. These warnings, voiced almost reluctantly by President Carter and Secretary of State Vance failed to convincingly convey any realistic possibility of strong U.S. reaction to Soviet movements into Afghanistan. Until Carter's statement after the invasion when he admitted his astonishment at the flagrant "betrayal" of détente, the Soviets were not made forcefully aware of strong opposition to their actions by those within the administration. Yet, had the United States tendered a more direct warning the Soviets would most likely have assumed that the United States would follow past behavior as in the case of Hungary, Czechoslovakia, Angola, and Ethiopia. Although U.S. intelligence knew the strength of Soviet troops massed on the Afghan border they did not or could not adequately communicate the significance of events to those within the State Department or to the president. As a result of several intervening factors—the taking of American hostages in Iran on November 4, the previous intelligence fiasco over the presence of a Soviet brigade in Cuba in September 1979, and the clash of personalities (Brzezinski and Vance) over the value of preserving détente and safeguarding SALT II—the strategic significance of the developments in Afghanistan was lost on all concerned.[32]

However well-informed the United States was as to Soviet intentions, the invasion on December 24 came as a surprise to Amin and his followers. On December 23, 1979 *Pravda* ran a statement denouncing the "U.S. rumor" that Soviet troops had moved into Afghan territory and said that, ". . . relations between the Soviet Union and Afghanistan are based on a strong foundation of . . . noninterference in the internal affairs of the other. . . ."[33] In the three days that followed 80,000 Soviet troops, including 10,000 airborne troops, and six motorized rifle divisions comprising the seven divisions of the Fortieth Army, poured into Afghanistan. Airborne battalions secured the remaining airbases at Herat and Qandahar and knocked out communications in Kabul and overran the Ministry of the Interior (secret police).[34] The Soviets relied on heavy air bombardment and ground attacks by tanks and APCs (armored personnel carriers), along with mine laying and comprehensive layered bombing. Helicopter gunships were used for the traditional roles of supply and transport and in their new capacity as elements of the command and control network and to provide concentrated firepower. The Soviets also used incendiary bombs and there have been numerous allegations of the Soviet use of chemical weapons.[35]

The Muslim guerrillas (*Mujahedin*) were organized into approximately seven large groups and numerous small strongholds, operating from bases in the mountains and in Pakistan. Through sabotage and hit-and-run raids they continued to control most of the countryside and could effectively interdict land supply, communications, and transport. Despite their capabilities the rebels were not sufficiently organized or equipped to meet the Soviet advance. There was little resistance or help from the shattered remnants of the Afghan army. Under these circumstances the Soviets rapidly took the capital and several larger urban areas including Herat and Qandahar without meeting significant resistance. After a bloody battle on December 27 between Soviet troops and Amin's loyal army and police guarding the palace Amin and his supporters and family were finally killed. According to the official line published in the Soviet Union in January and adhered to by the Soviet-backed government in Kabul, Amin had been backed by Western (CIA) intelligence sources in order to turn back the tide of revolutionary struggle in favor of the Muslim *Jihad*.[36]

Babrak Karmal, who had been in "exile" in Moscow and Eastern Europe, arrived (although the Soviets maintain he arrived and took control of Communist forces prior to the invasion) and was duly installed as head of the Soviet-controlled government (general secretary of the People's Democratic party, president of the Revolutionary Council, and prime minister).[37] The request for Soviet assistance in "resisting external challenges to the Democratic People's Republic of Afghanistan" came the same day.[38] Amin was characterized by Karmal as an agent of "external forces" and Taraki was resurrected in the role of "hero of the Afghan people." The references to "external" threats, characterized as Muslim fanatics and the spread of Western imperialism, has been the consistent justification of the Soviet presence in Afghanistan. A typical example of this form of propaganda is an excerpt from a "historical" primer for instructors in "newly liberated areas."

> Imperialism commenced the present undeclared war against the Afghan Revolution. The United States, other capitalist countries, as well as some Islamic countries are stinting no effort to "export counterrevolution" into Afghanistan. Basmachi . . . bands are being furnished weapons by the United States, China and Egypt, are undergoing training under the direction of U.S. and Chinese "advisors", and are being infiltrated into Afghanistan for the purpose of undermining revolutionary rule in that country and restoring a system to the liking of imperialism.[39]

Even as bodies and veterans returned in numbers too obvious to ignore the "presence" continued for over five years, the "limited" nature of the intervention remained a central theme of reports in *Pravda*. *Red Star*, the military daily, through its description of tactics, weaponry, battlefield life, and training gives a more accurate picture of what Afghanistan has become, a long-term war.[40]

Soviet Decision Making

Although the chaos engendered by Amin forced the decision to intervene militarily in Afghanistan it was not a significant departure from past

Soviet behavior. Prior to World War II the Soviets had invaded Iran in 1920 and 1941, China in 1929, Outer Mongolia in 1921, and Afghanistan three times in 1925, 1929, and 1930.[41] After 1946 the Soviets had not militarily invaded a Third World nation, although they had intervened militarily in Czechoslovakia and in Hungary in an effort to ensure their own sense of geographic and ideological security. The invasion of Afghanistan, historically perceived as a critical buffer zone in much the same sense as the countries of Eastern Europe, was merely an extension of past behavior and not an entrance into an unprecedented military phase in the Third World. Although the Soviets have not hesitated to use Cuban proxy forces in Angola and Ethiopia this should be construed as an even stronger indicator that the Soviets continue to take great pains to avoid the risks involved in the use of Soviet troops outside of what they consider to be their own sphere of influence. To consider Afghanistan as an independent Third World nation is a U.S. perspective that had little to do with Soviet decision making.

There were costs, however, in deciding to send troops to Afghanistan. By directly intervening in Afghanistan the Soviets had taken over a country whose leader was not in open defiance of Moscow, one who had attempted to follow faithfully, at least initially, the Soviet model of economic and political reform (although the Soviets may have thought his methods and vigor caused undue problems) and one who professed himself to be a strong, independent Communist. Although Amin had sought economic and military aid among pro-Western nations in the region he was still virtually dependent on Soviet loans, arms, trade, technology, etc. Even if Afghanistan had achieved some limited form of nonaligned status (such as Cuba or India) this would not have significantly lessened its dependence on the Soviet Union. The fact remains that because Amin had so successfully emulated the Soviet model he had also turned the entire population against him. The Soviets had to remove him if there was any hope of restoring Afghanistan in the long run. The only Soviet miscalculation may have been underestimating the deep-rooted animosity of the population for *anything* Soviet. A Muslim country in the midst of a holy war would not simply accept a new Communist leader and go on, even with the Soviet presence to guarantee its survival. The Soviets seriously miscalculated their ability to restore order and maintain Soviet influence without the long-term stationing of troops in Afghanistan. They also misperceived the degree of U.S. interest in the region and the effects an open challenge would have on a slowly suffocating détente.

Given the wide range of internal, regional, and international risks involved in the invasion of Afghanistan and the sense that gains would only be realized in the long term, the decision to escalate to military action was probably not easily taken, although the short time between Amin's takeover and the invasion suggests an overwhelming consensus among the members of the Politburo. This situation is in direct contrast to the prolonged decision-making periods prior to the Hungarian and Czechoslovakian interventions. Indeed, in an article in *Pravda* in January 1980 Brezhnev characterized the decision to intervene in Afghanistan as "very difficult." He further stated that "to have done otherwise would have meant to watch passively while a seat of serious danger to the security of the Soviet state was established on our southern border."[42] The deterioration of Amin's rule in Afghanistan threatened the Soviets with the overthrow of a Communist regime and its replacement with two unacceptable alternatives, Muslim nationalism or a pro-Western regime within their security zone. Although the internal political and ideological losses pressured the Soviet to interfere more directly in Afghan affairs the overriding issue of an imminent power realignment in the region elevated the question of the reliability of Afghanistan to one of national security.

Although the Soviets had made the decision in November to prepare to intervene militarily they still held out some hope that a political solution would make that decision unnecessary. However, when the U.S. hostages were taken in Iran on November 4, 1979 the calculus changed dramatically. The Soviets were faced with the sudden possibility that the United States would have to take direct military action in Iran and that any subsequent Soviet intervention in Afghanistan would be unacceptable to U.S. interests.[43] The necessity of ensuring that Afghanistan remain a reliable buffer state meant that the Soviets had no choice but to intervene militarily before the United States had time to react. Thus the international situation served as a trigger for Soviet actions.

The external dimension of Soviet decision making regarding the situation in Afghanistan before the taking of U.S. hostages provided the Soviets with no realistic obstacle to intervention. The Soviets had already foreseen the breakdown of detente. SALT II was in danger of not being ratified by the Senate even with Carter's wholehearted support. The United States had supported an increase in defense spending, the deployment of the MX missile system, and the Trident submarine. In addition, Carter had announced the creation of the Rapid Deployment Force (RDF) to counter problems in the Persian Gulf. NATO had also agreed to deploy new medium-range missiles in Europe and the United States was again trying to improve relations with China. The Carter administration seemed indecisive in Soviet relations, a perception strengthened by the Cuban brigade fiasco in September 1979 and the off-handed nature of the warnings regarding Soviet intentions in Afghanistan. The Soviets calculated that on the basis of past U.S. behavior (Czechoslovakia, Hungary, Angola, Ethiopia, and South Yemen), their preoccupation in Iran, their inability to rapidly project power into the region, and because of the timid nature of the warnings the United States would not risk confrontation over Afghanistan. There may also have been the sense that the Carter administration would not go public with its warnings on Soviet troop movements in an effort to retain the semblance of détente and to keep SALT alive.[44] The US had shown only minimal interest in Afghanistan since World War II and had refused to continue aid in February 1979 after the kidnapping and unsuccessful rescue of U.S. Ambassador Dubs by Afghan security police. Clearly, the United States had not anticipated or analyzed the effect of a Soviet intervention in Afghanistan given the new alignment of influence in the region after the fall of the Shah of Iran. If the Soviets gained major land and air bases in Afghanistan they could interfere with the production and export of gulf oil to the West. Although the United States was less dependent on foreign oil the other nations of the West still imported over 50 percent of their total reserves.

The Soviet decision to intervene militarily in Afghanistan was based on a series of internal and external contingencies and a complex assessment of risk. The invasion of Afghanistan had both short- and long-term costs, and gave impetus to a long-term military revitalization in both nations. The well-cultivated image of Soviet "benevolent" aid in the Third World and the long years spent rebuilding world opinion since the invasion of Czechoslovakia in 1968 were severely damaged. Any chance for improving relations with China or the Western nations was temporarily undermined by the blatancy of Soviet methods in Afghanistan, and the fear that the Soviet Union had embarked on a radical policy in the Third World. Client-nations, such as Cuba and India, that had nominally maintained their nonaligned status, despite Soviet backing, were caught in outright support of an invasion of a Third World nation that, at least superficially, emulated the Soviet model of political and economic development.

Such losses, however, were offset to some degree by a range of short- and long-term gains. By protecting the integrity of the Communist regime and installing a Soviet-trained leader the border with Afghanistan was secured as it had been in Hungary and Czechoslovakia. The presence of Soviet troops guaranteed the reliability of the new regime and prevented Muslim nationalists from overthrowing the Communists and threatening Soviet influence in the area. On a global scale the Soviets limited U.S. influence in the region by their presence in Afghanistan and their steady stream of arms and military aid to Iran, Iraq, and India. The Soviet presence in the gulf (Ethiopia and South Yemen) and their ability to threaten U.S. and Western interests is enhanced by Afghan airbases that could put Soviet Backfire bombers within range of the Strait of Hormuz and the U.S. carrier group in the Indian Ocean. As a side benefit to the invasion of Afghanistan, the Soviet presence puts them in a better position to influence regional power relationships (India and Pakistan, Iran and Iraq).

On a short-term tactical level the Soviet presence in Afghanistan allows the Soviet military a testing ground for weapons (attack helicopters, self-propelled artillery, chemical agents), technology (radars, communication nets) and tactics (close air support). In addition, the hit-and-run style of guerrilla warfare affords an opportunity for the Soviets to deploy their C³I network (Command, Control, Communication, and Intelligence) under battlefield conditions, and to train the officer corp, regular troops, MVD (border troops), and reserves in combat situations. Finally, taken from the Soviet perspective, the Soviet Union could demonstrate to the Western nations, its allies, client-states, and Third World trade and aid partners the extent of Soviet commitment to preserving Communist gains in the developing countries with the strength of Soviet military might. This is of course a severe warning to potential challenges of Soviet patronage from the Third World. In the face of U.S. losses and uncertainties in the region and recent widespread Third World challenges to Western foreign policy goals, the contrast in superpower behavior is especially relevant.

Finally the decision to intervene militarily in Afghanistan was taken not as a quick or easy solution to a manageable problem but as a last resort to preserve a critical security zone in a vital region. In other instances when internal political or covert solutions were possible, as in Poland in 1956, 1970, and 1980 or in Yugoslavia in 1948, the Soviet Union did not have to respond with force. In Afghanistan the question was perceived as one of national security not ideology or political expansion. Questions of international repercussions or U.S. response were secondary as were the estimates by the Soviet military of potential costs and the difficulties of armed invasion. Ultimately the Soviets intervened because they had tried everything and failed. Amin had become an unaffordable enemy that threatened their vital interests and security. The decision to stabilize the government of Afghanistan as a pro-Soviet state did not represent a change in Soviet foreign policy, it merely demonstrated its unfailing continuity.

Notes

1. Ludwig W. Adamec, *Afghanistan Foreign Affairs to the Mid-Twentieth Century: Relations with the USSR, Germany and Britain* (Tucson, Ariz.: University of Arizona Press, 1974), pp. 87–90, 107–8.

2. Thomas T. Hammond, *Red Flag Over Afghanistan* (Boulder, Colo.: Westview Press, 1984), p. 11.

3. Adamec, *Afghanistan Foreign Affairs*, pp. 110–12.

4. Hammond points out that Amanullah was Pushtun and very anti-British while the bandits were anti-Soviet. Although support of Amanullah was an easy choice the Soviets had also supported anti-British governments in Turkey and Iran at the expense of more revolutionary, Communist movements that failed to

win popular support. The need to outweigh continuing British influence in the region took precedence over furthering indigenous revolutionary movements. Hammond, *Red Flag,* pp. 113–15.

5. Henry S. Bradsher, *Afghanistan and the Soviet Union* (Durham, N.C.: Duke University Press, 1983), pp. 15–16.

6. Zahir's fear of a major Soviet domination in the region after World War II was largely unrealistic given the degree to which the Soviets had demobilized men and materiel and committed their already overtaxed resources to reconstructing the Soviet Union and consolidating their hold on Eastern Europe. See Cristann Lea Gibson, "Patterns of Demobilization: The US and USSR After World War Two" (Ph.D. diss., University of Denver, 1983).

7. Hammond, *Red Flag,* pp. 24–25.

8. Bradsher, *Afghanistan and the Soviet Union,* pp. 43–52.

9. Hammond, *Red Flag,* p. 32.

10. Hannah Negaran [pseud.], "The Afghan Coup of April 1978: Revolution and International Security," *Orbis,* vol. 23, no. 1 (Spring 1979), p. 100. Negaran says that Soviet pressure was exerted through the Communist party of India. Also see Anthony Arnold, *Afghanistan: The Soviet Invasion in Perspective* (Stanford, Calif.: Hoover Institution Press, 1981), pp. 57–65.

11. CIA, *Communist Aid to Less Developed Countries of the Free World, 1977,* ER 78–10478U, November 1978, pp. 1–2, 4–11.

12. Jonathan Steele, *Soviet Power: The Kremlin's Foreign Policy: Brezhnev to Chernenko* (New York: Simon and Schuster, 1984), p. 122.

13. For the size of the combined party see Louis Dupree, "Afghanistan Under the Khalq," *Problems of Communism* (July-August 1979) p. 40.

14. Robert Neumann, "Afghanistan Under the Red Flag," in *The Impact of the Iranian Events Upon Persian Gulf and U.S. Security,* ed. Z. Michael Szaz (Washington, D.C.: American Foreign Policy Institute, 1979), p. 137, and Cyrus Vance, *Hard Choices: Critical Years in America's Foreign Policy* (New York: Simon and Schuster, 1983), p. 384.

15. See the Constitution of the People's Democratic Party of Afghanistan reprinted as the appendix in Hammond, *Red Flag,* pp. 231–40.

16. Neumann, "Afghanistan under the Red Flag," p. 138.

17. *Vneshnyaya politika sovetskogo soyuza, 1978 qod* (Foreign policy of the Soviet Union, 1978) (Moscow: Mezhdunarodnye Otnosheniya, 1979), pp. 223–31.

18. Maj. I. Korelev, "Strengthen Friendship and Brotherhood," *Sovetskiy Patriot,* 4 December 1983, p. 3 in FBIS, 28 February 1984; and K. Selikov, "Neob'yavlennaya voya" (Undeclared war), *Sovetskiy Pisatel,* Moscow, 1983.

19. Korelev, "Strengthen Friendship and Brotherhood," p. 44.

20. Hammond, *Red Flag,* pp. 74–75 and Bradsher, *Afghanistan and the Soviet Union,* pp. 100–1.

21. Bradsher, *Afghanistan and the Soviet Union,* p. 104.

22. Raymond L. Garthoff, *Detente and Confrontation: American-Soviet Relations from Nixon to Reagan* (Washington, D.C.: The Brookings Institution, 1985), p. 902.

23. U.S. Embassy Kabul 5360, Confidential, July 16, 1979 and U.S. Embassy Kabul 5433, Confidential, July 18, 1979, in *Afghanistan* (Teheran: Moslem Stu-

dents Followers of Imam, 1981), vol. 1, pp. 167–69, 170–77. As cited in ibid., pp. 902–3, note 45.

24. East German Ambassador Hermann Schweisau in a conversation with American Charge d'Affairs J. Bruce Amstutz, reported in U.S. Embassy Kabul 5459, Secret-Exdis, July 18, 1979 in *Afghanistan,* vol. 1, pp. 179–84, as cited in Garthoff, *Detente and Confrontation,* p. 904, note 47.

25. Bradsher, *Afghanistan and the Soviet Union,* p. 112; and Jiri Valenta, "Soviet Decision-making on Afghanistan, 1979" in *Soviet Decisionmaking for National Security,* ed. Jiri Valenta and William C. Potter (London: George Allen and Unwin, 1984), p. 229.

26. Valenta, "Soviet Decision-making," pp. 229–30.

27. *Pravda,* January 3, 1980.

28. CIA Headquarters Message, Secret, September 19, 1979, in *Afghanistan* (Teheran), vol. 2, p. 162 as cited in Garthoff, *Detente and Confrontation,* p. 905, note 52.

29. U.S. Congress, House Committee on Foreign Affairs, *East-West Relations in the Aftermath of the Soviet Invasion of Afghanistan,* 96th Cong., 2d sess., January 24 and 30, 1980, 39–40.

30. See S. Enders Wimbush and Alex Alexiev, "Soviet Central Asian Soldiers in Afghanistan" (Santa Monica, Calif.: Rand Corporation, January 1981), pp. 16–17.

31. N. Muhammadiyev, "On the Way to a New Life," Taskent Ozbekiston, *Adabiyoti va san'ati* (in Uzbek) 27 April 1984, p. 7. in FBIS USSR Report JPRS-UMA-84–070, 5 November 1984, pp. 39–40.

32. See Cyrus Vance, *Hard Choices: Critical Years in America's Foreign Policy,* (New York: Simon and Schuster, 1983); Zbigniew Brzezinski, *Power and Principle: Memoirs of the National Security Advisor, 1977–1981,* (New York: Farrar, Straus, Giroux, 1983) and Jimmy Carter, *Keeping Faith* (New York: Bantam Books, 1982).

33. *Pravda,* December 23, 1979.

34. Bradsher, *Afghanistan and the Soviet Union,* pp. 176–79.

35. U.S. Department of State, "Chemical Warfare in South Asia and Afghanistan," Special Report 98, March 1982.

36. *Pravda,* January 19, 1980.

37. The establishment of a blatantly Soviet-backed government was a successful version of the attempt that was made to install a similar leadership in Czechoslovakia in August 1968.

38. *Pravda,* December 28, 1979.

39. Lt. Col. V. Lutskevich, "The Liberated Nations of Asia, Africa and Latin America," *Kommunist vooruzhennykh sil,* Moscow, no. 4, February 1982, p. 75.

40. For an account of the diversity of the Soviet press on Afghanistan see: Maj. P.V. Huisking, "Afghanistan and the Soviet Press," *Military Intelligence,* vol. 11, no. 1 (January-March 1985).

41. Thomas T. Hammond, ed., *The Anatomy of Communist Takeovers* (New Haven, Conn.: Yale University Press, 1975) and Hammond, *Red Flag,* pp. 9–22.

42. *Pravda,* January 13, 1980.

43. Carter and others hinted of a U.S. invasion to Soviet officials during this period. See Valenta and Potter, *Soviet Decisionmaking,* p. 228. Also see Brezhnev warning to US in *Pravda,* November 19, 1979.

44. Brzezinski, *Power and Principle,* p. 426.

17 CONCLUSIONS

Jonathan R. Adelman

This volume has chronicled the potency of repeated revolutionary challenges to superpower authority in the postwar era. Given the international context of revolution, the domestic desire of revolutionary movements to alter political authority structures poses a challenge to the reigning superpower of the region. The strong popular support, the political mobilization and radicalism immanent in revolutionary forces all threaten directly the interests of domestic allies of the superpower and indirectly the superpower. Perhaps the gravest result of the revolutionary situation from the viewpoint of the superpower is the weakened state of its domestic allies. Before the revolutionary transformation started, the superpowers, as Jack Goldstone ably depicts, could rely on the monopoly of levers of power available to their neopatrimonial allies. These states, heavily penetrated by their local superpower, maintained democratic trappings but relied heavily on executive control of bureaucratic institutions (especially the military), patronage, depoliticization of the masses, secret police control of opposition, economic growth, and limited economic autonomy to retain power. Such a system is highly vulnerable to mass dissatisfaction generated by economic difficulties and antisuperpower nationalism and elite dissatisfaction generated by exclusion from the political process and the liberal application of coercion.

The emergence of a strong revolutionary movement generally leads to the weakening or actual collapse of the neopatrimonial structure and leaves the relevant superpower in a quandary. For the United States this process has been painful since its policy has traditionally been one of strong support for and identification with such regimes and their authoritarian dictatorial leaders. Even though many U.S. policy makers may have wished to back off somewhat from unconditional support for such increasingly unpopular leaders as Chiang Kai-shek, Fulgencio Batista,

Ngo Diem, and the Shah—and even desired their ouster at times—they were unable to find a suitable replacement in a personalist regime. In such a situation the power of U.S. allies, generally identified with the corrupt and decaying Old Regime, was in sharp decline compared to that of the rising revolutionary forces. In this context U.S. decision makers found no easy solutions to the challenge posed to them.

In many ways the Soviet Union has also faced unpalatable alternatives provoked by the weakness of Soviet allies and growing strengths of generally hostile revolutionary forces. The collapse of the neopatrimonial regimes in Hungary and Poland (1956), Czechoslovakia (1968), Afghanistan (1979), and Poland (1980 +) in the wake of strong revolutionary mass activity created a dangerous situation for the Soviet Union. In all cases the allies on which the Soviet Union could rely—the Natolin faction in Poland (1956), the Bilak-Kolder-Indra bloc in Czechoslovakia (1968), the Parcham party of Karmal in Afghanistan (1979), and the Grabski faction in Poland (1980)—were relatively thin reeds on which to rely in the face of mass popular protest. And new governments generally led by Communists (as Nagy, Gomulka, Dubcek, and Amin) were not pliant tools of Moscow.

Under these circumstances and often in an atmosphere of crisis, the superpowers had to make critically important decisions in a complex environment. As Martha Cottam decisively demonstrates, such situations historically have not been conducive to the best decision making. Psychologists have shown that decision makers, selecting only information supportive of their ideas, have simplified views of revolutionary states as weak, hostile, and often willing tools of the other superpower. In this environment the traditional elements necessary for optimal rational decision making often do not exist.

Let us now turn to an analysis of elements involved in superpower decision making in revolutionary situations. These include history, international setting, information, view of the enemy, reaction of other superpower, cost/benefit calculations, and shifting bureaucratic coalitions. All of our authors have especially emphasized the historical context of these decisions. Quite important has been the historical relationship between the United States and Soviet Union on one hand and the newly revolutionary states on the other. Martha Cottam and Barry Rubin respectively ably chronicle how past U.S. policies toward Guatemala and Iran led the United States to seriously exaggerate its own power and underestimate the extent of possible opposition to its penetration of those countries. Similarly the long relationship between the Soviet Union and the various Eastern European states has often made it difficult at times for Moscow to fully appreciate the extent of opposition to its role.

Equally important have been the role of historical memories in influencing decisions. For as Martha Cottam has shown, important lessons are generally learned from only a few cases. These memories necessarily

shift over time. For the United States in China (1948), an important desire
was the wish to avoid involvements in a major Asian land war so soon
after the end of the Pacific campaign in World War II. The decision to support the Bay of Pigs invasion force (1961) was clearly influenced by the
success of covert operations in Iran (1953) and Guatemala (1954). And
after the rise of McCarthyism in the early 1950s in the wake of the China
"debacle," no Democratic president in the 1960s was eager to be vulnerable to the charge of abandoning Vietnam to the Communists. Similarly,
Soviet policy makers were sensitive to historical memories. Most important of all in invasion decisions have been memories of the consequences
of Soviet weakness and German control of Eastern Europe in World War
II. Too, the relative success of the 1956 Hungarian invasion undoubtedly
influenced subsequent invasion decisions in Czechoslovakia and Afghanistan.

The international context at the time of these decisions was extremely
important. Even superpowers seem unable to focus on more than one
crisis at a time and inevitably give priority to one over the other. U.S. policy toward Iran was heavily influenced by the priority given to Israeli-
Egyptian peace negotiations at the time. Soviet policy toward Hungary in
1956 was influenced by the Polish October (and Suez crisis). Similarly,
Soviet policy toward Iran was colored by the priority given to the emerging Afghanistan crisis at that time.

Perhaps one of the most interesting conclusions to emerge from this
study are the consistently grave difficulties encountered by the United
States and Soviet Union in receiving accurate and timely information on
the unfolding revolutionary situation and accurately interpreting it. On
one hand, this seems surprising given the massive expenditure of resources by both superpowers on intelligence gathering operations
through overt and covert sources. Yet revolutions invariably disrupt traditional lines of communication and challenge the conventional interpretations to which analysts have become habituated. And, as a consequence, the superpower becomes heavily dependent for information and
analysis on its dwindling group of allies who seek to use this channel as a
lever for regaining or consolidating power.

For the Soviet Union intelligence has been a very serious problem.
The purge of Beria's men and the attacks on the secret police in Hungary
seriously weakened Soviet knowledge of events there in 1956 (possibly
enhancing the role of Soviet Ambassador Yuri Andropov). Similarly intelligence deficiencies in Czechoslovakia and Afghanistan helped contribute to the illusion that the bulk of the populace would welcome or tolerate
a Soviet invasion.

For the United States this has at times been a serious problem. While
the quality of information and analysis on China (1948) and Chile (1970)
was quite decent, that on Guatemala (1954), Vietnam (1960s), and Iran

(1979) was seriously deficient and flawed. This was even more true of the quality of analysis than of the information itself. While Ernest May shows that the high quality of the China specialists contributed to a strong grasp of the dilemma facing the United States in China in 1948, Martha Cottam shows how the abysmal ignorance of Guatemalan politics influenced U.S. policymaking.

This carried over in both superpowers to the perception of the revolutionary forces as more hostile to the interests of the superpowers than they really were. The United States—as in Iran (1953), Guatemala (1954) and Chile (1970)—repeatedly saw nationalists and socialists as Communists and Soviet agents, even when they were not. In Vietnam, as Roger Hilsman makes clear, the predominant American hawks saw the Communists only as agents of a global Communist aggression directed from Moscow and Peking, totally missing their broad appeal and identity as anticolonial nationalists. Similarly, the Soviet Union tended to brand all opposition to its general line as degenerate and dangerous, even when it emanated from such authentic Communists as Alexander Dubcek, Josip Tito, or Mao Zedong. Thus the U.S. fear of Communist subversion was matched by an equally salient Soviet fear of capitalist restoration.

One of the critical aspects of the decision-making process for the superpower confronted by revolution was the reaction of the other superpower. In all three major Soviet intervention cases—Hungary (1956), Czechoslovakia (1968), and Afghanistan (1979)—there was little or no chance of U.S. intervention. In 1956 the United States was preoccupied with the Suez; in 1968 it was openly cool to the Dubcek regime; in 1979 it was little involved in a remote country traditionally in the Soviet sphere of interest. Indeed, the United States in practice conceded it had no intention of even considering the highly dangerous possibility of military intervention in the Soviet sphere of interest. However, in 1948 it did exhibit considerable interest in the fate of Yugoslavia and in the early 1980s in the fate of Poland. Similarly a major U.S. concern in China (1948) and in the decision not to invade North Vietnam (late 1960s) was possible Soviet reaction.

Although the evidence is not conclusive, our cases tend to support the applicability of a modified bureaucratic politics model to superpower decision making over revolution. In the U.S. cases our authors have repeatedly shown a strong conflict between "doves" and "hawks," liberals and conservatives, the State Department versus the Defense Department. Liberals repeatedly have urged restraint, a recognition of the limits of U.S. power, tolerance for nationalist chauvinism, and stress on political and economic weapons over military force. Conservatives, as in China, Vietnam, and Iran, have stressed a more Manichean view of the world with a marked preference for use of military force to prevent any possible Soviet gains.

Our authors, most notably Condoleezza Rice, Michael Fry, and Jiri Valenta, have found a similar tendency in Soviet decision making. In the Kremlin too there have been shifting coalitions of interventionist and noninterventionist forces, with a third force waffling in between. Interestingly, in 1956 this third force was led by Khrushchev, in 1968 by Brezhnev. And the resulting vacillations in policy in Moscow in these crises at least matched those displayed by Washington in other crises.

What is also apparent though from these cases is that a strong asymmetry in power and influence persisted throughout the postwar era between the United States and the Soviet Union. The power and extent of international capitalism and broad impact of American culture enabled the United States to act in a truly global context. The vast scope of its sphere of influence is reflected in our cases that range from Latin America to the Middle East and Asia. In this broad context the United States possessed a panoply of economic, political, and cultural levers of power as well as overt and covert military force. By contrast the Soviet Union acted predominantly as a great regional power in the center of the Eurasian continent. It is no accident that all of its cases occurred on or near its borders—and most involved Eastern Europe. In this limited context the Soviet Union lacked the political, cultural, and above all, economic levers available to its great rival. In this arena, then, a revolutionary threat, with all the danger of contagion, would seem especially threatening. The Soviets then have had to repeatedly resort to their own strong suit—the military weapon—to maintain their empire in the west and security in the south. This helps explain why in our seven cases the Red Army was called upon three times, the KGB once, and the Polish security forces once while in six American cases the army was used once and the CIA three times.

This naturally leads to our initial question in the first chapter of why force is sometimes not used despite great provocation. Our basic answer is that a strongly positive cost/benefit calculation must be perceived by the key policy makers before massive force will be used. For the Soviet Union in Yugoslavia (1948) this condition did not attain once covert actions failed. The Yugoslavian army and people would resist an invasion, the terrain was difficult, the United States would aid Tito, pro-Soviet forces were weak, and Yugoslavia was peripheral to Soviet security. Similarly in Iran (1979) there was hope for a continuation of anti-Americanism, the Iranian army and people would resist an invasion, the terrain was difficult, the Tudeh party was still weak, and Iran was not central to Soviet security. And the Polish October (1956), coinciding with the Hungarian revolution, showed the extent to which Moscow would accommodate local interests if necessary.

The U.S. cases are even more interesting, showing a marked preference for covert action. Only in Vietnam did the United States massively apply force to try to crush the revolution. Too, unlike the Soviet Union, the United States chose relative passivity in two cases, in China (1948) and Iran (1979).

How successful were the superpowers? The Soviet record was initially more successful. In five of seven cases it obtained its goal of gaining ascendancy over the revolutionary forces. Only in Yugoslavia and Iran, where it eschewed force, did it fail. By contrast, the United States was successful initially only in Guatemala and Chile where it used covert action. Its passivity did not keep China and Iran from becoming violently anti-American, its military force did not work in Vietnam, and covert action failed in Cuba. Yet a longer run perspective may be needed as well. The repeated use of military force has not solved the basic Soviet problem of achieving genuine support in Eastern Europe. And the nonuse of U.S. force in China in the late 1940s may well have ultimately helped China return to the U.S. camp in the 1970s.

Power, then, in that old truism, has its limits. And the significant differences between the two superpowers certainly cannot be ignored. Yet in the long run what is truly impressive are the basic similarities in the ways the superpowers have reacted when confronted with revolution.

INDEX

ABOUT THE AUTHOR

Professor Jonathan R. Adelman is associate professor in the Graduate School of International Studies at the University of Denver. A graduate of Columbia College, he received his Ph.D. in Soviet politics from Columbia University in 1976. After serving as Charles Phelps Taft Postdoctoral Fellow at the University of Cincinnati and Visiting Assistant Professor at the University of Alabama, he came to Denver as assistant professor in 1978. Recently promoted to associate professor, he spent the spring semester of 1986 on sabbatical leave as Lady Davis Visiting Associate Professor in the Department of Political Science at Hebrew University in Jerusalem, Israel.

Professor Adelman has also authored *The Revolutionary Armies* (1980) and *Revolution, Armies and Wars* (1985) and will author *The Dynamics of Soviet Foreign Policy* (1987). He will also author *Endgame: The Soviet and American Destruction of the Third Reich* (1988). He has edited *Communist Armies in Politics* (1982) and *Terror and Communist Politics* (1984). His articles have appeared in a number of journals, including *Studies in Comparative Communism, Armed Forces and Society, Survey,* and *Crossroads.* His work has concentrated in the fields of comparative communism, comparative revolutions, Soviet politics, and military affairs.